NATIVE
AND NATIONAL
IN BRAZIL

NATIVE AND NATIONAL IN BRAZIL

Indigeneity after Independence

Tracy Devine Guzmán

First Peoples
New Directions in Indigenous Studies

The University of North Carolina Press
Chapel Hill

PUBLICATION OF THIS BOOK
WAS MADE POSSIBLE, IN PART, BY A GRANT FROM THE
ANDREW W. MELLON FOUNDATION.

The paper in this book meets the guidelines for permanence and
durability of the Committee on Production Guidelines for Book Longevity
of the Council on Library Resources. The University of North Carolina Press
has been a member of the Green Press Initiative since 2003.

Library of Congress Cataloging-in-Publication Data
Devine Guzmán, Tracy, 1970–
Native and national in Brazil : indigeneity after independence /
Tracy Devine Guzmán.
p. cm.
Includes bibliographical references and index.
ISBN 978-1-4696-0208-0 (cloth : alk. paper) —
ISBN 978-1-4696-0209-7 (pbk. : alk. paper)
1. Indians of South America—Brazil—Ethnic identity. 2. Indians of
South America—Brazil—Politics and government. 3. Indians of South
America—Brazil—Public opinion. 4. Indians in popular culture.
5. Public opinion—Brazil. 6. Brazil—Ethnic relations. 7. Brazil—
Politics and government. I. Title.
F2519.3.E83D48 2013
305.800981—dc23   2012045725

cloth   17 16 15 14 13   5 4 3 2 1
paper   17 16 15 14 13   5 4 3 2 1

Portions of this work were previously published in different form as
"Diacuí Killed Iracema: Indigenism, Nationalism and the Struggle for Brazilianness,"
Bulletin of Latin American Research 24, no. 1 (2005), and "Our Indians in Our
America: Anti-Imperialist Imperialism and the Construction of Brazilian Modernity,"
Latin American Research Review 45, no. 3 (2010).

MIX
Paper from
responsible sources
FSC® C013483

For Marina and Siena

If you count
all the letters in
all the words on
all the pages in
all the books that
have been or ever will be written,
I love you more than that.

CONTENTS

ILLUSTRATIONS

ACKNOWLEDGMENTS

The stories behind the stories that I share in this book begin and end with serendipity and with love. As a graduate student in the late 1990s, having spent many months mired in education documents in the archive of the Serviço de Proteção aos Índios (Indian Protection Service, or SPI), I happened upon an image of a young woman in an unusual-looking wedding gown and stumbled, unwittingly, into a labyrinth of forbidden romance, political intrigue, and devastating loss. As I would come to learn, the events that culminated in that image had once been known as "the case of Diacuí," named for the Kalapalo teenager whose controversial "interracial" marriage in 1952 sparked a heated national debate about the relationship between indigenous peoples and Brazil, both as a place and an idea. I soon discovered the ultimate tragedy of her story, but it would take several years for me to grasp the magnitude of that tragedy, and longer still to piece together what it meant then, what came before it, and why it matters today.

In the end, this book is not really about Diacuí Canualo Aiute, but her life remains at its center in many ways. And so, my first words of gratitude must go to her, to her family, to the Kalapalo people, and to the indigenous peoples of Xingu and Brazil, whose struggles for freedom and justice endure today in the face of tremendous and growing odds. I especially wish to thank Ysani Kalapalo, who took time to speak with me about the legacy of her great aunt in August 2011, while we were both participating in the massive, peaceful demonstration that she helped organize to protest the construction of the Belo Monte hydroelectric dam in the state of Pará, now under way. Not much older than her aunt at the time of her untimely passing, Ysani, alongside many collaborators, continues to challenge received knowledge about indigeneity and Brazilianness, among other things. Ever inspired by their tireless labor, I count myself fortunate to have learned so much from them.

Many other people have guided me in my research, thinking, and writing about the questions explored in this work, and it is a privilege to recognize my tremendous debt to them here. I would like to express my deep appreciation to the scholars, writers, and activists whose ideas and lives I engage in these pages. A bibliography is, in some regard, the most important and sincere form of acknowledgment, for without it, there would be no meaningful discussion and no book. I am especially beholden to Eliane Potiguara, Daniel Munduruku, Lúcio Paiva Flores, and Florêncio Almeida Vaz, whose varied work in indigenous cultural production and digital scholarship has been key to my thinking about indigeneity and politics in modern-day Brazil, and thus crucial to the entire project. I am likewise obliged to Paulo Baltazar, Olívio Jekupé, Juvenal Payayá, and Marcos Terena for helping with invaluable information along the way.

I am greatly appreciative of the funding that has made research possible at different stages and would like to acknowledge the support of the Ford Foundation, the Mellon Foundation, the Tinker Foundation, numerous Foreign Language and Area Studies fellowships, and several grants and fellowships from Duke University, the University of North Carolina at Charlotte, and the University of Miami. In June and July 2010, I participated in a National Endowment for the Humanities (NEH) seminar at Newberry Library's D'Arcy McNickle Center for American Indian and Indigenous Studies that was crucial to the project's conclusion. My thanks to the NEH; to my fellow participants, for their sharing their ideas; to the Newberry staff, for their generous help in acquiring and copying materials; to John Powell, for his assistance in securing permissions; and especially to the center's director, Scott Manning Stevens, who led the seminar with relentless brilliance and good cheer.

Research in Brazil has taken me from Bahia, Brasília, Pernambuco, and Mato Grosso do Sul, to Minas Gerais, Pará, Rio de Janeiro, and São Paulo, and I am thankful for the support that I received in each of those places from archivists, librarians, colleagues, and friends. The Programa de Pós-Graduação em Antropologia Social at the Museu Nacional, and the SPI/FUNAI archives at the Museu do Índio provided me with crucial institutional backing and an intellectual home during the years I lived in Rio, and I am grateful to the people there who helped in so many ways. I wish to thank particularly Antonio Carlos de Souza Lima for facilitating my affiliation with the Museu Nacional, for allowing me to participate in his seminar on indigenist thought and practice in Latin America, and for offering helpful feedback on the earliest version of the project. I thank him, not least, for his groundbreaking scholarship, which has long been a cornerstone of my work. Carlos Agosto da Rocha Freire, whom I also first met at the Museu Nacional, shared valuable insights from his research regarding the history of Brazil's labyrinthine indigenous bureaucracies and generously helped decipher unlabeled images from the

Comissão Rondon. Bruna Franchetto invited me to discuss my work with her doctoral seminar on bilingual and intercultural education, where I also received helpful feedback and advice.

My beloved *comadre*, Rosely Rondinelli, led the textual archive of the Museu do Índio with generosity and contagious joy during the years that I did the bulk of my research there, and I can never thank her enough for her warm encouragement and many hours of engaging conversation. I am obliged to Denise Portugal and Renata Vaz, both from the audio-visual archive of the Museu do Índio, for their assistance with several of the images that appear the book, and to André Pimentel Mendes of Sagres Filmes for his help tracking down video materials. Many thanks to the staff at the Museu Emílio Goeldi in Belém; the Fundação Gilberto Freyre in Recife; the Fundação Casa de Jorge Amado in Salvador; the Museu Paulista in São Paulo (especially Ernandes Evaristo Lopes); and the Arquivo Nacional, Biblioteca Nacional (especially Elizete Higino), Museu de Belas Artes (especially Andrea Pedreira), Museu da Imagem e do Som, and Fundação Darcy Ribeiro, all in Rio de Janeiro, for their help in finding, copying, and securing permissions for various documents and images. I am indebted to Filipe Bastos, Jean Galvão, and Maurício de Sousa for the opportunity to reproduce their artwork in the book and to Wolf Lustig for allowing me to cite his research with nineteenth-century Guarani materials from Paraguay.

To colleagues, friends, and family in Brazil who shared work or ideas, helped with materials and references, and otherwise made life better, my profound thanks: Ditte Amskov, Silvina Bustos Argañaraz, Fernando de la Cuadra, Rafael Ehlers, Pierina Germán, Derval Gramacho, Leila Guzmán, Myriam Guzmán, Christophe Kirsch, Robin Lytle, Beth Machado, Ana Amélia Melo, Hélène Menu, Pedro Paulo Vítor da Silva, and Zé Luiz Viera Lacerda.

As the reader will surmise from my title, these histories are mostly from and about Brazil. The ideas and experiences that inform them, however, are from and about many other places as well. Although much of my work in those places has become part of a separate, ongoing project, I wish to thank those who have helped me to understand the relationship between indigeneity, politics, and national belonging in comparative terms, and to figure out, I hope, some of the issues and processes that are specific to Brazil and how they relate to similar issues and processes elsewhere. In Lima, am indebted to the staff and scholars at the Instituto de Estudios Peruanos (IEP) for material and personal support, and especially to Vicky García—a friend as well as an amazingly resourceful library director—who has helped me secure research materials for over a decade. The late Carlos Iván Degregori invited me to participate in a Rockefeller Foundation research seminar on indigenous peoples and globalization while he was director of the IEP, and I was extremely fortunate then to receive his valuable critique of my incipient project. At the IEP and the Pontífica Universidad Católica, Patty Ames, Manuel Marzal, Patricia Oliart, Gonzalo Portocarrero, and Francisco Verdera offered many helpful suggestions. Juan Carlos Godenzzi and Modesto Galvez Ríos of the Ministry of Education met with me on more than one occasion to discuss the benefits and challenges of managing interculturality. I wish to thank Pedro Godoy at the Biblioteca Benvenutto and the staff of the educational sector at the Biblioteca Nacional, the Centro de Estudios Andinos Bartolomé de las Casas, and the Archivo Regional del Cusco, for their help in locating and copying materials. Also in Cusco, Gina Maldonado shared her knowledge of Quechua language, history, and culture. For invaluable ideas and experiences in Apurímac, Ayacucho, Cajamarca, Cusco, Iquitos, Lambayeque, Lima, and Puno, I wish to acknowledge Braulio Allcca Sánchez, Félix Allcca González, Reina Altamirano Sánchez, Jaime Antezano, Francisco Boluarte Garay, Enrique Bossio, Alejandrina Carrión, Luz María Carrión, Milton Cordova La Torre, Nelva de la Cruz, Edwin Fernández Mañuico, María Vidalina García Zea, Rolando Hinostroza, Margarita Huayhua, Jorge Loayza Camargo, Tarcila Rivera Zea, Rafael Tapia, Jorge Vallejo Villavicencio, and Madeleine Zúñiga. I am grateful to Diana Balcázar, Miguel Calderón, Lali Cruz, Máximo Gallo, Claudia García, Jessica Soto, and María Amelia Trigoso for their support and companionship on cloudy days. Colossal thanks to Eliana Villar, comrade and confidante extraordinaire in Durham and Lima for seventeen years.

In Guatemala, I would like to thank the colleagues and collaborators in Chichicastenango, Guatemala City, Quetzaltenango, and Todos Santos Cuchumatán who spoke with me in their offices, homes, and churches about the ideas in this book. Demetrio Cojtí Cuxil and the facilitators of the Proyecto de Educación Maya Bilingüe Intercultural were especially kind to share some of their work. In Bolivia, Guadalupe Reque de Quinteros, Ronald Reque Valverde, Daniela Quinteros Reque, Lizeth Quinteros Reque, and Rene Saenz Reque treated me like family and opened up places and processes in a rapidly changing political context that otherwise would have been inaccessible to me.

My earliest dealings with these questions came about during my tenure as a graduate student in government at the College of William and Mary, and for their benevolent guidance during those years, I thank T. J. Cheng,

David Dessler, and Michael T. Clark, who led me into briar patches of pre-capitalist modes of production, Sandinista-Miskito relations, and related matters that have informed my thinking ever since. Maryse Fauvel, Teresa Longo, and Ann Marie Stock were magnificent advisors who helped me begin to build a theoretical bridge between political science and cultural studies. Ann Marie served as an outside reader of my thesis and offered, among other things, precious writing advice that has served me well over the years. When the road ahead was uncertain and steep, Maryse encouraged me to pursue my education, and for her inspiration, I am ever appreciative.

For their guidance and support during my doctoral studies at Duke University, I would like to express my immense gratitude to my wonderful teachers and mentors, especially Alberto Moreiras, my dissertation director, and John French, Walter Mignolo, and Leslie Damasceno, my dissertation advisors. Although that project did not become this book, many of the ideas herein percolated out of that work to preoccupy me for years to come. John has been a particularly spirited interlocutor since the day I first showed up to one of his classes. His encouragement and enthusiasm, shared from Brazil and the United States, have been crucial to this and many of my intellectual endeavors. Also while at Duke, I had the great fortune to study with Marisol de la Cadena, then at the University of North Carolina at Chapel Hill. As evidenced by these pages, Marisol's work has been central to my thinking about indigenous history, politics, and cultural production, and I cannot thank her enough for her support and friendship over the years. From sharing archival materials and commenting on proposals, to putting me in touch with intriguing people and stories, to, not least, caring about my development as a scholar, she has enriched my work and life for nearly two decades.

A community of dear graduate school friends (some enrolled, others not) has long sustained me with shared ideas, writing, travel, living space, good times, and some anguish on three continents. Wholehearted thanks to Sergio Alonso, Jon Beasley-Murray, Marc Brudzinski, José Luis Fernández, Pablo Filippo, Alessandro Fornazzari, Juanjo Frei, Jan Hoffman French, Adriana Johnson, Horacio Legrás, Ryan Long, Jorge Marturano, Anjali Prabhu, Freya Schiwy, Analisa Taylor, and Caroline Yezer. Idelber Avelar has been a model of intellectual political engagement since I first met him, back in the day, and I have been fortunate to count on his friendship and support, especially in recent years.

In Miami, I have been blessed with extraordinary friends who have seen me through the final and most trying stages of this work. George

Yúdice read the entire manuscript and offered comments, counsel, and steady encouragement throughout the process. I could not be more grateful to him for his generous support and for never failing to ask how things were going, even when he was nearly overwhelmed with his own massive amounts of work. Bianca Premo and Kate Ramsey, treasured friends as well as writing group partners, read and commented on several versions of several chapters, always posing helpful questions and offering insight and strong shoulders to make the whole process more fruitful and less lonesome. Hugo Achugar, with whom I had the joy of working for several years, has been a steadfast mentor and advocate, even when (and perhaps most especially) he has disagreed with me. A good friend and staunch ally, Bill Smith shared fabulous resources and much needed advice over the years—including helpful comments on portions of the manuscript. To Steve Butterman, my partner in Brazilian studies at the University of Miami (UM), who could not possibly have been more supportive or understanding, love and infinite gratitude. For their comments on one or more chapters at different stages of the writing process, I also wish to thank the UM Atlantic Studies Working Group (especially Eduardo Elena, Mary Lindemann, Michael Miller, Kyle Siebrecht, and Ashli White) and my dear and generous friend Tim Watson for facilitating that meeting; as well as my colleagues, Anne Cruz, Viviana Díaz-Balsera, David Ellison, Elena Grau-Llevería, and Ralph Heyndels. For her help with the intricacies of nineteenth-century Italian prose, my thanks go to Maria Galli Stampino.

For offering friendship, solidarity, and/or constructive critique from near and far, I would like to express my warm appreciation to Chrissy Arce, Ariel Armony, Molly Benson Prince, Rebecca Biron, Merike Blofield, Anabel Buchenau, Jürgen Buchenau, Otávio Bueno, Luis Cárcamo-Huechante, Christina Civantos, Jane Connolly, Colleen Culleton, Emilio del Valle Escalante, Evelina Galang, Laura Giannetti, Richard Gordon, Pam Hammons, Annette Jones, Barry Levitt, Andrew Lynch, Lillian Manzor, Jody McCourt, Martha Miller, Leah O'Leary, Gema Pérez-Sánchez, Jill Stark Koeppen, Rodney Roberts, Gustavo Rodríguez, Steve Stein, Michelle Warren, Subha Xavier, and Paul Youngman. Heartfelt thanks to Kunal Parker, whose wisdom, kindness, and humor made the last year I spent working on this book better in numberless forms.

I have had the good fortune at UM to work with a superb library staff and fantastic administrative colleagues and have counted on Elizabeth Desarov, Lilly Leyva, Matt Lubbock, Keyla Medina, and Michelle Prats for years of invaluable assistance. Many remarkable undergraduate and graduate students have helped me to think through some of the questions raised here, whether in class or in their own projects. I would like to acknowledge especially Eduardo Castro, Monique Labat, Américo Mendoza-Mori, Alfredo Palacio, María Gracía Pardo, Maisa Zakir, and two excellent research assistants: Sandra Bernal Heredia and Katherine Davis. You have taught me much, and I look forward to reading your books in years to come.

The staff at the University of North Carolina Press has been wonderfully supportive of this project for nearly two years. I would like to thank my editor, Mark Simpson-Vos, and his assistant, Zachary Read, for their patience and careful guidance; Alex Martin for his helpful suggestions and exceptional copyediting; Paula Wald for shepherding the manuscript through production; and Dino Battista and Beth Lassiter for their work in promoting the book.

Andrew Canessa, whose work I have long admired, kindly expressed interest in this project when I first contacted him regarding the First Peoples Initiative several years ago, and to him I am also sincerely grateful. The anonymous readers of my manuscript provided invaluable critique and advice, and I thank them for considering my work with such care and in the genuine spirit of helping me to make it a better book. While any value this project might now have is largely due to them and to all of the mentors, colleagues, and friends mentioned above, its shortcomings, of course, belong to me.

I wish, finally, to thank my family for their encouragement and patience. To my remarkable grandmother, Concetta, who, approaching her centenary, has seen it all, already, and charitably reminds me not to worry; to my godmother, Joanne, always a strong and precious ally; to my brother Matthew, who shares my incapacity to ignore the other side of the story; to my brother Patrick, who won back his life while I fiddled around with these pages and taught me more about courage than I ever cared to learn; and to my parents, Thomas and Jeanne, whom I could not love more, and who never wavered in their support, despite the fact that we disagree about many important things: my deepest gratitude. Words are insufficient to thank Eduardo, who accompanied this project with extraordinary generosity for over a decade, contributed to it in immeasurable ways, and gave me, during the same years, two most precious gifts: Marina and Siena, brilliant and challenging teachers who, as fortune would have it, graciously invite me to play on the seashores of their endless worlds.

ABBREVIATIONS

AIR   Acampamento Revolucionário Indígena (*sic*) (Indigenous Revolutionary Camp)

CNPI   Conselho Nacional pela Proteção dos Índios (National Council for the Protection of Indians)

COIAB   Coordenação das Organizações Indígenas da Amazônia Brasileira (Coordination of Indigenous Organizations of the Brazilian Amazon)

CPI   Comissão Parlamentar de Inquérito (Parliamentary Commission of Inquiry)

EBI   Educação Bilíngue Intercultural (Bilingual Intercultural Education)

FBC   Fundação Brasil Central (Central Brazil Foundation)

FINRAF   Former International Reserve of Amazon Forest (*sic*)

FUNAI   Fundação Nacional do Índio (National Indian Foundation)

GRUMIN   Grupo de Mulheres Indígenas (Group of Indigenous Women)

IIHA   Instituto Internacional da Hiléia Amazônica (International Hylean Amazon Institute)

INBRAPI   Instituto Indígena Brasileiro para Propriedade Intelectual (Brazilian Indigenous Institute for Intellectual Property)

NGO   nongovernmental organization

PAC   Programa de Aceleração do Crescimento (Accelerated Growth Program)

PT   Partido dos Trabalhadores (Workers' Party)

SIVAM   Sistema de Vigilância da Amazônia (Amazonian Vigilance System)

SPI   Serviço de Proteção aos Índios (Indian Protection Service)

UNESCO   United Nations Educational, Scientific, and Cultural Organization

UNI   União das Nações Indígenas (Union of Indigenous Nations)

VNA   Vídeo nas Aldeias (Video in the Villages)

NATIVE
AND NATIONAL
IN BRAZIL

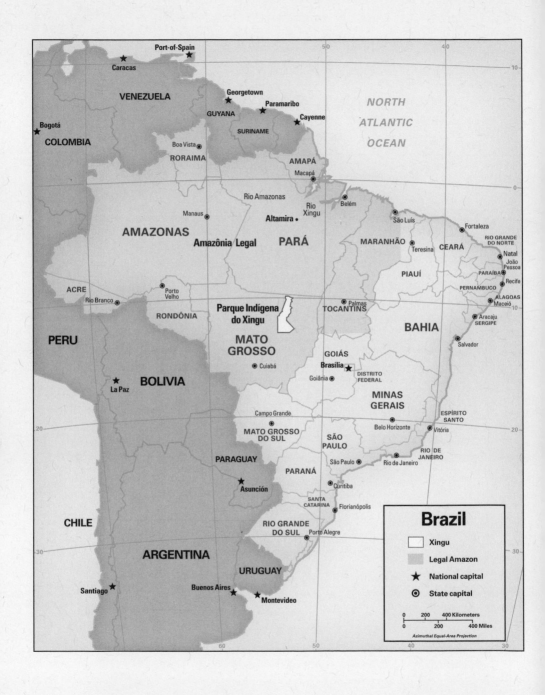

INDIANS WITHOUT INDIGENEITY

The Colonialist Renderings of the Present

PLAYING INDIAN, BRAZILIAN STYLE

In a crowded theater decorated with giant animated figures, multicolored helium balloons, costumed musicians, and thousands of tiny, flashing lights, dozens of small children sing, jump, and wave colored flags and pompoms in the air. Behind them, a huge pink spaceship looms above stage. In the foreground, blond teenagers dressed in toy soldier costumes and pointy feather headdresses hop around in circles. They surround another blond woman, slightly older, who wears a waist-length headdress resembling that of a Sioux warrior. Though she dances in a Rio de Janeiro TV studio, her jacket, embroidered and embellished with long fringe, is reminiscent of the U.S. Southwest.[1] Shaking a wooden maraca and bouncing until her huge headpiece finally slips off, she leads the group in a cheery tune: "Vamos brincar de índio!" ("Let's Play Indian!"). In broken Portuguese, meant to imitate "Indian talk," they all sing:

Let's play Indian, but without anyone to capture me!
Come, join my tribe! I'm chief and you're my partner.
Indian make noise. Indian have pride.
Come paint your skin so the dance can begin.
I grab my bow and arrow, my canoe, and I go fish.
Let's make a fire, eat the fruit of the earth.
Indian wants whistle but knows how to yell!
Indian doesn't fight. Indian doesn't make war.

Indian once owned this land. Indian all alone.
Indian want affection. Indian want back his peace [*sic*].[2]

Lost among the feathered performers, the ecstatic children, and the giant UFO is a small group of Xavante—four men and four young boys— who stand wide-eyed and stiff in the midst of the circuslike festivities.[3] Although they physically occupy center stage, they appear uncomfortable and out of place, making no sound or movement to accompany the performers or their audience. Holding spears and wearing red and black body paint and a few corporal adornments (but no headdresses), they serve as props behind the all the glitter, noise, and excitement. Since they say nothing, we can only imagine what they might have thought of the performance and their own awkward role in it.

While the Xavante stand ignored in the middle of the crowded stage, the blond powwow continues on for several minutes, complete with "Indian-style" drumming, tomahawk chops, and a chorus of shrill hand-over-the-mouth "war cries." Finally, star performer Maria da Graça Meneghel—better known as Brazil's most popular children's entertainer, Xuxa—stops dancing long enough to approach one stone-faced Xavante man and shouts in his face: "Little ones! Let's play Indian and teach people how to respect the Indian, which is living nature!" She then grabs the hand of one terrified Xavante boy and begins to skip around, dragging three others with her while showing them, presumably, how to dance like Indians. Goaded on, the humiliated children trudge forward while their blonde doppelgangers yell and wiggle until the song finally comes to an end.

While it is difficult to choose the most troublesome aspect of this ostensible appeal to the then-burgeoning ethos of multiculturalism, the conclusion of the presentation, when the "Indians" are shown how to "play Indian," is particularly jarring. Unfortunately for Xuxa and her *Xou* ("show"), the Xavante (perhaps chosen for the alliterative quality of their name) do not perform their assigned task particularly well. Alongside the costumed, hand-chopping, war-crying dancers, they seem, in fact, rather plain and uninteresting. Fixed on a stage where the performance of "Indianness" eclipses any presumable will to self-representation, the flesh-and-blood Natives cannot begin to measure up to their rendering by and in dominant Brazilian society, here represented by media giant Globo TV.

Xuxa's flat and mocking rendering of "Indianness" is a common one in Brazil, laden with sociocultural assumptions, political hierarchies, and interpretations of the past so deeply engrained in dominant society and cultural production that they make such performances seem not only unremarkable and acceptable, but also pleasurable, entertaining, and worthy of celebration. Since the time this show was produced in the late 1980s, its commodification and commercialization of Indianness have been witnessed by millions of spectators at home and abroad who have never have had any contact with indigenous peoples in Brazil or elsewhere. Even in a climate increasingly marked by political correctness, if not necessarily by heightened cultural sensitivity or tolerance, many enthusiasts still characterize "Brincar de índio" as innocuous children's entertainment—an expression of solidarity with the "Indian cause," as it were. Little does it matter to them, perhaps, that the "Indianness" it plays is in fact more evocative of an old Hollywood western or a controversial sports mascot than of the nearly 900,000 Native Brazilians who now reside throughout a vast and diverse country—from the Amazonian rainforests and the arid Northeast, to the Pantanal lowlands, and the outskirts of metropolitan São Paulo—that they increasingly claim as their own, and in explicitly national terms.

Xuxa is but one in a centuries-long line of nonindigenous Brazilians to exploit the idea and image of "Indianness" for personal gain and the amusement of others. But her show is significant for two reasons: First, because it was astonishingly lucrative and popular—not only in Brazil, but across Latin America.[4] And second, because it serves as a microcosm of the sociopolitical context in which staged and hyperbolic renderings of Native peoples have been relentlessly subsumed by and reproduced in the popular imaginary.

This book is about the ways dominant Brazilian society—intellectuals, scientists, civil organizations, journalists, practitioners of popular culture, political leaders, and state agencies, for example—has sought to represent "Indians" from the mid-nineteenth century to the present, and how the lives and ideas of indigenous peoples have informed, engaged, contested, and at times managed to decolonize those representations. I wish not, of course, to essentialize a nonindigenous Brazilian perspective,[5] but to highlight the consequences in hegemonic political discourses and cultural forms of the fact that Native Brazilians have rarely, if ever, had a say in official or dominant renderings of indigeneity, or in the long list of colonialist and assimilationist "solutions" that have been offered up since national independence in 1822 to address what has long been posited across the Americas as the "Indian question" or "problem": How do "Indians" relate to a dominant national project? The chapters that follow explore how and why indigenous peoples in Brazil have made this question their own, despite their perpetual exclusion from that project and ongoing treatment within the national polity as second-class citizens.

"Playing Indian"—which names not only Xuxa's song but also historian Phil Deloria's book on manipulations of Native imagery in the United States[6]—refers here to the ways indigenous peoples in Brazil have been silenced, infantilized, exploited, and mimicked in popular culture for profit and pleasure. As in Deloria's formulation, "Indian play" in Brazil feeds a collective fantasy about national origins and identity. Unlike in the North American context, however, the gesture in the Brazilian case does not "force an acknowledgement" of the social realities of living indigenous peoples.[7] Quite to the contrary, it points to a long-standing tendency for the state-backed "indigenist" bureaucracy[8] to supplant the potential for Native subjectivity (voice) and empowerment (movement) with predetermined and immutable ideas about who indigenous people are and how they ought to behave, leading over time to a phenomenon that anthropologist Alcida Ramos called the "hyperreal Indian."[9] Adapting philosopher Jean Baudrillard's concept of the simulacrum, Ramos wrote in the late 1990s that Native peoples, for motives ranging from the desire for land demarcation and educational opportunities to the urgent need for health care and reliable sources of income, had often been compelled to reproduce the far-fetched images of Indianness created by and for the dominant majority—and particularly by development workers and NGOs.[10] The Indian of traditional indigenist discourse thus came to reflect what Baudrillard called the fourth phase of the image—a figure so far removed from its original source that it would no longer bear any resemblance to reality at all.[11]

Likewise, in the video rendition of "Brincar de índio," the cheerless Xavante "performers" are entirely absent, leaving a plumed Xuxa to sing and dance alone alongside smiling cartoon "Indians" whose rendition of "Indianness" is more in keeping with the jubilant tone of her show. Continuing with the metaphor of indigenist politics, the Indian figures could never disappear entirely, because they stand in for a century's worth of state-sponsored "Indian protection," advocacy, education, and social programs that even now—more than a full decade into the twenty-first century—have never been led by a self-identifying indigenous person.[12]

The critique of this imagery and its enduring power is not to suggest that fantasy ought to be replaced by authenticity. As I will argue, along with others who have engaged in this debate, the roads to the authentic are congested and dangerous.[13] Nonetheless, as a social and cultural phenomenon, more than just a song, "Brincar de índio," reveals how capitalist

Maria da Graça Meneghel (Xuxa) "dressed in an Indian costume for Rede Globo's Xou da Xuxa Program," Rio de Janeiro, February 1989. Photo by Oscar Cabral. Courtesy of Editora Abril.

multiculturalism cannot be pulled free from its roots of exploitation and excess, regardless of the desires and intentions that it might hold in store. By failing to address the inequitable distributions of power and resources among dominant and subaltern groups, proponents of such discourses ultimately rearticulate colonialism in more prejudicial and thus more insidious ways.[14] If indeed, as Aníbal Quijano and Immanuel Wallerstein have argued, "there could not have been a capitalist world-economy without the Americas,"[15] then the story of Native peoples in Brazil is also the story of capital—from the spilling of what the Portuguese Jesuit Antônio Viera called "red gold" (indigenous blood) in the mid-seventeenth century,[16] to the parceling out of Native lands in the nineteenth and twentieth, to Globo TV's unabashed marketing of Xavante bodies on the eve of the twenty-first. There is, indeed, as Judith Friedlander observed in her classic critique of "cultural radicals" and "self-serving anthropologists" in northeastern Mexico, "no contradiction between growing interest . . . in Indian cultures and the expanding influence of global capitalism."[17] In a word, "Indianness" sells.

Any story of mere disempowerment, however, is woefully incomplete, for as I aim to show in these pages, indigenous peoples' creative engagements with politics and the market also continue to shape their lives, communities, and the national community in countless ways.[18] As I conclude this book in 2012, indigenous organizations across the country are ending a long and visible, if ultimately unsatisfactory campaign to elect the first indigenous president to the state's official indigenist body, the Fundação Nacional do Índio (National Indian Foundation, or FUNAI).[19] In staunch opposition to the ruling party's ongoing initiative to build Belo Monte—the third-largest hydroelectric dam in the world—in the Amazonian state of Pará,[20] the vice coordinator of the Coordenação das Organizações Indígenas da Amazônia Brasileira (Coordination of Indigenous Organizations of the Brazilian Amazon, or COIAB), Sônia Bone Guajajara, continues to argue for an alternative program of ethnodevelopment to which indigenous peoples could contribute with autonomy, recognition of their ancestral knowledge, and prior and informed consent regarding the use of their protected territories. "We are not against national growth," she explained in 2009 to an audience at the University of Chicago. "We are against the [government's] Programa de Aceleração do Crescimento (PAC) [Accelerated Growth Program], which doesn't work for us. . . . Brazil does need to grow, [but also] to take its people along—not abandon them to fate."[21]

"Indian play" is thus contested by Native Brazilians for what it ultimately signifies: the failure of the state to address satisfactorily, in social, cultural, political, economic, and juridical terms, the role of indigenous peoples in a nation famously marked by both a high degree of ethnocultural mixture [*mestiçagem*] and radical heterogeneity of every kind.[22]

Xuxa's ironic characterization of the Xavante as *natureza viva* (living nature) reiterates the long history of colonialist discourses that have sought to meld indigenous peoples into the measureless green rainforest or harness their knowledge of its resources for someone else's gain. The "Indians" on Globo's stage—rigid and static in their anger, embarrassment, or bemusement—bring to mind instead a *natureza morta* (still life), with all the liveliness and acumen of a bowl of fruit. Their projected incapacity to communicate, underscored by the "me Tarzan, you Jane" register of the Portuguese they speak through the mouths of Xuxa and her audience, has been reproduced in popular renderings of Indianness ever since Pedro Álvares Cabral laid eyes on Monte Pascoal in April 1500.

"Brincar de índio" further replicates dominant indigenist thought and policy by censoring the Xavante, ensuring that they will not utter a single word, and confirming the entrenched images of passivity and backwardness that are already held dear by so many members of Xuxa's real and virtual audience. Rather than "teaching people how to respect the Indian" or otherwise working to manifest understanding of, or empathy with the cultural specificities, social challenges, or political struggles of Native Brazilians, "Brincar de índio" is a performative utterance that does quite the opposite: It imposes silence and bolsters the notion that even if someone were willing to listen or able to understand them, indigenous peoples would not likely have anything valuable to say—not about themselves, and even less so about the broader national society and world in which they live.

Consider in this light the famous commentary on the *koro* (wood grubs) in Claude Lévi-Strauss's *Tristes Tropiques*, arguably one of the most widely read texts about "Indians" in Brazil (or anywhere) of all time. The anthropologist muses:

> The Indians now refuse to admit that they enjoy eating these creatures. . . . And if you enter an Indian house unannounced you can often see—just for a second, before they have time to whip it away—a cup in which the favorite worms are wriggling by the score. . . . All this makes it difficult actually to watch the *koro*-extractors at their work. We spent a considerable time plotting and planning how best to achieve it. One old fever-stricken Indian whom we found, all by himself in an abandoned village, seemed just the man to help us; we put an axe in his hand and tried to push or prod him into action. But to no avail: he feigned not to know what we were after. . . . Eventually we got him to a suitable trunk . . . where deep in the hollow of the tree, a network of canals lay waiting. In each one was a fat white creature. . . . The Indian looked on impassively while I cut off the head of the worm. The body oozed a whitish substance, which I tasted, not without some hesitation. . . . Thus baptized, I was ready for real adventures.[23]

By aligning Orientalizing images and the Indians' inability or reluctance to communicate with his own cunning and willingness to speak for them, the anthropologist's tale exemplifies the essential gestures of traditional indigenist discourse: By courageously eating the *koro* in preparation for "new adventures," he not only "plays Indian" but also "goes Native," thereby bolstering his own privileged role as a self-appointed conduit between indigenous and nonindigenous worlds.

Of course, anthropology's critique of its own power in the decades following the 1955 publication of Lévi-Strauss's classic study cast new light on that privilege and on the future of all ethnographic research, in Brazil and elsewhere. And yet, the overall record is by no means clear or simple. As I discuss at length in chapter 2 and highlight in chapters 3 and 4,

Brazilian(ist) social science, and anthropology in particular, have at times been complicit in the subjugation, abuse, and even murder of indigenous peoples. At the same time, anthropologists and ethnographers have also served as crucial advocates for Native Brazilians vis-à-vis the state, dominant society, and both national and international big business, at times providing key information about the ideas and experiences of individuals and communities whose lives seem to have seeped out of most official histories. Still, as I aim to demonstrate throughout the book and especially in chapters 1 and 5, ethnographic observation is but one way to gain insight into the life experience of subaltern "Others." Indeed, while years of my own work in the "field" inform and frame this study, my discussion also draws on a wide variety of self-fashioned representations through creative and political discourses that seek to address the always thorny question of what it means to be an "Indian," "indigenous," or "Native" person in Brazil from the mid-nineteenth century to the present.

The many meanings and contentious uses of this vocabulary are one central theme of this book and are highlighted throughout. Although my main interest here is Brazil, I refer frequently to Spanish- and English-dominant societies, so that the multiple filters of translation further complicate already complex questions of terminology, signification, and interpretation. Acknowledging what Michael Taussig famously called "the politics of epistemic murk" and the "fiction of the real,"[24] our starting point must be, I believe, to recognize the always contingent and thus imprecise function of each of these terms and its referents.

The individuals to whom I refer most often identify first with a particular people—as Xavante, Terena, Aymara, Guarani, or Mohawk, for example—and only second, often strategically, as "indigenous" or "Native." Although questions of language, meaning, and interpretation are a primary focus of chapter 1 and are contextualized constantly in light of the historical and political frameworks of each subsequent chapter, it is important to clarify that, in general, I use *indigenous* and *Native* interchangeably to refer to the realm of self-identification, and *indigeneity* to refer to the lived experience of that identification. In contrast—and appreciating that there are exceptions, including in Brazil, where the term *índio* is still frequently invoked in self-reference despite its bureaucratic and colonialist connotations[25]—I use "Indian" and "Indianness" to designate essentializing and Orientalist constructions in a wide range of discourse, from fiction, popular culture, and advertising, to state policy, education, and various forms of social science. Of course, because some of these referents inevitably overlap, their use can never be justifiably severed from the circumstances out of which they emerge. Paraphrasing philosopher and art critic Nelson Goodman, the best question may ultimately not be "*Who* is indigenous?" but rather "*When* is there an indigenous person?"[26]

In each chapter, I have sought to narrate my version of events within these parameters while making it clear that the "how and why" of the terminology original to my archival sources and used by my interlocutors changes constantly, oftentimes confoundingly, over time and across space. Differences between rural and urban, Amazonian and Northeasterner, older and younger, bilingual and monolingual, are a handful of the many factors that weigh into the ever-changing articulations of indigenous self-identification that unfold in the chapters that follow—all voices that reflect what anthropologist Andrew Canessa has aptly called a "social relation imagined in historical terms."[27] It is crucial to note, furthermore, that while some indigenous Brazilians are certainly caught up in the legal ramifications and sociopolitical impact of language use itself, many more are too busy navigating the startling proliferation of anti-indigenous public policy to dedicate much of their time or energies to such matters. This fact alone, of course, does not detract from the urgency of the terminology. As I argue throughout the book, and particularly in chapters 1 and 5, Native Brazilians working to reclaim the terms and concepts *índio* (Indian), *indígena* (indigenous), *indianidade* (Indianness), and *indigeneidade* (indigeneity), still have to rise above the colossal legacies of colonialist ideas and images—and perhaps particularly the well-intentioned ones—before they can even get started.[28]

COLONIALISMS PAST AND PRESENT

The tendency to negate indigenous subjectivity in the effort to interpret or showcase "Indianness" is an old one, evident in the earliest renditions of Brazil's colonial encounter. It begins with what is widely considered to be the country's founding document: a letter, long hallowed in popular and erudite renderings of the Brazilian past,[29] penned by Cabral's secretary, Pêro Vaz de Caminha, to King Manuel I of Portugal on 1 May 1500. Although Caminha's long and self-conscious missive told of the difficulties and wonders of the adventurers' long journey—of fatal illnesses and lost ships, lush landscapes, and vast riches—one primary interest was with those curious and "bestial people of little knowledge," and the ways in which they were different from, and occasionally, similar to "us."[30]

Caminha's comments included sweeping observations of cultural phenomena and social customs ranging from language use to hygienic practices and faith (or the presumed lack thereof), as well as a series of sanguine observations about attractive Native bodies, with an emphasis on skin color, nose shape, and uncircumcised and well-groomed *vergonhas* (pudenda, or as the term is more commonly translated "private parts").[31] Underlying this protoethnographic rundown of similarity and difference were the foundational colonialist assumptions that would ground dominant discourse on Indianness into the twenty-first century: first, that the Indians were empty vessels with scant valuable knowledge and few beliefs of their own; second, that they should be filled up with the knowledge and beliefs that "we" see fit to offer "them"; and finally, as I foreground in chapter 1 and examine in detail in chapters 3 and 4, that doing so successfully would ultimately be a matter of education—an investment of "our" time and effort to show "them" how to be more like "us." Acutely aware of his audience, Cabral's shrewd scribe observed: "They seem to be such an innocent people, that if we understood their speech and they ours, they would immediately become Christians, seeing that they neither have nor understand any belief, or so it seems. . . . *They can be stamped with any mark you wish to place upon them*. . . . If Your Highness sends someone here to spend some time among them, they will all be transformed and converted according to your wishes."[32]

Both with and without the power of the Church, the task of recasting and reimagining the Indians in "our" collective image only grew in importance and scope during the nineteenth-century development of Brazilian nationhood, which I explore in detail in chapter 2. Following the positivist tradition, in which faith in God would be supplemented or replaced by an equally vehement faith in "order and progress," the struggle for souls became a campaign to win not so much hearts and minds but *braços*— "arms to help build the country," as one concerned citizen put it candidly in 1952.[33]

Like the Christian proselytizing that came before it, then, positivist and nationalist proselytizing was tied to the rhetoric and practice of schooling—individual and collective, formal and informal—through which "Indians" would be transformed into useful "neo-Brazilians." Because indigenous peoples as such never vanished according to plan, however, many such educational processes became nothing more than self-perpetuating echoes of the colonial logic of "evolutionary development." As Caminha put it to the king at the dawn of the sixteenth century: "The best fruit to be taken from [the land] . . . [would] be the salvation of these people."[34]

Following independence, scientists, politicians, intellectuals, and artists debated the racial future of their predominantly nonwhite country in a context of intensifying scientific racism. After the abolition of slavery in 1888, and in the wake of the declaration of the First Republic in 1889, a small and rapidly dwindling indigenous population began to take on a disproportionately large role in the ever-amorphous notion of Brazilianness. As what Roberto DaMatta considers a human symbol of mediation between blacks and whites, embodying irreducible difference rather than the *mestiço* or *mulato* capacity for "encompassing opposition,"[35] the *figure* of the Indian as pure, genuine, and authentic has always been a potential thorn in the side of the dominant majority and the widely embraced narrative of single, mixed-race Brazilianness. To the extent that "Indianness" is muted, distant, powerless, or invented (i.e., "my great-grandmother was an Indian"), it is safe and acceptable, even a potential source of pride. When a self-identifying indigenous person gets too opinionated, however, too close, too demanding, or too real—by making claims to land, resources, education, or the leadership of FUNAI, for example—he or she moves out of the realm of what Charles Hale has called "authorized Indianness"[36] to become a threat, a source of fear and contention, or a target of loathing.

While the goal of transforming Indianness into something different and "better" has almost always been unidirectional, aimed at a future in which Indianness would be tempered or "improved" so much as to disappear into Brazilianness, it has also existed in conjunction with the symbolic exchange of cultural objects and practices—the colonialist desire to "play Indian," which also dates to the earliest encounters with Native Otherness. In his letter to King Manuel I of Portugal, Cabral's scribe recounted a legendary swap between members of the crew and "those people" who had come to greet the bearded arrivals to the "Land of the True Cross."[37] One cordial seafarer named Nicolau Coelho managed to convince an inquisitive and anxious group of bow-and-arrow wielding locals to lay down their weapons. Out of gratitude for their compliance, he presented them with the few items he had at hand: a red cap, a black hat, and a linen bonnet from his own head. The Natives, in turn, offered their own gifts: a string of beads—likely seed pearls, to be sent to the king—and a headpiece of red and brown parrot feathers.[38]

In between Coelho's headdress and Xuxa's headdress, between the writing of Caminha's earnest letter and the staging of "Brincar de índio," myriad cultural and political discourses about Indians and Indianness would

Oscar Pereira da Silva, Desembarque de Pedro Álvares Cabral em
Porto Seguro, 1500, *1922. Photo by Hélio Nobre. Courtesy of the Acervo
do Museu Paulista da Universidade de São Paulo.*

be put forth by generation after generation of intellectuals, politicians,
activists, scientists, writers, and artists from across the country. As David
Treece, Darlene Sadlier, and Lilia Moritz Schwarcz have all argued, the
cultural identification between Brazilianness and Indianness only deep-
ened after independence, as sovereign Brazilian subjects forged new political, economic, and cultural relationships with their former colonizers.[39]
Although the popularity and proliferation of nineteenth-century romantic
Indianism[40] initially had little to do with its real-life referents, ultimately,
as I show in chapter 2, it intensified their suffering and placed their lives
and livelihoods in even greater jeopardy. Later, as I discuss in chapters
3 and 4, state-backed indigenism beginning with the 1910 founding of
the Serviço de Proteção aos Índios (Indian Protection Service, or SPI)[41]
would be enthusiastically articulated in the best interest of the "Indians"
themselves because—paraphrasing Said, paraphrasing Marx—they were
"incapable" of representing one another.[42]

INDIGENEITY AND REPRESENTATION

The tendency to represent in this sense, to speak for or on behalf of as
proxy, must also be considered in light of the other dominant mode of

representing—that is, by concocting and reproducing an image or portrait.[43] The problem of representation is thus twofold: On the one hand, the political proxy represents without the consent, participation, or oftentimes even the awareness of those who are represented, thus revealing what anthropologist Alpa Shah has called "the dark side of indigeneity," and establishing an order that historian Ranajit Guha characterized in the case of postcolonial India as "dominance without hegemony."[44] On the other hand, this self-appointed and self-justifying mode of representation is predicated on an idea and image of subaltern and Native Otherness that has often, for good and for ill, reflected the needs, interests, and desires of those doing the projecting more than it has those of the projected. As a result, self-identifying indigenous peoples stand up, or are placed alongside the images created for them, and for a whole host of reasons—ranging from physical characteristics and language skills to geographical location and specific cultural practices (or the lack thereof)—fall short of the imagined ideal. The Xavante on Globo TV, after all, were not as good at "playing Indian" as Xuxa's audience might have hoped. And yet, as critic John Beverley concluded in his reflections on the much-debated testimony of Maya-Quiché intellectual Rigoberta Menchú Tum, the processes of representation also hold a potential for reciprocity through which indigenous and other subaltern actors can and do make use of interlocutors and their access to power and resources in ways that are often disregarded or ignored.[45]

However ambiguous or elusive, then, the motives and strategies behind different representations of Native peoples do matter as much as the ways they play out. If we fail to distinguish between ignorance and hatred, for instance, our efforts as students and educators will always be of negligible value, and any enthusiasm we might hold for the future of democratic heterogeneity—or, at the very least, a just and respectful acknowledgment of difference in what political philosopher Michael Walzer persuasively called the "thick" sense of the concept,[46] amounts to little more than folly or cynicism. In the case of Xuxa and Globo TV, any claim to social solidarity—even as a superficial but well-intended gesture—might have been grounded by inviting the Xavante to lead or join the celebration, rather than using them as a living backdrop against which non-Indians could carry out their performance of Indianness for other non-Indians.[47] Dominant renderings of indigeneity in politics and popular culture have long manifested a similar problem, tending to *speak for* rather than to listen, and to act *in place of* rather than alongside. The most cursory review of popular cultural forms in Brazil and across the Americas reveals the enduring power of racist stereotypes of Native peoples—including the continued popularity of Xuxa's "Brincar de índio."[48] In short, the Indian "question" or "problem" still has as much to do with imagined representations of difference (*Indianness*) as it does with lived experience (*indigeneity*) and thus serves not only as an important reminder of the popular tendency to conflate the two concepts but also of their ultimate incommensurability.

Why, then, as we mark a century of state-backed indigenism in Brazil, is the situation of indigenous peoples still so grave? Why is there no indigenous representation in the national congress? Why is FUNAI still led by a nonindigenous anthropologist? Why, in a country where the practice of racial discrimination has been outlawed since 1951,[49] are stereotypes and deprecating images of "Indians" still a popular source of entertainment? Who has and should have the authority to confront or contest such images? Which individuals, communities, and organizations ought to have the power to serve as the gatekeepers for legitimate (if never authentic) "Indianness"? Such questions are not easily answered because, of course, "Indianness" has always been a construction used or conferred with more or less legitimacy, depending on the actors and circumstances at hand. The Indian's "failure to become real" and "embody the natural" (to paraphrase Judith Butler's deconstruction of gender-based identities) is indeed the "constitutive failure of all . . . enactments for the very reason that these ontological locales are fundamentally uninhabitable."[50] In the end, there has never been and can never be a seamless match between Indianness and indigeneity.

But if these categories are always constructed to a greater or lesser degree, and if, as Butler puts it, "ontology is not a foundation, but a normative injunction that operates insidiously by installing itself into political discourse as its necessary ground,"[51] are all invocations of indigenous identity and identification but mere variations on Xuxa's unfortunate theme? In a word: no. All formulations of identity and identification can be more or less negotiable, more or less grounded in shared beliefs and lived experience, more or less representative of an ability or desire to connect with a collective, an ethos, a place, a past, or a set of convictions that lie beyond the realm of individual self-interest. But how have these constructions changed over time, and how have they remained the same? In what ways are they constitutive of *Indianness*, on the one hand, and *indigeneity*, on the other? How have they been recognized, employed, manipulated, and contested by different social actors—some self-identifying as indigenous, and others not? By and for whom, and to what ends? Finally, how can

Native and non-Native peoples talk to each other productively in light of the infinite constraints of language itself to collaborate toward common goals under the oftentimes unbearable weight of these legacies?

Although the colonialist appropriation of "Indians" and "Indianness" is alive and well throughout the Americas, the relationship between indigenous representation, social subalternity, and political empowerment continues to change in light of Native peoples' growing power to create and manipulate the images that are associated with them, and to engage in unmediated conversation and debate with the ideas and interlocutors who claim to speak on their behalf—either with or, as it has more often been the case, without consent and a claim to legitimacy. In Brazil, dozens of indigenous blogs, news columns, videos, Internet groups, and listservs now circulate thousands of open discussions regarding issues ranging from poetry and local elections, to the national leadership of FUNAI, to the future of state-indigenous relations in Brazil and around the globe. Although the "digital divide" makes access to resources uneven and the embrace of new technologies does not lead necessarily to social empowerment or positive political change, it is indisputable that some such technologies have already strengthened communication throughout the country and across international borders, promoting new forms of indigenous/nonindigenous collaboration and fostering more inclusive organizations, institutions, and processes in the realm of governance and popular cultural production.

The intense proliferation of indigenous political and cultural activism makes the enduring colonialist gesture of "playing Indian" both more predictable and more egregious. After all, the Indian-as-harmless-entertainment tends to garner more favorable attention from the dominant majority than nationally coordinated and globally engaged indigenous organizations armed with concrete social grievances and political demands. Consider for example the highly successful Globo TV soap opera *Uga, Uga* (2000) alongside the demonstrations in April of the same year by various Native groups to protest the whitewashed, state-sponsored celebration of the Brazilian quincentenary in Porto Seguro. At the same time that a melodramatic saga of a white boy raised in the Amazon by "good" Indians after his parents were murdered by "bad" ones garnered a massive audience, becoming one of the most popular *telenovelas* of all time,[52] Pataxó demonstrators were beaten by military police at the commemoration site and ridiculed for weeks thereafter in the national press.[53]

Leery of the "suspicious international NGOs" that must lurk behind any form of indigenous activism, Rio's municipal secretary for special projects, Sandra Cavalcanti, suggested that Native claims to political representation not only weakened national security and sovereignty but undermined the very project of Brazilian nationhood: "We are today a great, free, happy nation, open to the world—a paradise of racial mixture. No one in our country can suffer discrimination due to race or to creed. So let's stop with this paranoia of discriminating in favor of the Indians. For Brazil, the Indian is as Brazilian as the black, the mulatto, the white, and the yellow. *All those bloods run through our veins.* . . . I feel no obligation to ask the Indians for forgiveness during the celebration of Discovery. . . . Brazil is ours. It does not belong to the Indians. It never has."[54]

According to Cavalcanti, who derided the social agency and political claims of Native peoples while affirming her own distant claim to "Indian blood," Indianness can be overcome, overlooked, disparaged, and appropriated, all at the same time. As in decades past, the primary contention over the claim to indigenous alterity would boil down to the question of resources; the only thing worse than "discriminating in favor of Indians" would be to turn the country over to a nebulous cohort of "malicious" and "venomous" foreign interests.[55] Like the Brazilian elite of the late nineteenth and early twentieth centuries, then, Cavalcanti employed Indianness as a national(ist) symbol only when the "Indians" could be safely relegated to a present of gagged silence or a past of inferiority and backwardness that had, at least in her mind, happily been overcome.

Exactly one decade later, in January 2010, some 500 indigenous activists calling themselves the Acampamento Revolucionário Indígena (Indigenous Revolutionary Camp, or AIR [*sic*]) staged an extended demonstration in Brasília to protest Presidential Decree 7.056/09 of December 2009, aimed effectively at dismantling and privatizing FUNAI through the elimination of hundreds of regional offices and their services across the country. By mid-June 2010, the protestors seemed to have achieved a partial victory when the then justice minister, Luiz Paulo Barreto, agreed to raise several of the group's demands with President Luis Inácio "Lula" da Silva.[56] Nothing would ever come of these demands, however. Ridiculed by the local press and popular editorialists as a group of "fake" and "lazy Indians" out to milk the state, the AIR was removed violently from its campsite in front of the Ministry of Justice and forced to move its protest online, where it continues to the time of this writing.[57]

In its analogous preference for silent and acquiescent Natives, Xuxa's "Brincar de índio" was all the more unfortunate for the watershed moment in which it appeared: 1989—centenary of the First Republic; year of the First Encounter of the Indigenous Peoples of Xingu to protest the development of a series of hydroelectric dams in the Amazon;[58] and just months after the authors of a new national constitution closed the door on twenty years of authoritarian rule by limiting state power and safeguarding the "Fundamental Rights and Guarantees" of all Brazilian citizens.[59] For the first time in the country's legal history, "Indianness" would be considered a permanent ethnic marker rather than an inconvenient stopover on the teleological path to bona fide Brazilianness through dark forests of cultural assimilation, socioeconomic "progress," and the development of an appropriate political consciousness.[60]

As historian Seth Garfield has shown, the decades leading up to the 1988 Constitution revealed the Xavante to be adept negotiators in securing land rights and advancing their other key material interests.[61] In 1982, the Xavante cacique Mário Dzururá (otherwise known as Mário Juruna) became the first indigenous Brazilian elected to the national Congress.[62] Two years earlier, in November 1980, he had been at the center of a nation-wide debate about "Indian tutelage" after FUNAI denied him a passport and permission to leave the country to participate in the Fourth International Russell Tribunal in Rotterdam.[63] In 1977, he had become famous for recording and making public his conversations with indigenist bureaucrats who tended to forget important promises made behind closed doors. In January of that year, fearing that the FUNAI director of general operations would not keep his word, Juruna turned over a recorded discussion to journalists, who published it the following day in its entirety.[64] The tape recorder became a symbol and a weapon in the struggle for direct political representation in the years that followed: "The white man makes a lot of promises," he explained in an interview later that year. "Then he forgets everything. And the Indian can't prove it. Who's going to keep me from recording?"[65]

Despite such creative political efforts, years of strategizing, organizing, and carefully planned deployments of ethnic identification by Juruna and other indigenous leaders throughout the country could be eclipsed in minutes by the likes of Globo TV, which reinforces, instead, the familiar image of wordless, naive, passive "Indians" who can be manipulated not only by state policy and the whims of dominant society but also by a dancing pop icon and her adolescent sidekicks. Today, millions of people throughout Brazil and around the world remain enraptured with multimillionaire Xuxa and her many talents. Fewer will recall Juruna, who spent his final years impoverished, ill, and estranged from his community before dying of diabetes in 2002.[66] And while a handful of academics, politicians, NGO workers, and indigenist functionaries might be aware of the

Federal Deputy Mário Juruna (the first indigenous Brazilian elected to the National Congress) during the vote for the Dante de Oliveira Constitutional Amendment to restore the direct election of the Brazilian president, Brasília, 25 April 1984. Photo by Carlos Namba. Courtesy of Editora Abril.

contentious and violent history of power struggles between the Xavante (and other indigenous groups) and the state, millions more would see and accept instead the happy and more comfortable image of Xuxa's "cultural exchange" with a handful of nondescript "Indians."

Such renderings are, of course, never "harmless." To the contrary, they are perpetuated and embraced only to the detriment of Native and other discriminated peoples who must battle daily with the legacies of colonialist thought and practice, including but not limited to racism. Representation, in this sense, is a zero-sum game.

"Brincar de índio" thus serves here as a conceptual shortcut to a long-standing tradition in Brazilian politics and popular forms of cultural production of using the Indian as a liminal figure that symbolizes the ambiguous frontiers of the national community and the concept of national belonging itself, usually formulated in terms of citizenship. From the rhetoric of political and cultural independence to the development of anti-imperialist nationalism and popular discourses of multiculturalism, *the* Indian has always been a malleable figure to be molded or "played" expediently, according to the exigencies of the situation at hand. As in Deloria's study of "a characteristically American kind of domination" in the United States, "Indian play" in Brazil is often engaged with power struggles far removed from Native lives and interests. Yet, as other scholars have argued, and the growing industry of "aboriginal tourism" makes abundantly evident, the exigencies of cultural preservation and economic survival, and the postmodern politics of identity, also mean that nonindigenous peoples are not the only ones who engage in Indian "play."[67] After all, those who self-identify as indigenous must, like everyone else, select, emphasize, and make use of their personal attributes and life stories as best they see fit, in keeping with their needs, interests, skills, and resources, and according to the political demands on the horizon. In the end, we cannot discard the possibility that the Xavante men on Xuxa's stage may have found it necessary or desirable, for whatever reason, to be there.

BEYOND VICTIMIZATION

Writing in the late 1920s, the Peruvian philosopher José Carlos Mariátegui famously characterized *indigenist* writing as "still" the work of mestizos and prophesized about the social and political conditions under which "Indians" might be able to write for themselves so that a truly *indigenous* political expression might come into existence.[68] The implicit assumption of his analysis was that self-identifying "Indians" with pen in hand would automatically or naturally choose as their subject matter their collective histories and social conditions, thus providing the nonindigenous scholar with a direct conduit to Native subjectivity and unmediated and "authentic" views on "Indianness." Half a century later, testimonial narratives from throughout Latin America would be celebrated (and sometimes fetishized) as the next best thing to Mariátegui's dream, provoking endless debates in the academy over the nature of indigenous "authenticity" and its relationship to the representation of all subaltern peoples and voices.[69] As these debates have played out over the past three decades, the Americas witnessed a surge in the political participation and literary and cultural production of self-identifying Native peoples that would surely make Mariátegui's head spin and likely fulfill his prophetic wish—even if only to a limited degree in his native land.[70]

In addition to the most traditional literary forms, indigenous scholars, activists, and organizations throughout the Americas have also turned to a variety of visual media and the Internet as tools and channels for circulating their creative work and political platforms. For instance, the Vídeo nas Aldeias (Video in the Villages, or VNA) project, initiated nearly a quarter century ago by indigenist activist Vincent Carelli through the Centro de Trabalho Indigenista (Center for Indigenist Work), was a pioneering effort in this regard. Beginning in 1986 with collaborative work alongside the Nambiquara, VNA aimed to "support the struggles of indigenous peoples to strengthen their identities and their territorial and cultural patrimony" in the same social and historical context that Xuxa "played Indian" and Mário Juruna worked on behalf of the Xavante for land rights and representation in the National Congress.[71] Today, having produced dozens of videos and participated in a wide variety of educational and public information initiatives alongside indigenous peoples throughout the country, VNA is an independent nongovernmental organization—though not one entirely free of controversy.[72]

Despite the organization's clear dedication to social justice and indigenous rights, the issue of agency and the question of who is ultimately responsible for making VNA films remain open, even among some of the project's veteran facilitators. The VNA director and editor Mari Corrêa has posed the matter this way: "Are these films produced by us, theirs? What is the extent of our interference? What should we not teach? When will these films really be theirs? There are no easy answers to these questions, and we are not the only ones asking them. Although we don't have the answers, one thing is certain: they are films that they [the Indians] claim as their own. Let the debate begin."[73] As I discuss in chapter 5, even for the staunchest advocates of Native rights, including many who self-identify as indigenous, agency and authenticity return as the perennial chicken-and-egg of contemporary debates over the meanings of Indianness and indigeneity.[74] Corrêa's strategy of answering the question with questions hints again at self-identification as perhaps the most legitimate, if also always imperfect, answer. "Let the debate begin" points to the likelihood that, in reality, the most crucial aspects of the debate have indeed already been resolved.

But what happens when, contrary to Mariátegui's prophecies, Native peoples use their time, skills, and resources to talk about something *other* than Indianness or indigeneity? What if they prioritize different interests or emphasize distinct markers of identity, like gender, sexuality, class, nation, or vocation? What if they consider the notion of indigeneity to be an unwelcome imposition or disavow it altogether? Although such viewpoints are often discredited by indigenous advocates as a triumph of racism and other forms of colonialist thought, they point to the fact that the "Indian question" in Brazil can no longer be answered by the myriad political, social, and cultural entities that have historically claimed to speak for, or on behalf of, indigenous peoples. While self-preservation in the fullest sense of the term—what Anishinaabe critic Gerald Vizenor famously called "survivance"[75]—lies at the heart of Brazilian indigenous activism, Native commentary and critique are not now and indeed never have been limited to cultural traditions; community, local, and family histories; legends and myths; spirituality; or even concrete political struggles—however critical and interesting each of these issues may be. It now seems rather likely, in fact, that the intense focus on such matters as expressed in recent decades through the *testimonio* genre stemmed at least as much from the academic gaze and political interests that helped to shape that body of work as it did from the desire of "Native informants" to relay their stories with such themes in mind.

As Stuart Hall wrote over two decades ago in his theorization of a "new ethnicity," those who have seldom had an opportunity to be heard in their own voices are, unsurprisingly, eager to offer new versions of well-worn narratives and new interpretations of events that are already thought to be well understood.[76] And yet, as Hall also reminded us, "They are not prepared to be ethnic archivists for the rest of their lives. . . . They have a stake in the whole dominant history of the world [and] they want to rewrite the history of the world, not just tell my little story."[77] Likewise, while indigenous activists in Brazil and across the Americas have focused much of their work on political and cultural advocacy—calling attention to situations of crisis; working to recover and preserve communal lands, memories, and the languages in which they are embedded; rewriting and reinterpreting the histories that have been foisted on them, or from which they have been all but erased; and reforming educational processes and structures to make them more inclusive and representative—they have also worked to make the "little stories" relevant to "big" ones, and to place their ideas and priorities at the forefront of national and global political processes and social networks.

When communications guru Marshall McLuhan, author of the well-known phrase "The medium is the message," spoke of a global village and a metaphorical return to "tribal man" over half a century ago, his thoughts probably could not have been farther from the forests of Xingu.[78] McLuhan posited the metaphorical "retribalization" of the world as an involuntary and violent process through which the social role of individuals would be radically changed by the burgeoning influence of mass communications and mass production.[79] And yet, in an ironic twist on his uncannily prescient theories of communication, indigenous uses of "new" media in Brazil and elsewhere do, in fact, give credence to his prediction of a turn away from social and cultural forms and practices that revolve exclusively around individual experience and can be narrated in a strictly linear fashion. In many ways, the world does now function as a "single unit" or "tribe," as McLuhan put it in 1960, where "everyone gets the [same] message all the time," and the concepts that underlie dominant social behaviors and points of view are constantly in flux.[80] What he did not foresee, perhaps, were the countless ways in which tribal and other indigenous peoples from around the world would receive, interpret, re-create, and redeploy those messages and mediums in accordance with their own particular needs, interests, and beliefs, oftentimes subverting both the medium and the message in the process. As media scholar Freya Schiwy puts it, "The creative adaptations of indigenous rural communities have produced alternative spaces that are neither inside nor completely outside of the logic of capitalism, but rather, constitutive of an economic and epistemological border."[81]

In this sense, indigenous peoples in Brazil have been "rewriting the history of the world"[82] for a long time and in multiple ways, participating not only in local and regional politics but also in national and international debates over issues ranging from global warming and international terrorism to regional migration flows and the Arab-Israeli conflict. One important focus in these debates has been on how the local and the global relate to the national, and in particular, to the uneven state of Brazilian democracy by which indigenous peoples have always been marginalized, if not entirely excluded. Wapixana scholar and teacher Maria de Souza Delta has suggested that the project of "rewriting history" is inextricably tied to the power of interpretation and the level of cultural capital associated with distinct versions of the same story, past or present.

> Who writes history, whether a non-Indian or someone from the community, does matter. There are people who spend a year [in our community] and write things that are not quite right. I was analyzing a document that says things that are incorrect, "facts" that are incorrect. Oftentimes, the interpretation of one thing or another comes out wrong. The interpretations that others write of the Wapixana I find half wrong. . . . My professor . . . told me that I had to distance myself in order to write about my people. That's the nature of the work, with the Wapixana and others, and our cohabitation with the modern

world—the world of non-Indians. This is a process I see as natural. The important thing is that [the Wapixana] believe they will never cease being Indians. That's what really matters.[83]

Implicit in Delta's critique of the tendency to misrepresent Wapixana stories and versions of history seems to be some skepticism over the old ethnographic enterprise—that is, the notion that in a year's (or whatever) time, one can be endowed with enough truth and insight to serve as an interpreter or representative of the Wapixana people to the "outside world." Like Jorge Luis Borges's enigmatic ethnographer,[84] Delta points instead to the unsettling prospect that there is no "secret" to be revealed by ethnographic knowledge, that all interpretations of human experience are true and false in their "differences and contradictions" (epistemic murk, as Taussig would have it) and thus always limited, to some degree, in their power to interpret and to represent.

The truth that seems to matter most in Delta's case is the desire to self-identify with indigeneity (to "never cease being Indians"), in all of its complexity and potential ambiguity. But inasmuch as she questions her own ability to report "from a distance" on the community she takes to be her own, Delta does not propose a Manichean division of knowledgeable, capable "insiders" versus bumbling, mistaken "outsiders." She points, instead, to the "natural" distortion that occurs when we assign ourselves the task of translating an infinite number of possible versions of the story into one, and then have the audacity to call it "truth." Any claim to interpret or represent with legitimacy, she suggests, must also be accompanied by uncertainty and a healthy dose of humility.

The problem of indigenous representation in Brazil is compounded by another fundamental obstacle to communication. That is, the 2010 census identified more than 270 indigenous languages used throughout the country besides Portuguese. Although, as I discuss in chapter 1, this number is hotly debated by Native advocates and critics alike, indisputable is the limited circulation of academic and pedagogical materials in indigenous communities and their scant production in indigenous languages (and sometimes in Portuguese as well).[85] Such exclusions thus perpetuate a colonialist system of knowledge production that lacks even the token corroboration of its Native "objects of study"—many of whom, of course, already disagree vehemently among themselves about the most accurate and effective forms and means of self-representation. National- and regional-level meetings held in recent years to discuss the state of indigenous education, ongoing public discussions over the future leadership of

FUNAI, and contentious national debates over Amazonian development projects all attest to the fact that, aside from the basic recognition that some degree of political autonomy and the right to self-representation are crucial to the success of the Brazilian indigenous movement, there is no social or political consensus that stems organically from self-identification with indigeneity.[86] On the contrary, the very gesture of naming necessarily calls into question the many possible meanings that indigeneity holds, as well as differing perceptions of their relative compatibility.[87]

INDIGENEITY AND THE FUTURE OF POLITICS

The proliferation of diverging voices in this discussion over the past several decades makes it clear that Indianness can never be conceived as a transparent or exclusive representation of indigeneity. Whether through negation, comparison, or complementarity, dominant society's engagement with indigenous peoples must also be understood as a commentary on, and measure of, the idea of national identity and the always elusive notion of Brazilianness. The tensions between the political need for sociocultural homogeneity, the fetishization of multiculturalism, and the undying lore of Brazil's "racial democracy" thus play out continuously in the treatment of real and imagined Natives who are venerated as foundational First Peoples when it is convenient to do so and scorned as perpetual outsiders when it is not. Dominant Brazilian nationalism *needs* the colonial figure of the Indian, just as it *needs* those of the African and the Portuguese. The problem is that while the latter two have been largely (and of course, wrongly) reduced in the popular imaginary to skin color and subsumed into widely embraced notions of mixed-race nationhood,[88] indigenous actors project themselves tenaciously into the future as differentiated peoples—Brazilian, but also irreducibly indigenous. Dominant society longs instead for "Indians" without indigeneity.

Rejecting the colonialist discourses that have sought since the 1910 creation of the SPI to "include them" in the nation only on the condition of their de-Indianization and assimilation, many indigenous peoples, backed by the unfulfilled promises of the 1988 Constitution, identify not only as Maytapu, Munduruku, Pataxó, Payayá, Potiguara, Terena, Tukano, Wapixana, and Xavante (for example), but also as national—as distinctively *Brazilian* indigenous peoples.[89] Terena writer Lúcio Flores explains:

We carry with us the pride of being Brazilian, of having such notable compatriots, and such notable miscegenation. In this larger context we are part of Brazilian culture, and as a minority . . . we are questioned as to whether any trace remains of our traditional cultures. . . . *There . . . is a gap between our cultural practices and the visibility we are able to give to them*; the manifestations [of culture] in our communities are far from the sight of the mainstream media and major publications. Our reflections, our stories, our myths and our rites are of such greatness that they could be cited by the great thinkers of all times, because . . . our social and cultural values surpass many of humanity's frustrated attempts to exist in harmony. . . . Perhaps we will not be able to resolve some existing problems—like the future of the spaceship Discovery, or the struggle against terrorism—but still, we are crying in the desert that humanity is destroying itself, and that our old cultural baggage of living in harmony with nature is a window onto life.[90]

Rather than projecting himself and his fellow participants in the Brazilian indigenous movement as idealized remnants of a precolonial past or wishful protagonists of an "archaic utopia"[91] out to deny or undo the advances of capitalist modernity that have accompanied all of its destruction and horror, Flores posits his voice as one among many in an ongoing discussion about the future of his community, his country, and indeed, as he puts it, all of humanity. He does not purport to tell a "little story," to explain "merely" his worldview, or even to offer a narrative about the history of the Terena people. Instead, he questions the collection of assumptions about "Indianness" that grounds dominant understandings of nation, modernity, and progress, and recasts indigeneity as a source of knowledge to be tapped rather than a burden to be unloaded.

At the same time, Flores distances himself from the common images propagated by and in dominant cultural forms and traditional indigenist discourses of silent, stoic Indians frozen in time—or on Xuxa's stage—and the disempowering notions of purity and authenticity that typically accompany them. He embraces, instead, an interpretation of contemporary indigenous cultures as creative, dynamic, flexible, and open—necessarily so to have endured to our day. Indigeneity thus becomes a collaborative work-in-progress—a discourse of empowerment and optimism rather than one of persecution or amnesic glorification. He concludes: "At times we are mistaken for possessors of an 'ex-culture,' something backward, dead, prehistoric, and incapable of responding to the challenges imposed by postmodern life. . . . Faced with so many disastrous prognostications . . . , we too become overwhelmed and fearful. . . . Still, we bathe ourselves in life; in the power of our tradition and the depths of our cultures.

This potential propels us forward as owners of our actions, certain that we are more distant from the 'ex-culture' [but, at the same time,] unveiling a sculpture, which is ourselves."[92]

The nature of the "sculpture" to be unveiled is, once again, the subject of great debate, not only between indigenous and nonindigenous groups but also (to the extent that adapting to the challenges of postmodern life can be considered a choice) within and among indigenous communities. The willingness to confront the consequences of modernity head on—to embrace unfamiliar concepts, adopt new technologies, or open up to potentially threatening worldviews—is by no means unanimous. Certainly, there are as many opinions about the appropriate role for nonindigenous views and technologies in the future of indigenous life as there are indigenous peoples to express them.[93]

For some, like Flores, it is precisely the ability to adopt new forms of knowledge into Native societies and cultures and use them for their own benefit that have enabled indigenous Brazilians to reinvent and reestablish indigeneity into the twenty-first century. This vision is shared by Juvenal Teodoro, a Payayá cacique, activist, teacher, and writer from Bahia, for whom the incorporation of new information and modern technologies into indigenous life is, quite simply, a matter of life and death: "No people has remained outside the decision-making processes and control of the technologies of its time and managed to survive," he argues. "Failing to understand this, we will not have the means to fight for our own preservation."[94] And yet, without a specific idea of what *kinds* of technology are invoked in such assertions, of who will provide and have access to them, and at what price, the term alone means little. After all, some kinds of technology are easier to embrace than others; some are more compatible with the project of disseminating traditional indigenous knowledge and cultural forms than others. If tractors are not computers and transgenic foods are not vaccinations, who is to determine what is acceptable and what is not?

In an essay titled "The Corruption of the Ancestral Knowledge of Indigenous Peoples,"[95] educator and writer Daniel Munduruku argues against the notion that adopting new technologies—and biotechnology in particular—serves the long-term interests of indigenous peoples, their cultures, or their familial knowledge systems. He rejects the celebration of technology for its own sake and the various machinations of scientific "progress" that have "played Indian" by appropriating, marketing, and profiting from traditional forms of indigenous knowledge while reaping the material and other benefits of that "progress" for a select few. Even so, his stance and that of the Instituto Indígena Brasileiro para Propriedade Intelectual (Brazilian Indigenous Institute for Intellectual Property, or INBRAPI), which he directs, is not a traditionalist or reactive opposition to scientific investigation and "development." Rather, it calls attention to the ways the culling and exploitation of that knowledge have almost always taken place to the measurable detriment of indigenous peoples and communities. "The life that technology wants to offer is not life, but death," Munduruku surmises. If, as Alcida Ramos corroborates, "the tapping of indigenous knowledge and selected cultural features . . . has meant profits to non-Indians the dimensions of which the best informed Indians were until very recently unable to fathom,"[96] then crucial to the future of indigenous/nonindigenous relations and indigenous-state relations will be profit-sharing. Not in the circumscribed sense of divvying up earnings but rather as a radical reconceptualization of "development" that includes indigenous men, women, children, and their communities as coparticipants in and beneficiaries of "progress" rather than—as in the ongoing case of the Belo Monte hydroelectric dam—human fuel to be used up in the march to advance the well-being of others.

In her presentation of *Sol do pensamento* (*Sun of Thought*), an edited volume published in 2005 by INBRAPI and the Grupo de Mulheres Indígenas (Group of Indigenous Women, or GRUMIN), author and activist Eliane Potiguara reminds her readers that while contributors to the project deal primarily with modern technology and its impact on indigenous peoples throughout the country, many Native Brazilians still lack basic access to nutrition, healthcare, housing, and education.[97] Although these necessities might appear unrelated to the question of technology— or at least hierarchically related, with the need for immunizations taking precedence over the need for Internet access—Potiguara argues that the dichotomy is false, and that the fulfillment of basic needs and the opportunity to develop competence in modern technologies ought to be part of a single political initiative to expand and defend indigenous rights.[98] The majority of Brazilians, she affirms, are not asked to choose between vaccinations or e-mail, health or knowledge, body or mind. Indigenous Brazilians, of course, should not be compelled to do so, either.

Whether or not we accept Potiguara's position, it is clear that the "indigenous question" remains more crucial than ever in modern Brazilian society despite major advances on the fronts of political and cultural representation. For all of the local and international work and regional and global networking carried out by indigenous individuals, communities, scholars, activists, NGOs, and political organizations, as well as by their nonindigenous advocates and allies, the question of Native rights remains, as I argue throughout the book, inextricably tied to the state, which is still the ultimate guarantor or violator of those rights, and to the national society that will choose to prioritize them, or not. The issue, then, is not to fit "Indianness" into "Brazilianness" but to reimagine the nation and re-create its image to account for hundreds of thousands of Brazilians who refuse to see indigeneity and national belonging as mutually exclusive. Their belief in the ultimate coherence and complementarity of indigeneity and Brazilian nationhood is, indeed, the condition of possibility for contemporary indigenous political activism, intellectual practice, and cultural production.

CHAPTER OVERVIEW

Chapter 1 explores the gaps and overlaps in the treatment of Indianness and indigeneity in state policy and legislation, popular representation, and the self-renderings of Native peoples. I explain changing meanings of indigeneity in terms of lived experience and show how the question of "authenticity" intersects with broader struggles for resources, political power, and legal representation. In light of the challenge that the concept of indigeneity poses to Brazilian sovereignty and the ideal of mixed-race Brazilianness, the chapter illustrates why a relatively small indigenous population has played a significant role in shaping the ways that dominant society imagines itself as uniquely Brazilian. Far and above questions of "Indianness," indigenist thought and practice form a crucial political arena in which broad concepts like *humanity*, *modernity*, *citizenship*, and *progress* continue to be articulated and negotiated. Because the "Indian question" reflects changing perceptions of difference—as something to fear, eliminate, protect, or celebrate—it exists in constant tension with the ideal of a homogenous, *mestiça* nationhood. Indigenous Brazilians who challenge the evolutionary logic of traditional indigenist discourse and the ever-popular notion of the "Brazilian race" hence force us to examine what it means in political and theoretical terms to be Native and national at the same time.

Chapter 2 reconstructs the historical groundwork for these debates from the mid-nineteenth century through the early Vargas period. I show how the gap between indigenous experience and popular portrayals of "Indians" widened during the late 1800s as Brazil and "her" Native peoples became increasingly objectified and commercialized for national and international audiences and investors. As indigenous men, women, and children were enslaved as latex tappers during the rubber boom, scrutinized by legions of foreign "naturalists," drafted into the Paraguayan War, and hunted by those seeking to appropriate their lands, "Indians" were transformed through popular culture into caricatured tropes of Other and self: cannibals and Christians, as it were. The chapter explores the function of these hyperbolic templates of Indianness in diverse forms of cultural production, ranging from nationalist operas at the twilight of empire to celebratory interpretations of Brazilian exceptionalism on the eve of the Estado Novo. In the violent spaces of encounter between colonialist thought and the multiple processes of nation-building, "Indians" became the symbol of Brazilian nationalism while Native peoples began to forge their yet unfinished path to self-representation—political and otherwise.

Building on this dichotomy, chapter 3 shows how, over the mid-twentieth century, indigenous peoples became a national security threat while "Indians" were imagined as custodians of Brazilian borders and sovereignty. State-sponsored indigenism through the SPI thus sought to erase lived indigeneity while continuing to showcase "neo-Brazilians" as the embodiment of idealized nationhood. Exploring the ties between indigenist policy and broader nationalist discourses of modernity, the chapter illustrates how the rhetoric of education made improved and improvable "Indians" central to dominant ideas and ideals about scientific progress, economic growth, and national independence. At the same time, the practice of education was a biopolitical initiative that reconfigured traditional indigenous spaces and tied Native peoples more tightly to capitalist exploitation.

Chapter 4 widens the schism between Indianness and indigeneity by showing show how ethnographic, journalistic, and fictional discourses simultaneously shaped and undermined the state's policies for "indigenous protection." Framed by the legacies of the Indianist imagination and popular critiques of Brazil's April 2000 quincentenary "celebration," the discussion revolves around a controversial marriage between a *gaúcho* indigenist worker and a Kalapalo teenager in the early 1950s. Exploring academic debates and the strident outpouring of political support and public opinion for and against their "interracial" union, the chapter explains how the popular embrace of romantic fiction came to trump indigenous voice and experience—particularly those of the bride, Diacuí Kalapalo Aiute. Her story shows how Native women were triply burdened as subalterns: as objects for barter between indigenous and nonindigenous men, as victims of sexual and other forms of violence, and, in keeping with the hemispheric myth of what Deloria calls the "wilderness marriage,"[99] as suffering mothers of the romanticized *mestiça* nation.

In chapter 5, however, we see that women are now at the forefront of the Brazilian indigenous movement in terms of both cultural and political activism. I examine the ways Native scholars, writers, artists, and politicians across the country have worked over the last quarter century to dismantle the social discourses and political processes that configure them as "Indians" in the sense conceived by and in the dominant society. Although the battle over representation remains critical in light of the ongoing exclusion of indigenous peoples from national governance, legislation, and development planning, and their perpetual denigration in popular culture forms, Native engagement with national and international audiences through virtual social networks and personal media have also opened up new political fronts. By challenging dominant paradigms of sovereignty, education, and value while, at the same time, seeking public office at local, regional, and state levels, indigenous Brazilians are destabilizing mainstream renderings of indigeneity against great odds. As a key tool in this process, creative cultural production is vital not only to the movement but to Brazil, and indeed, to the future of politics in what promises to be a postindigenist era of representing indigeneity.

1

FROM ACCULTURATION TO INTERCULTURALITY

Paradigms for Including through Exclusion

On the indigenous post of Capitão Uirá, some 400 kilometers from the northeastern city of São Luis, a boy who had been given the Portuguese name Raimundo Roberto by local authorities penned a classroom assignment titled "Ditado" ("Dictation") into his school notebook. Adjacent to his sketch of the Brazilian flag, the Canela[1] student known as Kapêlituk by the members of his community transcribed a short dialogue as his teacher read it to the students in a language that was not theirs:

> Bentinho and Marieta sometimes discuss what they learn in school:
> *Bentinho*: It's like I tell you, Marieta. When Pedro Alvares Gabral [*sic*] discovered Brazil, everything here was just forest. There were no houses, no roads, nothing.
> *Marieta*: But Bentinho, the teacher told us that Indians lived here. They were just like us, kind of like Japanese people. The Indians didn't have cities back then.
> *Bentinho*: Of course not, Marieta. They walked around almost naked, hunted, fished for food, and organized themselves in groups called tribes. People say that some tribes were nomads, or wanderers.[2]

In mid-April of the same year, in preparation for the newly instituted Indian Day,[3] a regional director of the Serviço de Proteção aos Índios

(Indian Protection Service, or SPI) named Otto Mohn sent "Raimundo's" assignment and other samples of "well-developed" Canela schoolwork to the organization's headquarters in Rio de Janeiro. His cover letter to Education Sector director Herbert Serpa alluded to indigenous schooling as a "major problem [*problema magno*]" for Brazilian society and heaped praise on the patriots who were struggling against great odds to "teach the children of [their] indigenous brothers" and "open the doors of civilization to the SPI's little tutees."[4] Pleased by the pupils' progress and eager to see more of it, Serpa responded the next month with a letter of thanks to his colleague and a special reward for the Canela children: a set of Portuguese-language textbooks written for students in the capital city.[5]

Like schoolteachers on the dozens of Indigenous Posts of Nationalization (*Postos Indígenas de Nacionalização*) operating by the 1940s between Rio Grande do Sul and Roraima, Raimundo's teacher, Dona Nazaré, had been assigned the thorny task of educating students of different ages and representing differing degrees of "civilization" in a single classroom.[6] Her school, the Escola Capitão Pedro Dantas,[7] was located inside the SPI's Third Regional Inspectorate—one of eight such areas into which the country had been divided under the state's indigenist bureaucracy. Dona Nazaré shared with her SPI colleagues at Capitão Uirá and throughout Brazil the crucial and daunting mission of "facilitating the economic integration of . . . [Indians] in the final stages of de-Indianization."[8]

As suggested by Kapêlituk's assignments and SPI school records, renaming was a central component of de-Indianization—as important for its symbolic value as it was for any lived change it might have brought about. On the nearly 100 indigenous posts running throughout the country by the mid-twentieth century, rosters detailed the basic demographic information of the student body: Brazilian names, indigenous names, sex, and approximate ages. More elaborate reports also charted students' attendance history, academic performance, tribal membership, and nationality. Though the basic task of archiving this information remained in place until 1967, when the military regime dissolved the then floundering SPI and replaced it with the Fundação Nacional do Índio (FUNAI), the processes and formats used to do so were as uneven and subjective as other indigenist initiatives of the period. In keeping with typical SPI instruction, the documentation of indigenist education depended heavily, if not entirely, on the will, whims, interests, and organizational abilities of the teachers and administrators at hand. "Indianness" would mean, in short, whatever they wanted and needed it to.

List of Brazilian names given to indigenous students on the Laranjinha SPI Post (Paraná), 1 December 1942. Courtesy of the Museu do Índio/FUNAI Archive.

In the example of Kapêlituk's "Ditado," the precolonial past was reduced to nothingness and Indians were defined according to what they were like and what they lacked, rather than who they were, what they did, or what they thought. As the wobbly cornerstone of the state's twentieth-century indigenist mission, this characterization reiterates the long-standing ambiguity over the many meanings of Indianness, not only for representatives of the state and national society at-large, but also, inevitably, for the communities and individuals who were implicated by them directly. Since then, the problem has been compounded by the fact that those with the power to manipulate or fix such meanings in dominant and popular discourse have almost always remained distant, in space or thought (or both), from self-identifying indigenous peoples and communities.

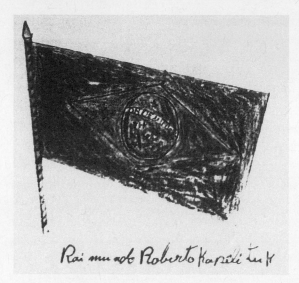

Over its five decades of existence, the SPI identified its protected tutees in a variety of ambiguous and sometimes incompatible ways: "Indian," "Brazilian," "neo-Brazilian," "Brazilian Indian," "Indian Brazilian," "Brazilindian," "civilized," "not yet civilized," "tribal," "unknown," or any combination of the above, depending on who was doing the judging and with what criteria. As evidenced by Mohn's letter and reiterated throughout contemporary indigenist discourse, however, at least this much was clear: the job of the SPI and its educators, in particular, was to move its subjects *away* from Indianness and *forward* to Brazilianness. In the minds (and mouths) of some indigenist functionaries, this shift meant bringing Indians "out of the Stone Age" and into modernity.[9] How this change would come about and when it would be complete, however, were never as self-evident.

Although educators, educational administrators, and students like Dona Nazaré, Otto Mohn, and Kapêlituk were not the only ones who lived, or were forced to live, with this question, they have been among the most important and influential. As an enduring promise of personal improvement, national belonging, and societal transformation, education has always been inextricably tied to the still open question of what it means to be "Indian" or Brazilian in Brazil. This is not to say that definitions have not been offered but, rather, as we have seen, that they have rarely if ever served or even considered the interests of those who self-identify with indigeneity.

Definitional issues are particularly difficult when working across languages, as the terms *Indian, Native, Native American, Amazonian, indigenous*, as well as the Portuguese *índio, nativo, ameríndio, silví-cola*, and *indígena* each have a unique etymological history and bring with them a particular constellation of meanings in different times and places. While each of these terms has its advantages and drawbacks, it is important to note that in Brazil, the most common and generic term—*índio*—does not *necessarily* have the predominantly pejorative connotation that the word *índio* does elsewhere in Latin America (Peru, Mexico, and Guatemala, for example). Although *índio* can certainly be used to imply insult, and although some would disavow it entirely, the term has also been revitalized in recent decades by intellectuals, communities, and social groups who claim indigeneity in their struggles for representation and autonomy. While many indigenous activists and writers identify first with their own peoples, communities, nations, or tribes, the words *índio* and *indígena* also sometimes serve as expedient if imperfect terms to invoke intertribal, intercommunal, and inter-national communication, collaboration, or alliance.[10]

This chapter surveys the terrain of twentieth-century indigenist state policies alongside and in a protracted relationship with popular ideas about Indianness, on the one hand, and indigenous efforts toward self-representation, on the other. While the hundredth anniversary in 2010 of the state's official indigenist venture marked how much this relationship has changed since the days when Kapêlituk received praise for his secular baptism into dominant national culture via SPI schooling,[11] it also pointed to the ways the colonialist nature of that relationship remains the same and serves, like a thorn in the foot of Brazil's deepening democracy and accelerating "development," as an enduring reminder that the liberties and relative prosperity of the early twenty-first century have been secured for some only at the expense of others.

INDIAN QUESTIONS, OLD AND NEW

Although the tension between lived indigenous experience and the inter-pretation, portrayal, and manipulation of that experience has existed since the earliest colonial encounters, it took on new meaning during the early 1800s, when elite intellectuals and everyday citizens had to ask how "Indians" and their "Indianness" would relate to a newly sovereign Bra-zil. Since the declaration of independence in 1822,[12] political leaders, art-ists, social activists, academics, and educators—along with the public at large—have engaged with this "Indian question" in drastically diverging ways. While some championed the protection of pre-Columbian ways of living and thinking by assigning to the state the responsibility to "preserve Indians" as "historical national patrimony," many more advocated phasing out Indianness and the transformation of Native peoples into "neocitizens"[13] who could help build and modernize the country. As in the case of Kapêlituk's schooling, indigenist thought postindependence posited the "Indian question" in national terms by tying the elusive concept of *indianidade* (Indianness) firmly to the equally elusive notion of *brasilidade* (Brazilianness).

As self-identifying indigenous peoples have become key protagonists in Brazilian politics rather than passive scribes destined merely to copy and internalize the nationalist "dictations" of their nonindigenous tutors, the old concept of Indianness and the notion of Brazilianness through which it has traditionally been framed have become increasingly unhelpful for understanding or describing the situation at hand.[14] Indeed, the work of the Brazilian indigenous movement and its supporters reflects what dominant indigenist discourses collectively failed to do: replace the monolithic, flat, imperialist notion of Indianness with a political recognition of indigeneity that prioritizes self-identification, in all of its heterogeneity and potential contradiction. This phenomenological task involves, on the one hand, establishing a nonessentialist politics of identity to accommodate individual and collective self-identifications. On the other hand, it means figuring out how concepts of legal differentiation and autonomy for Native peoples that are grounded in ethnic, cultural, and historical claims can be compatible with the democratic governance of a national society (and here is where the similarities with the U.S. case, as evidenced by Phil Deloria's work, fall away),[15] in which a substantial percentage of the overall population can lay a genetic claim to some degree of indigenous descent.[16]

At stake in these questions is the future not only of indigeneity and Brazilianness but also of modern politics. That is, despite the supranational reach of global economies, institutions, and laws, the politically sovereign nation-state remains the lynchpin of the international political system, and thus the most powerful guarantor (or transgressor) of individual and group rights. Inasmuch as questions of indigenous rights and the many possible definitions of indigeneity call state autonomy and the legitimate use of force into question, they impel a constant negotiation of national citizenship and the concept of sovereignty from which it is derived. This situation of legal and political limbo creates a complex predicament for self-identifying indigenous peoples and states that, as

Teme-Augama Anishnabai political theorist Dale Turner puts it, are constantly "forced to articulate [or acknowledge] metaphysical claims . . . as political arguments."[17]

Dominant notions of Indianness in Brazil are problematic not only because they fail to account for the always contingent nature of indigeneity but also because of the dominant majority's pervasive desire to administer and control it. That is, all meaning must also be considered in light of the social, ethnic, and cultural *mestiçagem* (mixing) that has long been hailed as a key product and producer of Brazilianness. Indeed, the fact of widespread miscegenation threw a wrench in the project of quantifying "Indianness" long before 1991, when "Indians" were counted as such for the first time through the national census.[18] A 1933 SPI report for the *Bulletin of the International American Institute* thus explained: "It has not yet been possible to conduct an official count of the noncivilized indigenous population of Brazil. . . . Regarding civilized Indians, they live almost entirely integrated into the mass of the Brazilian population as agricultural workers, cattle hands, boatmen, and workers in extractive or other industries, and in official population counts do not show up as Indians. Hundreds of thousands are being continuously diluted in the racial melding that occurs here, tending to produce the white type that is growing consistently because of immigration, while the aborigine and the pure black decrease every year."[19]

Despite the long history and powerful legacies of racist, scientific positivism, then, the realities on the ground have made it difficult to determine with exactitude the indigenous presence in Brazil since anyone ever bothered to try. And yet, the lived experience of the country's mixed ethnoracial makeup must also be considered with regard to the fact that, as Raymond Williams put it, "some important social and historical processes occur *within* language in ways [that] indicate how integral the problems of meanings and of relationships really are."[20] Lest we skate on the thin ice of census figures, any attempt to trace the trajectory of indigeneity and Indianness must dip into the well of popular, scholarly, and political thought that chronicles, however unscientifically, the malleable nature of all ethnoracial identities and identifications. The convoluted path by which a collective national protagonist has arrived at the present configuration of these names and meanings can never, of course, be retraced. But we can revisit some critical junctions on that journey to ask how and why the political and cultural significance of these overlapping terms and concepts have changed.

This excursion leads us through Plato's cave, where a massive Indian shadow still distorts the small but diverse indigenous population from which it is cast. Although nearly 900,000 people who self-identify as indigenous now live throughout the country,[21] the majority of Brazil's Native peoples reside in Amazônia Legal (the Legal Amazon),[22] far from the hubs of economic and political power in Brasília and the teeming metropolises of the northern coast and the industrialized Southeast. While urbanites and other "revitalized" Indians[23] who in decades past may not have been counted as indigenous now make up a significant percentage of the official Native population,[24] these massive distances still prop up colonialist racial paradigms, making it less likely that the 84 percent of Brazilians who reside in metropolitan areas will envision their indigenous compatriots as a diverse population with a wide variety of needs and interests.[25]

Accompanying the surge in Native self-identification and activism of the late twentieth and early twenty-first centuries, international attention to indigenous issues and rights grew in unprecedented ways, culminating in the United Nations' declaration of the Decade of the World's Indigenous Peoples in 1994 and 2005, and the adoption of the U.N. Declaration on the Right of Indigenous Peoples in 2007.[26] The ever-powerful presence of the *idea* of Indianness, however, has done little in Brazil to advance a critical understanding of indigeneity, or to make known the perspectives of the people who identify with it. Popular representations of Indians indeed continue to have quite the opposite effect.

Herein lies the ongoing influence of the nineteenth-century Indianists like Domingos José Gonçalves de Magalhães, Antônio Gonçalves Dias, and José de Alencar, whose allegorical tales channeled extremes of idealized and barbaric "Indianness" into an enduring rhetoric of racialized nationalism that has colored Brazilian cultural production ever since.[27] Despite the passing of 150 years since the heyday of romantic Indianism, Iracemas, Peris, Tamoios, and Timbaras continue to influence the suitable role many nonindigenous Brazilians imagine for "Indians" in their country.[28] This powerful imagery has been perpetuated not only through popular cultural forms like literature, television, music, film, and the fine arts, but also by and in national political debates, socioeconomic hierarchies, social policy, and—as in the case of Kapêlituk and his classmates—educational programming for Native and non-Native students alike.

Drawing on the poles of good and bad Indianness plucked from fiction and the hair-raising tales of colonial raconteurs, popular interpretations of indigeneity have tended to reflect Indians as victims or victimizers. The twentieth century presented us, on the one hand, with ingenuous Natives brutalized by corrupt bureaucrats and disease-carrying settlers. On the other hand, eyewitness reports offered detailed accounts of Amazonian headshrinkers, ferocious Indians fattening up prisoners for *rosbife*, and entire communities feasting on roasted *garimpeiros* (mineral prospectors) who were unlucky or stupid enough to be caught seeking treasure in indigenous territories.[29] While images of Native victimization were preferable to those of Indian "savagery" for the national project of "protecting" Indianness and making it compatible with the future of a modern Brazil, both extremes and seemingly irreconcilable views circulated until the turn of the millennium in a wide variety of popular media. Such hyperbole was disseminated alongside a steady flow of less shocking (and less sellable) accounts of indigenous lives—tedious logs of indigenist bureaucracy and land demarcation, for example—which competed unsuccessfully for space on the front pages and in the popular imaginary.[30]

Native peoples thus imagined as "good" and "evil" sit at opposite ends of a broad spectrum of Indianness on which "Indians" may or may not be considered promising raw material for Brazilian civilization and its future. In this regard, the philosophical, political, and ethical interrogation of the human and rational qualities of Native peoples that were laid out during sixteenth-century deliberations between Dominican friar Bartolomé de las Casas and theologian Ginés de Sepúlveda[31] have yet to be resolved. At one extreme, the imagined Indian (male or female) is still the transparent noble savage: innocent, at one with nature, inherently good, potentially redeemable, and therefore easily conceived as proto-Christian. At the other, he ("bad" Indians are almost always male) is utterly impenetrable: brutal, cannibalistic, evil, sometimes only bordering on human, and far from proto-Christian.[32] Popular discourses that invoke these images rely predominantly on Indians who live in the novels, poems, paintings, theories, reports, and policies of their nonindigenous architects. This thinking—dominant thinking—thus tends to lump all "Indians" into an amorphous category that is conceptually feeble and politically dangerous, for it fails to grasp the always contingent nature of indigeneity while ignoring even the possibility of an indigenous will to self-representation. For the vice coordinator of the Coordenação das Organizações Indígenas da Amazônia Brasileira (Coordination of Indigenous Organizations of the Brazilian Amazon, or COIAB), the largest Native-run organization in Brazil,[33] the term "'Indian' puts everyone in the same bag," whereas the notion of indigenous peoples (*povos indígenas*), "reflects differentiation and recognizes difference."[34]

Although this problem is not unique to indigenous peoples, and similar arguments might be made with reference to other historically marginalized groups, indigeneity as lived experience is particularly critical to the task of dismantling the misrecognition of racialized Otherness because the hyperbolic role that imaginary "Indians" play in the idealization of Brazil and Brazilianness has been diametrically opposed to the trifling historical role to which indigenous peoples have been relegated by and in national society at large. While the concept of "playing Indian" is easily recognizable in myriad popular cultural forms, political discourses, and social and economic structures, there is no clear cut equivalent or comparable notion of "playing Black," "playing Lebanese," or "playing German," for example.[35] Put crudely, "Indians" continue to be valued as emblems of Brazilianness not only because their ancestors were in fact "native" to the land, but also, conveniently, because the indigenous peoples who remain are relatively few in number, dispersed over a massive territory, and divided into hundreds of cultural and linguistic groups that until quite recently have lacked any meaningful access to self-representation.

INDIGENEITY AND THE LAW

Through their increased presence and participation in national politics and cultural production, self-identified indigenous peoples have worked for many years against the individuals, groups, institutions, and social practices that measure them according to their likeness to romantic Indianness or lack thereof. Seduced by images of painted warriors bearing bows and arrows and "uncontacted" tribes deep in the Amazon, however, dominant discourse still questions if not denies the authenticity of self-identifying Natives who wear jeans, use cellphones, speak no indigenous language, or write their own blogs. Likened to the "wannabes" of North America who are spurned by Native and non-Native critics alike, indigenous Brazilians who dissatisfy dominant expectations of Indianness face relentless accusations of racial hucksterism and opportunist posturing.[36]

The legal differentiation of Native peoples in recent years has inspired skepticism, protest, and terrible violence.[37] Piggybacking on opposition to polemical affirmative action measures that have aimed to provide enhanced educational and professional opportunities for economically disadvantaged Afro-Brazilians,[38] detractors of "Indians" have felt particularly aggrieved by legislation aimed at facilitating access for indigenous students to public universities and ensuring the exclusive indigenous occupation of demarcated indigenous territories—a policy they scorn as an unfair, unsound, and "racist" endorsement of *"muita terra para pouco índio* [lots of land for a few Indians]."[39]

Because measures for restitution and redistribution invoke college degrees and landownership in a country where tens of millions of nonindigenous people will for the foreseeable future continue to lack access to both, they have been one of the most contentious components of indigenous politics for the last three decades.[40] In response to an April 2009 decision by the national Congress that mineral extraction from indigenous territories would be subject to the approval of the indigenous peoples occupying them, one angry citizen voiced his disapproval by making the common accusation of "reverse discrimination": "My Lord in Heaven!! The lands do NOT belong to the Indians, they are OURS!!! This is absurd!! The subsoil belongs to the UNION. If they found mineral [wealth] on the property of any 'white' guy, the government would appropriate the land and pay an indemnity—end of story. In other words, they must be better than we are!!! Why? Because they are backward and primitive!"[41]

If everyone is supposed to be Brazilian in the present, the logic goes, why should any individual or group be privileged for injustices suffered in the past? Awash in the still powerful myth of racial democracy and armed with the notion of equal treatment under the law, such protest likens any legal distinction based on "race," ethnicity, or skin color to the importation of "North American style" racism while overlooking the fact that even 512 years after the Conquest, 190 years after independence, 124 years after the abolition of slavery, and 123 years after the declaration of the First Republic, Native peoples have, in fact, yet to be granted equal treatment under the law or the full rights of national citizenship.[42]

This condition of legal and social inequality is upheld by the 1973 Indian Statute that was enacted under the military government of Emílio Garrastazu Médici to formalize the juridical status of indigenous peoples and "regulate indigenous rights."[43] Of course, the authoritarian regime took these "regulatory measures" during the first decade of a twenty-year dictatorship that harshly curtailed the political liberties of all Brazilians— including free speech and habeas corpus rights.[44] Article 3 of the 1973 statute established that an Indian or forest dweller was "every individual of pre-Columbian origin who self-identifies and is identified as belonging to an ethnic group whose cultural characteristics distinguish him [*sic*] from national society." An "indigenous community" or "tribal group," in contrast, was "a grouping of families or Indian communities, whether living in a state of complete isolation in relation to other sectors of the national communion, or in intermittent or permanent contact with them but without being entirely integrated."

The fact that these loose and subjective descriptions functioned better on paper than in practice became evident in the decade following the statute's approval, when FUNAI leaders seeking to operationalize the government's definition devised an Indianness test based on phenotype and behavior: "Among the items [considered] were 'primitive mentality,' . . . 'undesirable cultural, psychic, and biological characteristics,' 'representative cultural traits,' enigmatic 'social characteristics . . . '[and] whether the candidate dressed, ate, and performed like an Indian."[45] As Alcida Ramos indicates, the aim of such a test was to use the ambiguity over indigeneity to prevent those deemed unworthy of state assistance from being able to self-identify as indigenous. At the same time, however, the ambiguity created opportunities for other individuals and groups to relinquish some citizenship privileges to gain rights to a series of state-sponsored benefits by identifying as what Jonathan Warren has called "posttraditional" Indians.[46] As anthropologist Jan Hoffman French has argued in the case of one such community (the Xocó from the northeastern state of Sergipe), the imprecise nature of the law governing Indianness has functioned as an "expandable and prismatic phenomenon" subject to "postlegislative negotiation."[47] Although the 1988 Constitution altered the legal condition of Natives to make "Indian" a permanent ethnic category rather than a transitory phase in the process of becoming Brazilian, the state's protective authority remains in place. Chapter 2, Article 7 thus maintains that, "Indians and communities who are not already integrated into the national communion are subject to the tutorial regime established in the Law."[48]

The tutorial gesture of this legislation in fact harkens back much further, as it became an official cornerstone of "Indian protection" during the early years of the First Republic.[49] According to Article 6 of the 1916 Civil Code, "jungle dwellers [would] remain subject to the tutelary regime established by special laws and regulations, which [would] cease as they [became] adapted to the civilization of the country."[50] In the decades that followed, indigenist functionaries expressed frustration over the "laws and regulations" mentioned in this code, claiming that their weakness and lack of specificity created a situation in which the legal tools created to protect Indians were just as often used to their detriment. The vagueness of indigenist legislation, they argued, enabled judges to consider those individuals with even the most perfunctory knowledge of Portuguese to be "adapted to the civilization of the country" based on language skills alone, reiterating, once more, education's centrality to the social construction of Indianness. Stripped of their lands and means of sustenance, these people were left with no aid aside from their compulsory assignment to nonindigenous "tutors." The declaration of minor status that accompanied official tutelage thus created a dynamic whereby the state perpetuated and even legitimized the effective enslavement of its indigenous "tutees."[51]

As one exasperated SPI worker complained in 1920, the lack of clear federal guidelines regarding Indianness meant that would-be exploiters had ample opportunity to practice corruption and abuse, while those working to better the lot of their "Native brothers"—those working inside the SPI or independently of it—were almost entirely beholden to the power of local authorities and political bosses. He lamented: "A solution for such evident violations of justice ought to exist out of necessity in the law; but for the Indians, the law will continue to be dead letter as long as Article 6 of the Civil Code lacks a competent entity to enact it—particularly in cases where the state governments are aligned with one of the involved parties."[52] The difficulty stemmed, once again, from the lack of a clear conceptualization or definition of "Indianness"—not only among nonspecialists but also inside SPI operations. A full decade later, another Ministry of Agriculture employee argued that two of the four official categorizations for indigenous communities established under Brazilian law were complete fictions, with no basis whatsoever in reality.[53]

On 12 July 1934, just days before the creation of Brazil's third constitution under the government of then embattled President Getúlio Vargas,[54] the formal responsibility for the state's "Indian protection" was transferred from the Ministry of Labor, Industry, and Commerce to the Ministry of War.[55] In keeping with the prevailing logic of national security, the Indians were declared "a precious element" of national society and praised for their outstanding "moral qualities, physical robustness, and climatic adaptability." It was in the country's best interest, therefore, "to take advantage" of this (human) natural resource, to "educate [them] by the proper methods . . . and call them to our [Brazilian] nationality before bordering countries call them to theirs."[56] Accordingly, Chapter 2 of the SPI Regulation Project, which was designed to carry out the 1934 decree but not finalized until the following year, was dedicated to the "nationalization and incorporation of the Indians."

This project outlined a multipronged, didactical approach to a renewed and nationally sanctioned indigenist mission that included five areas: (1)

"instruction of a hygienic nature," (2) "primary and professional schools," (3) "physical exercise and military specialization," (4) "moral and civic education," and (5) "agricultural and farming training."[57] Officially, the interrelated tasks would address the perceived needs of indigenous peoples with regard to their distinct levels of "civilization," and these distinctions, in turn, would help to determine the different categories of indigenous posts (*postos indígenas*, or PIs) established throughout the country.[58] As several scholars have pointed out, however, indigenous labor on the posts often had more to do with the economic interests of local (nonindigenous) populations and SPI functionaries than they did with the desire to protect the "protected."[59]

José Carlos Mariátegui was right about this: the issue of *how* land would be divided up for indigenous use by nonindigenous peoples has been the primary source of contention between advocates for and opponents of Native rights throughout the Americas since independence.[60] Some seventeen years and two constitutions after the institution of the SPI's 1935 Regulation Project, SPI director José Maria da Gama Malcher led an indigenist appeal against new federal legislation that aimed to resolve the ever-contentious issue of land occupation and ownership by parceling out traditional, communally held indigenous territories to self-identifying Indians and their families.[61] Citing the Dawes Act, which had failed in the United States during the late nineteenth century,[62] Malcher argued that the policy would be disastrous for Brazil because it did not account for the radically distinct relationships with and uses of land among different indigenous peoples (those living close to urban settlements in the Southeast, for example, versus those living in near isolation in the rainforest).[63] Any attempt to privatize or otherwise divvy up indigenous territories, he ventured, constituted a violent affront to traditional indigenous cultures and revealed a profound misunderstanding of Indianness: "It must never be forgotten that the Indian has [his] own culture within which development will be carried out. He lives in a community; his tribe is a small nation. We can never separate them from everything, from their nation, from their culture, unless we want to contribute consciously to their extermination."[64] While this vision went against the nationalist grain of his day, Malcher's allusion to a culturally autonomous indigenous "nation" would be perhaps more controversial today than it was then, for as the dominant majority has long assumed and expressed, the hard work of Native "civilization," "assimilation," and "integration" should, by now, have reached its conclusion.

Ignoring (or embracing) the paternalistic and discriminatory nature of indigenist legal history, trenchant "racial democrats" continue to oppose the legal differentiation of indigenous peoples and, in particular, claims to indigenous nationhood or autonomy. In April 2009, for instance, when Dionito José de Souza, the coordinator general of the Indigenous Council of Roraima, stated publicly that the Brazilian Army should have to ask for authorization to enter the 1.7-million-hectare Raposa Serra do Sol indigenous reserve, he elicited a barrage of indignant outrage from around the country, which was deeply divided over the political future of the area.[65] Echoing the FUNAI "Indianness test" of decades past, some critics decried the area's demarcation as indigenous land by questioning the authenticity of modern-day indigeneity and working to delegitimize those who claim it for themselves. Detractors complained: "The Indians want land to survive, but they cook on electric stoves, shop in markets, make microwave popcorn, drink whisky, and even speak English. Why so much land for [only] 19 thousand Indians? A tenth of that territory would already be an exaggeration."[66] "Those Indians, who produce nothing, are slothful, but very sly. . . . [They] don't even live in the forest, but in cities, like white people."[67]

Even if the guarantee of special rights under the law were once legitimate, the reasoning goes, those days are long gone. Politically savvy and equipped with modern gadgets, modern-day Indians are neither genuine nor credible enough to need or deserve such differentiated treatment. Of course, proponents of this thinking conveniently ignore the work of thousands of indigenous activists and scholars in Brazil and throughout the region who have been using a wide variety of old and new media, ranging from film and video, to e-books and specialized Internet listservs, to disseminate indigenous thought and cultural production for many decades.[68]

Another line of criticism revolves around the land itself, and holds that only "they" (nonindigenous peoples) hold the legitimate rights to Brazilian territories. As one "HARDWORKING BRAZILIAN" ranted:

WE HAVE LOST SOVEREIGNTY OVER THE AMAZONIAN REGION. WE HAVE LOST OUR VOICE IN THE LEGISLATURE AND THE JUDICIARY. . . . WE NEED TO ORGANIZE A NATIONAL STRIKE IMMEDIATELY. . . . THE BRAZILIAN ARMY NEEDS AUTHORIZATION TO ENTER AMAZONIAN TERRITORY[?] ANY BRAZILIAN NEEDS AUTHORIZATION TO ENTER AMAZONIAN TERRITORY[?] WAKE UP, BRAZILIAN PEOPLE[!] WE ARE BEING ATTACKED AND

MASSACRED. IF THE PEOPLE ARE NOT HEARD, THERE MUST BE WAR. THE BRAZILIAN ARMY CANNOT, MUST NOT, AND DOES NOT EVER NEED TO ASK . . . TO ACT IN DEFENSE OF THE TERRITORY AND SOVEREIGNTY OF BRAZILIANS. MY GOD, BRASÍLIA, WHAT A DISGRACE[!][69]

Another commentator, similarly perturbed, protested: "None of this coddling! For them, the billy club! They only want money. Money they know well! They only negotiate with millions!"[70] These arguments rest on deep cynicism over the possibility that land might hold any value beyond the realm of capital and feeds on the sneaky suspicion that all modern-day "Indians" see and use the benefits of their differentiated status as commodities to be pawned off—sometimes for goods and services entirely unsuited to Indianness!

Finally, still others hark back to the colonialist logic—associated most infamously with twentieth-century zoologist and Museu Paulista director Hermann von Ihering[71]—that the long-term survival of Native peoples was ultimately incompatible with the well-being of the majority and thus with a desirable future for the country. A third editorialist thus admonished: "When they get sick, send them to look for their medicine men and forest remedies. To study, go to an indigenous school. Those people who don't work and only think about exploiting whites need to be taught a lesson. . . . They are pissing people off, and those useless NGOs are only taking our money. Go to work."[72] However far-fetched they may seem, each of these deliberations points to the fact that the paradoxes of "modern Indianness" are not only a conjectural problem for scholars and a personal difficulty for those who self-identify as indigenous but also a lived political conundrum for the Brazilian nation, with legal, material, and ethical implications that transcend popular and intellectual discourses while being constantly reformulated in and by both.

The problem of authenticity, though unresolvable if we accept, acknowledging the tautology, that "authentic" Native peoples are those who identify as such, points us in two different directions. On the one hand, we can turn "outward" to address the physical and ideological construction of indigeneity in dominant national society and the influence that political practice, law, competing notions of citizenship, and discourses vis-à-vis Indianness ranging from the scientific to the artistic have brought to bear on the lives of individuals and communities. On the other hand, the problem can impel us "inward" to consider issues of ontology and epistemology, and to ask how experiences of and ideas about being indigenous (and "Indian") are molded by and contribute to racialized notions of self and

Other. These overlapping and mutually constitutive concerns might be summed up in two questions: First, what has indigeneity meant in terms of experience lived in a particular place and time? And second, how does the concept of indigeneity, whether self-ascribed or imposed, reflect on the human condition and the question of being-in-the-world?

The indigenous population has always played a powerful role in shaping how dominant national society sees and projects itself as uniquely Brazilian. At the same time, the many incarnations of indigenist thought and practice form an arena in which the most critical questions of personhood and nationhood have been repeatedly formulated, negotiated, contested, and reformulated. Unstable categories of "difference" (as something to fear, to eliminate, to preserve, or to celebrate) lie in constant tension with the undying ideal of homogenous *mestiça* nationhood. The paradoxes of indigenous citizenship—how to be "same" enough to guarantee the rights of national belonging yet "different" enough to ensure differentiation under the law—thus poses an unresolved challenge not only for indigenous peoples but also for the integrity of a society governed by the premise of "equality," "pluralism," and the "absence of discrimination."[73]

How then can the terms *Indian, Indianness, indigeneity,* and *indigenous peoples* be employed meaningfully if their referents are always relative, always in need of contextualization, always shifting? Is it possible to speak of an "indigenous identity" critically, or at least, as historian Rogers Brubaker puts it, without adopting "categories of ethnopolitical practice" as "categories of social analysis?"[74] Is indigeneity in Brazil an all-or-nothing category or should it be measured in degree? Is a monolingual Yanomami shaman from deep in the Amazonian rainforest more "authentically" indigenous than a bilingual Guarani schoolteacher working on the outskirts of São Paulo? Does making such a distinction help us to flesh out the many lived meanings of the concept, or does it mark a capitulation to the myth of stable, essentialized identities that postcolonial and subaltern critics have worked for so long to unravel? Finally, who stands to gain and to lose in these debates?

The fact that the United Nations chose, after nearly twenty years of deliberation among hundreds of delegates from around the world, not to define *indigeneity* or *indigenous* in the 2007 Declaration on the Rights of Indigenous Peoples is an indication of the pitfalls into which even a well-intentioned and well-informed attempt to delimit the baseline of commonality among such a heterogeneous group of peoples can fall. As Judith Friedlander argued from Mexico nearly forty years ago, definitive characterizations of indigeneity can also be used (or hijacked) to endorse

authentic essentialisms[75]—which in modern Brazil are particularly inju-
rious to "posttraditional" Native peoples and their allies. And yet, as
Brubaker reminds us, "if identity is everywhere, it is nowhere."[76] The openness vis-à-vis indigeneity as embraced in the international realm leaves
many indigenous peoples vulnerable at state and local levels to critiques
like those mentioned above, each of which seeks to delegitimize "dubious"
Indians and curtail their access to rights and resources.

In a country where nearly a fourth of the population could, in theory, lay
some claim to indigenous ancestry,[77] how should indigeneity be conceptu-
alized in social and political terms as a meaningful category of difference?
How too, in a country where a significant percentage of the entire national
population lives in poverty,[78] can any ethnoracial claim (as opposed to a
socioeconomic one) be linked to resources in a way that helps to promote
human rights, social justice, and democracy, but also hold wide (or at
least partial) support among the broader public? According to Hoffman
French, the legalization of Xocó identities toward the end of the twentieth
century merged communal claims to nontraditional indigeneity successfully with claims to land and other benefits.[79] Yet, even as the state came to
recognize constructed Indianness as "authentic" and with material compensation through a process she calls "legalizing identity," the ultimate
arbiters of that construction and guarantors of those benefits changed
little (if at all) from those who wielded the same power during the earliest days of the state's indigenist enterprise. On the one hand, a nonindigenous "indigenous expert" (anthropologist Delver Mellette) would have
the final word on the validity of the "new" Indians' claim to indigeneity.[80]
On the other hand, the collective fate of an entire community would be
decided, as in decades past, by the official indigenist bureaucracy and a
handful of jurists.[81]

In the end, the imprecision of the 1973 Indian Statute has served the
interests of newly declared indigenous peoples because, as Hoffman
French puts it, "if some people can cease being Indians, there is no impediment for others to become Indians."[82] That this can happen, however,
does not resolve the problem of legitimacy vis-à-vis the general population. The practice of reverse assimilation (or "becoming Indian," as other
scholars have called it in different contexts),[83] not only flies in the face
of the old indigenist credo, which almost always advocated for the eventual disappearance of indigenous difference,[84] but presents, as well, a
fundamental conflict with dominant ideas about Brazilian nationhood.
The midcentury melding of these two powerful agendas was expressed

succinctly by SPI director Vicente Vasconcelos at the height of racialized populism under the Estado Novo: "It is clear that the Indians, like the black, will have to disappear one day [from] among us, [so that] they will not form 'racial cysts' [and instead] dissolve into the white mass whose incursion is constant and overwhelming. . . . The point is to impede the abnormal disappearance of the Indians by death so that Brazilian society, aside from the obligation it has to take care of [the Indians], might receive in her breast the precious and integral infusion of indigenous blood that it requires for the constitution of the racial type that appeared here and is so appropriate for the environment."[85]

Vasconcelos's ideas point to the contradiction at the heart of the indigenist endeavor, for they lay bare the colonialist desire to appropriate an "essence" of Indianness without actually having to deal with Native peoples—for "Indians" without indigeneity, as it were. Though indigenous peoples would inevitably die off and "disappear," the mission of the indigenist body was, according to this view, to protect life as well as possible in the meanwhile. The general's pragmatic desire to turn Indianness into a benefit for national society was indeed always a powerful undercurrent of the state's indigenist mission.

Vasconcelos's statement appeared in print six years after the publication of *Casa grande e senzala* (*The Masters and the Slaves*) (1933), Gilberto Freyre's foundational endorsement of Brazilian *mestiçagem*. Despite the passing of nearly eight decades and the scrutiny of thousands of scholars, Freyre's image and ideas remain prevalent and powerful in the popular imaginary. This is particularly true of the erroneous attribution to him of the phrase "racial democracy,"[86] which is often invoked as a counterpoint to the activism of historically marginalized groups who identify, at least in part, in cultural or ethnoracial terms. Freyre is summoned so routinely in public discourse to signal the concept and practice of a particularly Brazilian miscegenation that his name itself has come to stand for the perceived benefits of cultural and ethnoracial "mixture."

For his "defense of *the mestiço* as *the* national ethnic identity of Brazil," Freyre has in recent years been distinguished as the "civic patron" of the so-called Movimento Pardo-Mestiço Brasileiro (Brown and Mixed-Blood Brazilian Movement).[87] This organization, also known as Nação Mestiça (Mixed-Race Nation),[88] opposes both the Indian Statute of 1973 and the 2010 Statute of Racial Equality, which became law after nearly seven years of congressional debate.[89] Characterizing affirmative action measures as "*mestiço*-phobic" and anti-Brazilian, leaders of Nação Mestiça refer to the

2010 legislation as the "Statute of Ethnic Cleansing" because it marks, in their view, the "official end" of "mulattos, *caboclos*, and all the *mestiços* of Brasil."[90]

For those who prioritize national identity above all other possible forms of identity, and who base their politics on the vision of a singular Brazilianness or *raça brasileira* (Brazilian race), there will likely never be room in the public sphere for the legal recognition of social or political differences that are grounded in ethnoracial or cultural claims. There is even less room, it would seem, for entitlement of any sort to be attached to such differences. According to Nação Mestiça and other manifestations of popular opposition to the demarcation or protection of indigenous-controlled territories, differentiated rights must be rejected *ipso facto* for their inherent "racism" and the ostensible threat that they present to Brazilian sovereignty.[91]

INDIGENEITY AND AUTHENTICITY

Certainly, many self-identified indigenous peoples share the experience of mixed ethnoracial heritage with advocates of the Nação Mestiça movement and could, like the majority of the Brazilian population, identify or be identified as *mestiços* in many contexts. That they have sidestepped this "escape hatch"[92] thus reiterates the increasingly accepted recognition of constructed ethnoracial labels, despite the enduring hegemony of Stuart Hall's "old" (essentialist) ethnicities.[93] At the same time, these choices reflect the fact that the "old" concept of Indianness has also changed forever. That is, more than phenotype, geographic location, language, communal recognition, cultural practices, social organization, philosophy, or spirituality, contemporary expressions of indigeneity in Brazil reflect agency and choice.[94] As André Baniwa put it in 2009, the year following his election as deputy mayor of the municipality of São Gabriel da Cachoeira (Amazonas state): "Being Indian means knowing one's own culture, traditions, and maintaining one's identity without failing to know the Brazilian state [and] the culture and tradition of the nation."[95] Indigeneity in this view is always negotiated, selected, and performed—not in the sense of disingenuous fabrication or pretending to be something one is not but rather, to paraphrase Judith Butler (drawing on Nietzsche), by constituting the very identity that one claims. If there is, in other words, "no 'being' behind the doing, effecting, becoming," then indigeneity must be "performatively constituted by the very 'expressions' that are said to be its results."[96]

Respecting and being faithful to said "performance," however, is not always or necessarily a fruitful task. Queried in 1998 about the long-term prospects for Native/non-Native relations, Yanomami leader Davi Kopenawa responded with an inversion of the old cannibalist metaphor: "There's no way out. The white man swallows the Indian whole, all of Brazil. The politician swallows the Indian. . . . There's no more life, no more people, nothing. It's over. That's the end."[97] Although his pessimism regarding the future of the Yanomami dovetails sadly with the colonialist goal of "disappearing" Native peoples through whatever means possible, he nonetheless reasoned that indigenous ways of being and thinking had to be defended because, quite simply, "[his] people are still alive. . . . Indians in Brazil still exist."[98]

Regardless of how it has been manipulated and squeezed into competing agendas, then, indigeneity can also be understood as the individual and collective lives through which it is perpetuated. More than "merely" a reference to "natural life" (a living body) or political life (civic existence), Kopenawa's position reflects what the Italian philosopher Giorgio Agamben called "bare life": life-exposed-to-death, or the violent power of sovereignty.[99] Agamben's study of "nativity and nationality" speaks to the paradox of indigenous citizenship as reflected in the twentieth-century indigenist discourse that cleaved the task of safeguarding Native bodies from the enterprise of transforming Indians into Brazilians ("de-Indianization"). In theory, the two charges overlap, but in practice, they have almost always functioned independently: the state's initiative to "save Indians" began in 1910 with the SPI, for example, while indigenous peoples were not granted political existence as Brazilians until the institution of the 1988 Constitution. And even so, the Yanomami leader reminds us, indigenous Brazilians are still situated mostly outside the polis, both in theory (law) and in practice.

In keeping with Agamben's proposal, then, Kopenawa's assessment morphs the so-called Indian question from one of authentic existence to one of existence itself. While it remains to be seen if a new way of conceptualizing sovereignty will bring about a necessary or inevitable commensurability of natural and political life,[100] the unresolved tensions between indigenous peoples and nation-states, on the one hand, and between indigeneity and nationhood, on the other, serve, at the very least, as a perpetual reminder of the always violent nature of their present incommensurability.[101]

Philosopher Linda Martín Alcoff has argued that interpellation in the neo-Marxist tradition and the necessarily essentializing gesture that it entails are part of the price that must be paid for the (political) recognition of many historically marginalized peoples.[102] She highlights, however, that the processes and outcomes of self-fashioning always transcend discourse to produce lived consequences that are acceptable or justifiable for some, and unacceptable and unjustifiable for others. On the one hand, Alcoff rejects strategic essentialism as an elitist position that disengages political practice from its theoretical commitments by exalting "knowing theorists" who wield identity strategically over "unknowing activists" who accept it (naively) at face value.[103] At the same time, she objects to the neo-Hegelian notion of an "essential self" that necessarily exceeds *all* forms of representation and must disavow it in all forms, including identity, as an automatic capitulation to power. "This makes sense," she argues, "only given the prior assumption . . . that the individual must be the final arbiter of all value. [But] why assume that giving any prerogative to the parent/community/society or the discourse/episteme/socius is in every case and necessarily psychically pernicious and enabling only at the cost of a more profound subordination?"[104] Echoing the value of the social voiced by activists like Baniwa and Kopenawa, Alcoff's embrace of community as idea and practice transforms the multivalent nature of indigeneity from a tragic flaw of the Brazilian indigenous movement into a vital strength. From this perspective, the "Indian question" can and must be understood as simultaneously existential, situational, and semantic.

Of course, "Indians" as such have always existed as a social and historical construction that is more or less acceptable, more or less expedient, depending on the circumstances and interlocutors at hand. But rather than accepting the assumptions of "perniciousness" that Alcoff characterizes as disempowering and counterproductive (for they can only lead to a theoretical and political dead end), indigenous peoples in Brazil have chosen more often to respond to the interpellation and "accept the hail" as a dynamic form of engagement with ongoing constructions of the self.[105] To reinterpret and redeploy historically marginalizing terms, concepts, and discourses is not necessarily a passive surrender to strategic marginalization or the most expedient (or least worst) option out there, because the *work* of resignification also presents new opportunities for thinking about the relationship between self and Other, and thus new possibilities for conceptualizing community. Acknowledging that these opportunities are never just battles over words, but in themselves vital forms of participating in the always incomplete formulation of one's meaning in the world, indigenous scholars and activists demonstrate repeatedly that there is no authentic indigeneity outside of the complex and contradictory processes of self-recognition. Because sociopolitical initiatives aimed only at proving or dismantling such affirmations do little to serve long-term Native interests or the interests of a heterogeneous and democratic national society, questions about authenticity are not, it seems to me, the most productive ones to be asking.

BEYOND ALTERITY

In light of the documentation of abuse and corruption inside Brazil's indigenist agencies, the historically antagonistic relationship between indigenist functionaries and Native peoples, and the long-standing goal of de-Indianization (official and unofficial, spoken and unspoken), it would not seem far-fetched to cast Brazil's long-standing indigenist mission simply as an extended exercise in subjugation—especially if we judge its work in light of the social and cultural mores of our day. Nearly twenty years ago, the eminent anthropologist David Maybury-Lewis characterized over half a century of work by the SPI as a protracted effort to keep Indians "out of the way" of national development.[106] A decade later, Alcida Ramos wrote that FUNAI, "either through outright criminal action or through omission . . . [had] been part of the problem more often than part of the solution."[107]

Certainly there is much truth in these statements if we consider the cumulative role that state-backed indigenism has played in Brazil's governing administrations since 1910. It is well known that the indigenist bureaucracy has been chronically overburdened, understaffed, and underfunded considering the magnitude and difficulty of its mission. And yet, while it can never be forgotten that Brazil's indigenous population has suffered horrific injustice at the hands of some of the very people sworn to uphold the sanctity of indigenous life, it is an oversimplification to characterize the indigenist endeavor only in such terms. Anyone who has stepped into the indigenist archive to study some of the hundreds of thousands of pages of memos, reports, budgets, letters, lesson plans, maps, and other forms of documentation produced since the early twentieth century by indigenist functionaries across Brazil must pause, at least, to consider the voices of dedication, respect, and even love that also occasionally speak through those pages. Against a regional backdrop of systematic indigenous extermination and "removal"[108] and cloaked in the narrative of benevolent neocolonialism so typical of early SPI discourse, such voices point to the simple but oft-ignored fact that not every gesture toward human difference is an imperialist one.

The mere recognition of institutionalized discrimination and racism, then, does little to help us understand the historical engagement of indigenists and indigenist discourse with avowals of social, cultural, and epistemological difference, whether self-generated or imposed. Likewise, acknowledging abuse does little to move us away from the problem, which is, of course, still present and real. At the same time, the notion that the debunked essentialisms of dominant indigenist discourse might be redeployed from a putative inside—that is, from a site of an unadulterated indigeneity that reconfigures old categories of racialized difference as somehow liberating and elective, rather than limiting and essentialist—replaces the problem of racism based on perceptions of phenotype and cultural practice into a reification of human experience that is based, instead, on an irreducible claim to ontological and epistemological differentiation. Either way, the results are far from satisfactory: If in the first case, the complexities of life were condensed into Eurocentric historiographies and dehumanizing scientific or pseudoscientific analyses of racialized Others, in the latter case, that Otherness is transformed into a series of impenetrable identitarian claims that place whole categories of human experience into a conceptual black box. Without access to the code, presumed outsiders can only make an educated guess as to what it might contain.

Surely there are ways of being and knowing that cannot be understood or analyzed through the Occidental rationalist canon or the entire archive of Western thought. But if the appeal to alternative ontologies and epistemologies aims to influence dominant political discussions, reconfigure widespread forms of sociopolitical representation, or expand the possibilities for a nonrepresentational, radically democratic politics, it must be more than a gesture that points to the black box.[109] While some scholars have accepted this challenge head-on, engaging with nonhegemonic concepts of time, space, labor, value, and progress, and using them to question the ways they live and premises from which they think, it is surely more expedient and common to summon imprecise notions of "difference" and non-European exceptionalism.[110] The second move begins to undo the primordial indigenist gesture, I believe, while the first one simply reaffirms and reinscribes it.

Just as self-declared Native peoples can identify more or less with the traditional knowledge, languages, belief systems, cultural practices, and ethical codes of their particular communities, nonindigenous peoples can, likewise, engage with indigeneity in ways that assume superiority, or in ways that question and seek to disrupt dominant configurations of social and political power. Is his "Discourse on Indigenous Resistance," Maytapu scholar and activist Florêncio Almeida Vaz argues: "The conquistadors did not defeat us and will not defeat us. . . . For it was the True and Only God that created us . . . and gave us this Land for which to care, saying that our spirit is eternal and free. He asked that we always sing and dance in the sacred circle so that He could recognize us as his children. And still today we dance and struggle for Land, Justice, and Liberty for all Indians: native Indians, black Indians, Palestinian Indians, white Indians. . . . All of them."[111] Although his self-identification is clear, Vaz moves beyond an essentialist notion of indigeneity by opening up the concept to accommodate a larger set of ethical and political convictions that are in keeping with his ethics and politics. Whereas Vaz seeks common ground among indigenous and nonindigenous interests and priorities, dominant indigenist discourse appropriated (or hijacked) the *idea* of Indianness as a handy symbol to stand in for interests and priorities that had little if anything to do with self-identifying indigenous peoples. Invoking Indianness as a nationalist, anti-imperialist gesture thus became an easy way for nonindigenous intellectuals to claim relative subalternity for themselves without having to question their own relative power vis-à-vis other marginalized groups—including "Indians."

Vaz's commentary underscores the obvious but often overlooked fact that indigeneity, as a reflection of lived experience, means different things to different people across time and space. Like their non-Native counterparts, Native peoples can choose, in Vaz's formulation, to dance/struggle, or not. As David Stoll argued in his controversial and rather unsympathetic take on the life and testimony of Rigoberta Menchú Tum, some indigenous people may defend collective rights based on traditional forms of knowledge and a spiritual connection to land and nature, while others may wish to chop down the last remaining forest and make a new start of things in L.A.[112] One of these options is certainly more in keeping with popular and romantic sensibilities about Indianness, but that fact alone, of course, does not make it more indigenous. Paradoxically, although Menchú rejected Stoll's investigation and his critique, she reiterated his repudiation of the same dominant (academic) Manichaean mindset regarding indigenous peoples that was purportedly a primary target of his book. This line of thinking, already subtly present in her 1982 testimony, was unequivocal in the memoirs she published fifteen years later. As she argued then: "No one can distinguish to what extent something is indigenous or not. . . . Absolutism is destructive. Absolutism generates sectarianism, intolerance, isolation, radicalism."[113] If we agree with her and Vaz (among others), then the concept of indigeneity only holds meaning in the unsettled, oftentimes uncomfortable realm of dialogue and negotiation. Its contingent nature is a necessary but not sufficient condition for the national and global political activism that must expand and deepen if Brazil's indigenous peoples are to flourish *as such* into the future.

INDIGENEITY AND INTERCULTURALITY

The growth of indigenous movements in Brazil and across Latin America during the 1980s and 1990s took place in the context of a regional transition to democracy after years and in some cases decades of authoritarian rule.[114] During the same period, a series of popular, political, and theoretical discussions addressing the power differential between subaltern and dominant groups developed around the notion of *interculturality*, which emerged out of the recognition that bilingual education was a question not merely of linguistic knowledge and skill but also of diverging cultural practices, values, worldviews, and interpretations of the past. Although the concept was born in the world of pedagogy and targeted primarily at monolingual indigenous communities,[115] it would come over subsequent decades to impact a much broader population and to herald the ideal of organizing heterogeneous and plurinational societies in more egalitarian ways.

Interculturality offered a radical reformulation of the "contact zone" between different forms of knowledge and ways of knowing.[116] Unlike nineteenth-century notions of acculturation and assimilation (which implied the absorption of subaltern cultural forms into dominant ones), the early twentieth-century concept of transculturation (which suggested an inevitable if unintentional melding of marginalized and hegemonic cultural forms),[117] later twentieth-century concepts of heterogeneity and hybridity (which would, in theory, mitigate the syncretic tendencies of acculturation and transculturation),[118] and the ever-popular discourses of multiculturalism (which evoke cordial coexistence among "diverse" cultures that remain forever intact and essentially unchanged by one another), interculturality would convey a deliberate, even exchange of cultural mores and forms among individuals and groups without regard to their social, political, or economic influence vis-à-vis the dominant majority.[119] On a conceptual level, then, interculturality represented a break with earlier ways of thinking about interpersonal and intercommunal contact inside national boundaries where, despite all possible differences, shared interpersonal identification is idealized to take place through national belonging and citizenship. By helping to foster the conditions in which subaltern ideas and practices can enter into productive exchange with dominant ones, without being subsumed or silenced by them, intercultural organizations, institutions, and policies ideally lay the groundwork for radical, direct, or at least more participatory democracy.

In keeping with broad goals of reciprocity, respect, and nonessentialism, educators and educational philosophers across Latin America elaborated the earliest notions of interculturality during the 1960s and 1970s.[120] Experimental programs in Educação Bilíngue Intercultural (Bilingual and Intercultural Education, or EBI) during subsequent decades posited intercultural exchange as a "dialogue among cultures that are grounded in their own cultural matrix, but can selectively and critically incorporate elements of Occidental and other coexisting national cultures."[121] By the mid-nineties, this notion had moved beyond the realm of pedagogy to inform new and professedly more inclusive models for national development and national identity formation. As Peruvian linguist Juan Carlos Godenzzi characterized it: "Recognizing the cultural diversity of the country as a benefit and not an obstacle . . . demands the formation of a *conscience* of interculturality[:] . . . willingness to engage in dialogue; openness to the unfamiliar; . . . recognition of one's own value; incorporating the new; and strengthening the traditions that serve to enrich life. . . . If we understand it in this way, our education will serve as the womb of national identity and an indispensable foundation for dialogue with others."[122]

On the one hand, then, the ethos of interculturality means that indigenous peoples have the right to study and learn in their own languages; to see their traditional cultural forms and epistemological practices as legitimate, valuable, and equal to that of non-Natives; and to embrace rather than relinquish those forms and practices as they adjust, along with everyone else, to the challenges of the twenty-first century. On the other hand, because the concept stems from and revolves around the ideal of reciprocity, interculturality can only succeed (in theory) if it also exists as an integral component of the broader matrix of power relations that structure national society.

In practice, of course, the lived realities of power often push this ideal out of reach. Even when subaltern peoples and practices gain equal footing in theory (in academic discourse or according to the law, for example), they are clearly less likely to do so in their day-to-day lives. As the possessors or practitioners of dominant cultural forms are rarely (if ever) asked to mirror the learning processes or outcomes expected of social, linguistic, and cultural subalterns, it is difficult to fulfill the ideal of sustained and equitable exchange that lies at the heart of intercultural theory and practice. Because the task of becoming knowledgeable about and competent in subaltern or historically marginalized languages and cultures is rarely assigned to the speakers of dominant languages and the practitioners of dominant cultural forms, bearing the burden of interculturality is frequently a one-way street, leading to what historian Dipesh Chakrabarty famously called the problem of "asymmetric ignorance."[123] In Brazil, for instance, while there is no shortage of theoretical and practical information about teaching the "indigenous theme" in nonindigenous schools (legally mandated since 2008),[124] nonindigenous students in Rio de Janeiro, São Paulo, Belo Horizonte, and Brasília (for example) are rarely able to consider Native-authored sources as part of their study, and even less often expected to develop competence in Native languages, philosophies, or cultural traditions as a long-term educational or civic goal.

The uneven practice of interculturality is further challenged by the conceptual and political paradox that has long been the Achilles' heel of subaltern studies: subalternity. For even when subalternity, like the concept of power out of which it is derived and the question of "Indianness" through which it has been channeled, is contextualized and understood in relative terms, the basic paradox of representation remains. In other words, the cultural and political projects that have sought to affirm the social, cultural, linguistic, and philosophical traditions of marginalized peoples by subscribing to an ethos of interculturality are not *necessarily* more liberating or democratic than the prevailing indigenist discourses of the twentieth century. At the end of the day, some individual or group has to assume responsibility for selecting elements suitable to a properly indigenous perspective.[125] Although the very fact of this selection presents an opportunity to deconstruct and reconstruct the concept of indigeneity through questioning, analysis, and negotiation, it also leaves room to essentialize and dictate, and thus runs the risk of truncating the discussion or burdening it with dogmatism.

TOLERANCE

Early theorists and practitioners of intercultural projects in the Americas stood on the shoulders of Paulo Freire, the Pernambucan philosopher and educator who in the early 1960s developed a revolutionary "pedagogy of the oppressed" to oppose what he called the dominant "banking conceptualization" of education.[126] Rather than treat pupils as unknowledgeable, empty "accounts" into which all-knowing teachers deposit their knowledge, Freire argued, learning should be grounded in a dialogical relationship between teacher and student as two already-knowing subjects. Although Freire's early work grew out of a materialist conceptualization of social relations in which racial, ethnic, and cultural identities and identifications were subordinate to class structures and their relationship to political and social power,[127] he later theorized the precarious situation of ethnoracial minorities—not only in terms of their social and cultural marginalization in and by the dominant majority but also in terms of differentiated epistemologies and ontologies.[128] While he did not work closely with indigenous communities in Brazil, his recognition of the subjective nature of truth claims and embrace of many ways of being and knowing in the world grew out of decades of work with individuals and groups whose conceptualizations of rationality and science diverged radically from those most commonly accepted in and perpetuated by the broader societies in which they lived.

Rather than compare the "mathematical precision" with which different kinds of knowledge could describe or explain the world, Freire questioned the conceptual grounds on which dominant societies erected and institutionalized hierarchies of "superior" and "inferior" forms of life and thought. These hierarchies informed or generated educational structures that posited certain individuals and groups as auspicious possessors of knowledge and others—like Native peoples—as perpetually needy beneficiaries. He therefore countered, "The curiosity that motivates, drives, and pushes knowledge is one and the same—that of the Indian, mine, and yours. There is no pure curiosity—neither the Indian's nor ours; there is [only a relationship of] domination in the encounter of [different] findings. . . . With regard to understanding reality and the world, we search rigorously for the object, and can find it with more precision. However, this does not mean you invalidate the Indian's findings."[129]

Like the concept of intercultural reciprocity, then, Freire's assessment works against the foundational indigenist postulation that traditional indigenous knowledge is necessarily invalidated by dominant, modern, or scientific knowledge. He likewise opposed the twentieth-century "educational corollary" to this position: that the state's architects of progress must, in keeping with the teleological march of history, replace indigenous cultural practices and knowledge—typically reduced to myths, superstitions, and family histories—with "superior" cultural forms and the Western knowledge necessary to usher in modernization and development.

For Freire, the precision with which particular kinds of knowledge might reflect a scientific (Western) rendering of the world was not the sole or most important criteria with which to judge its relative worth. His "indigenism" thus reflected a "pedagogy of tolerance"—not in the condescending sense of one person or group having to accept or embrace the shortcomings of another but, rather, as a reciprocal acknowledgment of engagement with and respect for differences or disagreements that appear irreconcilable at face value.[130] Consistent with an ethos of interculturality, Freire's thinking pointed to the then burgeoning notion that indigenous knowledge has "a future in the project of productive conservation as it increasingly complements more conventional forms of environmental management."[131] While the question of *how* to mold this future without simply "commodifying the Indian" remains a challenge,[132] indigenous intellectuals, activists, and community leaders argue that the integrity of demarcated territories, the valorization of ancestral knowledge, and the right to direct and prior consultation regarding new legislation and public policies that impact their lives and livelihoods are all conditions necessary for such work to succeed.[133]

Unlike traditional indigenist discourses, which sought to re-create the indigenous world in the image of dominant society, Freire's work envisioned social heterogeneity as a motor for intellectual growth and the progressive democratization of national society. If "legitimate tolerance teaches [us] . . . that when faced with another's experience, [we] can learn from difference,"[134] all encounters with Otherness present opportunities for mutual education and thus mutual benefit. Projected into the realm of relations between the indigenous and the nonindigenous, the Freireian notion of tolerance opens up the possibility for indigeneity to replace Indianness as an integral part of Brazilianness and Brazilian society, and emphasizes the need for subaltern and dominant groups alike to share in the work of interculturality. Linguist Eunice Dias de Paula has argued that meeting this challenge with regard to education requires not just incorporating the "indigenous theme" into mainstream schools but, much more important, reevaluating the fundamental goals of indigenous and nonindigenous learning alike.[135]

Embracing the concept of reciprocity ultimately means transferring the authority over pedagogical processes and structures from the indigenist apparatus to indigenous peoples themselves. Contrary to the twentieth-century version of the civilizing mission, whereby indigenist education—as in the case of Kapêlituk and the Escola Capitão Pedro Dantas—moved from centers of state power into indigenous communities, Dias de Paula proposes that the ideals of interculturality will only begin to be served when the education of indigenous children moves into a classroom.[136]

An enterprise much older than interculturality and, indeed, an enterprise much older than Brazil, indigenous education, has of course always existed in indigenous communities—whether independently from, in conjunction with, or in spite of the state and its Dona Nazarés.

Transferring power to indigenous peoples to implement their own educational programs turns the colonialist legacy of Indian education on its head. Like the polemical demarcation of indigenous territories, it raises crucial questions about the nature of indigenous citizenship, about the constitutionality of differentiated treatment for indigenous individuals and communities, and about the sovereignty of the Brazilian state. Namely, if indigenous people in Brazil are indigenous *and* Brazilian, rather than Indians-perpetually-on-the-way-to-Brazilianness, how should their membership in the national community be reflected in their classrooms and their lives? How much autonomy is enough? How to draw the line between the national thought and practices reflected in civic education and the neocolonial de-Indianization campaigns of the past? Native Brazilians continue to negotiate answers to these questions and the weight they bring to bear on the state's institutionalized relationship with indigeneity—mostly, but not exclusively, through FUNAI.[137] Although their interventions are far from homogeneous, they are bound by the recognition that any meaningful form of autonomy will ultimately, if also paradoxically, be granted by the Brazilian state. While many indigenous peoples rebuke the Brazilian government for the colonialist structures and policies that still shape their lives, they also recognize that it is precisely by participating in that government—and therefore, by working with the implicit and explicit cooperation of the wider Brazilian populace—that such policies and structures can be transformed.[138] How this situation has come to pass since the nineteenth century, and how it continues to unfold in the twenty-first, is the focus of the chapters that follow.

2

ON CANNIBALS AND CHRISTIANS

The Violent Displacements of Nation Building

When *Il guarany* opened on 19 March 1870 at Milan's Teatro alla Scala, the Brazilian composer Antônio Carlos Gomes could hardly have imagined that he was destined to become a national icon, or that the overture to his third European opera—a tale of Indians as cannibals and Christians—would one day be hailed as Brazil's second national anthem.[1] The Italian-written libretto had been based on José de Alencar's successful novel, *O guarany* (1859), and though presented in simplified form, the tale remained largely the same:[2] In 1560, a clever Guarani warrior named Peri foils a Spanish conspiracy to kill the Portuguese fidalgo,[3] Antônio de Mariz, and in so doing, befriends the nobleman's chaste and beautiful daughter, Cecília. When "Ceci" is captured by Aimoré cannibals seeking retaliation for the death of one of their women, Peri saves her just in the nick of time. A happy ending seems assured until the man-eaters, together with the plotting Spaniards, lay siege to Dom Antônio's castle.

Facing this gruesome fate, Dom Antônio entrusts his daughter to Peri's care on the condition that the Indian renounce idolatry, accept a Christian baptism, and deliver the young woman safely to Rio de Janeiro. As the Aimoré move in, Peri escapes with Ceci through an open window while ignoring her desperate pleas to die alongside her father. The old Don Antônio, however, will not be an easy victim. Before falling to his enemies, he detonates the castle and everyone in it while the young couple observes his Pyrrhic victory from a hilltop in the distance. Thus freed from the double bind of European patriarchy and native savagery, they depart into

Frontispiece of the copy of Il guarany *given to Dom Pedro II by Antônio Carlos* Gomes, 1870. Courtesy of the Acervo da Fundação Biblioteca Nacional—Brasil.

the wilderness, united by love and faith in God to found the harmonious, mixed-race Brazil of national and nationalist myth.[4]

The celebration of Gomes's Indianist nationalism would culminate seven decades later on the centenary of his birth, hailed in 1936 by National Institute of Music director Guilherme Fontainha as the "grandest event of all time in the world of Brazilian music" and thus deserving of its own national holiday.[5] Planned months in advance, the commemoration inspired schoolroom productions, a special meeting of the Brazilian Academy of Letters, an international conference sponsored by the Universidade do Rio de Janeiro,[6] and a monument to honor the composer in his hometown of Campinas. Attendants at a much-touted commemorative concert held in the capital included not only ministers of state, the federal diplomatic corps, high-ranking officials from the armed services, "select circles" of socialites and artists, and key representatives of the national press corps, but also President Getúlio Vargas and *primeira dama* Darcy Sarmanho Vargas.[7] The *New York Times* reported the next day that similar events had been staged in France and Germany, and that favorite sections of *Il guarany* had been transmitted live from Milan to Carlos Gomes's adoring compatriots on the other side of the Atlantic. As one enthusiastic reporter observed from Rio de Janeiro, "all of Brazil, in a manifestation of spiritual solidarity and civil exaltation to the memory of her most preeminent figures, pulsated and throbbed on that day of glorification."[8] Hence a loyal monarchist who had declined a presidential invitation to pen the anthem of the First Republic became an unlikely hero of Brazilian cultural nationalism on the eve of the Estado Novo.[9]

Over a lifetime spent between Campinas, Rio de Janeiro, Milan, and (briefly) Belém,[10] Carlos Gomes had no contact with the Native peoples of his country, and most of his work had nothing to do with Indians. But it was precisely for their representation, and *Il guarany*, in particular, that he would be (and continues to be) most remembered and celebrated. The 500-page *Revista Brasileira de Música* that was dedicated to his work by the National Institute of Music in observance of the centenary offers not a word from or about indigenous peoples but is adorned throughout with "ornamental motifs" of the Guarani and other *índios brasileiros* whom the organizers judged at the time to be extinct.[11]

Despite such fanfare, the posthumous characterization of Carlos Gomes as a treasured national symbol was not an accurate reflection of his difficult and sometimes tragic life, which was marred by poverty, illness, dejection, and, toward the end, an acute sense of estrangement

II - O homem e sua arte

"The Man and His Art: Ornamental Motif of the Extinct Indians of Marajó Island." From Revista Brasileira de Música 3, no. 2 (11 July 1936). Photo by Ricardo Pimentel.

from his homeland and its people.[12] Nevertheless, at the height of Vargas's nationalist populism, the collective construction of Carlos Gomes's iconic status was already well under way. The 1936 festivities followed an already substantial demonstration of patriotic enthusiasm for his work and its projected ideals, particularly among the aspiring and dominant classes. From the end of the nineteenth century through the first decades of the twentieth, generations of intellectuals and political leaders embraced the composer as a symbol of national talent and promise. Along with *Il guarany*, they showcased the other major piece of his Indianist repertoire— *Lo schiavo* (*The Slave*), from 1889—for its idealized rendering of Native redemption, making harmonious and markedly Brazilian processes of miscegenation popular entertainment for select audiences at home and abroad.

In the postabolition Brazil of the late 1880s, when many elites were skeptical of their country's racial future and deeply invested in the powerful logic of racial improvement, Carlos Gomes meant "Indians," only better.[13] If *Il guarany* served to revitalize the Indianists' backward-gazing search for Brazilian roots in a precolonial past, the nationalist appropriation of Carlos Gomes's work and persona during the early twentieth century point to what Hermano Vianna calls the "imaginative recreation of those roots."[14] Bolstered by Gilberto Freyre's rethinking of racial mixture as a positive and potentially unifying national force, and by President Getúlio Vargas's campaign to consolidate official Brazilian culture over racialized and classist regional loyalties, the dominant majority of the 1930s equated nationalized *mestiçagem* with social improvement and embraced Gomes's contribution to its promotion.[15] The son of a brown-skinned music teacher and mother of mixed-indigenous descent, Gomes was called a *caboclo*[16] at home and dubbed (not without admiration), the "savage of the opera" in Europe.[17] Guilherme Fontainha thus explained in his centenary homage: "Carlos Gomes deserves everything the Brazilian people have to give. He . . . proved the musical value of *our race* overseas . . . because the staging of his operas has always been a resounding triumph for the author and an immense glory for the land he loved so much. . . . [Gomes's work] meant recognition for us, at the time so little known in the Old World, especially in the field of art.[18]

This statement, while doubtless sincere, is deeply ironic on several counts. First, it elides the fact that Carlos Gomes died with great love for Brazil but great disdain for the First Republic, by which he felt betrayed.[19] Second, like most posthumous invocations of the composer, whether favorable or not, Fontainha's statement politicized Gomes's work despite the fact that he was a staunchly apolitical thinker who bluntly expressed his unwillingness to "get involved in any 'noise' other than music." His allegiance to the emperor and the royal family was not ideological but personal and professional.[20] Finally, Gomes's contribution to the popular construction of the *raça brasileira*, like that of José de Alencar and his Indianist cohort, never impacted indigenous peoples in any positive material way. On the contrary, I will argue, operatic and literary Indianism hastened the destruction of Native lives and livelihoods by bolstering fables of benevolent colonialism and cordial miscegenation during extended periods of anti-indigenous violence.

While the romantic notion of Indianness grew increasingly important over the nineteenth and early twentieth centuries as a hallowed essence of Brazilianness, Native men, women, and children fell victim to the Paraguayan War (1865–70); became slaves for landowners in the North and Northeast; served as guinea pigs for legions of foreign craniometrists, eugenicists, and "naturalists"; and were hunted like animals by settlers and prospectors in search of land and valuable resources. Indian Christians and cannibals were staged with resounding success at home and abroad at the same time Laiana, Quiniquináo, Guaná, Chooronó, Terena, Guarani, and hundreds of other indigenous peoples were collectively "cannibalized" by the brutality that was unleashed on them not only by slave-runners and latter-day *bandeirantes*, but also by representatives of the nation that showcased them as its valued and "protected" subjects.[21] "The Indian," as David Treece puts it, "became the embodiment of the very nationalism that was engaged in his own annihilation."[22] By the mid-twentieth century, a Native population that in 1500 numbered between 3 and 6 million fell to some 100,000 souls. Surely not a "relatively untraumatic history" by their calculations, or by those of their modern-day descendants.[23]

It may seem paradoxical at face value that the popular reverence for Gomes and his *Guarany* developed over the same period that so many Native communities were shattered by the growing onslaught of nation-builders, but romantic Indianism and indigenous destruction, in fact, went hand in hand. Several scholars have addressed the fact that Brazilian intellectuals from statesmen to poets engaged in intense and extended debate over the fate of their Native compatriots.[24] As the gap between indigenous experience and portrayals of Indianness widened, Brazil and "her" Native people became increasingly objectified and commodified—not only for national policy and pleasure, but also, as in the case of Carlos Gomes, for people and markets abroad. Foreign and foreign-influenced renderings of Brazilian Indianness in art, science, and political discourse were in countless ways "out-of-place" on Brazilian soil, but as Roberto DaMatta reminds us, "what is startling . . . is not the existence of contradictions and cynicism, but the enormous tolerance of the system . . . [and] a social logic that . . . exploits the ambiguities of its intermediate ranges."[25] Indeed, idealized Indians and indigenous peoples have continued to exist in this symbiotic relationship because it is generally more expedient for members of the dominant majority to embrace the ideal of a democratizing *mestiçagem* if they also hold the power to determine its meaning and to claim Indianness, in whatever imagined or distant form, as their own. Revisionist emplotments and their hyperbolic tropes of self and Other—cannibals and Christians—have thus been recycled repeatedly into the twenty-first century. It is only against this backdrop of colonialist imagery and the violent processes of nation-building that have accompanied it that Native Brazilians have begun to forge their still-unfinished path to self-representation and differentiated citizenship.

ITALIAN INDIANS AND THE MARVELOUS CITY

Although Italian critics generally assessed Gomes's *Il guarany* favorably, its debut on Milan's booming opera scene in March 1870 was not quite as "triumphant" as some twentieth-century scholars wished to suggest.[26] Well-known columnist Filippe Filippo, for example, writing for Milan's *La Perseveranza* one month later, characterized Gomes's work as "inspired" and "at times original" but also ambiguous, uneven, lacking in coherence, and "short on dramatic color."[27] Antônio Ghislanzoni of Casa Ricordi's *Gazetta Musicale de Milano*[28] surmised that the young Brazilian had made "good music" despite the "mediocre" libretto on which the opera had been based and concluded that such an achievement had been no small feat, "for a beginner."[29]

In contrast to this ambiguous reception by the guardians of Italian high culture, folks back home hailed Gomes as a national hero—the first Brazilian, and, indeed, the first Latin American artist, ever to win such international acclaim for his art. Word of his "great success" arrived to Campinas in a letter that Carlos Gomes penned to his brother, José Pedro Sant'Anna Gomes, who forwarded the news to the local press. The people of Campinas wasted no time appropriating the improbable triumph of their native son and his operatic Indians as their own:

> Our distinguished compatriot . . . received his grand European baptism, thereby bolstering the legitimate fame of his artistic merits. The great opera, *O guarany*, was performed in Milan's Scala Theater with great success, and the maestro was called back to the stage more than twenty times to the resonance of frenetic applause. This glory belongs in large part to Brazil, and particularly to this province, which considers that illustrious *campineiro* one of her most beloved sons and one of the most notable embellishments of her artistic fame. We *paulistas* must not be indifferent to this occasion. We must pay attention. Carlos Gomes, whose musical career has begun so brilliantly, should . . . be our source of pride, our brightest star in the field of fine arts. . . . As is fitting and just, Campinas broke into celebration upon hearing the great news. The musical crowd . . . joined together . . . and paraded through the streets along with a large number of citizens whose shouts of approval and brilliant speeches gave wings to the immense jubilation of the entire population.[30]

In an odd mix of regional and national pride, these zealous fans were but a tiny wave in the ocean of patriotic sentiment that engulfed Carlos Gomes and his "Guarany" crooners over the century to follow.

Opera had become a pastime in the capital city in the mid-1840s—"a consuming passion of every educated and aspiring inhabitant of Rio," as historian Eric Gordon described it nearly a century later.[31] When *Il guarany* crossed the Atlantic in November 1870, nine months after its Milan debut, Carlos Gomes's European success grew by several degrees of magnitude. Opening night at the Theatro Lyrico Fluminense was set for 2 December to coincide with the birthday of the composer's patron and friend, Dom Pedro II, and popular hype crescendoed into a flurry of renewed enthusiasm for the empire. The debut announcement read: "Performance in grand, national celebration . . . honored with the August Presence of Their Imperial Majesties. After the National Anthem, . . . the grandiose opera-dance of the Brazilian *maestro* A. Carlos Gomes will take the stage."[32]

In keeping with Marcos Terena's observation that indigenous peoples under colonialism were either "innocents" or "barbarians,"[33] the tale was constructed around the basic distinction between the protonational, Christian Guarani and the demonic, man-eating Aimoré.[34] Beneath the list of Italian performers appeared an *aviso*: "The grand march and Indian dance is directed and composed by choreographer Sr. Poggiolesi. In it take part the same Gentleman, the leading female dancers, . . . the dance troupe, choruses, extras, the Italian band, and the band of savages."[35] Imagined Europeans and Amerindians thus fulfilled their expected roles in the patriotic narrative of national myth, occupying center stage, while Brazil and Brazilians would be inferred from the idealized encounter between the victorious forces of the good. As was the case with the ample body of cultural production associated with the Indianist moment, Carlos Gomes's masterwork folded indigenous cultures, languages, epistemologies, and histories into well-defined tropes of sameness and alterity that would endure for decades to come.

Il guarany was a smash in the capital city. Advertisements ran for weeks in the *carioca* dailies, and the opera played some thirteen times in the first two weeks of December 1870 alone. Classified ads offered the original score arranged for piano and voice with the headline banner: "*Il Guarany*, Grande Successo!"[36] After the closing performance on 17 December, an extensive article highlighting the genius and splendor of Carlos Gomes's work appeared on the front page of the *Jornal do Commercio* in the space typically reserved for a popular *folhetim*.[37] Local critics reiterated the success of *Il guarany* abroad as a personal victory for the composer, a crowning achievement for the Brazilian people, and a testament to the emperor's wise investment in the burgeoning industries of a distinctive national culture.

Although Carlos Gomes was heralded at home and abroad as a *maestro brasileiro*, *Il guarany* was promoted on Brazilian soil as "*ópera italiana*"—a

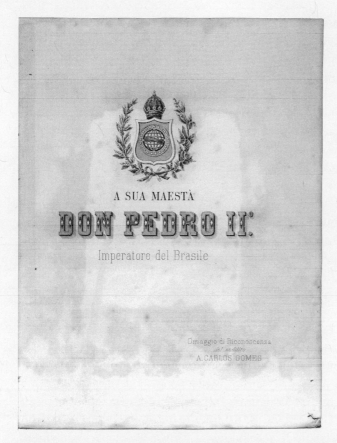

Dedication page of the copy of Il guarany *gifted to the emperor in 1870: "To His Majesty, Dom Pedro II: Emperor of Brazil. A tribute of gratitude from [your] subject, A. Carlos Gomes." Courtesy of the Acervo da Fundação Biblioteca Nacional—Brasil.*

label aimed to boost the cultural capital of the work among an audience teeming with Europhiles. *Il guarany* was superior to its Indianist precedents, including José de Alencar's original novel, because it reinterpreted the cherished legend of Euro-Indian romance not only in European terms and in a European genre, but also with Europeans performing in a European language: In Milan and Rio de Janeiro alike, Italian Indians hit the stage singing in Italian. Carlos Gomes triumphed at home in large part because—adapting Edward Said's formulation—"the quasi-ethnographic displays afforded by European expositions" were emptied of local content and "associated with consumerist leisure based in Europe."[38] The enthusiastic reception of operatic Indians in Rio and São Paulo was thus mediated by, and to some degree, predicated on Brazil's budding reputation on the other side of the Atlantic and honorary affiliation with the most civilized of nations.

The hyperpatriotic, proto-*ufanista* mindset[39] that celebrated the portrayal of Brazilian "Indians" abroad while (at best) ignoring and (at worst) facilitating the persecution and disappearance of indigenous peoples at home was especially important in the work of Carlos Gomes because of its simultaneous interpellation of, and power to influence regional, national, and international audiences. The aggrandizement of his work at each of these levels, though staggered and uneven, indicated the enduring power of the Indian as a malleable symbol that could be easily divorced from any real-world referent and tied to a seemingly endless variety of social, political, and cultural issues. Turning a blind eye to the imperiled indigenous population, elite and middle-class urbanites already sold on the promises of racial improvement could accept and even applaud the representation of their still-young nation through ideas and images of Indianness as long as the Indians in question sported silk and belted out arias for elegant crowds in Europe and across the Americas.[40]

And yet, Carlos Gomes was not without his homegrown critics. Among those less than enthusiastic about *Il guarany* was Alencar himself, for whom the libretto adaptation by Italians Carlo d'Omerville and Antonio Scalvini was a disappointing caricature. He complained: "Gomes turned my *Guarany* into a nameless mess, full of nonsense. . . . I forgive him for everything, though, since perhaps in times to come, because of his spontaneous and inspired harmonies, many will read or reread the book, which is the greatest favor an author could possibly deserve."[41] Alencar's equanimity served him well: many an Indianist novel would be sold to the readership born of Gomes's "mess." Of course, in keeping with the Indianist movement that would in the following century become synonymous with his name, Alencar's sense of entitlement to his subject matter and indignation over its distortion held no trace of alliance or solidarity with indigenous peoples. Devoid of any fidelity to a Guarani past or present, the author's only touchstone for a proper rendering of *Il guarany* would be his own fruitful imagination.

The Indianists' Janus-faced rhetoric was "foundational," however, not only for ideologues of Brazil as a national project, but also for the Native peoples who have been chipping away at those foundations ever since. Concepts like *selvagem* (savage), *silvícola* (jungle dweller), *primitivo* (primitive), *bárbaro* (barbarian), and *bugre* (bugger)—the lingo of nineteenth-century Indian policy—are still among the building blocks of indigenist discourse and thus influence what Peter Hulme called the "archeological labor" of piecing together a history that can never be fully reconstructed and has yet to reach its conclusion.[42] Indeed, representatives of the "progressive" Serviço de Proteção aos Índios (Indian Protection Service, or SPI) couched relations between indigenous and

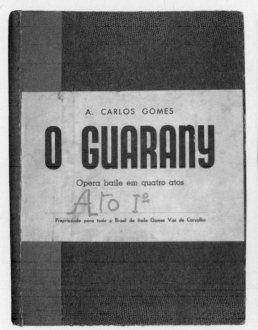

Original score, labeled "Property for All Brazil," from Carlos Gomes's Italian-born daughter, Ítala Gomes Vas (sic) de Carvalho, and the "furious" chorus of the cannibalistic Aimoré, no date. Photo by Catherine Gass. Courtesy of the Newberry Library, Chicago. Case MS 1500 G63g.

nonindigenous peoples in sixteenth-century terminology well into the twentieth: "For better or for worse, the extreme physical and moral acuity of the Indian mean that if we are not to ruin and lose entirely the already realized *conquest*, [success] will depend on the continuity of action carried out by the same person . . . who is already known and credible [to them]."[43]

The flipside of such efforts to undo Indianness, of course, is indigenous peoples' work to redefine indigeneity despite the ultimately unbridgeable gap between individual and collective modes of self-fashioning and the multiple processes of social identification. On the one hand, this work entails wrestling with the Sausurrean dilemma of reconciling the structures of language with its historicity—or the not-so-simple reality that all meanings change over time[44]—and on the other hand, trying to understand such changes across the multiple fields where they are at play, from politics and social discourse to journalism and creative cultural production. Because the work and legacy of Carlos Gomes are implicated in each of these contexts, they remain consequential for indigenous peoples, even if indigenous peoples were never of much consequence to Carlos Gomes or his Indianist work.

THE PARAGUAYAN WAR AND THE OTHER GUARANI

Il guarany was Gomes's most popular opera in Brazil not only because of its artistic merit and positive reception in Europe but also because news of its success landed on Brazilian soil shortly after the conclusion of the War of the Triple Alliance, known in Brazil as the Guerra do Paraguay (1864–70).[45] Although the united forces of Brazil, Argentina, and Uruguay occupied the Paraguayan capital of Asunción in January 1869, fighting had dragged on for more than another year. The war would not end officially until 1 March 1870—just eighteen days before *Il guarany* debuted in Milan—when Brazilian troops killed the defiant Paraguayan president and military leader Francisco Solano López at Cerro Cora, some forty kilometers from Paraguay's border with the then-province of Matto Grosso (later, Mato Grosso). After hundreds of thousands of deaths and devastating material losses on all sides, the allied forces had finally brought their long-suffering neighbors to their knees.[46]

Patriotic sentiment in Brazil was high despite a pervasive sense of exhaustion with the war and its mind-boggling expenditure of life and capital—losses that would not be quantified until decades later and are, indeed, still passionately debated.[47] The general public revered the sacrifices and sufferings of the Brazilian armed forces and transformed them into various forms of cultural production, ranging from popular journalism and personal memoirs to theater pieces and poetry.[48] Brazil's nationalist embrace of Carlos Gomes's *Il guarany* thus took place in the wake of a highly racialized confrontation in which the Paraguayans obsessively disdained the Brazilians as an empire of "black stinking monkeys" and "black dirty pigs"[49] and were scorned, in turn, by their Brazilian and Argentine enemies as a (second) Guarani Republic—a people shockingly tenacious but hopelessly uncivilized.[50] Paraguayan journalists referred to Pedro II and the Brazilian forces with racist language targeted at drafted slave soldiers while identifying themselves as "Indians" who "had no reason to be refined"[51] but nonetheless wished to distinguish themselves from the "savage" Mbayá-Guaicuru peoples on the other side of the border who had been "recruited" into the Brazilian army.

In his detailed record of the ground war, the young military officer Alfredo d'Escragnolle Taunay[52] launched a career in writing that would lead him years later to coauthor the libretto to Carlos Gomes's *Lo schiavo*.[53] His

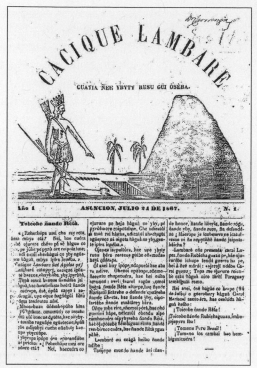

The newspapers Cabichuí (*13 May 1867*) and Cacique Lambaré (*24 July 1867*)
racialized Paraguay's struggle against Brazil during the War of the Triple Alliance.
The caption of the later issue reads "Toicobe ñande Retà [Long Live Our Fatherland]."
Guarani-Spanish translation courtesy of Dr. Wolf Lustig.

double-edged representation of the Paraguayans in his most famous war
memoir, *A retirada da Laguna*,[54] ranged from a reluctant appreciation of
"inexorable" fighters and "great scouts" to loathing for "cruel," "cowardly,"
"boastful," and "hateful" savages who would burn their enemies alive,
dig up the dead to steal their clothes, and assassinate Brazilian victims
of a cholera outbreak en masse as they begged for mercy.[55] Although the
Paraguayans embraced the Guarani language and culture for symbolic
ends, publishing the state-backed Guarani-language newspaper *Cacique
Lambaré* and using Guarani words and images in support of their anti-
imperialist struggle,[56] Brazil, its allies, and even Solano López's compatriot
foes sought to do away with the language and traditions of a people whose
lack of civilization they attributed to the decades of despotic rule and isolation perpetrated on them by their wayward if not fanatical leader. For the
heads of the Brazilian-backed interim government, the backwardness and
abject poverty of postwar Paraguay were "spit in the face of civilization":

On Cannibals and Christians / 75

The Paraguayan people, escaping their horrible martyrdom thanks to the . . . triumphs of the Allied Armies; destroyed and dispersed; naked and hungry; prisoner to disease and annihilated by sufferings, arrives and is received at the door of their own home, freed from the order of the tyrant by a foreign population that honors civilization with the humanity of its acts and the philanthropy of its sentiments. . . . The Triumvirate . . . will adopt as the norm of its government and foundation of the national reorganization the principles, guaranties, and rights consecrated constitutionally by the freer peoples of the American continent. . . . Taking this first step onto the terrain of its high obligations to fulfill that which in the normal order of societies is entrusted . . . to the discretion of the head of the household—providing the food, clothing, and shelter of the child—the Provisional Government is the father of the Paraguayan family.[57]

In keeping with the desire of Paraguay's postwar leaders to "catch up" with "civilization," an important undertaking of this "freer" and "more liberal" society would be to do away with the lingua franca of the Paraguayan majority (Guarani), starting in public schools. Reversing the wartime effort to valorize the language,[58] a national decree passed on 7 March 1870 required teachers to use and demand the use of Spanish in their classrooms.[59] Such policies meant that Carlos Gomes's *Guarany* graced the stages of Rio de Janeiro at precisely the same time state-backed efforts to bolster Guarani language and culture across the border were systematically truncated with the backing of Brazil and the triumvirate postwar authority.

In the months that ensued, up through the December 1870 staging of Gomes's opera in Rio, journalists, critics, and citizens recounted in personal memoirs and the popular press the tales of their soldiers—the so-called Voluntários da Pátria[60]—and their moments of torment and triumph during the deadliest war fought on Latin American soil since the Conquest.[61] Although the conflict had taken an enormous toll on Pedro II—personally, because of poor health and troubled family relations; and politically, because of the escalating costs of war and diminishing support for his rule—the surge of patriotism fashioned the emperor as an adept leader heartily devoted to his nation and its people.[62] When the final commander of the Brazilian armed forces returned to Rio de Janeiro at the war's end, he was greeted with such joyous "delirium" that it was nearly impossible, according to eyewitness André Rebouças, for those present to "to keep their feet on the ground."[63]

The same day, on 29 April 1870, an Italian enthusiast named G. Berga-maschi dedicated an original sonnet to the Brazilian people on the front page of the *Jornal do Commercio*: "Al Brasil: In occasione della sua festa per lo splendido trionfo ottimo dalle sue armi nel Paraguay!"[64] Praising Brazilian soil, the poet speculated that the bones of her martyrs exulted for joy underground, and concluded: "Gloria o Brasile a te possente Imperio! Gloria al tuo deffensor Pietro Secondo! Gloria agli eroi che eterno onor ti diano!"[65] Since the waves of Italian immigration sought by the ruling elite to whiten their country would not begin for over another decade,[66] when abolition was in sight and a shortage of agricultural workers loomed on the horizon, the heightened interest in Brazilian affairs among Italians was likely due, in part, to the rising fame of Carlos Gomes and *Il guarany* across circuits of European high culture. What was evident, in any case, was that at the conclusion of the Paraguayan War, the only empire in the so-called New World—a slaveholding empire with fresh indigenous blood on its hands—still enjoyed substantial political support both at home and abroad. And yet, in less than thirty years' time, such patriotic sentiment would morph into a front of anti-imperialist nationalism powerful enough to banish the emperor and his family from their homeland just three days after the declaration of the First Republic on 15 November 1889.

Although the republican movement had been afoot since the early nineteenth century and grown during the postwar period among disgruntled veterans and military leaders, it was in the early 1870s still a relatively toothless threat. On 3 December 1870—the day following the emperor's lavish birthday celebration and the debut of *Il guarany* in Rio—the Republican Manifesto appeared in the first run of *A República*—a short-lived publication of the Partido Republicano Brasileiro that was produced in collaboration with the Clube Republicano. It read:

> The war we had to sustain for six years allowed us to see with the occupation of Matto Grosso and the invasion of Rio Grande do Sul how critical and disastrous centralized government is to the task of safeguarding honor and national integrity. The federal government—based . . . on the reciprocal independence of the provinces, raised to the category of proper States, united only by the bond of nationality and the solidarity of great interests in representation and exterior defense—is that which we adopt in our program as the only way to maintain the communion of the Brazilian family. If we needed a formula to emphasize . . . the effect of both regimes, we would sum it up as follows: Centralization = Dismemberment. Decentralization = Unity. . . . Strengthened by our

right and our conscience, we stand before our fellow citizens, resolutely flying the flag of the Federal Republican party. We are from America and we want to be Americans.[67]

Fewer than sixty people put their names to the original document,[68] but *A República* grew from a tiny, three-day-per-week operation to a highly influential publication with a daily distribution of some 10,000 copies.[69] Scholars have disagreed as to why the paper closed down a few years later, some attributing its demise to a lack of readership and others to threats of physical violence made against the journalists.[70] Undeniable, in any case, is that the paper opened the floodgates of republican journalism and popular critique. Dozens of similar publications cropped up across the country in the years that ensued, including more than twenty new titles nationwide by the end of 1872 alone.[71] The *Revista Illustrada*, founded in 1876 by the Italian-born satirist Angelo Agostini, was among the most influential, offering an unrelenting critique of Pedro II, the royal family, and the hypocritical, slaveholding elite that had characterized Brazil as a nation of free peoples vis-à-vis the Paraguayans at the conclusion of a disastrous war just a few years earlier. Playing up the hackneyed appropriation of Native images as a nationalist trope, Agostini's work addressed conflicts between indigenous populations and nonindigenous settlers, and constantly invoked "Indians" to symbolize the Brazilian people living under conditions of always politicized duress—from economic hardships and excessive taxation, to corruption and the reviled institution of slavery itself.

Notwithstanding such rustlings of discontent, the power of Dom Pedro and the royal family remained intact for time to come. With the support of his second postwar cabinet led by José Maria da Silva Paranhos (the *visconde* do Rio Branco) from 7 March 1871 to 25 June 1875, the emperor staved off brewing insurgency with legislation to target contentious issues ranging from electoral reform and military pensions to the modernization of national infrastructure and the elephant in the room: slavery.[72] On 28 September 1871—four months into her first regency and still seventeen years before abolition—Princess Isabel signed the Lei Rio Branco,[73] making all children born to slave mothers free upon their birth, at least in theory.[74] Infants "emancipated" by this legislation would not see freedom until their twenty-first birthdays, and even then, their parents and older siblings would remain in indefinite bondage. Republicans and abolitionists found such adjustments palliative, for as historian Roderick Barman put it, they changed "everything and nothing."[75] For the nineteenth-century

Brazil as "Indian": Francisco Manuel Chaves Pinheiro, Alegoria do Império Brasileiro, *1872. Molded terracotta, 192 × 75 × 31 cm. Photo by Jaime Acioli. Courtesy of the Coleção Museu Nacional de Belas Artes/Instituto Brasileiro de Museus/Ministério da Cultura.*

literary scholar Sylvio Romero, the brutal losses of the Paraguayan War opened up a series of social and political crises that made it impossible for the dominant majority to perpetuate the alluring mirage of romantic nationalism any further. Except, as it would turn out, where "Indians" were concerned.

While the cause of abolition made some jolting progress with regard to national legislation and popular opinion, the situation of indigenous peoples continued to backslide on both fronts despite the still privileged place of romantic Indianness in the popular imaginary. "Indians" had been "tutees" of the provincial governments since the mid-1830s, and

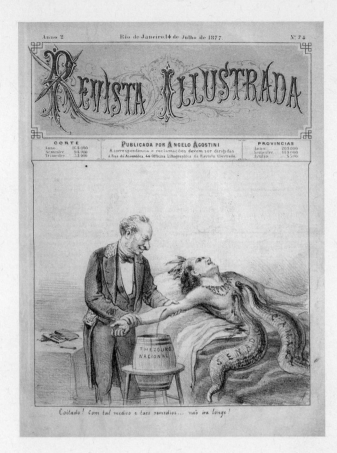

Brazil as "Indian," leeched by the Senate and the Câmera, and bled by the Barão de Cotegipe (João Maurício Wanderley), president of the Tribunal of the National Treasury. *From* Revista Illustrada, *no. 74 (14 July 1877). Courtesy of the Acervo da Fundação Biblioteca Nacional—Brasil.*

provincial legislation dedicated in large part to the official takeover of indigenous territories (not to mention informal takeovers of those territories) was markedly anti-Native. The most significant national indigenist legislation of the empire did not pass until a full decade later, creating the Regiment of Missions for the Catechism and Civilization of Indians by Decree 426 on 24 July 1845. The law recognized that the tricky work of civilization might be best carried out by missionaries and established an imperial administration for Indian affairs wherein each province would have a general director of Indians (*diretor geral de índios*), and each *aldeamento*, a community director (*diretor de aldeia*).[76] On the ground, however, this neat scheme did not always play out as intended. Many Indian directors were appointed by provincial governments rather than by the emperor or his cabinet. Others assumed such positions *ipso facto* and sought official recognition only later, if at all.[77]

The Land Law,[78] which passed five years later, on 18 September 1850, determined for the first time that land could be bought and sold among private parties and without governmental approval and mediation. A regulation of the law on 1 January 1854[79] required those occupying particular tracts of land to document their ownership with the state and provided the legal mechanism through which "unoccupied" lands (*terras devolutas*) would revert to state ownership and control.[80] Some scholars have argued that indigenous lands were at the time considered "original" and "inalienable" per the Carta Régia of 2 December 1808.[81] However, as the document states nothing to that effect, this interpretation remains open to debate.[82] Aside from advocating for the effective enslavement of indigenous peoples by anyone with the resources to "civilize them," and mandating the "just" corporal punishment of any "Indian" seeking refuge from his or her "civilizer," the law justified the Crown's appropriation of lands that had been "abandoned," were "not duly occupied," or whose once-Indian tenants were so thoroughly "mixed in" with the non-Native population so as not to merit Indian status. The Carta stated: "On the territory newly rescued from the incursions of the Botocudo or any other Indians, you shall consider *devolutas* [unoccupied public property] all the terrains that, having been distributed previously in *seismarias* [sixteenth-century land grants] have not yet been demarcated or cultivated."[83] As anthropologist Manuela Carneiro da Cunha has pointed out, these distinctions might be read as an early attempt to delimit the boundaries of "authentic" Indianness.[84] Imperial reason and, as I argue hence, reason of state,[85] had it that the primary difference between *índios brabos* (wild Indians) and *índios mansos* (tame Indians) was the right of the former to be killed in "just wars" and of the latter to occupy particular tracts of land until the work of civilization or elimination was complete. A future of "civilized Indians" thus meant a future of landless Indians or one of no Indians at all.

The provinces wasted no time tying the power to distinguish "wild" and "tame" Indians to the authority to (re)distribute land and wealth to non-Natives who were already both landed and wealthy. In 1875, for instance, individuals and communities determined to be "non-Indian" in Pernambuco province were asked to pay for the demarcation of their claimed territories, which they would then lose for not being "wild" Indians in the eyes of the very authorities who required them to pay for the land survey in the first place.[86] Following this tautological logic, the provincial government would subsequently "indicate the best way to take advantage of lands [deemed] not necessary to the communities, [which would then] . . . revert . . . to the state due to the illegitimate titles of those who occup[ied] them."[87] Thus ends a foundational and devastating chapter in the ongoing saga of indigenous land rights.

For all of the upset and unrest that developed out of the social and political crises of the 1860s and 1870s, the dominant majority was deeply ambivalent in its desire for significant social and political change. Republican discontent and the relative freedom of the press bred the popular lampoons of an aloof, backward-looking monarch that appeared midcentury and proliferated in the fading glow of postwar patriotism. The emperor's critics depicted a man whose affinity for "useless" knowledge and pretensions of erudition made him incapable of addressing the changing needs and interests of his people. At the same time, however, Dom Pedro's widely acknowledged love for his homeland and deep sense of responsibility for guarding the welfare and honor of its people were mirrored back to him even after the fall of empire in the unshakable loyalty of those subjects—among them Antônio Carlos Gomes and the *visconde* de Taunay—who continued to see their leader as the greatest and most diligent patriot of the fatherland. First Lieutenant E. C. Jourdon, for example, dedicated his 1871 *Atlas histórico da guerra do Paraguay* to the emperor as "First Citizen of Brazil"; to the Army, Navy, Volunteers of the Fatherland, and the National Guard; "and to the . . . Valiant, suffering, . . . heroic people, who, having to battle a bloodthirsty enemy for five years in the midst of ghastly horrors [and] every possible deprivation, proved to be always dignified in their glorious mission."[88] Absent from this and most other dedications, however, was yet another group of "patriotic volunteers" who have been all but erased from the official record: the indigenous communities of Matto Grosso province, where Paraguayan troops made their first incursions into Brazilian territory.[89]

One of the reasons for this erasure, perhaps, is that aside from its scant documentation, the story of indigenous involvement in the extended conflict is complex and ambiguous, resisting any neat or comfortable incorporation into a seamless narrative of resistance, alliance, triumph, or nation-building. If we add an indigenous perspective to the dominant narratives of national security and nationalism, it becomes clearer, however, that noncompulsory indigenous participation in the war stemmed primarily from the desire to recover and protect the lands lost to "purutuyé" ranchers beginning in the late eighteenth century.[90] Pedro II had pledged protected lands in exchange for Native wartime service, but his promise was only partially fulfilled. Indeed, it was not until decades later that the newly inaugurated SPI would begin a demarcation process that even today remains contentious and incomplete.

Ranchers who took over the Native territories vacated in the wake of wartime violence brought more disease and destruction to the beleaguered border region by co-opting or forcing indigenous peoples into servitude when they returned home at the conflict's end. Descendants of some displaced families recounted their ancestors' postwar struggles in a history written for Terena students. As one Genésio Farias explained, part of this trap meant burdening returnees with new debt: "The Terena found themselves out of their communities, working on the ranches in conditions of near slavery. They were working without remuneration and oftentimes the ranchers took advantage of the Indians and lied when settling their expense accounts, saying, 'You still owe money, so you have to work for another year.' And at every meeting to settle accounts they would repeat the same thing."[91] João Menootó' Martins, in contrast, explained Terena imprisonment as a consequence of physical mistreatment and fear: "People were afraid . . . because they remembered the master who whipped them on the ranch. My deceased grandfather told me that whoever was late for breakfast was beaten. . . . As punishment, people had to pull [sharp] brush with their bare hands. . . . They had to finish fifteen fathoms, and if they didn't complete the necessary amount in one day, the next day they would measure all over again so that the work just accumulated."[92] Finally, Honorato Rondon expressed coercion in terms of separation from sociocultural norms and a communal structure: "My father, Belizário Rondon, from the Passarinho community, was a prisoner of the Surucri Ranch. In order to keep time, he would go by the new moon, and to settle accounts with the master he would put notches into the handle of his machete to mark the days of the month."[93]

In light of the Paraguayan War's tragic outcome for the Native peoples of the Miranda region, contemporary indigenous narratives still refer to the years following the conflict as *os tempos da servidão* (the time of servitude)[94]—an expression that acknowledges indigenous defeat despite or perhaps, for some, because of Brazil's victory. As veteran activist M. Marcos Terena put it to me—contrary to popular lore and dominant historiography—it is indeed difficult to maintain that the Terena and Guaicuru peoples fought for Brazil or on behalf of the Brazilians.[95] Both indigenous and nonindigenous sources suggest that Native communities responded to the Brazilians and the Paraguayans in various strategic ways, ranging from material collaboration and armed support, to subtle resistance and guerrilla warfare. But when caught between a rock and a hard place—between likely abuse at the hands of one foreign power (Brazil) and likely death at the hands of another (Paraguay)—most people, of course, opted for their own survival.

THE VOLUNTEERS WHO WERE NOT

As far I have been able to determine, the most detailed written account of Native participation in the conflict belongs to Alfredo d'Escragnolle Taunay—Carlos Gomes's friend and eventual collaborator on *Lo schiavo*—who was honored with the title of viscount on the eve of the First Republic, in September 1889. Taunay wrote of the indigenous peoples he encountered in battle with sentimental distance and protoethnographic description typical of the postindependence period. Native peoples were always peripheral to his principal objective of documenting the Brazilian war effort, but his curiosity and creativity sometimes got the better of him—or at least of his writing.

Taunay's earliest chronicle of the war, *Scenas de viagem* (1868),[96] presented his ambiguous take on the indigenous peoples of the "Miranda District" (located between the Aquitaine and Aquaria Rivers)[97] and their potential contributions to the Allied struggle. Although much had been written about the Indians, he explained in 1866, it was worth considering the "special practices" of those who had maintained their "very characteristic type" despite years of contact with the dominant majority.[98] "During our long stay," he explained "we aimed to analyze the character of the Indians, their most salient trait, to investigate the degree of civilization in which they found themselves, and [to determine] the result of their cohabitation with whites."[99] He divided his subjects into two "Indian races": first, the Guaycurú (*sic*)—a name given to the "nearly disappeared" Guaycurú and the relatively "wild" Cadiuéo (*sic*) and Beaquiéo (*sic*); and second, the Chané, by which he meant mostly Terena peoples but also the Laiana, Quiniquináo, and the "docile and civilized" Guaná or Chooronó.[100]

Hence with the most imperial of eyes and a copy of Jean de Léry's sixteenth-century chronicles under his arm,[101] Taunay set out to determine the lay of the human landscape and found that he could not offer any definitive interpretation of the people he encountered. Through the wearisome task of cataloguing their traits and behaviors, he discovered that the diversity of the peoples in his midst made it exceedingly difficult to incorporate them into one consistent narrative. Taunay's eventual allies, the Terena, were "agile," "active," "tall," and "robust," for example, but their astute intelligence also "predisposed them to evil." Perhaps because of their strong will to freedom, he surmised, "they only accept[ed] . . . [Brazilian] ideas with difficulty."[102] They expressed hatred for the Portuguese language and, annoyingly, insisted on speaking their own language whenever possible.

The Laiana, in contrast, were a "transitory type" with "good instincts" that made them less hostile and more willing to speak Portuguese. They were also "less lively and intelligent" and, in general, their women were "ugly."[103] The Quiniquináo, he found, were attractive and at times even beautiful (*bellas*). But they were also "apathetic," "placid," and lazy: "They spend their days lying around on hides of leather, without nostalgia for the past or fear of the future."[104] Finally, the Guaná, having all but "disappeared" through intense miscegenation, were an attractive people of "potentially Venusian" beauty[105]—beauty that Taunay ultimately appropriated for himself in the form of a fifteen-year-old Chooronó girl he called Antônia, whom he "bought" from her father for a cow, a bull, and a few bags of beans, corn, and rice.[106]

After offering this rundown of Chané "types," the young soldier failed in the 1860s to account for the Guaycurú in comparable detail. We learn only that they were "unusually tall," "extremely vigorous," and potentially valuable as support for the Brazilian troops.[107] Nearly seventy years later, however, in the posthumously published *Entre os nossos índios* (1931), Taunay revealed that he had little contact with the Guaycurú during the war. He made up for it by dedicating to them two chapters of the later volume based almost entirely on his reading of an eighteenth-century account by Portuguese commander Francisco Rodrigues do Prado: *História dos índios cavalleiros ou da nação guaycurú.*

Taunay's analysis reinscribed with new detail vague impressions from the war and reiterated the "terrible," "savage" nature of the "bloodthirsty," "ferocious," and "cruel" Guaycurú relative to other Native peoples of the region.[108] Among his reflections on the infamous "Indian horsemen,"[109] Taunay highlighted a penchant for body paint and "hideous" mutilations; infanticide and abortion; sodomy, through the figure of the *cudinho*;[110] "repugnant" foods; "brutal" games among adults and children; the "excessive" use of tobacco and alcohol; "humble and stupid" stories of origin; and the "cruel" treatment of Indian slaves from other nations.[111] Despite this litany of grievances, Taunay found it fitting to toss in some backhanded praise for his subjects. He admired, for example, that the Guaycurú treated children with great affection; that they respected the dead—even slaves— and buried them with great ceremony; and above all, that they and "other branches of their nation" had developed the remarkable horsemanship

Rondon Commission's registration of Terena men whose uniforms apparently dated to the Paraguayan War, no date. Courtesy of the Museu do Índio/FUNAI Archive.

that, together with their bellicose nature, made them attractive allies in the war.[112] The Paraguayans likewise loathed the Guaycurú, he noted, and (as corroborated by the wartime publications *Cabichuí* and *Cacique Lambaré*) referred to them as "Mbayás."[113]

Like the Indianists and other would-be ethnographers of his day, Taunay identified a clear correlation between indigenous behavioral and physical traits and their potential usefulness to the Brazilian cause. Nevertheless, his reflections in the late 1860s were often tentative and contradictory: While some Native peoples "embraced [Brazilians] in the nicest and most cordial manner" and "fawned over [them] with great demonstrations of respect,"[114] others were dismissive and treacherous—preferring to cede their livestock to Paraguayan thieves, for example, before handing them over to starving and impoverished Brazilian refugees.[115] Some, like the Terena, possessed physical abilities of which Taunay and his ilk could "only dream" and thus proved to be valuable scouts and auxiliaries,[116] while others, like the Cadiuéo, "caused as much damage to the Brazilians as [they had] to the enemy" and "deserve[d] no confidence whatsoever."[117]

Taunay was therefore perplexed and fascinated by the cultural and social diversity of the peoples and communities he saw. He found indigenous demonstrations of friendship "edifying and sometimes even touching," but was horrified by the Indians' "total ignorance" of religion and capacity for violence, including what he referred to as the rape (*estupro*) of girls and adolescents by their adult husbands.[118] Finally, he was disenchanted by the lack of deference to elders on par with the traditions of North American Indians, "whose customs," he recalled, "Chateaubriand had made into the subject of a poem."[119] Hence, even in the midst of war, the image of those poetic Indians—of a different place and time, and written by a French plume, no less—set the bar that would forever make the lives of the living seem substandard.

Although Taunay's uncertainty regarding the suitability of Native peoples as prospective allies against a skilled and tenacious Paraguayan enemy surfaced throughout his writings on the war, his misgivings were accompanied by the nagging fact—corroborated by Brazil's heavy and infamous reliance on slave soldiers—that the emperor's fighting forces faced such dire shortages of human and material resources that they could not afford to be selective in choosing their "volunteers." Hence Taunay railed against a host of indigenous customs and practices while embracing the contributions of his sometimes "savage" collaborators in the struggle against the equally or even more "savage" Paraguayans. Indeed, his frequent characterization of both groups in disparaging terms fashioned him and his (white) Brazilian compatriots as a force of civilization up against so much backwardness and barbarism—both compounded by the madness of war itself.

His report on an early 1866 trek between the Taquary and Aquidauana Rivers included detailed commentary on the Brazilian contingent: "There are in total 130 Indians serving in a support capacity to the force. We have to visit . . . two [more] communities, one Quiniquináo and another Laiana, which [should] raise the number of men and provide some bushels of rice and corn. . . . The character of the Indians is warlike: they profess cruel hate toward the Paraguayans, with whom they are in a constant guerrilla war, where the cruelty and ferocity of both sides has brought about mutual fear and apprehension. Still, the inconsistency of their temperament and dedication . . . makes them suitable only as jungle shooters and guerrillas."[120] A later observation on the size and strength of enemy forces laid bare his earnest views on the Terena and Quiniquináo working in his

Pedro Américo, Batalha do Avaí, *1872/1877, depicting one of the bloodiest conflicts of the Paraguayan War, fought on 11 December 1868. Oil on canvas, 600 × 1,100 cm. Photo by José Franceschi. Courtesy of the Coleção Museu Nacional de Belas Artes/ Instituto Brasileiro de Museus/Ministério da Cultura.*

service: "Interrogating diverse *people and Indians* [*pessoas e índios*] that have visited places still occupied by [enemy] forces, we have gathered . . . information on a total of 810 men."[121]

ROMANTIC INDIANS AT THE TWILIGHT OF EMPIRE

Back in the capital city and far from the destruction of lives and livelihoods on the front lines, the success of Gomes's romantic Indians gave the other "Guarany" an extraordinary new life. Alencar's novel was reprinted and remarketed in the surge of patriotic sentiment that accompanied Gomes's success in Europe and anticipated arrival in Brazil.[122] Advertisements appeared alongside news of the operas—beginning in March 1870 with the Milan debut of *Il guarany*, and continuing until after the September 1889 presentation of *Lo schiavo* in Rio de Janeiro. From notices of "vividly printed" new editions to convenient *publicações a pedido* (prints-on-demand), offers abounded for the best deal in town. The Congresso Literário Guarany in Rio's sister city, Nictheroy (now Niterói), hosted a wide variety of presentations, conferences, and other literary events related to Indianist and other popular works through the late 1880s. At home, in Europe, and across the Americas, the composer's power as a symbol of Brazilianness tied his work to the novel *O guarany* and helped to consolidate Alencar's position at the head of an Indianist movement that would endure in various incarnations for nearly another half century.

Conveniently, both the opera and the novel were set during the early colonial period,[123] allowing audience members and readers alike to distance themselves and their lives from "Indian" realities, which in the dominant imaginary were mostly things of the past. Reflecting years later on his own work, Alencar explained: "In *O guarany* the savage [was] an ideal, . . . poetize[d] and . . . stripp[ed] . . . of the crude façade imposed by the chroniclers and [freed] from . . . the ridiculous image projected by the brutish *remnants of that nearly extinct race.*"[124] Far from addressing the indigenous diversity of his day, acknowledging Native participation alongside Brazilian troops in Paraguay, or imagining the resurgence of "modern indigeneity" in the twentieth century, the Indianist desire revived by Carlos Gomes catapulted onto the national stage an enduring representation of Indianness that juxtaposed tongue-tied "savages" with the eloquent and charming Peri, described alternatingly throughout the novel and the libretto as "king," "friend," "angel," and "Christian."

Differentiating his work from the realist and socially engaged writing of North American novelists,[125] and drawing on a childhood wilderness trek from Ceará to Bahia, Alencar "floated in fantasy"[126] to fashion Native heroes and villains who would long outlive the nineteenth century.[127] A figure powerful enough to supplant those "ridiculous" and "brutish" relics of Indianness who were fast on their way to extinction, Peri came to represent the ideal male prototype: "Standing in the middle of the space formed by the large dome of trees . . . was an Indian in the flower of his youth. A simple cotton tunic secured at the waist by a string of scarlet-colored feathers gave him the thin, svelte figure of a wild reed. . . . His copper-colored skin glowed with golden light; his black hair was cut short, his skin smooth; his eyes were large, with the exterior corners pushed up toward his forehead; his pupils black, active, shining; the strong, well-formed mouth, equipped with white teeth gave the slightly oval-shaped face the rustic beauty of grace, power, and intelligence."[128] The idealized Native, redeemed not only by his attractiveness but by his self-sacrificing love for a white woman and embrace of her father's Christianity, was also an extension of Brazil's venerated natural wealth. By imprinting Peri as a beautiful, resilient, and clever "plant," Alencar and Carlos Gomes immortalized the colonialist conflation of Indians with their putative, proper habitats.

Long after his return from the Paraguayan War, the *visconde* de Taunay recalled the impact of Alencar's novel in the capital city upon its original publication in 1859: "I still remember vividly the enthusiasm it awakened, [the] true emotional novelty unknown in this city so devoted to . . . worries of business and the stock market. . . . Moved and enraptured, Rio de Janeiro read *O guarany* and followed the pure, discreet love of Ceci and Peri, and with great sympathy accompanied the varied, dangerous luck of the protagonists . . . , perfumed by the exotic flowers of our luxurious virgin forests [as they navigated] . . . the dangers and traps of the savage buggers."[129] Easily converted into expedient symbols, such simple and flat Indian prototypes lent themselves over the decades that ensued to reappropriation by a battery of politicians, intellectuals, and artists (among them Taunay), who used them to represent the extremes of human nature and to imagine how those extremes had shaped national history and politics. The themes of good and evil, purity and decadence, love and hate, civility and savagery, innocence and corruption that structured the novel, the opera, and the majority of Indianist cultural production through the end of the empire would inform all subsequent discourses on Brazil's "indigenous problem" over the century to come—even those of scientific inquiry and public policy. The association between unspoiled Indians and unspoiled lands, both needing and deserving state "protection," would in fact never be undone and instead blossomed into the dominant nationalist metaphor of the late twentieth century.[130]

As an aging Carlos Gomes watched the Brazil he loved but no longer knew or understood crumble before his eyes, the enduring promise of romantic Indianness would lead him in the late 1890s in a failed attempt to recycle the themes of his greatest commercial success. The long twilight of empire had seen the country's slave-based economy increasingly under attack—not only by abolitionists and the mounting republican movement but also by monarchists, members of the royal family, and—however reservedly—the emperor himself.[131] Growing international debates over "race," skin color, modernity, and social progress influenced dominant ideas about the role of indigenous peoples and Afro-descendants in the future of Brazilianness in powerful ways. Increasingly haunted by harsh foreign critiques and cataclysmic social prognostications for their predominantly nonwhite country, the national intelligentsia embraced the ideology and practice of *branqueamento* (whitening) as Brazil's ticket into the community of "civilized" nations.[132]

In conjunction with the intensifying national discussion over slavery, the disputes that evolved out of the racial theories of scientists and statesman like Swiss ichthyologist Louis Agassiz[133] and French diplomat Arthur (*comte*) de Gobineau[134] helped justify the intensification of "desirable" immigration during the decades leading up to abolition and the fall of the empire. By facilitating the influx of "attractive," "industrious," and, most important, white or light-skinned workers, governing elites aimed to dilute and eventually eliminate the majority black and African presence that had been eliminated from the Brazil imagined on paper and onstage by the likes of Alencar and Gomes. The exclusion was not particularly remarkable in the broader trajectory of a movement that sought to re-create Brazil through a Native-European alliance untainted by the "sons of Ham,"[135] but it became especially egregious in Carlos Gomes's second Indian-themed work, *Lo schiavo*, which he dedicated to Princess Isabel two months after she signed the Lei Áurea that ended slavery on 13 May 1888.

Gomes's penultimate opera debuted in Rio de Janeiro one month shy of the declaration of the First Republic on 15 November 1889. Penned by fellow monarchist Alfredo d'Escragnolle Taunay[136] nearly two decades after his service in the Paraguayan War, the libretto portrays the subversive love of Américo—Brazilian son of the slaveholding Portuguese Count Rodrigo—and Ilára, a "Brazilian indigenous woman" born into servitude on his *fazenda*. Defying powerful family alliances, entrenched social hierarchies, and jealous desire, the "mixed-race" couple overcomes a series of mishaps and misunderstandings to escape sure death at the hands of "hordes" of rebellious and heathen Tamoyo "savages."[137] Amid much commotion, the nominally Brazilian lovers choose one another over their kinfolk and intended spouses, hence defying the colonialist social norms of their day and adding yet another "wilderness marriage" to the Indianist collection. The French Countess de Boissy, chosen by Count Rodrigo to rescue his son from his debasing love for Ilára, scoffs indignantly at Américo's preference for the Indian lass over her own European charms.[138] Of course, the renegade couple's final getaway is made possible only through indigenous demise: Overcoming his own burning passion for the slave girl and "with the faith of a king,"[139] Indian hero Ibarê sacrifices himself so that Ilára can escape with her true (white) love. "Victory! Love triumphs!," cries the heartbroken Native hero as he plunges a dagger into his own chest.[140]

When *Lo schiavo* opened in Rio de Janeiro the year following abolition, it was hailed by many as an extraordinary musical creation but raised eyebrows, even among an elite that was deeply divided and anxious over the rapidly changing social and political landscape of their country, for

representing slaves as plumed Indians rather than as people of African descent. Two days after the debut performance at the Cassino Fluminense on 27 September 1889, *carioca* critic Oscar Granadaliso complained that an excess of anachronisms made Gomes's piece implausible and attributed them to the Italian Rodolfo Paravicini, who had reportedly modified Taunay's work for the stage.[141] He complained: "This work beckons the responsibility of national men of letters. . . . Even if we disregard the time frame, the drama is bad and the libretto awful. . . . Carlos Gomes saw only one thing—the national question; the Tamoyo, the rancher, the *inúbia* (bamboo flute), the savage tribes in the forests. . . . The Brazilian savages are monotonous . . . ; the African is more passionate, more alive and more melodious than the inhabitant of the Brazilian jungles. . . . In the end, [though,] one could not hope for more than our maestro has achieved. Carlos Gomes can return to Italy and say that . . . *Lo schiavo* has received the baptism of applause. The Italians can applaud him with the same enthusiasm that we . . . applaud . . . Bellini, Rossini, Ponchielli, Boito, and Verdi."[142]

The maestro and his troupe might have been able to get away with such shenanigans in the Old Country, these comments suggest, but a politicized and somewhat skeptical national public acutely sensitized to how the "race question" was playing out on its own soil would not be so easily duped. In light of the multiple authorship of the libretto and a series of complex legal and logistical difficulties that forced the production of *Lo schiavo* to Brazil (rather than Milan, as Gomes had intended), generations of critics have yet to reach consensus over whose decision it was to represent Indians rather than Afro-descendants onstage. In 1988, the president and artistic director of the Ópera Brasil do Maranhão, Fernando Bicudo, attributed the switch to Paravicini's whims and Italian racial prejudice toward Afro-descended peoples, including Carlos Gomes himself.[143] One year later, in its edition commemorating the centenary of the declaration of the First Republic, *Veja* magazine attributed the preference for indigenous slaves to Gomes's dire straits and mockingly accused him of "succumbing to the temptation of easy success" by trying to repeat the financial triumph of *Il guarany*.[144] Carlos Gomes's finest biographer, Marcus Goés, also attributed the decision to the composer, observing that he had penciled into the margins of his original score "Tamoio sou; Tamoio morrer quero [I am Tamoio; Tamoio I wish to die]."[145] Due perhaps to his general aversion to politics and polemics, Goés speculated, Gomes moved the opera's action from the nineteenth to the sixteenth century. "It was abolitionist," Goés observed, "*ma non troppo*."[146]

Although the cantankerous Granadaliso had suggested in 1889 that the creator of *Lo schiavo* either "head to Paris to submit himself to the influence of [stylistic] evolution, . . . or cease composing altogether," subsequent waves of patriotic verve eventually eroded such harsh critique and replaced it with an abundance of nationalist sentimentalism. Modern-day critics not only consider *Lo schiavo* Gomes's "most perfect and beautiful opera" but also "the symbol of . . . enormous cultural patrimony [and] the foundation of [Brazilian] Citizenship."[147] In any case, whether for pleasure or intrigue, the popularity and commercial success of the original opera are clear: It ran for eight performances rather than the scheduled four, allowed Carlos Gomes to pay off part of his weighty debt, and earned him a promotion to the rank of Grand Dignitary of the Imperial Order of the Rose—a distinction he had first received some four decades earlier.[148]

As the disparity among these sentiments indicates, popular enthusiasm for Carlos Gomes and his work did not leave him without a fair number of outspoken detractors, both during his lifetime and after his death from cancer in 1896. Among them were the self-proclaimed *modernistas*—predominantly white, upper-middle-class writers and artists, also from São Paulo, who beginning in the mid-1910s distanced themselves from a nineteenth-century aesthetic by revolutionizing the relationship between art and Brazilianness. The beloved son of Campinas was an easy scapegoat for the movement and earned the intense loathing of one of its best-known leaders, Oswald de Andrade, who condemned Gomes's work as a naive, uncritical, and self-loathing imitation of Europe. During the Semana de Arte Moderna—a famous and controversial arts festival held in São Paulo in February 1922—Andrade laid out his antagonism: "Carlos Gomes is horrible! We've all felt it since we were little. But because it's about family glory, we swallowed all that melodious blathering of *Guarani* and *Schiavo*—unexpressive, ostentatious, nefarious. . . . From one success to another, our man managed to denigrate his country in the most profound way— . . . through 'Peris,' who donned tea-colored leotards and flashy feather dusters to bellow . . . indomitable might in horrid scenarios."[149]

The disdain for Carlos Gomes and his Christian Indians must also be considered, however, alongside the fact that Andrade soon thereafter adopted the opposing figure—the cannibal—to represent his own nationalist countermovement. In 1928, he published his oft-cited "Manifesto antropófago" in the debut issue of a short-lived cultural and literary magazine called the *Revista de Antropofagia*, based in São Paulo. Rather than returning to a vanquished, racialized (indigenous) past, he proposed, the modern Brazilian artist or intellectual seeking to produce genuine national work ought not imitate the ideas and forms of the so-called developed world but, like the autochthonous cannibal, "devour [*deglutir*]" any and all ideas, forms, theories, discourses, and materials of value or interest. Turning the tables on an Indianist tradition grounded in centuries of colonial(ist), Christian thought, Andrade derided baptized Peris and self-sacrificing Ibarês to champion the metaphorical *antropófago* who, "against memory as a source of habit" would "absorb the sacred enemy" and "turn him into totem."[150] This anthropophagous methodology, which has endured in various forms into the twenty-first century as a touchstone of national popular culture, would produce an authentically Brazilian product that was, at the same time, a parody of authenticity.

Andrade's take on the ideas of indigenous peoples and their diverse histories and cultures was simultaneously satirical and deferential. More certain was his contempt for the architects of Indianist romanticism, whose work he attacked directly in his founding statement. Woven into the "Manifesto" we find a brief but biting critique of his opera-writing nemesis: "[We are] opposed to the torchbearing Indian, the Indian son of Mary, godson of Catherine de Medici, and son-in-law of D. Antônio de Mariz."[151] Against Carlos Gomes, then, Andrade was hostile not only to Peri as the romantic Indian but also to the Christian Indian, the Indian-as-spectacle for Europeans,[152] and the "Uncle Tom Indian," who, like Alencar's protagonist and Carlos Gomes's star tenor, would bow before the figures, laws, institutions, and ideas of European authority.

Another monumentally ambiguous cultural gesture vis-à-vis indigeneity and Indianness appeared soon after the "Manifesto antropófago" as *Macunaíma*—the second novel of Oswald de Andrade's fellow modernist militant, Mário de Andrade, who published the beginning of his enigmatic text in the second issue of the *Revista Antropofágica*, also in 1928. Born in Roraima to a Tapanhuma mother, Andrade's black and indigenous protagonist, Macunaíma, is a contradictory, amorphous, frequently grotesque figure—a hero with "no character," according the novel's subtitle—whose skin morphs from black into white; whose man-sized body is topped by a tiny, child-sized head; and who is so perpetually slothful that he cannot help but to exclaim, "*Ai, que preguiça!* [Oh, I feel so lazy!]" at every turn.[153]

The narrative revolves around the enigmatic hero's ill-fated search for a stolen, power-granting *muiraquitã* (amulet) given to him by his *companheira* (lover or partner), Ci—the Mother of the Forest—who perishes from desolation after the accidental death of a child conceived when Macunaíma rapes and beats her with the help of his brothers.[154] Macunaíma's exploration leads him from the heart of the rainforest to the megalopolis of São Paulo, where as a boorish jungle man he suffers a series of mishaps. Managing against great odds to recover the amulet, he eventually returns home to the Uraricoera River only to learn that all of his siblings—his entire tribe—have disappeared.[155] Forlorn and alone, Macunaíma recounts his sad saga to a parrot shortly before falling prey to the malicious intrigues of Vei (the sun): On a scorching morning, seeking desperately to relieve an intense sexual desire by bathing in a cool lake, the lonesome antihero is beguiled by a beautiful maiden he glimpses in the water. He dives in after her, only to be attacked by a fierce *uiara* (*mãe d'água* or lake mermaid), this time losing not only the amulet but also several of his limbs.[156] Although he manages to recover parts of his body from the belly of the beast, one leg and the amulet have disappeared forever. Suffering, he heads to the "vast fields of the sky" to meditate all alone, as a star.[157]

Drawing on Andrade's contradictory commentary on this work over the course of many years and its long if uneven trajectory of success, scholars have reached different conclusions about his objectives in crafting the complex and popular tale—and particularly its enigmatic protagonist.[158] Andrade's notes and correspondence suggest that he considered *Macunaíma* a *brinqueido* (plaything), *pura brincadeira* (a pure joke), and "satire"—even one marked by his "plagiarism" of ethnographic texts. In a letter to Raimundo Moraes published in the *Diário Nacional* on 20 September 1931, Andrade defended his *deglutição* (devouring) of German ethnographer Theodor Koch-Grünberg, for example, with characteristic irony: "I am obliged to confess . . . : I copied Brazil, at least that part where I was . . . satirizing Brazil with Brazil. But even the idea of satirizing is not mine, 'cause it's been around since [seventeenth-century Baroque poet] Gregório de Mattos. Shucks!"[159] The first draft of the novel, he once claimed, was penned over "six uninterrupted days of hammocks, cigarettes, and cicadas at the country house in Pio Lourenço, close to the nest of light that is Araraquara."[160]

Alongside the portrayal of Macunaíma as an absurd and repulsive figure, these pronouncements work against the suggestion that Andrade sought to share the wisdom or experience of traditional indigenous oral histories and legends, or to ensure that they be taken seriously by a nonindigenous audience.[161] Indeed, like generations of nonindigenous writers before and after him, Andrade's *Macunaíma* manipulated the *figure* of the Indian and the *idea* of Indianness as expedient cultural, social, and political signifiers precisely *not* to speak of indigenous peoples, of indigeneity, or of indigenous intellectual and cultural production but rather—and paradoxically, considering his strong distaste for the Indianists who found themselves in the crosshairs of the *modernista* movement—to make a foundational statement regarding the *figure* of the Brazilian and the *idea* of Brazilianness, however critical, slippery, and counterfoundational it might have might have been. That in doing so Andrade represented "Indians" roguishly, placing them in line with colonialist stereotypes as lazy, unattractive, dishonest, dim-witted, and violent, did little to shift his contribution to Native representation away from the "imperial center of Europe,"[162] regardless of any "authentic" indigenous narratives he might have appropriated along the way as grist for his "war machine" of conjured transculturation.[163]

Of this, of course, Andrade was well aware. But beyond poking fun at nineteenth-century romantics and their "ridiculous" attempts to nationalize Indianness into something Brazilian, *Macunaíma* went a step further to jeer at the legion of European and North American scientists and adventurers who had planted a booted foot on Brazilian soil, compass and anthropometer in hand, to study and explain away the "Indians" to other Europeans and North Americans. Andrade sensed, furthermore, that for elite and uninformed foreign audiences overseas, all Brazilians were in fact "Indians," whether they hailed from the muddy shores of the Tapajós River, or from the Centro Velho of São Paulo. Hence the modernists' indignation over Carlos Gomes's "defamation" of his homeland through the promotion of "leotard-wearing" figures like Peri. After all, Carlos Gomes was himself a "savage" in Italy because, as Goés had it, "Brazil [was] mistaken . . . by cultivated European societies as an entity [and] delimited psychologically by a general idea . . . from centuries earlier: that . . . everything on the other side of the ocean are the Indies, West or East."[164]

Placing a sardonic critique of this "general idea" in the mouth of his narrator, Andrade concludes his novel by pointing to the problem of misrecognition and the propensity for foreigners not only to misread Brazil but to promulgate their misinterpretations with the blessing of the Church, the backing of European civilization, and the implied authority of modern science and all rational thought. The narrator wryly observes: "They say that a professor—a German, naturally—went around saying Ursa Major had one leg because she was Saci.[165] Wrong! . . . Ursa Major is Macunaíma."[166]

If the acceptance of such erroneous ideas among foreigners on foreign soil was bad, their embrace by Brazilians on Brazilian soil was for Andrade all the more troubling. It laid bare not only a host of irreconcilable contradictions and the abundance of Roberto Schwarz's "out of place" ideas but also what Roberto DaMatta has described as the lived tensions resulting from the constant encounter between progressive, postcolonial desire and the cynical or unwitting perpetuation of colonial legacy.[167] "The interpretation of our reality through patterns not our own," as Gabriel García Márquez famously observed some fifty years after *Macunaíma's* publication, would be Latin America's great source of "solitude," for it could only lead to more self-alienation and less freedom.[168] Faced with this tragically probable, but not inevitable, trajectory, Andrade's antihero offered a retort: "Patience, brothers! No! I'm not going to Europe. I am American and my place is in America. . . . European civilization deteriorates the integrity of our character."[169]

From this *modernista*, counterhegemonic perspective, then, Carlos Gomes's rendering of Brazilianness on foreign soil and influence on Brazilian society could only be construed as negative. Not only did the composer work in a decadent and colonized art form with long dead material, he also had the questionable judgment to portray his homeland as a partially civilized, exotic land, and the nerve to cast himself—a *caipira* and poor teacher's son, no less—as the conduit to her partially civilized, exotic people.

In light of this mostly implicit but sometimes explicit critique, Mário de Andrade managed like his associate, Oswald, to slip a dig at Carlos Gomes into his text: Recovering from a harsh and extended illness, a nearly browbeaten Macunaíma heads to downtown São Paulo to "look for some mange to scratch." Ruminating and meandering aimlessly around town, and feeling exceptionally weary, he decides to rest before continuing his journey, and takes a seat in Anhangabaú Park, right below "the monument to Carlos Gomes, who had been a famous musician and was now but a little star in the sky."[170] The statue, which sits in front of the Municipal Theater in what is now known as the Vale Anhangabaú, was dedicated to the "great Brazilian spirit" of Carlos Gomes and the "Italian colony of São Paulo" on the centenary of national independence in September 1922. It is one of dozens of geographical and architectonic tributes to the loved and loathed "savage of the opera" distributed across the country—from the tiny municipality named in his honor in the southernmost state of Rio Grande do Sul, to a legendary opera house in the heart of the Amazonian rainforest.

CIVILIZATION IS BARBARITY

The Teatro Amazonas rose with Brazil's first rubber boom (1850s–1920s) and fell into decadence following the 1922 centenary of independence, as the country slid into a financial crisis that paved the way for Getúlio Vargas's coup and rise to the presidency in 1930. For nearly seven decades, the Amazonian capital of Manaus had played an important symbolic role in the growth and modernization of the national economy, even as most rubber commerce flowed in and out of Belém, located some 1,064 miles up the Amazon River. Seventeen years under construction and with a price tag of 20 thousand *contos de réis*,[171] the infamously lavish building opened at the height of the boom in December 1896—just two months after Carlos Gomes died in Pará, where he had assumed directorship of the state's music conservatory. Venetian chandeliers, Bavarian mirrors, and Louis XV furniture sat beneath a 2,368-square-foot ceiling embellished with European murals of the deceased composer's operas. In one adjacent ballroom, frescoed walls depicted what one foreign journalist, apparently unfamiliar with Brazilian opera, took to be "an Indian rescuing a Portuguese girl from a burning plantation house"—that is, Peri carrying Ceci from Antônio de Mariz's castle shortly before its destruction.[172]

The relative opulence of Manaus challenged the regionalist discourses that placed São Paulo and its majority Euro-descended population at the head of Brazilian culture and "civilization." Political, cultural, and scientific debates about race, modernity, and resources during the second half of the nineteenth century and its tumultuous years of war, rising republicanism, and the abolitionist movement all fed racialized notions of geography that pitted the wealthier, whiter, more modern, and "civilized" South against a poorer, darker-skinned, less modern, and "barbaric" interior, North, and Northeast. As historian Barbara Weinstein has argued, intensified regional loyalties never managed to supplant Brazilian nationalism, but they did provide the raw materials out of which changing national identities would be reimagined and recirculated.[173] Because rival *regionalist* discourses and their intellectual and political proponents had to vie for the opportunity to project through a *national* spotlight onto the *international* stage of Brazilianness, it made perfect sense that Carlos Gomes's fellow *campineiros* would claim his unprecedented success in Europe as a local victory, as well as a national one.

That a racialized geography of southern affluence and modernity versus northern poverty and backwardness still pervades national and international discourse on Brazil is, at best, a truism—albeit one that is increasingly called into question by its scapegoats.[174] The dichotomy not only obfuscates the great diversity of both regions; it also ignores the notoriously uneven distribution of resources that has always existed *within* them. At the turn of the twentieth century, for instance, the Amazonian elite and droves of foreign capitalists enjoyed electric lighting, telephone service, paved streets, public transportation, piped gas and water, ornate architecture, lavish parks and gardens, along with a "refined" cultural calendar that included opera, before many Southeasterners even dreamed of having access to such amenities.[175]

The urban centers of Manaus and Belém burgeoned in the middle of the world's largest rainforest thanks to wealth earned off the backs of indigenous and *caboclo* rubber tappers who worked in dangerous conditions, under coercion, and oftentimes as indentured servants or slaves.[176] For the hundreds of Native communities occupying the Brazilian Amazon during the early twentieth century,[177] the harsh treatment associated with the *ciclo da borracha* meant violent insertion into an atomizing global economy and the end of a way of life. In countless cases, of course, it also meant the end of life itself. Reflecting on the human costs of the still growing rubber enterprise across the region, the head of the Botanical Museum of Amazonas, João Barbosa Rodrigues, inverted the familiar civilization/barbarity paradigm to reconstruct a decades-long conflict between one indigenous group commonly taken to be "savage" and the non-Native residents of Moura—a small Amazonian settlement north of Manaus.[178] By the early 1870s, he noted—at precisely the same time Antônio Carlos Gomes traveled between Europe and the Americas with his Italian *Guarany*, and while Taunay wrote of Guaicuru and Terena participation in the Paraguayan War—that once-limited skirmishes had escalated into warfare when belligerent Indians "failed to show gratitude" for the *brindes* (trinkets or presents) bestowed upon them by migrant settlers in (compulsory) exchange for their lands and general subservience.[179]

In 1873, after years of bloody conflict, numerous requests to local political and military leaders for personnel and ammunition, and countless lives lost on both sides, an exasperated Colonel João do Rego Barros Falcão wrote to the president of Amazonas with a suggestion and request: "I cannot fail to call to Your Excellency's attention the need for an energetic means to contain these Indians that *infest* the margins of the Rio Negro, from Jacaré Beach to the falls of the Rio Branco. . . . I recognize that using force against them is not ideal, but it is my duty to tell Your Excellency that either we take hold of that resource or abandon those settlements and relinquish that zone—*so ripe for agriculture*—to the savages."[180]

Falcão's thinking was not original, of course, as intellectuals and political leaders throughout Brazil had expressed similar desires long before him and would continue to do so well into the twentieth century. Notable among them was the German-born founder of the Museu Paulista, Hermann von Ihering, who a few decades later found even "tame Indians" unfit for membership in national society and advocated openly for their annihilation. Reflecting on conflicts between Native populations and European settlers in the Southeast, he observed: "One cannot expect serious and continuous work from the civilized Indians, and since the savage[s] . . . are an impediment to the colonization of the backland regions that they occupy, it seems that there is no option at hand except their extermination."[181] Both men's comments, it seems to me, encapsulate the constellation of social, cultural, political, and economic issues at stake for the dominant majority in the "indigenous question" as it played out across the country in the lead-up to the 1910 birth of the SPI: First, land occupation; second, prospects for commercial development; and finally, the future of civilization itself. The language of these influential thinkers indicates clearly that for them and for many of their contemporaries, "the Indians" were still something quite less than human—an inconvenient nuisance that like vermin "infested" valuable terrain and hindered the lives and livelihood of civilized, Christian people.[182]

One year after the SPI'S founding, an enthusiast of the new state-run initiative returned to Barbosa Rodrigues's accounts of the 1870s massacres to draw public attention to the still-dire situation of indigenous communities in the Southeast, and to voice support for the fledgling agency that would, in theory, protect them from self-serving Jesuit and Capuchin friars, *bugreiros* (Indian hunters), and any other contemptible soul inclined to embrace the macabre prescriptions of von Ihering. "In Amazonas," he wrote, "the spectacle [of exploitation] has been truly woeful."[183] But the situation in the purportedly more "civilized" South was no better. According to his grisly report, enlightened and sophisticated São Paulo was among the most barbaric regions of the country with regard to the treatment of Native peoples.

Where operatic Indians had been celebrated on the front pages of Carlos Gomes's hometown newspaper and enthusiastically applauded on the stages of São Paulo's opera houses just days before the fall of the empire,[184] "unhappy" Kaingang were annihilated under the *paulistas'* proverbial noses. The journalist lamented: "The situation of the disgraced race is one of crucifying martyrdom. The most barbarous scenes of slaughter have developed. . . . The . . . great and powerful State of São Paulo is . . . a *theater of scenes of the most horrific cannibalism* against the miserable indigenous race."[185] In keeping with Barbosa Rodrigues's critique of "civilization and barbarity," the journalist's reference to "cannibalism" had nothing to do with the eating of human flesh but evoked, instead, a category of violence proper to what Michael Taussig, writing much later of the "Putumayo affair," would call the cultures and "economies of terror."[186]

Probing the possibilities and impossibilities of recounting such unfathomable violence, Hayden White argued that all human horrors, including the Holocaust, challenged but never defied representation. "Genocide . . .

is [not] any more unrepresentable than any other event in human history," he argued. "It is only that its representation . . . requires the kind of style . . . developed . . . to represent the kind of experiences that social modernism made possible."[187] For the historian, that style meant something akin to Roland Barthes's "intransitive" writing, or the pouring of oneself onto paper in a way that makes what is written inseparable from both the writer and the event that he or she narrates (rather than merely an author's reflection on an external event). In this light, the efforts of Barbosa Rodrigues and the later *O Paiz* journalist were crucial not only for shedding light on a human tragedy that went ignored by the dominant majority but also for seeking to destabilize and redefine the widely accepted notions of "civilization," "barbarity," "order," and "progress" that lay at the heart of a still-new national project. The journalist concluded:

> The scenes become all the more shameful when it is certain that while the indigenous man is limited to defending himself with his rudimentary arms—the bow and arrow—the civilized man has multiplied and perfected the elements of attack, operating with a superior armament of extraordinarily deadly force. The arm of the Indian is raised; the bow is held taut; the arrow flies and the white man falls victim. He [the Indian] is a savage—a barbarian—they say. The white man invades a river, binds the hands of its inhabitants, sells them, takes them to houses of oppression and vice, sets fire to their *teyupares* [straw dwellings], robs the honor of their sons. He is a civilizer.[188]

Against the celebratory backdrop of national growth, modernization, burgeoning wealth, booming cultural industries, and opera houses, then, dissident opinions such as these offered a critical if far less common rendering of the "Indian questions" of the day. In short, they highlighted voices sympathetic to the goal of indigenous survival[189] and focused on the real human costs of "development": *correrias* (Indian-hunting expeditions), massacres of entire communities as they slept, bow-and-arrow wielding warriors gunned down by semi-automatic weapons, the elderly burned alive in their homes, intentional poisonings of water and food, the rape of Native women and girls, and the capture and murder of indigenous children.[190] Still, while the tone of these communications indicated outrage, their underlying premise was that the days of Brazil's indigenous peoples, already having been reduced to living "ruins" or "remains," were indeed numbered. Lamenting from the capital city the deterioration of relations between Indians and non-Indians, the journalist continued: "In our backlands, in any of the States where there still exist the *remnants* of

Captured Kaingang children, circa 1912: "After the slaughter of the Indians—men, women, and children—Martinho Marcelino [seated in the center of the canoe] transports the children who escaped to distribute them to their parents' assassins in Santa Catarina." Courtesy of the Museu do Índio/FUNAI Archive.

the valiant indigenous tribes, . . . organized attacks have been repeated with . . . ferocity and inhumanity."[191]

In July 1888—two months after the Lei Áurea abolished the slavery of Africans and Afro-descendants to "[win] the commendation of the civilized world," and a year before *Lo schiavo* debuted in the Theatro Dom Pedro II—reports circulated internationally, attesting to the genocide of Native peoples near the Paranapanema River in São Paulo province.[192] A *New York Times* journalist citing Brazilian and British sources attributed the imperial government's failure to investigate to the fact that "Indian hunting" was "so common" a practice across Brazil that the horrific accusations were neither noteworthy nor deserving of particular attention. "Thus far," he avowed, "it has not been shown that the people of any South American Nation except for Brazil have tried to solve the Indian problem as the Australians sought to exterminate their rabbits—with poison."[193]

Brazilian chargé d'affaires J. August Da Costa flatly repudiated the accusation and its sources: "I was sorry to see . . . such prominence [given] to the matter after the official denial. . . . If such a case were to happen, no doubt the murder would meet with the severest punishment allowed by law, because it is the policy of the Brazilian Government to afford the most efficient protection to its Indian population."[194] Despite the fact that the emperor himself, just weeks shy of removal, would express interest in getting to know his enigmatic Native subjects as people, rather than as caricatures,[195] it would take four more decades for the state to begin to mirror that interest in any substantive way.[196] During the long interlude, the only Indians suitable for imagining "order and progress," it would seem, were the ones who appeared onstage.

3

ANTI-IMPERIALIST IMPERIALISM
AND OTHER CONSTRUCTIONS
OF MODERNITY

THE FORMER INTERNATIONAL RESERVE
OF AMAZON FOREST

Images of the "Former International Reserve of Amazon Forest [*sic*]" (FINRAF) have been circulating as part of an Internet chain letter since the year 2000. Alleged to be an excerpt from a geography primer used in U.S. middle schools, the contentious message depicts the Amazon on a map of Brazil and neighboring countries and explains, in poor English, why the world's "most important rain forest" has been seized from the "illiterate" and "primitive" peoples of South America and appropriated for safekeeping by the United States and United Nations. The textbook's supposed author, neoconqueror "David Norman," justifies the confiscation of national territory from the "irresponsable, cruel and authoritary [*sic*] countries" of the region by endorsing protection of the "lungs of the World" and positing the "valuable lands" of the Amazonian rainforest as the patrimony of "all humanity."[1]

Titled "A Amazônia é nossa!" ("The Amazon is ours!"), the anonymous e-mail message created by an unspecified group of Brazilian nationalists led Internet users from a wide variety of political persuasions to believe that children in the United States routinely study the necessary takeover of Brazilian territory and its conversion into FINRAF as part of their school curriculum. Indeed, during the early 2000s, the bogus book persuaded so

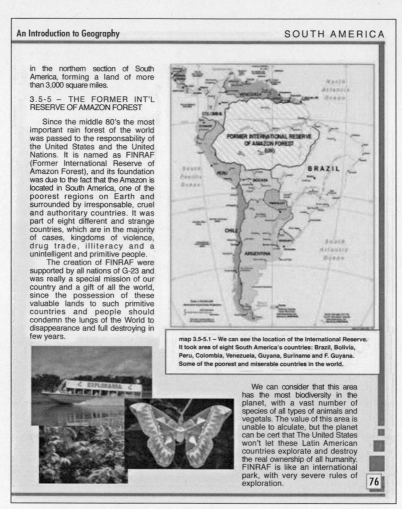

in the northern section of South America, forming a land of more than 3,000 square miles.

3.5-5 – THE FORMER INT'L RESERVE OF AMAZON FOREST

Since the middle 80's the most important rain forest of the world was passed to the responsability of the United States and the United Nations. It is named as FINRAF (Former International Reserve of Amazon Forest), and its foundation was due to the fact that the Amazon is located in South America, one of the poorest regions on Earth and surrounded by irresponsable, cruel and authoritary countries. It was part of eight different and strange countries, which are in the majority of cases, kingdoms of violence, drug trade, illiteracy and a unintelligent and primitive people.

The creation of FINRAF were supported by all nations of G-23 and was really a special mission of our country and a gift of all the world, since the possession of these valuable lands to such primitive countries and people should condemn the lungs of the World to disappearance and full destroying in few years.

map 3.5-5.1 – We can see the location of the International Reserve. It took area of eight South America's countries: Brazil, Bolivia, Peru, Colombia, Venezuela, Guyana, Suriname and F. Guyana. Some of the poorest and miserable countries in the world.

We can consider that this area has the most biodiversity in the planet, with a vast number of species of all types of animals and vegetals. The value of this area is unable to alculate, but the planet can be cert that The United States won't let these Latin American countries explorate and destroy the real ownership of all humanity. FINRAF is like an international park, with very severe rules of exploration.

76

Entry for the "Former International Reserve of Amazon Forest" in the bogus textbook, An Introduction to Geography.

many people of its veracity that the U.S. State Department and the Brazilian embassy in Washington, D.C., were compelled to post disclaimers on their respective websites stating that its claims were false.[2]

Like other perceived infringements of national sovereignty, spurious or otherwise, FINRAF draws on a telluric anti-imperialism that pervades dominant Brazilian politics, social discourse, and cultural production and has associated the country's interior with the heart and soul of Brazilianness since long before the declaration of the First Republic in 1889. From nineteenth-century romantic fiction and twentieth-century musical

"They want to 'eat' our forests!" Cover of the Revista Bundas, *23 May 2000.*

nationalism to popular outrage over rumors of foreign takeover at the turn of the millennium, the Amazon and its inhabitants emerge repeatedly as a patriotic trope to represent the whole or imagined essence of the country.[3] Over time, the accumulation of such "outsider" renderings has tended, as critic Candace Slater argues, to shroud the social and cultural diversity of a complex and massive territory under a green, "one-dimensional" world populated exclusively by "natural peoples" and marked by colossal and exotic wonders of every possible sort.[4] In policy initiatives and the popular imaginary alike, nationalist responses to the potential violation of Amazonian sovereignty have triggered the preemptive takeover of "virgin" lands deemed to be lacking occupation, control, and suitable proprietors. Consider, for example, the imagery of sexual possession used in popular media responses to rumors of Amazonian takeover, which intensified in October 2000 after George W. Bush suggested that "third-world debt" might be traded for "valuable rain forest lands."[5]

This chapter considers the overlap of Amazonian imaginaries, the unfinished processes of Brazilian modernity, and anti-imperialist articulations of national identity in relation to fictitious "Indians" and the indigenous peoples whose collective fate has been powerfully implicated in all three sets of discourse. I aim to show that the bogus textbook's abusive and imperialist logic of rightful possession is in fact analogous to the state's historical rationale of interior occupation and border defense—the very logic of modernization and national security that for generations of Native Brazilians has meant, as we saw in chapter 2, the diminution or forfeiture of traditionally occupied lands and often of life itself. Although the dominance of colonialist reason is, of course, rooted in the sixteenth century, it would take on new impetus following independence, as transportation and communication technologies opened up the "hinterlands," as the rubber boom sparked the hasty and uneven "development" of the interior, and as the Terena and Guaicuru peoples on Brazil's western border were conscripted as "volunteers" for the Paraguayan War.[6]

Notwithstanding the anti-imperialist sentiment behind the Internet chain letter, the imperialist logic of FINRAF echoes a century of state-backed indigenism—also an anti-imperialist doctrine, but one that sits at the opposite end of the political spectrum and has been implemented precisely through education—or, more broadly, the authority that anthropologist Antonio Carlos de Souza Lima aptly labeled "tutelary power."[7] It is ironic that the masterminds of the fake geography textbook sought to rouse anti-imperialist sentiment by inventing a pedagogical discourse positing all Brazilians as "primitives" in need of "civilized" guidance and enlightenment, for that is precisely what the country's dominant majority has been saying about "their" Native peoples in the Amazon (and elsewhere) for most of the last two hundred years.

Both indigenist discourse and the international plot to take over the Amazon invoke the role of indigenous peoples in the processes of Brazilian modernity by positing the legitimate superiority of "modern" knowledge and reason over "backward" traditions and myths in order to impose new and specific configurations of time and space. Though touted as "objective" and "scientific," this temporal and spatial reorganization presents a colonialist rendering of the physical world under the guise of universal truth and in the name of "all humanity." In both cases, "superior" cultures have been deployed to supplant "inferior" ones by bringing with them what Anthony Giddens called the "consequences of modernity," which foster relations between peoples, institutions, and ideas that in premodern times would have been unlikely to cross paths.[8] Thus was the thrust of Brazil's indigenist enterprise, which—like the fictitious FINRAF takeover—reconfigured "primitive" places through "protection," on the one hand, and the dissemination of positive images of that protection, on the other.

The goals of educating "strange," "underdeveloped," "illiterate," and "primitive" peoples and equipping them with books, weapons, and new technologies to safeguard Brazilian territory was a direct result of national development policy beginning in the early twentieth century. The republican push to develop and modernize the interior became President Getúlio Vargas's "Marcha para o Oeste" during the thirties and forties and President Juscelino Kubitschek's "Cinqüenta anos em cinco" campaign during the fifties, finally culminating in the inauguration of Brazil's hypermodern capital—Brasília—in 1960.[9] In the midst of the development flurry, Vargas's vice president, João Café Filho, charged a committee of indigenist "specialists" with a feasibility study for a new indigenous reserve in the then-unified state of Mato Grosso: the Parque Indígena do Xingu.[10]

The committee concluded that Xingu would facilitate the protection of the nation's "indigenous factor" in "human, animal, and plant forms" and emphasized the value of fusing the state's indigenist mission to help "Indians" find their place in Brazilian society with its broader technological, security, and economic interests. More than a buffer zone between "uncivilized" Natives and the dominant majority, Xingu would provide a tactical military zone. The study concluded, "In the Xingu Indigenous Park, the Brazilian Air Force and commercial air navigation would find a point of utmost strategic importance . . . for flight security. Scientists would be guaranteed a sample of pristine Brazil where they could contribute to a more profound understanding of our land and our people. And our generation would redeem itself from the devastation that. . . . is being inflicted on the Brazilian environment, thus reserving a sanctuary where it would be preserved intact."[11]

President Jânio Quadros finally approved modified plans for the Parque Nacional do Xingu some nine years later, in 1961.[12] Equipped with landing strips and radiotelegraph stations, the reserve would drag the nineteenth-century association between indigenous protection and the militarized takeover of Native lands into the second half of the twentieth century. The postindependence desire for defensive dominion over the prized but "empty landscape" thus fashioned Native peoples as one of the many material resources to be exploited in the interest of technological progress, national security, and economic development. Together forming a trinity of Brazilian modernity, these goals interpellated "Indians" primarily through education—a rhetoric and practice of anti-imperialist imperialism that grounds the historical relationship between indigenous peoples and the society of the dominant majority.[13]

Although indigenous peoples are in some ways more empowered than ever to represent themselves on the national and international stage in politics and various forms of cultural production,[14] the colonialist tendencies to "vanish" them into nature or subordinate their ideas and agency to comfortable romantic images and the exigencies of nation-building are also alive and well.[15] Indeed, the nationalist critique of imperialism behind the FINRAF facade points to a long-standing metonymic relationship between "our Indians" and "Our America"[16] in which the idea of "Indians"—and expressly not the thought or experience of indigenous peoples—stands in for Brazil, and vice versa. By tracing the modernizing discourses of science, security, and development in the rhetoric and practice of indigenism and the thought of those interpellated by it, we can see how a wide variety of imperialist discourses—real and imagined, foreign and domestic—have appropriated and manipulated the idea, practice, and image of indigenous education to reconfigure traditional notions of space and time as part of the ongoing construction of Brazil's colonialist modernity.

FROM XINGU TO SIVAM: WHO IS PROTECTING WHOM?

The seeds of indigenist modernity that were planted during the early twentieth century blossomed many decades later as the Sistema de Vigilância da Amazônia (Amazonian Vigilance System, or SIVAM), characterized by its Brazilian and U.S. infrastructure providers as the largest environmental monitoring program and law enforcement system in the world.[17] A massive configuration of surveillance radars, environmental sensors, airborne systems, and on-ground coordination centers, SIVAM would be the technological infrastructure for monitoring 5.2 million square kilometers of Amazonian rainforest.[18] The Brazilian Air Force and the U.S.-based Raytheon Corporation, which amid great controversy won the contract to provide the Brazilian government with infrastructure and technological expertise, developed the project between 1994 and 2005 in collaboration with Brazilian companies Embraer and ATECH. With a price tag of US$1.395 billion, SIVAM was initiated during the administration of Fernando Henrique Cardoso but was born of a Vargas-era desire to control Brazilian airspace that intensified under military rule in the 1970s and early 1980s.[19] As allegations of corruption surrounded its thorny passage through Congress for approval of international financing, the project brought scandal to Cardoso's administration, leading to an official investigation (by the Comissão Parlamentar de Inquérito [Parliamentary Commission of Inquiry, or CPI]) and the dismissal of four top officials.[20]

Shadowed by this controversy, SIVAM advocates pitched the project to the general public as a means to protect valuable and endangered national territories. Their rationale justified this effort at protection with language that resonates almost perfectly with the fake textbook's justification of FINRAF. The governmental website stated:

> During the 1980s, the Amazon was considered the lungs of the world, and we Brazilians, the arsonists who were doing away with the oxygen of the planet. Other countries with an eye on our resources said they were worried about the health of the Earth and that they wanted to keep abreast of everything that was happening in the Amazon. At that time, the region was plagued by drug trafficking, uncontrolled settlement, the invasion of indigenous areas, smuggling and predatory actions—primarily by illegal loggers and miners—and a whole series of other crimes. In reality, with the difficulties of communication and control in the region, it was hard for the Brazilian government to know what was really going on in the Amazon.[21]

That SIVAM might deter countries with their "eyes on Brazilian wealth" was contradictory, however, considering that foreign sources funded 97 percent of the initiative. Earning 8.5 percent interest on nearly US$1.4 billion in loans over two decades, the "other countries" in question would manage to accumulate massive amounts of Brazilian "riches" legally and with the approval of the National Congress.[22]

While SIVAM's political and scientific significance as part of a regional history of military and environmental defense is unquestionable, the social and cultural ramifications of the project are also significant and have been largely ignored. Particularly relevant to the question of indigenous representation was the multifaceted educational and publicity campaign used to promote SIVAM between 1997 and 2000 as part of a communications operation to improve public opinion regarding what had become known in the mainstream press as the "project of scandals."[23] Brainchild of the SIVAM project coordinator, Brigadier Marcos Antônio Oliveira, the pedagogical undertaking originated in Rio de Janeiro with members of a Social Communications Advisory Team, who decided to represent the government's technological security initiative with a cartoon image—first, a parrot that ended up looking too much like the Petrobras mascot; and then, a young indigenous boy named Sivamzinho ("Little SIVAM").[24] The promotional materials explained: "This nice little Indian is Sivamzinho, mascot of the SIVAM project. He's the number one friend of the children of the Amazon."[25] A light-skinned, monolingual Portuguese speaker sporting shorts, a T-shirt, and a Yanomami-looking haircut, the "nice little Indian" would be the centerpiece of 1,028,000 pieces of pedagogical material distributed to schoolchildren and teachers throughout the region, including the twenty-three locales targeted as installation sites for SIVAM infrastructure.[26]

The 115 tons of notebooks, posters, calendars, rulers, and pencils—all showcasing the SIVAM mascot—aimed "to generate a legion of Sivamzinhos" throughout the Amazon who would identify with the "little Indian's" "spirit of adventure" and "love of the land."[27] Part environmentalist and part spy, Sivamzinho was also the protagonist of a series of educational comics that depicted him protecting the rainforest, advocating for sustainable development, and turning over wrongdoers to the Federal Police. In two such comics, *O garimpo que não deu certo* (*Mining Gone Wrong*) and *Estão levando os animais* (*They're Stealing the Animals*), he foiled smugglers dressed like foreign tourists as they sifted stolen gold and trafficked protected animals deep in the heart of the rainforest. Other editions showed Sivamzinho preventing deforestation and river pollution, thwarting improper fishing practices, and praising the enhanced production levels and improved quality of life brought about by SIVAM.[28]

With an emphasis on individual and communal responsibility in policing the hinterlands, Sivamzinho served as the metaphorical eyes and ears of the Brazilian state and the poster child, quite literally, for nearly a century of "indigenous protection." He was *the* "educated Indian": authentically Native enough in his abilities and interests but also sufficiently whitened by the knowledge that he had gleaned from dominant society and that he sought, in turn, to impart to his less-enlightened brethren. Above all, Sivamzinho was a patriot who embraced the responsibilities of his national citizenship. Five hundred thousand "educational notebooks" circulated through Amazonian schools depicted him hoisting the Brazilian flag and singing the national anthem.

As a human symbol of SIVAM and mouthpiece for the national interests it was supposed to represent, Sivamzinho put a positive spin on a complex international initiative that the newspaper-reading public had reduced to the eternally popular and not unfounded idea that foreigners—and particularly U.S. foreigners—were preparing to take over the Amazon.[29] At the same time, the mascot reflected the colonialist tendencies to put expedient words in the mouths of silenced Others and place an Indian

The cover of the Sivamzinho Educational Notebook reads: "Hi, little friends! I am Sivamzinho. I am very proud to live in the Amazon. Sometimes I get very angry when someone destroys my home [by] cutting down trees, polluting the rivers, and invading our lands.... Only from now on, with your help, I will be here to help protect the Amazon." Courtesy of Filipe Bastos.

face on the aspirations of the dominant majority—all in the purported best interest of the Indians themselves. Although the pedagogical materials were undoubtedly popular in the poverty-stricken schools where they were distributed, SIVAM's critics contended that the local population would have benefited much more from investment in small-scale infrastructure and basic human services. As local priest Nilton César de Paula argued, "If SIVAM is going to bring satellites, let them bring some decent radios and telephones, too. Lots of people die from snakebites in the communities of Rio Negro because they don't have a phone to call for help."[30]

NEO-BRAZILIAN PATRIOTS IN THE SPOTLIGHT

Despite the futuristic nature of the SIVAM initiative, the conflation of Indian education with national development and the technological militarization of indigenous lands is an old phenomenon. By placing soldiers, science, and "desirable" settlers in frontier regions during the early 1900s, the young Republic was forced to confront its most "imagined" constituents in the Native peoples who lived there, frequently ignorant of their own Brazilianness.[31] Presaging the turn-of-the-millennium anxiety over precarious Amazonian borders by nearly a century, Brazil's civil and military leaders, along with the newspaper-reading public, evoked the "illiterate, unintelligent, and primitive" inhabitants of remote national terrain in order to justify its takeover by the indigenist patriots who were, at least in theory, willing to risk their lives for the future well-being of the nation. Following the declaration of the First Republic, in the aftermath of the Canudos War (1896–97),[32] and a long-standing series of violent confrontations between Native communities and settlers infringing on their traditional lands, indigenist pioneer Cândido Mariano da Silva Rondon tasked the newly minted Serviço de Proteção aos Índios (Indian Protection Service, or SPI) with forging a pacific and enlightened passageway into modernity.[33] A military officer and engineer of Bororó descent, Rondon directed SPI indigenists to "die if need be, but never kill [*morrer se preciso for, matar nunca*]."[34] Grounded in this conviction, he sought to "pacify" indigenous communities, organize them on *postos indígenas* (indigenous posts), and place them under the protective arm of the state. During the first decades of the twentieth century, the SPI established more than one hundred indigenous posts across the country, each designed to carry out its own version of the civilizing mission.[35]

In 1925, senior indigenist functionary Luiz Bueno Horta Barbosa explained in an interview with *O Paiz* that the SPI's indigenous posts were micromodels of national modernity, equipped with electricity, efficient agricultural technologies, innovative infrastructure, and, most important, self-sacrificing and patriotic personnel.[36] To address the particular needs of each newly settled community, however, the tools of positivist change would be insufficient without that most important motor of positivist change: capital. He reasoned: "In order to attend to other nuclei of sparse, savage peoples still at risk, [we need] . . . funding proportionate to the demands of such a worthwhile and onerous undertaking. Congress's erudition and competence should lead it to reflect more carefully on the nearly resolved problem of the Indian, and to give the SPI the resources it needs to fulfill its great, pious mission of humanity and patriotism."[37] The indigenist mission was thus couched in commercial terms that tied indigenous education and training to the Indians' capacity for manual labor and economic productivity. Because foreign investment was critical to the national development initiatives under way (as it would be with SIVAM, so many years later), SPI indigenous posts would need to become

Map of SPI Indigenous Posts nationwide, 1930.
Courtesy of the Museu do Índio/FUNAI Archive.

self-sustaining in order to survive the international financial downturn looming on the horizon.[38]

As Horta Barbosa had feared, the political and economic crises of the thirties crippled the state's indigenist apparatus with massive budget reductions exacerbated by Rondon's failure to support the revolutionary coup that brought Vargas to power in October 1930.[39] On 12 July 1934, the president removed the weakened SPI from the Ministry of Labor, Industry, and Commerce and transferred it to the Ministry of War. Placing the SPI under the Inspetoria Especial de Fronteiras (Special Inspectorate of Borders), he ordered the minister to address "border defense" and "Indian nationalization" as interrelated problems and to revise SPI legislation accordingly."[40] The SPI propaganda films that followed these changes thus spotlighted the indigenous posts—and particularly their schools—as an extended experiment in the militarization of everyday life.

Touted by their sponsors as microcosms of positivist humanism, the "hygienic and comfortable" posts would be islands of Brazilian civility in a dark and dangerous sea of barbarism, aimed and equipped to accommodate the "aspirations and customs" of those destined by order and progress to call them home. As one 1942 propaganda film explained:

In the middle of a zone once wracked by battles against the Indian who stood up to protest the takeover of his lands, today we find this Post with its . . . pacified Indians. As the first habitat built by civilized people inside indigenous territory, it represents an arduous task. . . . Raising livestock is one of the primary ways to maintain an indigenous post. It's also a great way to introduce Indians to the notion of money. . . . [Another] principle factor in the life of an indigenous post is agriculture, which . . . sets the Indian on the road to rural Brazilian civilization. . . . The school . . . introduces new habits and socializes the little Indians. Oftentimes, Indian and civilized children learn at the same school, thereby initiating the social communion that the Post aims to intensify later among adults."[41]

By emphasizing the relationship between manual labor and the consolidation of a modern economy, SPI propaganda made little distinction between the people and livestock residing on the posts, but promised a "new" and "productive" life to those who "worked happily and satisfied, alone or in groups." In keeping with the SPI's founding principles, technology and capital would enable the indigenists to integrate their Native tutees—and particularly school-aged children—socially and economically into dominant society while at the same time harnessing their innate, virtually untapped industriousness to help build the nation.

As the film reveals, the educational thrust of the state's development initiative conflated the "indigenous problem" with a long-standing battle between people and the environment—"green hell [*inferno verde*]" or the "backlands [*os sertões*]," as the case might have been[42]—and posited both in terms of a regional, postindependence interrogation of civilization and barbarism. A final scene depicts Kaingang women in discreet Western dress, weaving traditional cloth as uniformed pupils hoist the Brazilian flag over their school under their teachers' approving gaze. The narrator exclaims: "The Indian woman obeys tribal tradition, working tenaciously on a ceremonial tapestry. Her fingers never tire, and her ability is indeed impressive. In her physiognomy—calm and serene—flow the remembrances of other times, now happily vanquished. There is hope for civilization!"[43] The camera then moves in to show the hands of one woman as she tugs adroitly on a few of the thousands of threads that make up her massive tapestry—a reminder, perhaps, of the challenge of plaiting a single nation from so many ethnic, cultural, and social strands. Staring expressionless into the distance, the woman suddenly breaks a small smile as she glances at the flag-raisers. The narrator raises his voice over a crescendo of classical fanfare to conclude: "Cloaked in the national flag, the SPI aspires to carry out its sacred duty to civilize and protect Brazilian Indians."[44] We are left with the image of the Native schoolchildren, one line for boys and another for girls, gazing up as their new flag is unfurled in the winds of felicitous change.[45]

Throughout SPI discourse, this paternalism interpellated not only children, but also indigenous men and women of all ages, who according to the 1916 Civil Code were legally minors and thus forever in need of state supervision and guidance.[46] In keeping with a long trajectory of authoritarian thought encapsulated by Simón Bolívar's depiction of colonialism as a state of permanent childhood,[47] the trope of everlasting infancy and its accompanying tutelary apparatus rationalized and justified the marginalization and "underdevelopment" of indigenous peoples and truncated the possibilities for Native self-representation by equating Indianness with "relative incapacity."

In 1945, three years after the SPI produced the film on the Curt Nimuendajú and Icatu Indigenous Posts, President Vargas instituted National Indian Day, thereby formalizing the state's recognition of the indigeneity within Brazilianness. In his commemorative address, the head of the SPI's Educational Sector, Herbert Serpa, linked the messianic indigenist mission to the need to safeguard the physical integrity of the nation: "It is to the Indians that we must turn our thoughts when we raise the flag of the free America that they symbolize so perfectly. . . . In order that fearsome nature not defeat the light of human intelligence, Rondon tamed the jungle man, so that, hearing for the first time the call of the fatherland, he would emerge from the forest to raise the green and yellow pennant in his fist, as if to say to the people on the borders: '*The soil of the Brazilian fatherland begins here!*'"[48] Until 1967, when the military regime dismantled the SPI and replaced it with the Fundação Nacional do Índio (FUNAI), this prophecy of racialized modernity would depict *neo-brasileiros* hoisting the Brazilian flag over the Amazon to consolidate national power over the precious metals, gems, minerals, timber, rubber, petroleum, and other potential sources of wealth found therein.[49] These

widely circulated images would be the precedent to Sivamzinho's raising the "green and yellow" and safeguarding the Amazon from foreign predators some fifty years later, at the turn of the millennium. In both cases, the "Indian" voice was not indigenous, and the "protection" at hand was, for the most part, a fiction.

Because, according to SPI doctrine, Indians in frontier regions near Bolivia and Peru had to be seduced from nomadism, settled, nationalized, and trained to secure the contentious international borders, indigenous education was also a vital question of national security in keeping with the later "geopolitics" of influential military thinkers like General Golbery do Couto e Silva.[50] Modernization and its burgeoning capitalist order were thus overlapping projects of biopower that relied on the controlled insertion of human beings—in this case, both individuals and communities—into a statist but increasingly global machinery of production that would sustain agricultural exports and service the country's mounting external debt before later being put to use to consolidate an economy based on import-substitution industrialization.[51] Brazil's modernity thus meant not only the appropriation and transformation of traditional indigenous spaces—a process that Souza Lima characterized brilliantly as "a massive siege of peace"[52]—but also what Michel Foucault might have called "the calculated management of [indigenous] life."[53] The process of interior development was twofold: On the one hand, it meant the demarcation, takeover, and settlement of traditional indigenous lands; and on the other, it meant the demarcation, takeover, and settlement of indigenous bodies, which would be squeezed into uncomfortable clothes, national consciousness, and imaginary citizenship through a system of production and propaganda that evokes clearly the slave-based economy that had been abolished officially in Brazil more than half a century earlier.

The staging and visual documentation of these efforts point to how, as anthropologist Deborah Poole has shown in the case of Peru, fictions of racial progress circulated physically and ideologically inside and beyond national borders. Through the still-burgeoning arts of photography and film, the SPI documented heroic arrivals to distant lands and its power to transform the peoples living there. Inside the SPI's photography archive, thousands of "after shots" reveal "improved" Indians frozen under the invasive gaze of the indigenist photographers whose Orientalizing images would become essential blocks of the racialized nation-building project under way. As Walter Benjamin would argue not long after these pictures were taken, the mechanical reproduction of such imagery had the power to disrupt familiar configurations of time and space. Passing through the hands of indigenist specialists and everyday newspaper readers, alike, carefully staged photographs helped to make nameless "Indians" and their exotic, distant, and parallel worlds more personal and more familiar, shattering the aura of romanticized, Amazonian alterity, and replacing it with images of uncannily modern subjects who could be reimagined and inserted into the dominant majority's preferred representation of Brazil and its people. The incomplete, fragmented documentation of these subjects and their lives suggests that personalized details were of limited value to the visual architects of indigenist modernity or the consumers of their imagery. More important was the notion that positive (and positivist)

Karajá community registered by the Rondon Commission, circa 1910.
Courtesy of the Museu do Índio/FUNAI Archive.

change was possible, and that it could be accomplished through that most modern of republican institutions: the school.

The goal of making Indians useful through schooling was not, of course, unique to Brazil but reflected a central component of the pan-American indigenist initiative that flourished across the region beginning in the first half of the twentieth century. Supranational indigenism had culminated with the Inter-American Indigenist Congress of April 1940 in Pátzcuaro, Mexico, and the formation of the Instituto Indigenista Interamericano that December. As the proceedings commanded: "The countries of America [had to] provide their indigenous masses with an education that [would] later permit them to participate directly in the life and development of their respective countries."[54] Even at the regional level, then, Indian "usefulness" was tied to civic responsibility as well as to economic productivity. By linking indigenous peoples to their self-appointed protectors, the Instituto helped to institutionalize—and to imagine—an international educational apparatus as the central mechanism through which geopolitical mappings of Indianness and nationhood would take place across the Americas.[55] As the documentation from these schools reveals, the indigenous pupils were expected—like Kapêlituk from the

SPI classroom on the Rodolfo Miranda Indigenous Post in Amazonas, circa 1922. Courtesy of the Museu do Índio/FUNAI Archive.

Escola Capitão Pedro Dantas, or the "legion of Sivamzinhos," so many years later—to internalize and reproduce the very forms of knowledge by which they would be marginalized.

In 1940—the same year the Instituto held its first Congress and seven years after Gilberto Freyre published his foundational manifesto in praise of Brazilian miscegenation (*Casa grande e senzala*)—Rondon made a public address to President Vargas, who had just completed a highly photographed and widely publicized visit to Karajá communities on the Ilha do Bananal.⁵⁶ On behalf of the SPI's newly formed governing body, the Conselho Nacional pela Proteção dos Índios (the National Council for the Protection of Indians, or CNPI), the general used his speech to pose a rhetorical question—"What is the Indian?"—and offered his rhetorical response: "The greatest treasure that we encounter on our March westward."⁵⁷ Thus conflating the indigenists' goal of protecting and developing "Indians" with Vargas's desire to protect and develop the "West," Rondon proposed that one key strategy of the joint endeavor be to create among Native communities new material needs through the provision of modern tools, thereby turning them into consumers as well as producers of new wealth.⁵⁸ Hence the market logic of modernity would reconfigure indigenous peoples from within the indigenist imaginary—modifying their status as "obstacles" to national progress to vital (if also unwitting) agents of the same. In the overlapping processes of the modernist incursion into the Amazon, victims would be warriors, commodities would be consumers, and slaves would be citizens.

"CIVILIZATION FOR THE INDIANS OF THE AMAZON": AN INDIGENOUS PERSPECTIVE?[59]

At the outset of the SPI's crisis decade, a Guarani man named Inhanderu sought an interview with a major newspaper in the nation's capital in order to let the world know of his deepening personal crisis. "Mário Cardoso," as he was called by his "civilizers," had been expelled from his community in Anahy (Paraná) because of his outspoken "defense and love of his race."[60] Harkening back to the infamous Putumayo reports from two decades earlier on the mistreatment, torture, and murder of indigenous rubber workers on the Peru-Colombia border,[61] the young man alleged physical and mental abuse at the hands of SPI functionaries and appealed to the minister of agriculture to intervene on behalf of his besieged people. He decried the impunity with which SPI workers approached their mission and claimed that the beneficiaries of "state protection" were in fact not indigenous peoples but the indigenists themselves. He lamented: "SPI functionaries are torturers of Indians. They force us to work, and at the littlest complaint, order our capture and imprisonment. . . . The Indian has no rights at all. . . . [We] work from sunrise to sunset . . . and in compensation receive only abuse and imprisonment."[62] Inhanderu's testimony thus reiterates not only that the SPI brutality that the Figueiredo Commission would document in horrendous detail in the late 1960s had in fact been taking place for over half a century, but also, and just as important, that some of its victims had long sought redress from other state representatives on their own behalf.[63] Not least, his allegations cast a new and grim light on the cheery images of "fruitful Indian labor" that the indigenist apparatus under Vargas would showcase so prominently under the banners of "national progress" and "development."

One generation later, Lyrio Arlindo do Valle, a self-declared "cacique of the Tembé Indians," echoed Inhanderu's claims in a letter he sent to Getúlio Vargas in the fall of 1945, weeks before the fall of the Estado Novo. In the name of "all the Indians and rural poor living in the *sertões*," he explained to his president, he "had come to solicit . . . protection." Valle self-identified as a "civilized Indian" from the state of Pará who had studied with Catholic priests, served in the Brazilian Navy, and supported the

1930 "Revolution" that brought Vargas to power. Having worked for years as an SPI functionary, often under coercion and without remuneration, he was deeply frustrated with the broken system yet eager to "redeem his fellow Indians" and make them "useful to the fatherland." He pleaded for the immediate dissolution of the SPI: "The real protection of Indians will require a new organization."[64] Reiterating Inhanderu's complaints, he added, "I ask that you not accept false information about Indian protection, as I do not accept it, because the SPI protects whites, not Indians."[65] A radical suggestion then accompanied Valle's primary admonition: "Your Excellency knows that the Indian is best suited to protect the Indian; [there are] civilized Indians who want to be well used [*índios civilizados que querem ser aproveitados*]."[66]

Reasoning that Rondon, by then old and tired, had "forgotten about the Indians," Valle made the case for (his own) indigenous leadership of a different public enterprise for Native advocacy. His desire for this "new beginning" was, however, remarkably in line with the existing apparatus of state tutelage. Likewise, his revolutionary proposal for indigenous control of the state's new indigenist enterprise—as of 2012, a proposal that has yet to be realized[67]—invoked national modernity as science, security, and development through the then-familiar rhetoric of education. Valle made it clear, for instance, that if appointed to a position of indigenist leadership, he would found schools to train Native communities in new agricultural techniques and ranching technologies. As testament to his readiness to counter the audacity of "foreign invaders" and fight for a "free Brazil," he likened himself and his two sons (both Brazilian soldiers) to colonial legend Poti, whose spirit they carried in their "blood and minds."[68] Finally, like Sivamzinho, the Tembé leader was heedful of his civic duty and eager to see Native peoples driving Brazil's capitalist engine into the future. He promised: "If Your Excellency is disposed to help us, in two years there will appear in Belém the first products made by the Indians of Brazil, which will really have an impact on the national economy."[69]

Valle's plea was also presented against the backdrop of the state's successful penetration of the hinterlands, which had managed, unlike in the lawless Putumayo region just over the border, to rein in the illicit exploitation of land and people—particularly *seringueiros* (rubber tappers). For this progress, the cacique expressed enthusiasm and heartfelt appreciation: "I give thanks in the name of all the *seringueiros* of the Amazon, because it was Your Excellency who put an end to the traffic of people from Ceará to the backlands of the Amazon. . . . Those *seringueiros* who today express their gratitude are paying you back to the best of their ability because Your Excellency did away with the slavery of rubber soldiers."[70] Valle thus condemned the flawed execution of indigenist policy but dared not address its imperialist rationale or the imperative of Indian transformation on which it was premised.

In keeping with the developmental trajectory of the Vargas administration, then, the educated and "civilized Indian" lamented the gravest SPI shortcomings while linking the state's ability to rectify them to an endorsement of indigenous colonization and transformation. It is perhaps for this implicit agreement, after all, that the cacique's letter eventually found a home in the state's indigenist archive. Given the great and dangerous constraints in which Valle lived—and presumably, wrote—we will never know, of course, the sincerity of his esteem for Vargas or the state's indigenist endeavor. But whatever else it might have been, his effort, like that of Inhanderu, must be considered as part of a struggle for indigenous self-representation that began long before them and continues on, in various forms, into the twenty-first century.[71]

"CIVILIZATION FOR THE INDIANS OF THE AMAZON": AN IMPERIALIST PERSPECTIVE?

In 1947, two years after Valle wrote to Vargas, and after the end of the Estado Novo, the United Nations Educational, Scientific, and Cultural Organization (UNESCO) undertook an investigation of "fundamental education" in the Hylean Amazon.[72] Led by Bernard Mishkin, a naturalized North American anthropologist, military officer, and businessman, and under the auspices of the Instituto Internacional da Hiléia Amazônica (International Hylean Amazon Institute, or IIHA), the study considered obstacles to educational initiatives serving indigenous and *caboclo* populations across the Amazon Basin.[73] The Brazilian press hailed the project as the advent of "civilization for the Indians of the Amazon"—especially those who were still living "a primitive existence comparable to that of [their] Stone Age ancestors."[74] Mishkin's report, which appeared later that year in Mexico City and Paris, offers a unique perspective on indigenous schooling in relation to national and international modernizing discourses vis-à-vis scientific progress, national security, and socioeconomic development. Despite its evident bias, the anthropologist's vision serves, alongside the accounts of Inhanderu and Valle, as a counterpoint to SPI policy and other forms of state documentation that have been used to tell the official story of Native peoples in Brazil.

The gist of Mishkin's report—that indigenous protection in the Amazon was consistently inconsistent—is familiar: While some regional leaders were efficient and dedicated, others were "hopelessly corrupt" or "usually drunk."[75] Although some respected a minimal-intervention policy in the Rondonian tradition, others aimed mostly to "implant the concept of productive labor [and] educate the Indian to work."[76] In the state of Amazonas, where most people eked a living from the various "extractive industries" that were available to them, SPI employees established lumber camps and auctioned off wood on indigenous lands that were supposed to be protected.[77] In contrast to Valle's praise for the improved treatment of rubber workers under Vargas, Mishkin observed *seringueiros* toiling as slaves or in slave-like conditions, and he recounted the miserable living standards of non-Native Amazonians, many of whom he perceived to be perpetually overworked and chronically underfed.

Notwithstanding the scope of these observations, Mishkin's primary task was to surmise the state of the educational system showcased by the government as a crowning achievement of the indigenist nation-building enterprise and evidence of its enduring promise. Instead he observed that schools were seldom located in Native villages and that many indigenous children had no access to education whatsoever. The limited instruction offered to them was available exclusively in Portuguese, and indigenous authorities had little or no say regarding the programs that targeted their own communities.[78] Mishkin sized up the Bororó schooling on the indigenist post of Córrego Grande (approximately 155 miles from Cuiabá) as follows:

> It is difficult to estimate the number of days per year the school actually operates. . . . I would guess . . . two mornings a week, for one reason or another—the students do not appear; [or perhaps] the teacher is indisposed and wants to catch up on her housework. . . . There is only a three-year programme; no students have ever reached the fourth year. The textbooks used . . . are: 1st year—Meu Livro [My Book]; second year—Meus Deveres [My Homework]; third year—Minha Pátria [My Fatherland]. All three books have been prepared for instruction in the City schools and make as much sense to the Indian as the atomic bomb.[79]

Mishkin concluded that the schools were "alienating," and that the education they offered was "worthless" since it had "no connection" whatsoever "with the life of the Indian."[80]

Such comments regarding indigenous schooling must also be considered, however, against the broader backdrop of regional education, where, even in urban areas, "exhausted and malnourished" students sat in "badly lighted, crowded rooms" to receive instruction from "tired teachers through hopelessly outmoded and inadequate texts."[81] What is more, the 1933 Vargas Report that Mishkin cited in his study had determined that only 3 percent of the national population had completed an elementary-level education. By underscoring UNESCO's goal of comparing "underdeveloped" areas across Latin America and around the globe, then, Mishkin's analysis offered a counternarrative to the propagandistic documentation and activity logs maintained by SPI administrators and teachers over the same period. Alongside his indigenous counterparts Inhanderu and Valle, the anthropologist critiqued the indigenist mission by impelling readers to question the efficacy and justice of teaching arithmetic, history, geography, hygiene, natural science, civics, and Portuguese to monolingual indigenous children who, even as adults, would never enjoy the full rights of Brazilian citizenship.[82]

Shortly after completing these assessments, Mishkin published a harsh and controversial critique of the Good Neighbor policy in *The Nation*. Contrary to what one might expect from the author of the UNESCO reports, the anthropologist, who would later be investigated by the FBI as a communist spy,[83] called not for a softening of political and economic imperialist practices but for their intensification:

> Any attempt to save democracy in South America would . . . put the United States in the position of a doctor who rushes into a house to discover that the patient not only is not ill, but does not live there. In none of these countries is there a democratic basis of government. . . . The continent was compelled to stew in its own juice. A juice whose salient characteristics were and are a backward economic structure, feudal mentality, poverty, . . . ignorance, illiteracy . . . and acute despair. . . . South America is made for exploitation, gets a living from it, precarious though it may be, and is unprepared for any other kind of existence. The exclusion of foreign imperialism at this point would bring disaster.[84]

Mishkin went on to dismiss concerns over an impending communist takeover of South America and argued for a massive investment of U.S. capital to help finance electrification, industrialization, irrigation, and the modernization of agricultural technologies across the region. Acknowledging that these "necessary changes" would likely encounter resistance from the powerful—landowning elites, the Church, the military, and others with "vested interests in the status quo"—he added that "coercion may have to be used" and concluded, "The . . . points presented here may appear to reestablish the framework of an aggressive imperialist policy in South America. If they suggest imperialism, however, it is an imperialism of a sort not hitherto practiced by the United States. In reality, these are the first principles of a revolution calculated to break up an anachronistic social system whose continued survival is inimical to the interests of the United States."[85] Considering that these comments—also eerily reminiscent of "David Norman's" textbook—were published just fifteen years before a U.S.-backed military coup ousted Brazil's democratically elected government under President João Goulart, it seems that some in Washington were indeed sympathetic to Mishkin's call for a heightened U.S. presence in the region.[86] As is well known, the authoritarian regime that seized power in 1964 would make the intensified industrial exploitation of the Amazon a cornerstone of national development policy, devastating the lives and livelihood of thousands of indigenous (and other) Brazilians in the process, and planting the seeds of SIVAM (and FINRAF) along the way.

OUR INDIANS IN OUR AMERICA

Sociologist Anthony Giddens has argued that the advent of modernity brought about not only a radical reconfiguration of traditional temporal and spatial relations but also the "dislocation of space from place."[87] If social practices in "premodern" societies were linked temporally and geographically to particular locations and specific moments, Giddens proposed on the eve of the new millennium, then conditions of modernity undo these ties and reestablish them in relation to countless additional influences, many of which are distant in time as well as in space. Like the "reflexively applied" knowledge that in modernity comes to question its own certainty and restructure itself accordingly, fixed relationships between particular ways of being and knowing and their purportedly "proper" locations are undone in and by conditions of modernity to become "free-floating."[88] *Place*, for Giddens, thus refers to an identifiable location on the map—a location that once delimited most of the social dimensions of life—while *space* invokes the broader, potentially infinite social dimensions of modernity, many of which exercise their influence even from afar. *Place* and *space* can, therefore, coincide or overlap, but the consequences of modernity make the occasions for coincidence and overlap increasingly infrequent. As a result, he offers, "what structures the locale is not simply that which is present on the scene; the 'visible form' of the locale conceals the distanciated relations [that] determine its nature."[89]

From the SPI indigenous posts to Xingu, and from the UNESCO study to SIVAM and FINRAF, the ongoing (re)construction of national modernity through indigenist thought and practice thus helped to convert the Brazilian "hinterlands"—and particularly the Amazon—from *places* into *spaces*. Through real, perceived, and imagined power to influence and alter "premodern" configurations of time and space, indigenous schooling became a key mechanism through which traditional Native communities would be reconfigured as both "modern" and "national"—or at least always on the fringes of the nation and at the threshold of national belonging. The expansion of Brazilian modernity in and through indigenist policy and discourse brought with it a renewed politics of anti-imperialist imperialism. FINRAF, after all, ultimately reiterated the neocolonialist function of decades of state-backed indigenist and "development" initiatives through a hyperbolic rendering of SIVAM, which ultimately represents just one of the real and ongoing initiatives—such as the highly controversial Belo Monte hydroelectric dam—to restructure the Amazon and the lives of the people who live there, indigenous and not.[90]

The processes of disjuncture that for Giddens convert *places* into *spaces* are also useful for thinking about the social transformations impelled by indigenist policy through the biopolitical ordering of individual and collective bodies. The "disembedding" of knowledge, culture, and social praxis from modern centers of political and economic power and their violent insertion into traditional communities organized predominantly according to precapitalist modes of production provided the political, social, and economic mechanisms through which the private places of indigenous life would be usurped as public spaces that, in turn, were appropriated to represent—and to imagine—the nation.[91] This manipulation and transference have enabled generations of nationalists, regardless of their political orientation, to equate Brazil with "the Amazon," "the Amazon" with "the Indian," and "the Indian" with "the people."[92] Never mind that eight countries besides Brazil make up the international Amazon,[93] that less than 10 percent of Brazilians reside in the Amazon, or that "Indians" in Brazil represent hundreds of ethnic groups speaking hundreds of languages and yet account for less than 0.5 percent of the overall national population.

Four decades ago, the celebrated novelist Antônio Callado alluded to the association of these metonymic terms—*Brazil/Amazon, Amazon/ Indian, Indian/people (índio/povo)*—in his condemnation of the military regime's decision to "decapitate" the Xingu Indigenous Reserve by building the Federal Highway BR-080.[94] In doing so, he conflated the yet unresolved indigenous struggle for territorial demarcation with the colonialist circumscription of "Indians" to the jungle. Why not, he wondered, merge the Instituto Brasileiro de Desenvolvimento Florestal (Brazilian Institute for Forest Development) and FUNAI into one organization? After all, "where there are Indians, there are forests. The patrimony to be preserved is one and the same."[95]

Callado took the metaphor one step further, suggesting that not only the future of Brazil's Indians but indeed the future of the entire national community was at play—and at risk—in Xingu: "In the midst of many sinister and nonsensical acts, President Jânio Quadros, in a sober moment, created the Xingu Indigenous Park. It's up to another president to ensure the preservation of Brazilian nature, and the Indians who give it life and soul. Like a specter, the headless Park demands expiation to redeem us as a people."[96] "Our Indians" were thus not only "our dead," as in journalist Edilson Martins's notorious formulation,[97] but also the potential root of "our" demise. At the same time, Indian protection and redemption, if executed properly, would pave the path to "our" salvation. The indigenist desire to situate Indianness geographically would be a double-edged sword, leading to marginalization and exploitation, on the one hand, and security and "emancipation," on the other. In practice, of course, the former "wolf" has most frequently come dressed in the sheep's clothing of the latter.

Years earlier, on the threshold of dire institutional crisis, the SPI's interim director, José Bezerra Cavalcanti, explained the institutionalized takeover of indigenous communities and the appropriation of their lands as one and the same enterprise: "Above all," he explained, "we aim to protect *our* Indians wherever they may be. We assemble them in convenient locations and . . . teach them how to work and save the fruits of their labor. Regarding teaching materials, the principal intent is to provide them with knowledge and customs of farming, raising animals, and . . . [other] tasks that are within reach of their intelligence. For these reasons, the national territory has been divided up into a particular number of special zones [*inspetorias*]."[98] Each *inspetoria* was then divided further into the nationwide network of *postos indígenas* that I have examined here, where lives were not so much "protected" as they were assessed and managed in accordance with the regional, national, local, and inevitably, personal interests reflected in the dominant indigenist agendas at hand.

Forty years before the Brazilian government would begin to document the abuse perpetrated by some SPI representatives on the very populace they were meant to safeguard, Cavalcanti cut to the heart of the agency's fatal contradiction by inadvertently disclosing to a journalist that a de facto open visit policy was at work under his supervision. His admiring interviewer reached an exultant conclusion: "Anyone who wants to can, on any day and without special license, visit any of the SPI establishments."[99] The director's assertion thus contradicted nearly two decades of official indigenist policy—still at odds with itself today—regarding the SPI's mission to safeguard indigenous peoples precisely by safeguarding indigenous lands. Long before its precipitous decline, the state's tutorial apparatus was already deeply flawed—not only by its typical indigenist paternalism or the quixotic mission of turning people into something they were not, but also, as Cavalcanti unwittingly exposed, by its tragic vulnerability to unpredictable and at times arbitrary administration. Whose interests did the SPI ever represent? Whose interests does FUNAI represent today?

By making private indigenous space public—physically, as in the case of Xingu; rhetorically, as for Cavalcanti; and ideologically, through the notion of education—the state's indigenist apparatus indeed implemented quite the opposite of protection. This ambiguity, as we now know, would be a harbinger of dark days to follow—dark days still lived by the indigenous and nonindigenous peoples of Pará as I once again revise these pages. In continuity with the imperialist pulling apart of time, space, and place that hailed Brazilian modernity, the work of indigenist protection, Indian schooling, and "development" would go hand in hand with the division, distribution, and swallowing up—*deglutição*—of Native peoples and their lands. As in David Norman's imaginary and not-so-imaginary world, where impunity reigns and the Amazon is ever subject to the whims of power, "undoing primitiveness" in the name of science, security, and progress would become the patriotic task of the hour. And the eternal question would remain, How do we turn a profit off of our Indians in our America?

4

UNRAVELING INDIANIST
HEGEMONY AND THE MYTH OF THE
BRAZILIAN RACE

Despite the fact that Native peoples account for less than 1 percent of the Brazilian population, "Indians" real and imagined have been key figures in intellectual and political debates over the meaning of Brazilianness since the zenith of romantic Indianism nearly two centuries ago. From the saga of "Indian protection" at the turn of the twentieth century to passionate clashes between indigenous communities and the architects of national development at the turn of the millennium, the idea and experience of indigeneity have always existed in perpetual tension with politicized imaginings of a singular and cohesive Brazilian nationhood. More than three quarters of a century after Oswald de Andrade's cannibalist manifesto gave disgruntled *modernistas* a nationalist metaphor,[1] popular notions of Indianness and Brazilianness continue to feed off one another in "anthropophagous" symbiosis.

Although "the Indian" has typically been imagined, alongside the Portuguese and the African, as one pillar of a uniquely Brazilian *mestiçagem*, indigenist thought and practice have also served as a counterdiscourse to the concept and programmatic endorsement of nation-based homogeneity. Even during the Vargas period, at the height of the state's suffocating and transformative embrace of the so-called Brazilian race, indigenist discourse would not rise above the racialized essentialisms at the heart of its own social and political critique. Dominant indigenist discourse developed across the region in response to the European scientific racism that was refined in human labs on American soil, as well as to the looming cultural imperialism and racial segregation policies of the United States.[2] But when the Brazilian nationalist project of preserving Indianness came face-to-face with competing nationalist projects to "whiten" and "improve" the overall population through programmatic miscegenation, age-old colonialist configurations of "race" and power were inverted, rather than dissolved. "Pure" and "unadulterated" Natives would be idealized and fetishized in accordance with the powerful legacies of the Indianist imagination.

Sociocultural critics have considered the "racially democratic" notion of Brazilian *mestiçagem* in the context of overlapping and sometimes competing paradigms of mixture and change across the Americas, beginning with *assimilation, acculturation,* and *transculturation* during the first half of the twentieth century, and shifting through *heterogeneity, middle ground, hybridity, multiculturalism,* and *interculturality* during the second.[3] In its diverse and oftentimes contradictory iterations, Brazilian indigenism has been implicated in each of these discourses, both in theory and in practice. Transculturation's celebration of *mestiçagem,* which corresponded roughly to the dominance of the national-popular state formation in Latin America,[4] would promote "Indian" assimilation into dominant national societies as inevitable but also always incomplete, while the theories of heterogeneity and hybridity that grew out of the violent crises of national populism posited *mestiçagem* instead as a guarantee of further marginalization for forms of being and knowing that were already marginalized vis-à-vis the dominant majority. Late-twentieth-century discourses of multiculturalism and interculturality were born of this exclusion but would address it in different ways: the former by advocating for social and cultural "diversity" among groups that would "tolerate" but remain essentially unchanged by one another, the latter by calling not only for "tolerance" but also for the egalitarian exchange of ideas and cultural forms despite the sometimes monumental power differentials between subaltern and dominant groups.

The symbiotic relationship between this overarching trajectory of ideological adjustments and shifts and the transformation of indigenist thought and practice was, of course, uneven, inconsistent, and highly contentious. Nonetheless, it would have momentous consequences for the individuals and groups who were interpellated or coerced by it, whether directly, through particular social policies, or indirectly, through the circulation of dominant sociocultural paradigms.

It is now obvious, of course, that the early- and mid-twentieth-century predictions of indigenous disappearance into dominant Brazilian society through assimilation, acculturation, or extermination were entirely off the mark. For reasons including improved (if uneven) access to higher education and health care, shifting perceptions of ethnoracial identity and identification, and the relatively recent possibility for Brazilians to self-identify vis-à-vis the state in terms of "race" and skin color, the official indigenous population more than doubled between 1991 and 2000 and has increased exponentially during the first decade of the twenty-first century.[5] In light of indigenous mobilization around the issue of representation, intellectual and popular debates over the uses and abuses of "Indian" images have taken on a new set of consequences. For anthropologist Veena Das, "the links between aesthetic, legal, and political forms of representation are . . . at the heart of the problem in the theorizing on the relation between culture and power. Yet, if we were not willing to experiment with how much one's own voice finds recognition in other voices—and, conversely, with when it is that in speaking for oneself, one is also legitimately speaking for another—it would be hard to conceive of any democratic processes at all. Hence the category of shared experience as a ground from which this recognition may stem has some attractive possibilities, provided we do not slip into the idea of a pregiven subject to whom experience happens."[6]

Although in the case of indigenous peoples, such "pregiven subjects" indeed abound and remain powerfully informed by colonialist imaginaries, the question of what happens when dominant ideas about "Indians" come up against indigenous experience has changed in many ways since the Brazilian state's attempted co-optation of Indianness some seventy years ago. Following on the patriotic glorification of Carlos Gomes's Indianist operas in the nineteenth and early twentieth century, and the simultaneous exploitation of indigenous lands and lives during the early Vargas period, this chapter considers the ways the growing breach between Indianist ideals and indigenist practice played out on the national stage and in the lives of indigenous peoples from the mid-twentieth century to the turn of the millennium.

O CASO DIACUÍ: "NOT A STORYBOOK ROMANCE"

What became known as the "case of Diacuí" began in August 1952, when Ayres Câmara Cunha, a thirty-five-year-old *gaúcho* from Uruguaiana, located in the interior of Brazil's southernmost and historically "whitest" state,[7] decided to seek legal union with a young Kalapalo woman named

Diacuí Canualo Aiute. Cunha had worked in the Xingu forests for over a decade and was employed as a *sertanista*, or backlands explorer, by the state-run Fundação Brasil Central (Central Brazil Foundation, or FBC).[8] Though rapt with Aiute from their very first encounter, when she was just thirteen years old, Cunha traveled in and out of her community and her life for five years before "capricious Destiny" finally united them as lovers.[9] One of several state employees accused of having improper relations with indigenous women that year,[10] Cunha was found guilty in an official FBC inquiry and threatened with the loss of his job and definitive expulsion from Xingu. Faced with a sentence that would have punished him for cohabiting with Aiute in her *aldeia* of Kuluene for six months, Cunha sought an alternative outcome for the illicit romance: In response to the guilty verdict, he publicly declared his love for the young woman and announced his desire to make amends for his alleged transgression by marrying her in civil and religious ceremonies. However, because the eighteen-year-old Aiute, like all indigenous peoples in 1950s Brazil, was legally a ward of the state,[11] Cunha would have to seek permission for the marriage from her official guardians at the Serviço de Proteção aos Índios (Indian Protection Service, or SPI), which by that time had been removed from the War Ministry and integrated into the Ministry of Agriculture.[12]

While the SPI began deliberating a judgment on the proposed union, Cunha left Xingu for Rio de Janeiro, seeking to meet with indigenist officials and to plead his case for the marriage. His professed intention, as he would explain years later, was to "live forever in the forest among his indigenous friends and help them morally and materially."[13] But his dreams would be dashed: At their first meeting, SPI director José Maria de Gama Malcher heard the *sertanista*'s appeal with indifference, instructing him to put his request in writing and return at a later date for an official verdict.[14] Two days later, with requested paperwork in hand, Cunha was received instead by SPI ethnographers Darcy Ribeiro and Eduardo Galvão, who dismissed his petition as ludicrous and advised him that the request to marry Aiute would never be granted, regardless of any argumentation he might have been able to offer. Angry but unwavering, Cunha went on record as having responded: "Well, you all should know, once and for all, that with or without the consent of the SPI, I will marry the Indian girl!"[15]

Thus faced with the all but certain denial of his request, Cunha released his story to the national press corps with the assistance of the powerful and politically connected newspaper baron Assis Chateaubriand.[16] Within days, newspapers throughout the country transformed the affair into a Romeo and Juliet production intriguing enough to rival modern-day

Brazilian soap operas. An initial interview published in Rio de Janeiro's *Diário da Noite* on 4 October 1952 set the tone for a melodramatic media campaign that lasted for months. The headlines read: "White Man Wants to Marry Kalapalo Indian: 'I Really Like Diacuri [*sic*]; It's Not a Story-book Romance.'" The interview read as follows:

> Beckoned by Mr. Arquimedes Perreira Lima, president of the Central Brazil Foundation, to give details in an interview conceded yesterday to the same organization, FBC employee Aires [*sic*] Câmara Cunha added a curious bit of information to the report.
>
> "I'd like to take advantage of this opportunity to make an appeal, through the press, for the appropriate authorities to add a clause to the rules of the SPI permitting the marriage of whites to Indians. . . .
>
> "I'm crazy about a Kalapalo Indian woman whose community is located on the banks of the Kuluene River. I really like her, it's not a storybook romance, the kind you see in bookstores."
>
> "And you want to marry her?" was the general question. . . .
>
> "Diacuri, daughter of a Kalapalo medicine man, a svelte and pretty young woman she is my chosen one."
>
> "How do you say 'my darling' in Kalapalo?"
>
> "Ah! I don't know. I haven't yet had the chance to learn. I've known Diacuri for a long time. I know she likes me a lot, but I always respected her."
>
> And concluding the report, Mr. Aires Cunha added:
>
> "Don't forget to make my appeal. Do it for me and for the friendship that I devote to Diacuri."[17]

Cunha's tactic worked: In the wake of Vargas's heavy-handed cultural management, and in the postwar context of heightened awareness of eugenics and opposition to "European-style" racism, the prospect of a pro-hibited "interracial" marriage sparked endless debate about the "Indian problem" and the SPI's appropriate role in solving it. Reflected in and nourished by sensationalist coverage, the controversy hit the press at a critical moment in the history of indigenism and the cultural politics of "race" across Brazil.

By the time Cunha and Aiute became front-page news, the SPI's indig-enist practice had evolved dramatically since the institution's 1910 found-ing to reflect both diminished confidence in the enterprise of Native assimilation and the increasing conviction that indigeneity was, perhaps, an immutable social, cultural, and ethnic marker that would not be so readily undone by covering people in Western dress and teaching them

Portuguese. Contrary to its original mission as a civilizing agency of the state, this retailored perspective within the SPI sought to "accommodate the Indians' resistance, understand its role in assuring their right to live according to traditional customs, protect them from the violence of civilized invaders, and guide their progressive integration into regional life in a manner that would guarantee survival."[18] Official indigenism in the early 1950s hence began to acknowledge its frustrated assimilationist ambitions and to consider the pervasive indigenous subversion of traditional assimilationist ideas and policies, yielding instead to the project of "improving" Indians rather than trying to do away entirely with them or their Indianness.

The slow evolution of indigenist practice within the state's primary indigenist body was, however, also taking place in the broader context of President Getúlio Vargas's proactive, citizen-making populism, which outlawed racial discrimination for the first time in national history while sanctioning racist practices in public institutions ranging from schools and museums to government agencies.[19] Building on a model of social liberalism that intellectuals had for decades raised up in radical contrast to segregationist governance in the United States, Vargas embraced the powerful Freyrean assessment of Brazil as a would-be utopia of racial mixture in order to round out the administration's complementary strategies for the economic, social, and cultural development embodied in the Marcha para o Oeste (March to the West).[20] Cunha's employer, the FBC, was indeed one of the organizations fashioned by Vargas's regime to expedite westward expansion by developing the interior and securing the country's precarious western and northern borders. As a centerpiece of the authoritarian regime, the expansion initiative embodied for the president an "integrated alliance between the campaign of the founders of Brazilian nationality—namely, the *bandeirantes* and *sertanistas*—and the processes of modern culture."[21]

In the overlapping aims and operations of the state's indigenist bureaucracy and the burgeoning administration of national development, "the Indians"—despite their relatively small numbers—took on a major role in the drama of frontier expansion that played out in the popular press. In contrast to the anti-assimilationist contingent of the SPI, who aimed to preserve some form of Indianness in an enhanced and hence more acceptable form, Vargas's sociocultural agenda vis-à-vis Indianness was more in keeping with the early-twentieth-century goals of doing away entirely with cultural, social, racial, and linguistic difference and homogenizing the Brazilianness of all Brazilians. Indigenist doctrine under *varguismo* thus continued to bestow great importance on the symbolic Indian while working to make indigenous peoples fade into an expanding *mestiça* and increasingly "developed" sociocultural landscape (*paisagem*).

The diverging social and political goals of the Vargas administration and the leadership of its foremost indigenist agency would become glaringly evident in the case of Cunha and Aiute. Although indigenist officials disagreed deeply over the *sertanista*'s request to marry, the initial verdict of the SPI's governing council—the Conselho Nacional pela Proteção dos Índios (National Council for the Protection of Indians, or CNPI)—was negative.[22] Their decision was based on the premise that the primary goal of "Indian protection" was to assure that enduring, "uncorrupted" Indians remained so for as long as possible.[23] In this view, the legal union of a white man and Native woman would set a dangerous precedent and potentially jeopardize the physical well-being and moral integrity of indigenous peoples in all government protected areas. Some SPI leaders also frowned on the fact that Cunha and Aiute neither spoke nor understood a common language,[24] adding that as a member of an "extremely primitive" tribe, the young Kalapalo woman was simply still "too Indian" to marry a "civilized man." Such coupling could only rightfully be considered, they argued, when the Indian in question had been tempered with enough of dominant national culture to be considered a *neo-brasileiro*.[25]

Darcy Ribeiro—the young SPI ethnographer who would later become a well-known educator, politician, and novelist—was serving as the head of the SPI's Educational Sector at the time the *caso Diacuí* developed. When asked to testify to the CNPI, he adopted the concept of "neo-Brazilianness" to justify his own strong opposition to the marriage. In characteristically impetuous and impassioned style, he submitted:

The forty years of indigenist activity in which the SPI has not only allowed but encouraged interracial marriage in the majority of its [Indigenous] Posts demonstrate that marriage is not a process of assimilation, but the result of acculturation in its final stage. . . . The Indians of the Guarani, Iawano, Kadiwéu, Bacaerí [*sic*], Tembé, and so many other tribes that marry civilized people do not behave like Indians linked to tribal life but like neo-Brazilians, who are integrated into our customs, speak our language, and have a concrete idea of what awaits them in married life. Countless concrete cases tell us that such marriages frequently result in happy unions. However, for a Xavante, a Urubá, a Caiapó, and a Xinguano who live isolated in their territories, which have yet to be reached by our society, who don't speak any language other than their own, and [who] understand marriage [only] in terms of the emotional associations of their tribes, the union with an outsider is an adventure with zero possibility of success.[26]

Ribeiro's unyielding position was shared by the majority of CNPI members, who after days of intense debate refused Cunha's request by a vote of six to one.[27] On 11 October 1952, the *Folha da Tarde* simplified the council's decision, settled only after countless hours of philosophical, political, and scientific discussion, into one banal argument: "If whites become interested in Indians, Indians won't have anyone else to marry."[28]

While the CNPI and the SPI were busy deliberating the nature of Indianness and the racial future of Brazil, the media support that Cunha had sought and received from Assis Chateaubriand following the SPI's disapproval of the marriage had begun to generate a torrent of public opinion about the implications of the case for Brazilian society at large. In 1952—eight years prior to the inauguration of Brasília and before the widespread use of television across the country—indigenous areas were inaccessible to many residents of the increasingly urban Southeast, where most of the debate over the prospect of "interracial" marriage took place. The limited nature of national travel, especially to places like the Alto Xingu, meant that most Brazilians would have to rely on a handful of personal and journalistic accounts to catch even a glimpse of the more "imagined" members of their national community.[29] Faced with an abundance of sensationalized and ethnographic interpretations, public recourse to the realm of the imaginary made the influence of popular and canonical (if not necessarily widely read) Indianist novels even more significant. For many urbanites, Diacuí Canualo Aiute would in fact be fatefully transformed into José de Alencar's indigenous protagonist Iracema, whose name gave title to his most famous novel, first published in 1865.[30]

A prevalent figure in the national and nationalist imaginary since the late nineteenth century, Alencar's tragic heroine was the "honey-lipped virgin" whose illicit and ill-fated romance with a white soldier (Martim) resulted in the *mestiço* love child Moacyr—the "son of suffering." When Martim tired of his Indian lover and abandoned her for travel and wartime adventure, Iracema's soul dried up with her breast milk. Shriveled in body and spirit, unable to nourish her newborn son, and unwilling to face the prospect of life without her beloved, she would perish from heartbreak after placing Moacyr safely in the arms of his hard-hearted father, just back from exciting and victorious battles fought alongside Native friends and allies. While Iracema thus disappeared, her mixed-blood progeny came to embody (albeit not without opposition)[31] the idealized fusion of Old World civilization and New World vitality at the heart of the nineteenth-century Indianist movement.

Its title an anagram of "America," *Iracema* has been treated by prominent literary scholars as an allegory of the colonial encounter that was politicized in support of a particular set of intellectual nation-building projects.[32] Building on those analyses, critic David Treece has examined the vigorous political upheavals and profound social reformulations that served as the backdrop for Alencar's interventions into debates over much broader issues, including abolition and republicanism, as well as the burgeoning notion of Brazilianness itself. "Once combined with the concept of miscegenation," Treece observes, "Alencar's mythology acquired an ideological force that reached far beyond the Indianist movement itself. . . . This notion of a conciliatory, collaborative relationship between races . . . is the first manifestation of . . . a tradition of *mestiço* nationalism that is best known in its twentieth-century form as elaborated by Gilberto Freyre and associated with the phrase 'racial democracy.'"[33] Thus Alencar, like his early Indianist contemporaries Antônio José Gonçalves Dias and Domingos José Gonçalves de Magalhães, used Indian images to advance a politicized interpretation of empire and the racialized legacies of colonialism while championing a new sense of nationhood that might do more than replicate Europe. Working to loosen dominant intellectual discourses either delicately or forcefully from their Portuguese roots, romantic Indianists would engage the most divisive politics of their day, planting the seeds for explorations of Brazilian national identity that would flourish well into the twentieth century and coalesce tragically around the lives of an ambitious *sertanista* and a smitten Kalapalo teenager.

The immediate result of Cunha's collaboration with news mogul Assis Chateaubriand was a passionate public debate over the indigenist veto of his proposal to marry Aiute. Ironically, the saga of the contentious union would play out like a modern-day *folhetim*—the popular serial form in which another famous tale of white-Indian romance (Alencar's first novel, *O guarany*), had appeared with such success nearly a century earlier.[34] Although the editorial pages revealed some resistance among the general population to the idea of indigenous peoples marrying outside their communities and living outside their proper surroundings, public opinion was overwhelmingly favorable to Cunha and critical of the "racist" indigenist authorities who had so coldheartedly denied his request. With the influence of sympathetic politicians, including Minister of Agriculture João Cleofas, who finally reversed the SPI decision,[35] public enthusiasm aroused by the spirited media crusade paved the way for Cunha to meet his fiancée at the altar.

By mid-November 1952, Aiute received SPI authorization to accompany Cunha to Rio de Janeiro. Hyped by stirring headlines, her visit to the Cidade Maravilhosa was an elaborate and awkward spectacle during which she either fulfilled or frustrated the Indianist fantasies of the tens of thousands of *caraíbas* (nonindigenous or "white" Brazilians) who flocked to see her. A massive throng of spectators witnessed the couple's arrival at the Santos Dumont Airport, creating havoc as they sought a glimpse of the Flor dos Campos (Flower of the Fields). The following day, the *Diário da Noite* headline read, "Indescribable Delirium at the Airport: Diacuí in Rio—Crowd Breaks through the Cordons!"[36]

Straight from the forests of Xingu and lacking venerated romantic graces—like honey lips and a light, airy stride—the young Kalapalo woman fell short of the prevailing ideal of Indian comeliness held by many of her urban critics. To rectify the problem, she was treated to a well-publicized Helena Rubenstein makeover, embellished with "Indian-looking" necklaces, and cloaked in colorful (but civilized) outfits. Journalists who marveled over her "exotic beauty" and easy adaptation to life in the big city showcased her skill with a toothbrush, a comb, heeled shoes, a sewing machine, and even a book: *Beleza e personalidade*—the "key to success of any civilized woman."[37] Elite bridal shops scrambled in competition for the privilege of creating the much-anticipated wedding dress, and the winning gown, adorned with white dove and heron feathers, was "inspired by jungle themes."[38] Wedding arrangements were covered with minute detail and editorial pages revealed a mix of delight and disgust over the logistical details and bureaucratic intricacies leading up to the blessed occasion.

Finally, on 29 November 1952, Cunha and Aiute wed in the presence of more than 10,000 onlookers, who flooded to Rio de Janeiro's famous Candelária cathedral to watch the historic ceremony.[39] The bride would only make it to the altar with her dress in tatters and missing her petticoat, which had been tugged off by the adoring crowd as she made her way down the packed aisle. One reporter described the onlookers as a "sea" of women who engulfed the bride and her *padrinho* ("godfather" or sponsor) while clapping and yelling, "Diacuí is precious! What a beautiful dress! She is Brazilian, more Brazilian than we are."[40]

As Cunha had promised to Kalapalo and indigenist authorities, the couple returned to Xingu after the wedding, and the newspaper debates tapered off. Nine months later, however, public interest stirred once more

"The Kalapalo Bride [Diacuí Canualo Aiute] in her gorgeous white dress, with a brocade taffeta skirt and a blouse covered in heron and dove feathers. The diadem stood out from her black, silky hair." From Gurgel, "Abençoada." Photo by Badaró Braga. Courtesy of the Acervo Jornal Estado de Minas/O Cruzeiro.

when news spread that Aiute had perished in her *aldeia* less than a day after giving birth to her first child while Cunha was on the road, ostensibly occupied with work.[41] In fact, as his young wife agonized in her final hours of life, the *sertanista* was busy traipsing along the banks of the Kuluene River with filmmaker William Gericke, whom he had contacted to make a documentary about his own halting progress in locating the so-called Minas dos Martírios—fabled gold mines sought for centuries by generations of ill-fated explorers and adventurers.[42] Although "transformed" with grief upon learning the terrible news, the *sertanista* would never again lay eyes on his young bride: In keeping with their traditional funerary and mourning rituals, the distraught Kalapalo buried their famous daughter on the very day of her passing.[43] Absolved of a traditional mourning seclusion by his father-in-law, the cacique Kumátse, Cunha declined the community's proposal that he wed one of his wife's siblings (what ethnographer Ellen Basso calls a "brother-sister exchange marriage"),[44] and departed Xingu for his mother's home in Uruguaiana.[45] Accompanying him was his newborn daughter, who would be robbed of the birth name

given to her by her mother's community (Uacapú) and baptized Diacuizinha, or "little Diacuí."[46]

The tragic turn of events revived prenuptial controversies and debates
over the propriety of "Indian-civilized unions," and despite the fact that
Diacuí Canualo Aiute's untimely death had little to do with her unusual
marriage, the SPI's early efforts to prohibit it were largely vindicated in
the public eye. The legion of "indigenist experts" who had opposed the
controversial relationship lamented her demise by reiterating the absolute and exclusive nature of the state's power over the indigenous peoples
within its borders. Notwithstanding its mounting reputation for incom-
petence, inefficiency, and corruption, the SPI was able to reaffirm, albeit
momentarily, its symbolic function as rightful protector of Brazil's indigenous peoples. The somber lesson of Diacuí's death, they contended, was
that the state's indigenist authority ought not be subject to the whims of
an unsophisticated and poorly informed public. Even Cunha's take on the
matter would become ambiguous. Reflecting on his experiences many
years later, the older and wiser *sertanista* announced that he would no
longer "recommend the marriage of whites and Indians," and he reiterated, instead, the discourse of his erstwhile foes in the SPI. As he had
surmised from his ill-fated marriage, "the cultural unevenness was just
too great an obstacle to the full union of both [parties]."[47]

THE "REAL STORY" OF DIACUÍ

Cunha characterized his early memoirs as a two-pronged effort through
which he sought, on the one hand, to reflect "scientifically" on many years
of cohabitation with the Native peoples of the Alto Xingu and, on the other
hand, to relay a behind-the-scenes version of his inauspicious love affair in
the midst of so much hype and speculation (mostly initiated, of course, by
him).[48] Following in the footsteps of colonial chroniclers who captivated
far-away readers with unabridged and "truthful" versions of the Conquest,
Cunha beguiled his audience with an epic tale titled *Entre os índios do
Xingu: A verdadeira história de Diacuí* (*Among the Indians of Xingu: The
Real Story of Diacuí*). The commentary of Willy Aureli, editor of the Club
do Livro publishing house that would issue one of Cunha's later books,
underscored the power of one man to interpret "savage" and "mysterious" realities by producing adventurous ethnography for readers who had
little if any contact with indigenous peoples in Brazil or elsewhere. He
observed: "Ayres is no novice in the field of literature. His book . . . reveals
his true value as a narrator, observer—and why not say it?—historian of

indianistic [*sic*] realities almost entirely unknown to the public at large. I truly hope that he reaps great rewards from this additional undertaking, which reveals his magnificent and valuable contribution to the study of a world that is new, savage, beautiful, and profound, like the mystery of the majestic and impressive jungles."[49]

Cunha's rendering of the story read like a romantic fantasy in which he appeared as an upstanding citizen and passionate hero, who out of disillusion with the greedy and frivolous nature of bourgeois society sought a simple and peaceful life in the Upper Xingu. He explained: "I married Diacuí only for love. I was a *sertanista*, already thirty-five years old, and felt rather disappointed by the outside world. I didn't expect anything else from mankind. I wanted only to finish out my days in the isolation of an indigenous village, far from Civilization and social conventions. Perhaps the consequence of my profound dismay was a lack of love—that irresistible feeling that consumes destinies, reforms delinquents, modifies temperaments, and transforms the life of the powerful."[50] Cunha also recognized, however, that his relationship with Aiute was much more than a forbidden romance. It was also a symbolic covenant for the future of Brazil between white and indigenous, conqueror and conquered, modernity and antiquity. As he put it: "The desire of the Kalapalo bride and the white man became . . . a true national petition. The people, from their different walks of life, together with high civilian and military authorities, wanted the wedding because everyone saw . . . in the union of the couple from the forests of Xingu, more than just happiness; . . . [they also saw] the harmonization of the Brazilian races and a process for the gradual integration of jungle dwellers into the national community."[51]

Positioning himself in opposition to the "racists"[52] who had spoken out against the marriage, Cunha recounted how even "primitive" indigenous leaders had been forward-thinking enough to embrace the union: "I agreed to the conditions of the Kalapalo. I would marry Diacuí and live with her forever in the Indian village. Hence was settled the racial romance between a white man from the Atomic Age and a little jungle woman from the Stone Age."[53]

Consistent with the cultural propaganda of *varguismo*, Cunha posited that "nonracists" had endorsed his union with Aiute because they favored the "racial unity" of national society. Those who disputed the "scientific" opposition of the SPI and CNPI, he pointed out,[54] had applauded his marriage as a valuable extension of his years of generous service to the country.[55] By marrying Aiute, it followed, the patriotic *gaúcho* had helped to drag the "uncivilized" young woman out of her backwardness and into the nation. Considering that no verbal exchange was likely to have occurred when Aiute and other members of her community met with Vice President Café Filho,[56] the minister of war, the minister of agriculture, and members of the National Congress on her trip to the nation's capital, the calculated symbolism of such encounters far exceeded any practical result they might have brought about and were perfectly in line with the institutionalization and consolidation of "cultural management" that evolved out of the Estado Novo.[57] Alongside Cunha, Cândido Rondon, and Vargas himself, these state representatives were welcoming Diacuí Canualo Aiute not to Rio de Janeiro but to civilization and neo-Brazilianness.

Outside the principal indigenist apparatus, the patriotic duties carried out by representatives of the Vargas regime spoke to one of the most widespread criticisms of the SPI and CNPI during the middle of the twentieth century: that they were not doing their job quickly or effectively enough. As one editorialist lamented, "The Brazilian Indian can and should be incorporated into the active populations of the country. We have inside [our] national territory at least 500,000 pairs of arms that could be producing for the well-being of us all. We do nothing to make that a reality."[58] Where, in other words, were all the "neo-Brazilians"? For many of the SPI's urbanite critics, the resolution of the "Indian problem" was long overdue considering that the SPI had already been in place for over four decades.

The nature of "neo-Brazilianness" in SPI and public discourse was customarily indistinct, although arguments in its favor alluded predominantly to questions of language ability and the value of material labor to serve the collective national good. To those ends, the idea and institutionalization of indigenous education would be fundamental to neocitizenship.[59] Upon learning of Aiute's death, President Vargas intervened personally to guarantee that her motherless child would have a "proper education." Even naysayers who had expressed distaste over the circumstances that brought Diacuizinha into the world were heartened by the administration's effort to guarantee Cunha's daughter an opportunity, at least, to become Brazilian.

At the same time, however, others expressed the desire for some aura of pure Indianness to remain—an aura that harked back to the dreamy Indianist tradition of a timeless world unscathed by the corruption and disappointments of modernization and urban life. One editorial writer waxed sentimental: "President Getúlio Vargas has demonstrated an attitude that has moved the whole country: he decided to save the little girl by providing resources for her education. . . . The leader of the Nation is in touch with the sentiments of the Brazilian people. . . . Confronted with the extraordinary, moving story of Diacuí, we have but one abiding desire: that the Kuluene River send to the civilized people of Guanabara other Indian girls as mystical and delicate as the Flower of the Fields, so that we might feel, from time to time, a bit of rustic poetry in the midst of so many urban falsities and lies masquerading as beauty."[60]

UNRAVELING THE INDIANIST FANTASY

In the intellectual and political bastions of the dominant majority, Diacuí Canualo Aiute and her love affair with "civilization" were simultaneously real and imaginary, fact and fiction, theory and practice. Likened by the general public to the mythical characters of Indianist literature for her "Indian beauty" (despite the complaints regarding her lack thereof), Aiute was at the same time subjected to the scientific scrutiny and bureaucratization of the state's indigenist apparatus. Never was she treated as an individual with ideas and opinions about her own situation, let alone about the rapidly changing world in which she lived. In hundreds of pages of materials that document her short life, the fact of Aiute's speech is indeed noted only in the memoirs of her husband, who sparsely interjected her "Indian talk" into his text to infantilize his "childlike" bride even further;[61] and twice by the *carioca* paparazzi who chronicled relentlessly her every move on their turf. On the first occasion, she "yelled a bunch of words in Kalapalo" on the way to the altar as zealous admirers tugged at her clothing, but no one bothered to report what the words were, or even speculated as to what they might have meant.[62] On the second occasion, Aiute expressed a "sonorous yes" to the question—reportedly posed through a translator—as to whether she really wanted to marry Cunha.[63] In the public saga that chronicled these silences, the young woman's self-expression would be limited to a few shy smiles and awkward poses for the photographers looking to circulate her "naked innocence" to the papers.

While state functionaries quarreled over the rationale and execution of official "Indian policy," popular judgment on the *caso Diacuí* brought to light the vacuous nature of much of the academic and legal discourse upon which that policy had been based. The goals of the SPI became, at best, ambiguous and, at worst, absurd for a general public who perceived the "interracial" scandal as an affront to cherished notions of nationhood and national belonging. Drawing attention to an area of public policy that had gone largely unseen by mainstream society, the controversy became a thorn in the side of the indigenist bureaucracy, calling into question what the SPI and its collaborators had been doing for all those years with

The Diário da Noite *headline of 21 October 1952 read: "Symbol of the National Communion: The wedding, in Rio, of the little Kalapalo Indian to the white sertanista." CNPI member Heloisa Alberto Tôrres cited such "scandalous" photographs of Diacuí Canualo Aiute, otherwise known as "A Flor dos Campos," as evidence to support her position against the marriage of Aiute to Ayres Câmara Cunha. Courtesy of the Acervo da Fundação Biblioteca Nacional—Brasil.*

public resources that were supposed to be churning out neo-Brazilians on "Indian posts" across the country.

Public indignation over the official prohibition of the marriage thus encapsulated the cynicism that had arisen by midcentury over the state's overall handling of indigenous affairs. One irritated commentator protested:

> Only a crazy person could permit these racist principles in a Fatherland like ours, whose glory lies precisely in its ethnic patchwork, completely stripped of the prejudices that there—outside, in the old civilizations— are only unearthed to protect economic interests. . . . According to the "big wigs" of the Serviço de Proteção aos Índios, the marriage is impossible for three reasons: (1) because of the rule that would give so

much happiness to the little soul of the deceased Comte Gobineau;[64] (2) because of *mestiçagem*, which the good sir considers inferior; and (3) because of the zero-culture of the lovely Diacuí, with [her] splendid smile and big, naked breasts. . . . More audacious idiocies have yet to be declared below the tranquil and pleasing skies of our land! . . . If the protection that they give our poor Indians is this spectacle of racist segregation, . . . why continue to spend so much money with these mongrels of the jungle, so abundant in beards and stupidity?[65]

Such condemnation stemmed, in large part, from the idealized notions of a "Brazilian race" propagated through conventional historiography in which Vargas's populist discourse had found a comfortable home. Criticism proliferated: How could the indigenists adhere to rigid, *foreign* notions of racial difference while progressive intellectuals and politicians were struggling to heal the deep social wounds inflicted by so many generations of Eurocentric racism and imported racial engineering? Why keep indigenous peoples isolated from "mainstream society" when influential thinkers like Gilberto Freyre, Cândido Rondon, and even President Vargas himself were hard at work promulgating Brazil as a harmonious amalgam of diverse "races" and cultures?

Significantly, the national debates over the *caso Diacuí* took place during the same year that the recently established UNESCO undertook an extensive study of Brazilian race relations. Its aim was to demonstrate the relative success of ethnic and cultural assimilation and "interracial" harmony in Brazil, as opposed to legal segregation in the United States and other manifestations of racial discrimination and violence across the Americas. Investigations carried out in the states of Bahia, Pernambuco, Rio de Janeiro, and São Paulo all demonstrated, however, that quite to the contrary of national and international expectations, the systematic and individual discrimination of Afro-descendants ("*negros*" and "*mulatos*") was patent in all four cases.[66]

Ethnographer Darcy Ribeiro—a key SPI authority from the *caso Diacuí* and a lifelong spokesman for Brazilian exceptionalism—was charged with the portion of the UNESCO project examining indigenous assimilation into dominant national society. In keeping with his unfavorable verdict on the Cunha-Aiute marriage, he generated a report that disappointed aspiring racial democrats for its obliteration of popular imaginings about the success and inclusive power of nation-based *mestiçagem*. He argued:

In every case that I was able to observe, no indigenous group was converted into a Brazilian village. It is true that . . . some locations previously occupied by Indians became neo-Brazilian communities. But there was no assimilation that transformed Indians into Brazilians. The Indians were simply exterminated through various forms of biotic, ecological, economic, and cultural coercion. Their old habitat, occupied by other people with whom they never identified, grew based on other forms of ecological adaptation and quickly became independent of any contribution by the indigenous community.[67]

Like the contentious Diacuí debates, then, the unexpected and unwelcome findings of the UNESCO report confirmed that the progressive racial attitudes and cordial racial politics showcased by the Vargas administration were in fact counter to widespread social and economic realities.[68] As far as the architects of official culture were concerned, such unpleasant scenes would best remain out of the national and (especially) the international spotlight.[69]

By favoring Aiute's "improvement" through marriage, antagonists of SPI "racism" upheld the belief that caring persuasion could provide a desirable alternative to civic education and brute force in working toward the goals of national unity and progress. After all, what motivation more powerful than love to expedite the arduous processes of civilization and integration that would continue to be so vital to modernization and development? In light of this rhetorical uncertainty, the concept of neocitizenship that had been used initially to deny Cunha and Aiute the right to marry would also hold the redemptive possibility of Brazilianness. That is, the nation would only be possible if the real *as well as* the symbolic union of whites and Indians could prevail. The pervasive criticism spawned by the censure of one such union hence reflected not only an ongoing interrogation of the "Brazilian race" and national identity but also the growing divergence between a burgeoning civil society and the contradictory cultural authority of the state. The *caso Diacuí* marked a watershed moment in ethnoracial politics and the question of indigenous representation, for the clash between the "protection"-based mandate of the indigenist apparatus and the pro-*mestiço*, citizen-making agenda of the Vargas administration meant that the state's manipulation of Brazilianness had ultimately come into conflict with itself.

"DIACUÍ KILLED IRACEMA"

Although Aiute and Cunha's short-lived relationship was summarily reduced to ethnography and political debate, the symbolic value of their marriage would eventually outweigh its scientific and legal consequences. While lawyers, politicians, bureaucrats, and academics considered the matter in technical terms, the broader population was caught up in issues too passionate to be contained by the technical scrutiny and bureaucratic conundrums of the hour. Notwithstanding the inconsistency of popular and intellectual notions of Indianness, Brazilianness, and *mestiçagem*, the case revealed a common conceptual contradiction across a broad spectrum of indigenist thinking and its different points of intersection with the politics of identity and identification. That is, while "Indians" were the unqualified referent of all versions of indigenist discourse, ranging from those seeking the eternal preservation of Indianness to those seeking its swift disappearance (and all the positions in between), there was no underlying ideological or operational scheme in place to establish what it might mean to "be Indian" in lived human experience, in Rio de Janeiro or in the forests of Xingu. Simply put, who would be considered "Indian," by whom, and on what grounds?

Although Darcy Ribeiro's 1952 reflections on neo-Brazilianness and subsequent elaboration of "ethnic transfiguration" would approximate these questions,[70] a comparable examination at the crossroads of indigenist thought and indigenist practice was never documented in relation to the case at hand. What is more, the "criteria for Indianness" charted by state indigenist officials nearly thirty years after the death of Diacuí Canualo Aiute indicated that superficial and indeterminate notions of Indianness would long outlive the SPI, which was disbanded by the military government and replaced by the Fundação Nacional do Índio (FUNAI) in 1967.[71]

The colonialist distribution of power at the heart of the *caso Diacuí*, like other political manipulations of Indianness both before and after 1952, indicated how the bureaucratization and administration of indigeneity required taking a step back from the materiality of daily life into fictitious or scientific abstraction with little or no capacity to represent the individuals or groups identified or self-identified with it. Apart from the sensationalist coverage of recently "discovered" or "pacified" groups and echoes of white-Indian conflict on the expanding borders of "civilization," flesh-and-blood indigenous peoples were not particularly newsworthy in midcentury Brazil, despite the Vargas administration's best efforts to fashion "Indians" into passive protagonists of the nation-building enterprise. In perpetual conflict and contradiction with the realm of lived experience, Indians of idealized national history became evermore real as people tightened their embrace of the comfortable and convenient visions of treasured Indianist fantasy. One concerned citizen was inspired to comment on the Aiute-Cunha affair after an unpleasant encounter with a small group of indigent Natives near her home in São Paulo:

> Yes, a remarkable case, that of the charming Indian girl who arrived with the chief of the tribe in an airplane, and ended up, like in fairy tales, marrying the prince. But there was no need for so much worry over the effects of marriage, those questions about race and adaptation and the effects of civilization. . . . There are many Indians on the loose, abandoned to die on street corners or beg for charity, who are more in need of protection than their more intelligent brothers who stayed in the jungle—without clothing, it's true, but dressed with a bit of their dignity. Iracemas and Moemas, Ubirajaras and Peris, where are the glories and beauty, the songs of poets and gurgling, green oceans? After this, neither Gonçalves Dias nor José de Alencar could, on a Saturday afternoon, write a poem or tell a tale of the rustic beauty of the Indians of Brazil.[72]

Even if the essence of Gaúdio's criticism was her immense displeasure over the fact that so much time, energy, and money had been spent on Aiute while the situation of indigenous peoples elsewhere remained deplorable, the only benchmark by which she would—or perhaps, could—assess their collective well-being was the Indianist fiction that predated the foundation of the SPI by half a century and its romantic re-creation by the likes of José Maria de Medeiros, who in 1884 was granted the title of officer of the Ordem da Rosa for his painting of Iracema.

As another writer expressed, the enthusiastic proponents of Aiute's marriage to Cunha were united in their shock and grief upon learning of the young woman's passing: "The whole country bears the painful death of Diacuí. . . . Around her nearly legendary feminine silhouette, in which we discovered the sleeping beauty of Iracema, was fashioned a halo of admiration, both sublime and ineffable. Rio prepared to receive Diacuí as if to take part in a religious procession, or watch, with due distinction, the wedding rituals of a royal princess. . . . Without a doubt, she embodied that other little Indian girl 'with lips of honey' that José de Alencar gave to us in our childhood through his immortal work."[73] Still others remained unconvinced by the hype over Aiute and her "legendary feminine silhouette." One commentator found inspiration for some misdirected hostility in the polemical photographs that had become a centerpiece of Cunha's crusade for "racial justice." For him, Aiute's life served merely to extinguish a cherished illusion:

José Maria de Medeiros, Iracema, *1884. Oil on canvas, 168.3 × 255 cm.
Photo by Romulo Fialdini. Courtesy of the Coleção Museu Nacional de
Belas Artes/Instituto Brasileiro de Museus/Ministério da Cultura.*

Diacuí is, without a doubt, some type of indigenous beauty. Everyone
saw her physique when the first photos were published *ao natural*
[*sic*], without a bikini bottom, or anything. In all frankness, we have
to recognize that it was not pleasant. And those who read our Indianists were disenchanted. Was Iracema like that? Would the lack of
harmony, the overabundance and flaccidity of body tissue, be compatible with the ideas held by many about the honey-lipped virgin? Would
the White Warrior have fallen in love with an Indian lacking elasticity,
whose sluggish, heavy steps do nothing to evoke a moonbeam skim-
ming across the grass? Diacuí, it seems, came to kill off the charm of
a national legend. Perhaps it was in order to save Alencar's romantic
tradition that they dressed the daughter of the Kalapalos in such haste.
Beauty salons, hairdressers, stylists, everything was mobilized. But it
didn't do any good. Diacuí killed Iracema.[74]

Whether favorable or not, popular interpretations of the *caso Diacuí* thus reflected the enduring hegemony of the nineteenth-century
Indianist imagination and its foundational logic of sentimentalized,

"mixed-race" nationhood. While the indigenists transformed Aiute into the embodiment of an abstract social problem, the public at large made her over, quite literally, into the protagonist of a well-worn romantic plot. The tragedy of Aiute's story thus centers on not only her untimely death but also how her life revealed the inevitable schism between the theorization of the "Indian question" and the interminable flow of words and deeds put forth with the intention of answering it. Abstract reflections on Indianness and national identity at midcentury were seldom considered in relation to the material conditions of indigeneity that would have made it possible or impossible to transform theory into practice, and they thus existed independently from the diverse peoples whose interests and desires those "answers" were supposed to serve and protect. In that pervasive gap, perpetuated through the state's indigenist bureaucracy into the twenty-first century, lies the fundamental contradiction that continues to make it impossible for nationalist discourse to absorb Brazil's indigenous peoples into dominant society through a homogeneous and homogenizing set of political, social, or cultural discourses in accordance with the aspirations and imagination of the nonindigenous majority.

That Diacuí Canualo Aiute was exploited to advance an "antiracist," pro-*mestiço* nationalism and a segregationist, racialized identity politics at the very same time illustrates how the figure of the Indian has been made to stand in for self and Other in both popular and intellectual discourse.[75] If dominant desire still creates a violent disjunction between fetishized Iracemas and people of flesh and blood who have been repeatedly subjected to political maneuvering and ethnographic prodding, it is partly due to the fact that state-backed indigenist politics still engages abstract notions and symbols of Indianness without having resolved, in collaboration with self-identifying indigenous peoples, what indigeneity means in a postmodern society marked by radical heterogeneity of every sort. Although twenty-first century Native activism confronts the same thorny question from the other side—that is, from the presumption of self-identification—it nevertheless stands apart from the colonialist happy ending of assimilationist *mestiçagem*, which either negates indigenous difference altogether, or rests comfortably on the metonymical claim that, as novelist Antônio Torres puts it, "the Indian is the people [*o índio é o povo*]."

Elite hegemony in the creation and imposition of vacuous ethnic and cultural markers continues to govern the real and the imaginary, conferring on subaltern categories like Indianness an interminable and thus highly problematic malleability. As we also know, however, the steady if uneven and incomplete democratization of information and communication technologies means that the "Indian simulacrum" has become increasingly subject to controversy and contestation by self-identifying Native peoples (among others).[76] Nearly sixty years after Aiute's passing, indigenous political and cultural activism in Brazil and across the region intensifies its challenge to the colonialist manipulation of ideas and images that marked her life with tragedy while working to disseminate the indigenous ideas and aspirations markedly absent from her case through a growing variety of nontraditional channels.[77]

BRASIL 500 ANOS

From the streets of Rio de Janeiro at the outset of the new millennium, it was impossible not to notice the scheduled commemoration of Brazil's five-hundredth anniversary of "discovery." In preparation, the all-powerful Globo TV network displayed enormous countdown clocks in strategic locations across the country, including the hub of national and international tourism, Copacabana Beach. Adorned with a map of Brazil superimposed on a globe, the gigantic timekeepers counted down the days remaining until 22 April 2000. The marking of five centuries since Pedro Álvares Cabral arrived on what would eventually become Brazilian soil was expected to inspire patriotic sentiment and festivity, and numerous official activities were planned accordingly. Foremost among the scheduled events was a symbolic and ceremonious meeting of Brazilian president Fernando Henrique Cardoso and Portuguese president Jorge Sampaio in the city of Porto Seguro—not far from the spot where Cabral's crew first arrived to secure the Portuguese foothold in the New World.

Less conspicuous than Globo's massive clocks, perhaps, was the popular reaction they inspired. A typical *carioca* response to Copacabana's imposing timepiece, which cheerfully read, for example, "100 days left till Brazil 500!," was a cynical, "100 days left till that clock goes away." The skepticism was telling, and, as it turned out, the festivity was remarkably subdued on 22 April. Instead, protest rocked the official celebration sites, where violent confrontations between demonstrators and military police dampened enthusiasm for the events and called into question the administration's jubilant tone in organizing them in the first place.

Protestors who hailed from across the country were of all ages, backgrounds, and ways of life. Indigenous groups, *sem-terras*,[78] Afro-Brazilian organizations, and university students, for example, came together to question the celebration of the colonial encounter, whose legacies continue to scar Brazilian society, and to critique a broken and unjust order of which many posited themselves as victims. Reminiscent of 1992, thousands of indigenous activists representing Native peoples from across the country repudiated their compulsory role in the commemoration as the "discovered" tokens of a whitewashed, multicultural "encounter." In light of the violent suppression of their demonstration, the Pataxó, in particular, stood out from the diverse group of protestors as protagonists of anticolonialist sentiment. Images of unarmed "Indians" in confrontation with the military police hit the press almost immediately. In the days and weeks that followed, they became emblematic of indigenous repudiation of "Brasil 500 Anos" and widespread cynicism over the uncritical nature of the intended commemoration.

Despite the indigenous protestors' integration into their opposition platform of specific appeals for legislative and institutional reform, including attention to the unfulfilled rights guaranteed to them by the 1988 Constitution, the symbolic power of their presence swiftly overshadowed the content of their political message.[79] Exploiting the entrenched imagery of Native "resistance" as the flipside of Native suffering, the popular press interpreted the demonstrations metaphorically rather than literally. Indian cartoons and caricatures proliferated, for example, while indigenous protests and political activism, rather than being taken seriously and at face value, were readily appropriated as popular symbols of social subalternity and discontent. Print media reproduced the images with irony and humor, mocking the 22 April "fiasco" and exploiting "the Indian" as an expedient personification of civic distress over Brazil's high ranking on the list of the world's most inequitable societies. Harking back to the *caso Diacuí*, the chaotic quincentennial sparked new reflection on the enduring legacies of colonialism by revealing and recycling the workings of the "Indian simulacrum" at the dawn of the new millennium.

In 2000, however, unlike in 1952, the circulation of colonialist attitudes in the mainstream media brought about two noteworthy changes to an otherwise familiar story: first, visible and vocal indigenous participation in an impassioned national debate over racism and social inequity; and second, an organized indigenous critique of the cavalier exploitation of "Indian" images by and in the mainstream press. In timing with the 22 April protests, for example, members of the National Indigenous Conference drafted a statement to the Human Rights Commission of the Câmera de Deputados (House of Representatives) to protest the negative and ridiculous portrayal of Native Brazilians on a popular Globo soap opera called *Uga! Uga!* The program, they maintained, was damaging to the collective interest of indigenous peoples because it portrayed them as

"Indians" and Brazil's quincentennial celebration of April 2000.
Courtesy of Jean Galvão.

"circus animals used to get the attention of television spectators."[80] Their open letter appeared in Rio's *Jornal do Brasil* and concluded: "We want to make it very clear that we are peoples with living memory. We have not forgotten what happened in the last five hundred years. . . . We have our cultures and we demand respect for our customs and traditions."[81]

A few months later, Xavante filmmakers from the Pernambuco based Vídeo nas Aldeias media initiative projected scenes from *Uga! Uga!* inside São Paulo's bustling Praça da Liberdade subway station and collected testimony from random passersby regarding the perceived merits and shortcomings of the program. The short production, called *Índio na tevê* (Indians on TV), was hosted by Hiparendo Xavante and filmed on 18 September 2000 to commemorate the fiftieth anniversary of Brazilian television. In the film, the young Xavante host, wearing Western dress and earplugs, along with a Xavante cameraman sporting shorts, flip-flops, and body paint, juxtapose the harsh criticisms of some interviewees with other viewers' esteem for the cultural and educational "value" of the soap opera—all the while interspersing images of traditional Xavante ceremonies with melodramatic scenes from *Uga! Uga!* as the backdrop to their metro-station dialogues. Thus portraying, simultaneously, the long road traveled and the steep road ahead, the filmmakers encapsulated the many-layered complexity of indigenous representation in a production that runs just over five minutes.[82]

INDIGENEITY BEYOND IDENTITY

The preference for the imaginary that marked the controversy surrounding the relationship between Diacuí Canualo Aiute and Ayres Câmara Cunha in 1952 was as evident in the nineteenth-century intellectual endeavors to romanticize the Indian into a national icon as it was to the country's five-hundredth anniversary commemoration, where dominant ideas of Indianness proved to be more influential in the popular imaginary than the indigenous people who showed up to voice their opinions about the event. Ironically, the melding and exchange of the real and the imaginary that informs all indigenist discourse, past or present, is at the same time the condition of possibility for the formulation and proliferation of any politics of indigenous identity or identification. At the crossroads of Native activism and indigenist policy, the Indian simulacrum holds the potential promise of democratic heterogeneity alongside and in tension with the potentially dangerous claim to "authenticity," and the political dilemma posed by any assertion of identitarian truth with the power to delegitimize the experience of others. Certainly, self-identifying indigenous peoples are, like the indigenists or other non-Natives, subject to the perils of the hyperreal. Yet without the willingness to brave the tightrope of personal truth over the bottomless pit of authenticity and to experiment, as Das puts it, "with how much one's own voice finds recognition in other voices," there can be no representation of indigeneity—or subalternity, for that matter—that does not always already reinscribe a condition of relative disadvantage.[83]

If we recognize that categories of "race," ethnicity, nationality, and culture are social and historical constructions laden with meaning and irrefutable real-world consequences, then the identities and identifications derived from these markers will always be an articulated means to other ends that may or may not be particular. After all, if communication and understanding among diverse people and peoples has ever been possible, it is surely not only because of our individual, inimitable life stories or the sum of their parts—call them "races," ethnicities, nationalities, or cultures—but, indeed, in spite of them. Whether intended to stand for tolerance or intolerance, to create justice or protect privilege, to ensure rights or to trample them, the tale of one remarkable individual can never reflect the "whole reality of a people" because there is, quite simply, no such thing.[84] There are only the infinite heterogeneities that we condense into and imagine through our chosen and assigned communities, nested like so many Chinese boxes, so that we can try to go on with this difficult business of life.

And while the infinite heterogeneity of all sociopolitical actors means that all discursive practices and social formations evolving from them are also infinitely heterogeneous, the governance of democratic society must ultimately rely on some degree of categorical assumption that can suspend the infinite heterogeneity of every sociopolitical actor, every discursive practice, every social formation. If that suspension is not intentional and strategic, however, social justice can never be served, for any compulsory suspension—the denial of the very right to be what one is, for example—obliterates any democratic *potential* of a social contract that rests, as it always does, on the precarious and precious border between liberty and tyranny—or, as for the Native peoples of the Americas, on the border between life and death. By disavowing a tautological politics of identity that merely feeds on and nourishes "pre-given subjects to whom experience happens,"[85] then, and embracing instead the infinite heterogeneity of those subjects and its purposeful suspension, we might broaden the ground of shared experience and goals beyond the realm of oppressive essentialisms with the simple certainty that, as the saying goes, *cada pessoa é um mundo* (every person is a whole world).

The lessons of Brazil's indigenist history continue to destabilize popular, exclusionary notions of national community by inviting us to question the very notions of self and Other on which they are based, and to acknowledge, at the same time, the radical transformation of indigenous sociopolitical subjectivity that has occurred since the days in which a hushed Kalapalo bride probed the meanings of community and belonging by gracing the front pages of the daily papers. These many years later, securing respect and legal protection for different ways of being and knowing entails not only dismantling the colonialist concepts of Indianness and Brazilianness that shaped the ephemeral existence of Diacuí Canualo Aiute but, even more important, recognizing the heterogeneity *within* indigeneity and all social experience that might have allowed her to be herself, instead of an always imperfect Iracema.

It is to this possibility that we now turn.

5

A NATIVE CRITIQUE OF
SOVEREIGNTY

The Brazilian Indigenous Movement
in the New Millennium

"I can be what you are without ceasing to be who I am," is a slogan that has been circulating in Brazil for over three decades. For the protagonists, collaborators, and sympathizers of the Brazilian indigenous movement, it is a well-worn mantra and manifesto. For the ruling minority, some of whom may be familiar with indigenous history and the legacies of indigenist politics, it is an obscure if not outright hostile claim. And for the dominant majority—those who believe that "Indians" belong to the past, to the jungle, or both—the expression remains as unknown as the cause of Native self-representation itself. "I can be what you are without ceasing to be who I am" is a simple phrase, but deceptively so. After all, who am *I*? Who are *you*? What does it mean to "be what someone else is" or to "cease to be oneself"? What have been and what can be the political consequences of such an enigmatic claim, such a curious feat?

This tenet of the Brazilian indigenous movement defies the dominant nationalist discourses from throughout the region that have long endorsed an expedient move away from "deficient" Indianness through shifting and overlapping paradigms of "cultural loss" and "racial improvement"—ranging, as we have seen, from assimilation, acculturation, transculturation, and *mestizaje/mestiçagem* during the first half of the twentieth century, to hybridity, heterogeneity, multiculturalism, plurinationalism, and inter-culturality beginning in the late 1960s. In the case of Brazil, the claim undergirding the slogan also exists in tension with the enduring ideals of a racially and culturally inclusive nationhood and national identity that are still often invoked in popular discourse as the *raça brasileira*—the so-called Brazilian race. More than the mere affirmation of a differentiated "indigenous identity," though, the idea of becoming like another without ceasing to be oneself posits an indissoluble relationship between indigenous ontologies (ways of being) and epistemologies (ways of knowing), and situates the Native subject in the context of the modern nation-state, where he or she exists in constant contact and potential conflict with dominant forms of being and knowing and, derived from them, with dominant notions of community, belonging, nationhood, citizenship, and sovereignty.

Non-Native scholars have responded to the notion of a distinctive indigenous metaphysics in a variety of ways. In what might be characterized as the methodology of classical anthropology, some researchers, backed by the repertoire and implicit authority of dominant Western thought, have chosen to study, select, and "translate" their interpretations of indigenous being and knowing into the lingua franca of the academy, thus necessarily distorting and simplifying them while, at the same time, playing with the fire of "authenticity" (i.e., whose version of the story to choose?). In 1959, Margaret Mead explained the basic subject-object relationship in her ethnographic research as follows: "The anthropologist understands a great many things about the savages which they do not understand themselves. . . . Although many savages may become good friends who spend long hours helping him [the anthropologist]—dictating stories slowly so he can write them down, patiently explaining just how one man is related to another—they do not understand what scientific work is."[1] As Maori scholar Linda Tuhiwai Smith reiterates, anthropology was, of course, not the only Western field of knowledge to "employ the practices of imperialism in devastating ways."[2] But it has been among the most systematic in its denigration of Native peoples, oftentimes carried out with the best of intentions, including what Trinh Minh-Ha calls the "imperative of making equal."[3]

A second tack among scholars of indigeneity and subalternity has been to assert that differences between indigenous and nonindigenous metaphysics are no more significant than the differences between any two human beings; that the "secret" of Indianness is not so much a hidden truth as it is a carefully deployed stratagem in a larger struggle for political power; and that the very language of "secrets" and impenetrable ways of being and knowing are the stuff of Orientalism, hucksterism, or both. Such interventions, the argument goes, are not merely unhelpful but in fact prejudicial to the interests of so-called subalterns, indigenous or otherwise.[4]

Finally, a third scholarly response to assertions of differentiated indigenous metaphysics has been to affirm that "alternative" (non-Western) indigenous ontologies and epistemologies indeed exist; to attest to their legitimacy and importance vis-à-vis dominant society and history; and to establish or at least announce a politics of solidarity based on the fact of that legitimacy and importance rather than undertake any sustained engagement with the particularities of its content. Self-identifying indigenous and nonindigenous scholars have tended to justify this position quite differently. The former do so by asserting personal regard for and belief in the sacred (frequently expressed in relation to the natural world) or exasperation over the imposed role of "Native informant." The latter do so without being able or daring to speak *for* beliefs, traditions, and ways of life they cannot claim as their own without being construed as charlatans, wannabes, or "New Age Frauds and Plastic Shamans."[5] These nonindigenous scholars refuse to engage in what some social scientists, aggravated by the paralyzing effects of too much "postmodernist critique," have denominated "good-enough ethnography."[6] Such a collection of strategies might be described as the "black box" approach to indigenous metaphysics when employed by self-identifying Native peoples (i.e., what's inside?) or the "Fred Murdock" approach when employed by those who do not identify as indigenous. Either way, those who adopt it manage, like Jorge Luis Borges's enigmatic ethnographer (Murdock),[7] to decipher the "secret" of their indigenous subjects through great insight and personal sacrifice but are ultimately unwilling to subordinate the knowledge gleaned from that discovery to the social and political institutions of the dominant majority or the colonialist intellectual bastions of the ivory tower.

This chapter begins, then, with the sense that each of these approaches, despite their various merits and important differences, leads us to a similar impasse vis-à-vis the possibilities for understanding and collaboration between indigenous and nonindigenous peoples, and with a conviction I share with many of the scholars and activists whose ideas I engage here, that we must continue to work toward a more constructive and respectful way of thinking about the relationship between indigeneity, scholarly discourse, and the political. Seeking to avoid the easy dismissals of mockery and negation, on the one hand, and the pitfalls of distortion, appropriation, and essentialism, on the other, these pages point to the emergence of a postindigenist politics—born not only of the aporias of representation examined in this study but also of the possibilities they present for staking out common ground and creating prospects for solidarity and collaboration in the face of radical and, at times, seemingly irreconcilable difference.

A DOUBLE BIND

M. Marcos Terena, author of the phrase "I can be what you are without ceasing to be who I am," was born in 1954 in the then-unified state of Mato Grosso, in an indigenous *aldeia* called Taunay.[8] He entered the public sphere in the late seventies as a founding member of the União das Nações Indígenas (Union of Indigenous Nations, or UNI). The creation of UNI marked a critical reformulation of the national indigenist politics that culminated in 1988 with the approval of Brazil's most recent constitution, guaranteeing for the first time the right to be simultaneously indigenous and Brazilian—Native and national.[9] In 2010, after nearly three decades of work in political activism and advocacy on behalf of indigenous peoples, Terena won space on the ballot in his home state as a candidate for *deputado federal* (representative in the National Congress). Winning the election would have made him the second Native congressman in the history of republican Brazil.[10]

Over the course of a long and varied professional and political trajectory, Marcos Terena has worked in various capacities to chip away at the colonialist relationship that the Brazilian state initiated with "its" Indians in the years following independence and institutionalized nearly a century later, in 1910, with the Rondonian indigenism of the Serviço de Proteção aos Índios (SPI).[11] Along with dozens of indigenous leaders across the country,[12] he has sought to multiply and expand the spaces of autonomy from which Native Brazilians can represent themselves in every sense of the word, and particularly in the realms of cultural production and national politics. Where Indianist writers and indigenist functionaries once spoke uncontested on behalf of their Native compatriots through the arts and state policy, indigenous Brazilians have increasingly surmounted political, social, cultural, geographic, and linguistic obstacles to debate, create, and disseminate their own diverse images and political platforms—even if these are not always duly noted by the society of dominant majority.

Traditional indigenous knowledge, once passed orally from generation to generation and now shared through a wide variety of media ranging from home videos and print newspapers to e-books and blogs, often derives from lived experience (as opposed to the abstract or secondary accounts transmitted in a classroom environment) and is characteristically grounded in the notion that the natural world is sacred.[13] In this light, Marcos Terena's personal and professional dedication to the cause of Native self-representation within a broader context of democratic rule is intimately related to his own experience with misrepresentation—or lack of representation—by and in the society of the dominant majority.[14]

As a pilot for the Fundação Nacional do Índio (FUNAI) during the final years of Brazil's military dictatorship (1964–85), Terena made a living flying "pacifying" indigenist missions to the "hostile" and "dangerous" Native communities that other pilots were unwilling to visit.[15] He later went to work for state indigenists as chief of staff for then-FUNAI president Jurandy Marcos da Fonseca. Paradoxically, in order to receive professional training from the Brazilian Air Force and serve as a FUNAI aviator, Terena had to deny his own indigeneity for over a decade. As he explained years later to journalist Zózimo Barroso, he strategically acquiesced to his frequent misidentification as "Japanese" (i.e., of Asian descent and thus "white," or at least non-Indian) in order to circumvent the restrictions of the 1973 Indian Statute and its categorization of indigenous peoples as relatively incompetent before the law.[16] In the long run, however, this utilitarian de-Indianization would not sit well with the man who would later be known not only as a key protagonist in Brazil's indigenous politics but also as one of the most influential Native intellectuals in the Americas.[17] He recalled:

> Arriving in Brasília, I encountered FUNAI and discovered that I was a "tutee" [of the state]. I met great indigenous leaders who spoke of their struggles for land demarcation—a language unknown to me. . . . They wanted me to explain the law to them. I explained, and I was ensnared. By the Indians, as brothers. By FUNAI, as a threat to order and convention. Between becoming white again and continuing my career as a pilot, and becoming Indian again—even a "subversive" Indian—I opted to return to my origins and felt like a true prodigal son. I knew how to read, write, speak Portuguese and Spanish, and to understand English and French. I knew how to analyze the political, economic, and social situation of our country. I didn't fit into any standard mold

of Indianness that existed in the minds of the FUNAI leadership. As punishment, I was banned from flying for three years because it was, according to them, impossible for an Indian to fly a plane.[18]

Terena's experience was at once extraordinary and exceedingly common. On the one hand, he was one of the few Native Brazilians ever to hold a position of relative power in the state's indigenist bureaucracy (or indeed, at any level of government). On the other hand, his confrontation with the widely held conviction that Indianness was incompatible with professional training and work, and thus unsuitable for the exigencies of "civilized" life makes his story emblematic of the paradoxes of lived indigeneity at the outset of the new millennium. Indeed, his experience speaks to that of millions of Native peoples worldwide who continue to struggle against the perception that "Indianness" is something one must abandon or overcome in order to play a productive role in modern society or deserve the full rights of national belonging.

The ambiguities of "differentiated" indigenous citizenship laid out in Brazil's 1973 Indian Statute and subsequent indigenist legislation recall what philosopher Giorgio Agamben, drawing on the work of Carl Schmitt, has theorized as the *state of exception*—the condition through which an "accursed" or "sacrificed" man (*homo sacer*) is included in the juridical order of the state precisely through his exclusion from that order.[19] Adapting this notion to the case at hand, we see that *the* Indian's inclusion in Brazil, as a nation and as a legal order, has always been contingent, imperfect, and incomplete—a condition referred to euphemistically over the past century with terms like "neocitizenship" and "neo-Brazilianness."[20] Institutionalized anti-indigenous discrimination was weakened by the 1988 constitutional proviso that Native peoples would no longer have to cease being "Indians" in order to also be Brazilian in the eyes of the state.[21] But the presence of such "proindigenous" policies on the books has had little impact on the deeply rooted colonialist mindset that has framed official indigenist policy into the second decade of the twenty-first century and continues to perpetuate, through popular culture, widespread ideas and images of Native Brazilians as incompetent and backward.

It has become an unfortunate truism of Brazilianist scholarship that the formal, legal guarantees of progressive social justice are not necessarily (or frequently) reflected in the experience of the Brazilian people—a reality that adds an extra layer of theoretical complexity and an additional set of logistical challenges to the already thorny question of indigenous representation.[22] The 1988 Constitution, for example, called for the complete demarcation of indigenous territories within five years. More than a quarter century later, that promise has not been met, and thousands of Native people across the country are indeed increasingly under siege.[23] What is more, the revival of dictatorship-era development projects in the Amazon under the administrations of Presidents Luis Inácio Lula da Silva and Dilma Rousseff presents a major threat to indigenous lands—including some that have supposedly already been protected.[24]

A key symbol of twenty-first century neocolonialism and indigenous and popular opposition to it in the twenty-first century is the Belo Monte hydroelectric dam, first proposed for construction in the state of Pará during the 1970s by Brazil's military government, which named its project "Kararaô."[25] During the decade that followed, a massive outpouring of indigenous, national, and international protest forced the regime to shelve its plans to divert the flow of the Xingu River and flood dozens of Native and riverbed communities—actions that critics argued would cripple the local fishing industry, destroy rare plant and animal species, pollute the environment with methane gas, and attract tens of thousands of migrant families to the region who would subsequently have no place to work or reside.[26] In 2012, arguments against a new and purportedly less prejudicial Belo Monte initiative—already in the works for well over a decade—raise the same objections and involve, once again, a wide variety of indigenous, national, and international organizations—a coalition complicated by the fact that the dam project is no longer the brainchild of a military dictatorship but the pet project of a highly popular (and populist) "progressive" government.

Clearly this kind of "progress" favors some and victimizes others. Indigenous activists who organized against the construction of Belo Monte during the centenary of state-backed indigenism considered it not only prejudicial to the interests of their particular communities but also a powerful symbol of everything that has gone wrong with national indigenist policy, the development goals of the governing Partido dos Trabalhadores (Workers' Party, or PT), and the state's cozy embrace of global capital in some of its most culture-razing forms.[27] Native activist Kretã Kaingang thus wondered of the Lula government, "What kind of progress does this syndicalist administration want for us? We believed very much in this administration. They wanted to get there, and they did. They wanted to pass laws and they passed several. But many of the laws are contrary to the rights of indigenous peoples. Many of us . . . put those people into power, and now they have come out against us."[28] This assertion points to the frequently obscured reality that the political Left in Brazil and throughout

Latin America has been historically—alongside the political Right—a relentless exploiter and oppressor of Native peoples.[29]

Kaingang's statement also indicates that the struggle on the horizon is not just over Belo Monte or even the dozens of other hydroelectric dam construction projects already on the books but, indeed, raises the greater and more urgent goal of keeping Native ways of being and knowing alive in the face of a state-sponsored development agenda that has been around in various forms for nearly two centuries and has only recently morphed into the so-called Programa de Aceleração do Crescimento (Accelerated Growth Program, or PAC).[30] Up against this locomotive of "progress" and the widely accepted premise that "history is about development,"[31] the executive director of the Coordenação das Organizações Indígenas da Amazônia Brasileira (Coordination of Indigenous Organizations of the Brazilian Amazon, or COIAB), Marcos Apurinã, laid out the stakes of the controversial enterprise for the people and communities he sought to represent: "Money is not more valuable than nature, than our traditions. . . . We are not going to sell our blood, sell our children to big capital. We are going to fight. We will never give up."[32]

Indigenous political leaders and activists who share with Marcos Terena the desire for meaningful representation and direct participation in the realm of state politics do so from within a tricky double bind, knowing that any intervention they might undertake in that system—already against great odds and at great personal cost—unavoidably reinscribes, to some degree, the erasure, exclusion, and delegitimization that has characterized the indigenous-state relationship since its inception.[33] Their efforts to participate in national governance and international political bodies despite these distressing circumstances might be framed as the groundwork for a realist, postindigenist politics. Or they could present the least-worst option available to individuals and communities whose ways of being and knowing are constantly at risk of disappearing forever. Teme-Augama Anishnabai political theorist Dale Turner describes a similar predicament among Native peoples of North America:

American Indian intellectuals . . . should make it clear that the relationship between the tribes and the American government is, to borrow a phrase from John Rawls, "political, not metaphysical." The reason we do this is to assert from the outset that our ways of knowing the world are not up for negotiation. . . . I am unable (and unwilling) to explain these metaphysical differences; instead, I will focus on the political dimension of asserting that these differences exist in the first place. . . . If American Indians want to have their rights and sovereignty recognized by American legal and political institutions, they must do so using the already existing legal and political discourses of the dominant culture. . . . The normative concepts that drive these discourses have evolved with little or no influence from American Indian intellectuals. American Indians must use a foreign language to explain the content of their rights, have very little to say about shaping its philosophical worth, and engage the institutions that enforce the decisions created by these discourses. Why? The answer is simple: to survive.[34]

While there is certainly no consensus among indigenous intellectuals and scholars regarding the most appropriate or desirable relationship among Native philosophies, spirituality, and indigenous political and cultural activism, the shared imperative "to survive" is, of course, irrefutable. But what does "survival" mean for those implicated in these debates, as well as for their nonindigenous partners, advocates, and interlocutors? What would be the best possible outcome for the future of state-indigenous relations? Considering that indigenist political and cultural discourses in Brazil and across the Americas have almost always stemmed from and referred to renderings of "Indians" by non-Indians, what can we conclude after a hundred years of state-backed indigenism about the ever-changing relationship between indigeneity and representation?

Indigenous academics, activists, writers, and artists throughout Brazil continue to work and fight for survival in predominantly national terms, recognizing, like Marcos Terena, the opportunities for political self-representation that are afforded by their "double bind" even as they work to loosen themselves from it. At the same time, they participate ever more frequently in an intensifying dialogue about the relationship between indigeneity and representation that also spills beyond national borders. By working to restore and strengthen traditional ways of being, knowing, and speaking; by claiming authority over their images and intellectual property; and by seeking to secure land rights, educational autonomy, and formal (elected and appointed) roles in state governance, indigenous peoples are turning on its head the premise of a traditional indigenist politics—representation through tutelage, or in Agamben's terms, "inclusion by exclusion." By doing so, they impel a reformulation of indigenist and national politics and a critical rethinking of the nature of politics itself. That is, the sovereignty claims of indigenous peoples as expressed, for example, in Marcos Terena's claim to multiple, coexisting, overlapping ways of being and belonging destabilize dominant (Western) theories and practices for organizing and administering states. Although collectively they still endure the "tyranny of the alphabet"[35] and exclusion from a "lettered city" notorious for its impermeability,[36] indigenous intellectuals, artists, and especially writers are playing a new and crucial role in this reformulation. Their interventions bring new meaning to the ever-changing notion of indigeneity and to the concept of Brazilianness itself.

SOVEREIGNTY

The statement "I can be what you are without ceasing to be who I am" was formulated in the midst of Brazil's "modernizing" military regime, which intended to do away at all costs with "backwardness" and "underdevelopment"—particularly that of the indigenous peoples fortunate (or unfortunate) enough to occupy valuable or strategically vulnerable tracts of land. It was then and is now an affirmation of Native self-identification and an appeal for differentiated citizenship—in a nutshell, for the right to be indigenous and to participate in national society and government both as indigenous peoples and as Brazilians. Just as crucial, however, has been the effort to bring together radically diverse Native individuals and communities from across the country and unite them around a shared and urgent goal: not survival as a collective grasping on to what philosophers from Viktor Frankl to Agamben have characterized as *naked* or *bare life* (that is, life in its minimal, biological sense), but rather, as a common political existence born of a shared awakening or reawakening *as Native peoples*—what Frantz Fanon articulated half a century ago as an interpellation into a political community.[37] The notion that, as Mohawk political theorist Taiaiake Alfred has claimed, "being born Indian is being born into politics,"[38] exemplifies the melding of the biological and the political in and through biopower. For Native peoples, of course, all politics since the Conquest have been biopolitics.

Agamben's contention that the militarized and neoliberal order of the twenty-first century subjects all bodies, indigenous or otherwise, to the reign of biopower may indeed be true. "Every attempt to rethink the political space of the West must begin," he writes, "with the clear awareness that we no longer know anything of the classical distinction between *zoē* and *bios*, between private life and political existence, between man as a simple being living at home in the house, and man's political existence in the city."[39] Clearly, however, the stakes of a pervasive biopolitical order are not the same for all. If the imperative for self-identifying indigenous peoples is not just "survival" or "resistance" but, indeed, influencing national and international politics and the multiple relations of power that make them possible, then perpetuating indigeneity into the twenty-first century means cultivating Gerald Vizenor's "sense of presence" not only as lived experience but also at the level of ideas and discourse—the initiative Native scholars have long referred to as decolonizing thought itself.[40] As the militant Aymara theoretician Ramiro Reynaga argued in the early seventies: "Only mental colonization can explain the survival of economic and political colonization. Domination of the mind permits the domination over wealth, work, governments. . . . Economic imperialism and mental colonialism are each cause and effect—an untiring and ever-growing process."[41] Disheartened with the revolutionary Left and convinced of the need to "Indianize Marxism,"[42] Reynaga called for nothing less than "the rebuilding of brains": "Four hundred and fifty years ago they cut off our head. Since then, we've been walking around blind, following one invader or another." In concert with Terena's dictum, he concluded: "The danger is not in learning what is foreign, but in forgetting what is ours. Knowledge is growing and learning without having to forget."[43]

In Brazil, where indigenist discourses and practices have for the last century channeled not only the state-backed "protection" of Native territories and peoples but also their state-sponsored usurpation and destruction, the political task of persisting into the future, regardless of how we ultimately choose to label it, could not be more critical. Terena's ambitions, like those of Reynaga and countless others before and after them, resonate clearly with the interwoven social, political, and cultural movements of indigenous peoples worldwide—a diverse collection of initiatives that Tuhiwai Smith characterized on the eve of the twenty-first century as "a new agenda for indigenous activity [that extends] . . . beyond the decolonization aspirations of a particular indigenous community [and moves] . . . towards the development of global indigenous strategic alliances."[44] Dakota-Chickasaw scholar and activist Phil Lane Jr. corroborates the growing interest among indigenous peoples to collaborate across boundaries of state and nation: "In every nation-state in the Americas, including the Caribbean, there is some form of an Indigenous movement emerging and joining with others. . . . The primary challenge . . . in rebuilding the Americas . . . is disunity."[45] The 2007 adoption of the U.N. Declaration on the Rights of Indigenous Peoples, after three decades of transnational work among indigenous leaders from around the world, helped set the stage for Lane's vision, which has been increasingly realized through North-South and South-South solidarity movements and collaborative political work among Aymara, Guarani, Lakota, Mapuche, Maya, Kichwa, and Quechua peoples, for example.[46]

Considered in this comparative context, Marcos Terena's assertion that "I can be what you are without ceasing to be who I am" exceeds the realm of identity politics and cuts to the heart of the political—that is, the boundary, however ambiguous or porous, between self and Other and the infinite possibilities for identification, recognition, and representation across that threshold. What is more, Terena's claim engages the dominant (Western) notion of sovereignty as "supreme authority within a limited territory"[47] and places it under scrutiny as the constitutive basis of the modern political system. He urges us to consider who has and should have the power to delimit and enforce the boundaries of inclusion and exclusion among the many communities to which we all belong, and that we continue to define and deploy, whether explicitly or implicitly, in predominantly political terms. Which of these communities—"racial," ethnic, linguistic, cultural, tribal, national—are the most propitious for self-identifying indigenous peoples and their collaborators in the twenty-first century? How do current articulations of indigeneity impel us to rethink these categories, to specify or redefine their limits, and to understand and employ the notion of sovereignty not for violent exclusion but in ways that might be conducive to goals of freedom, peace, and social justice to be shared by indigenous and nonindigenous peoples alike?

Employed by statesmen and theorists to understand and govern modern states since the seventeenth century, the notion of sovereignty in the post-Westphalian, Hobbesian tradition has typically produced and legitimated violence as a necessary if (for some) regrettable reality of political life.[48] The concept has a long and complex yet still unfolding history that begins for our purposes with the 1493 *Inter caetera*—the papal bull singed by Alexander VI,[49] claiming ownership of newly "discovered" territories for the Spanish monarchy. It continues one year later, when the Treaty of Tordesillas (in Portuguese, Tordesilhas) gave the disgruntled Portuguese the land mass now known as Brazil;[50] and leads us all the way into the twenty-first century, with hosts of unsettled Native land claims across the Americas—from Maine to Oaxaca to Rio Grande do Sul—and annual petitions to the pope by indigenous groups worldwide to repudiate the Church's historical complicity in their collective subjugation.[51]

Early theoreticians of international law, like Francisco de Vitoria in the sixteenth century and Hugo Grotius in the seventeenth century, contested the Church-sponsored notion of title by discovery established by the *Inter caetera* while endorsing the notion of "just war" by which Europeans laid claim to Native lands and their occupants.[52] The result for indigenous peoples, of course, would be the same: colonization. As eighteenth-century diplomat Emmerich de Vattel argued in his 1758 *Law of Nations*, the "free, independent, and equal" nature of nations derived from the natural rights of their constituents, and "the general and common right of nations over the conduct of any sovereign state [was] only commensurate to the object of that society which exist[ed] between them."[53] Denied status as independent nations or as states (terms Vattel used interchangeably in his writing), indigenous peoples would have no rights as distinct communities. Legal scholar James Anaya elaborates: "The very idea of the nation-state . . . is based on European models of political and social organization whose dominant defining characteristics are exclusivity of territorial domain and hierarchical, centralized authority. By contrast, indigenous peoples . . . typically have been organized primarily by tribal or kinship ties, have had decentralized political structures often linked in confederations, and have enjoyed shared or overlapping spheres of territorial control."[54]

Dominant (Western) notions of sovereignty thus run counter to the traditions, needs, and interests of most self-identifying Native peoples and have been employed historically by both individual and state actors to their detriment—oftentimes violently and fatally. In Max Weber's early twentieth-century formulation, the sovereign state defends the use of the violence deemed "necessary" for its own preservation, and that preservation, in turn, undergirds the state's ability and "right" to use such violence with legitimacy, whether against other states or against its own subjects.[55] Those who failed to recognize the legitimacy of such violence or to accept the corollary claim that "it is *not* true that good can follow only from good, and evil only from evil" were thus reduced, in Weber's view, to political "infancy."[56] The necessary violence of sovereignty hence reproduces the conditions of its own necessity.

Philosophers Gilles Deleuze and Félix Guattari proposed during the mid-twentieth century that the state manifests the violence of sovereignty as an "apparatus of capture" that serves at once to organize and police human life. In Brazil, this "capture" might refer to the state's "right" to appropriate and control indigenous territories by "capturing," as the philosophers put it, "while simultaneously constituting a right to capture."[57] In this formulation, the "primitive" exists only in the always incomplete process of becoming something else (i.e., "civilized") or in relation to his or her degree of interaction with the nonprimitive (i.e., "*the* civilized").[58] History thus "translates" the coexistence of different forms of being and knowing into dominant paradigms of succession and evolution—paradigms that scholars like Marcos Terena, Ramiro Reynaga, and Linda Tuhiwai Smith (among many others) challenge with the affirmation that cultural change does not necessarily imply the cultural loss and acculturation expressed thorough the popular tautological argument that "real" Indians belong to the past and "modern" Indians are not "real."

In the case of Brazil, the state imperative to protect and expand the frontiers of order, progress, and civilization fashions the violence of sovereignty as legitimate, if not inevitable, while attributing the primary responsibility for the violence to its victims.[59] The state is continually erected through violent inclusions and exclusions to generate, as Benedict Anderson argued so famously, the collective subjectivity of a community that imagines itself as national while simultaneously articulating its Other—in this case, the so-called *primitive* whose backwardness must be contained, forced outside the limits of the sovereign state, or erased altogether. Hence, as Souza Lima put it, the state's historical initiative for Indian "protection" can be characterized as a "siege of peace" whereby the question of territorial occupation is always at stake.[60] The fact that many nonindigenous advocates of indigenous rights have opposed anti-indigenous violence and indeed given their lives to prevent or to stop it has not increased popular support for the protection of indigenous lands or otherwise succeeded in making indigenous interests a priority on the national agenda. Even in 2012, as political opposition to Belo Monte finally begins, perhaps too late, to gain a foothold among some fraction of the dominant majority, that opposition is articulated more frequently in relation to economics and the environment than it is in relation to indigenous or human rights.

After a century of state-backed indigenism, the primary challenge posed by the Brazilian indigenous movement is no longer the recognition of indigenous difference as real, enduring, and legitimate in the eyes of the dominant majority. Nor is it to bring marginalized Native populations into the fold of the national community and "neocitizenship," with all of the rights thereunto pertaining. Above and beyond the still crucial work for recognition and inclusion, Native Brazilian intellectuals, artists, and political leaders question the injustices faced by their communities in the twenty-first century as a consequence of their long-standing "inclusion through exclusion" per the hegemonic logic of dominant sovereignty. After all, self-representation within a network of political, economic, and sociocultural power that is colonialist and racist in its very constitution is a necessary but always insufficient condition to guarantee Native self-determination, to consolidate a system of governance that serves the needs and interests of indigenous and nonindigenous peoples, or to reframe those needs and interests as ultimately complementary rather than as the always conflicting forces of a zero-sum game. If the current indigenous question stems from the notion that violence and exclusion are *natural* and *necessary* consequences of state sovereignty, part of the answer must lie in the possibility of rethinking sovereignty and reconceptualizing social belonging and self-determination in ways that posit state violence and exclusion instead as *unnatural* and *unnecessary*.

Political theorist Karena Shaw has observed that "the reconstitution of the political that addresses the historical violences of sovereignty . . . must happen in a context of understanding them not as givens, but as complex social, economic, political, and material productions."[61] She goes on to consider the nature of this reconstitution, but in doing so she limits the parameters of worthwhile inquiry to the trajectory and boundaries of dominant (Western) thought, avowing her own "lack of interest" in indigenous "worlds, cosmologies, modes of social and political interaction, and so on."[62] The result is productive in terms of those limits, but as she notes, unsatisfactory with regard to the central ("Indian") question at hand. She concludes: "I, like . . . many others, thus think that Indigenous political movements pose the question of the day, but I am not sure we even know what this question is with much precision, let alone have an answer to it."[63] Both the articulation of the problem and this ambiguous conclusion thus imply that Native peoples who are unable or unwilling to speak in the tongue of Western philosophy have little to contribute to the discussions of which their existence is the primary focus.[64]

Counter to this assertion, indigenous scholars and activists in Brazil and across the Americas insist that some of the solutions to the problem of dominant sovereignty as articulated by Native intellectuals and movements can, in fact, be found among the very political and cultural projects that are articulated under that rubric. The existence of contemporary indigenous movements *as such* raises theoretical questions that vary according to the circumstances in which they are articulated and cannot be truncated from the lives and thoughts of their protagonists without betraying the desire for self-representation of which they are born. Acknowledging this fact means that scholars and students of indigeneity, indigenous or not, perhaps ought to be "interested" at some level in the "worlds, cosmologies, and modes of social and political interaction" of the people without whom work and study would be impossible—even if access to those worlds and cosmologies is incomplete or otherwise imperfect, and even if their "modes of social and political interaction" are not always (or ever) articulated through or informed by the canon of Western thought.

The conviction that nonindigenous thinking can or ought to be "critically reformulated" in reference to indigenous peoples without engaging them as subjects and interlocutors and without taking their views seriously is akin to putting them (back) to work as so much "raw material" in the service of dominant interests—political, social, economic, and cultural.[65] As critic John Beverley argued with regard to the widely commented testimony of Maya Quiché activist Rigoberta Menchú Tum,[66] such an intellectual practice relegates Native peoples to perpetual "informants" who, like Margaret Mead's proverbial "good friends," lack the capacity to understand, develop, or sustain political interests or agendas of their own and can only be manipulated as pawns in someone else's game. Such, too, is the message of the popular political discourses that would ascribe all motivation and agency in the protests against Amazonian development projects to Hollywood movie stars and pesky foreign NGOs.[67]

In light of such conflicts, which in Brazil have to do not only with occupying land but also with how and for whom that land will be used, one way to rethink the grounding of modern politics in the violence and exclusion of dominant sovereignty is to rearticulate the ontological and epistemological foundations of its citizen-subjects. That is, who is to choose what count as acceptable ways of being and knowing within the boundaries of the sovereign state? Native Brazilian intellectuals and organizations are of course intimately involved in this enterprise, which for the last several decades (and in some instances, for much longer),[68] they have channeled into constructing indigeneity as compatible with Brazilianness rather than as prior, antithetical, or exterior to it. It is precisely the perception of this compatibility, after all, that enables Marcos Terena to straddle the shores of self and Other and leads the Brazilian indigenous movement to call itself precisely that. In keeping with these important linguistic gestures, one activist explained to me in July 2010 that in protest of the state's dismantling of FUNAI he would cloak himself in the Brazilian flag and set flame to the flag of the governing Partido dos Trabalhadores. The problem for him and his fellow protestors was not with Brazil as a concept, a place on the map, or even as a body of legislation by which they are made to feel marginalized, but with a specific set of political leaders and their penchant for anti-indigenous development policies.[69]

In their willingness to embrace expedient forms of self-identification with the state, contemporary indigenous activists in Brazil differ from many of their counterparts across the region—including (English-dominant) North America—where for some, political loyalties rest less with the United States or Canada than with the Native nations and tribes whose leaders once entered into political treaties with their colonizers.[70] Despite the fact that it may have diverse meanings at the community level, sovereignty vis-à-vis the colonial state and dominant society, for these peoples, still harks back to its Hobbesian origins, indicating distinct nationhood, allegiance, symbolism, and documentation of citizenship, including passports.[71]

In contrast, as a tiny fraction of the overall population, Native Brazilian activists express little interest in advocating for mutually exclusive national separatisms or in following in the footsteps of their neighbors in Bolivia by gaining control of the state government and economy (though certainly the control of natural resources is a shared concern). Between these two poles, indigenous intellectuals and communities in Brazil articulate, instead, a desire for the state to respect the promises and premises of its own Constitution and to honor the international legal agreements to which it is signatory.[72] At the same time, they challenge the dominant majority to live up to its preferred image of Brazil as a *"país de todos* [a country that belongs to all],"[73] where racism, discrimination, and acts of violence are considered just as egregious and unacceptable when perpetrated against indigenous peoples as when they are perpetrated against other sectors of the population.

This trajectory of indigenous political and cultural activism shows us that rethinking dominant notions of sovereignty requires dismantling the colonialist relationship between the state and its Native subjects and rebuilding it anew. What might be the consequences for national and international politics if, for instance, the state served no longer as the primary vehicle for the "capitalist axiomatic,"[74] and thus for the gradual homogenization of human experience, but, rather, as a critical purveyor of heterogeneity? What if it did this not through the multiplication of "diversity" or the predetermined political identities of neoliberal multiculturalism but as the productive coexistence of difference in the Bhabhian sense, or as in the Zapatistas' now familiar "world in which many other worlds can fit."[75] What if, rather than occupying the "uncivilized" fringes of the imagined national community—either to be ignored as irrelevant or craftily usurped into multilateral development initiatives that recycle old "modernization" initiatives as new and "proindigenous" political agendas—Native ways of being and knowing held a place at the very center of the "new social and political reality" as imagined by Alfred and so many others?[76]

AN INDIGENOUS CRITIQUE OF SOVEREIGNTY

Native intellectuals in Brazil and elsewhere have suggested several philosophical and political alternatives to the intrinsically violent notions of sovereignty that developed in the Western tradition and now lie at the heart of contemporary state politics. The specificities of these proposals vary significantly through time and across space, but some common ground has been established and continues to grow thorough transnational indigenous activism and indigenous/nonindigenous legal and political collaboration at national and international levels. Although the 2007 U.N. Declaration on the Rights of Indigenous Peoples makes no statement with regard to sovereignty other than to reaffirm that of the signatory states,[77] nine of the forty-six articles of the declaration uphold Native rights with reference to traditional "lands, territories, and resources,"[78] thus indicating the centrality of land to indigenous political initiatives worldwide.

Unlike dominant Western understandings of sovereignty, which are derived from a colonialist impulse, grounded in a history of violence, and sustained by the overt or implicit threat of additional violence, contemporary indigenous notions of sovereignty stem from a principle of mutual respect, noncoercive forms of authority, and the notion that human society and the natural world can coexist in a partnership through which value is expressed in terms of longevity and equilibrium rather than extraction, surplus, and profit. As Alfred puts it, the "primary goals of a [traditional] indigenous economy are the sustainability of the earth and the health and well-being of the people."[79] An alternative to sovereignty as a "violent production,"[80] or what Alfred considers a social construction that represents "the triumph of some ideas over others," is a "nonintrusive" "regime of respect" that "builds frameworks of coexistence by acknowledging the integrity and autonomy of the various constituent elements of the relationship."[81] These principles echo the writings of Native activists and scholars in Brazil with regard to their own ambiguous position in national society, which is often articulated in relation to a two-tiered struggle for the demarcation of indigenous territories, on the one hand, and legal representation vis-à-vis the state, on the other.

That the "Indian problem" is a "problem of the land," as José Carlos Mariátegui wrote famously in the early twentieth century, is indeed still the case, although not only for the reasons he imagined when contemplating the need for agrarian and political reform in the Andes.[82] Yet contemporary indigenous theorists in Brazil share with the father of Peruvian socialism a critique of capitalist modes of production, land title, and material labor. As organizers of the Acampamento Revolucionário Indígena in Brasília put it during their 2010 protests of nonindigenous FUNAI leadership and national indigenist policy more broadly, "The Indian *is* land, and from it cannot be separated."[83] The gamble inherent in such an assertion is twofold: On the one hand, the statement inadvertently validates the common and dangerous misperception that urban and other "posttraditional" indigenous peoples are inauthentic, or at least less authentic than their counterparts who live in traditional communities.[84] On the other hand, it risks disappearing Native peoples into the rainforests and subsuming their needs and interests into competing discourses of environmental protection and development.

Of course, many nonindigenous peoples also have important historical and affective ties to specific territories, and not all Native peoples embrace ancestral (or any other) ties to particular lands. Many of the indigenous scholars and activists whose work I engage here are, indeed, urbanites. Despite this fact, the indigenous movement today *is* very much about the urgency of protecting indigenous lands and demarcating territories in accordance with the unmet promises of the 1988 Constitution. In light of the devastating development projects on the horizon, many indigenous leaders and young people express a dire need, regardless of where and how they, personally, choose to live, to ensure that those who want to live on traditional or protected lands will be able to do so into the foreseeable future. Many indigenous urbanites also return to their *aldeias* or communities routinely, as a matter of choice. The issue at stake, then, is that these positions can and should be able to coexist, and that they are perfectly reconcilable because, returning to Terena's dictum, it is not only conceivable but urgent to be oneself and yet like another at the same time.

Of course, the perceived desire of some indigenous peoples to have their proverbial cake and eat it, too, can also be a source of great resentment. Embracing the "too much land for two few Indians" argument, sociopolitical antagonists point recurrently to those who deviate from tradition— that is, from seeming markers of Indianness—as hucksters out to bleed the state. Documented cases of Native individuals and groups who have been willing to sell their lands or its resources for financial gain, for example, are a hot news item that adds fuel to this fire. And certainly, it has long been the case that for an infinite number of reasons and in keeping with dominant expectations, some people are quite happy to disassociate themselves from traditional indigenous ways of life, leave their communities, and never return. But those who do self-identify with indigeneity in political terms, regardless of where and how they live and work, tend to prioritize the land and its protection—some in terms of the sacred, some in terms of environmental preservation, and some in terms of both positions, which they see as not only compatible but indivisible. This association provides key linkages to a transnational indigenous politics and the growing inter-American (and global) indigenous movement and serves as one common ground for the alliances between indigenous and nonindigenous peoples that will continue to be necessary if the movement is to project indigeneity into the future as a form of self-identification, a politics, and an ethics of which non-Natives might also partake.

On the occasion of the 2000 Brazilian quincentennial, educational scholar and writer Daniel Monteiro Costa (Daniel Munduruku) explained the relationship between Native communities and territories thus:

> The land is not . . . a good to be exploited and plundered but . . . something alive, the holder of a protective spirit, a guardian. . . . In order for life to continue, indigenous peoples learned to relate to nature with respect, and for that reason developed an entire body of knowledge regarding fauna and flora. They use the land for a period and then move . . . so that plants can grow back and the soil can be replenished. After a while, they return. . . . The obsession with penetrating the Earth to extract her riches has inspired many peoples to organize in defense of their rights as guaranteed by the 1988 Constitution. Indigenous organizations know that the land is sacred and that everything done to her today will impact everyone on the planet sooner or later. . . . Indigenous society does not accumulate goods but lives the necessity of the moment.[85]

Hence for Munduruku and many others, the inviolability of the land and its centrality to traditional indigenous cosmologies and cultural practices make it impossible to separate indigenous metaphysics entirely from an indigenous politics.[86] As the Guarani writer Olívio Jekupé puts it: "We are a philosophical people tied to Mother Nature, and it is through her that we learn to live and to understand the world."[87] Turner corroborates from a North American context: "Indigenous peoples have been forced to articulate metaphysical claims that gain their normative force within tribal oral traditions, as political arguments. These political arguments are articulated in the Western European discourses of law and politics, the main consequence of which is that Indigenous metaphysics must be subsumed within the already existing legal and political practices of the dominant colonial culture in order for them . . . to make sense."[88] Turner's assertion thus brings us back to the double bind within which Native scholars and activists are compelled to adopt the lexicon, syntax, and implied values of a colonizing political discourse precisely in order to free themselves from it.[89]

In an effort to offset romanticized perceptions of indigenous peoples and introduce non-Native audiences to some basic tenets of Terena spirituality, writer Lúcio Paiva Flores underscores the diversity among the hundreds of indigenous peoples living inside Brazilian borders and emphasizes the varying degrees to which they have embraced dominant religious forms, such as Christianity, and melded them with their own beliefs and practices. Like Munduruku, Jekupé, and Alfred, he emphasizes the importance of working toward a harmonious relationship with the natural environment and observes that "this practice is increasingly discovered and lived by other [non-Native] peoples."[90]

One does not, of course, have to live or want to live in or near Amazonia in order to respect the Earth, but "it is in the forests, in rivers, and alongside the animals," Flores suggests, that indigenous peoples replenish their dreams and construct their utopias to bring about "harmony between humans and nature so that they can develop into one sole being."[91] Such harmony, in his view, requires and produces social sustainability and equilibrium: "Complete order is not ideal; neither is disorder. It is [a] dual principle of complementarity, unlike Occidental philosophy, which sees us [humans] as antagonists in a constant battle that someone has to win—a struggle internalized by the human being, who is tempted and can give in, or not. From that kind of [dualistic] thinking derives the scheme of salvation that is absent from indigenous thought. Without the never-ending struggle between heaven and hell, who is there to save? And from what?"[92]

Flores goes on to explain how the balance at work in the natural world also exists, ideally, in the human world, thus transforming human qualities and experience into an undivided continuum rather than a series of opposing forces and interests that can only be realized at another's expense: "The eternal struggle for the side of good is a human tendency that, in turn, condemns that which is evil. The difficulty perhaps rests on the boundary where one ends and the other begins, if there is such a boundary. . . . In indigenous thought, evil is not so evil, and . . . life without it would not need to be tipped in the other direction on the scale [because] there would be no such scale. 'Balance' would not be necessary because everything would already be on just one of the two plates, with no counterweight."[93]

Like several indigenous writers whose work I address in this study, Flores suggests that the inevitable connectedness of all human life and experience makes social conflict and enmity nonsensical, for to do harm to others is, ultimately, to do harm to oneself. Mutual respect, in contrast, is a social, cultural, and political obligation without which community as an abstract concept would be meaningless, and community as a lived project would always be predestined to failure. As Alfred writes, "Indigenous conceptions and the politics that flow from them maintain in a tangible way the distinction between various political communities and contain an imperative of respect that precludes the need for homogenization."[94] Without the "assimilative impulse" of the Western tradition, peaceful coexistence can be achieved without violence and the whole host of political, legal, social, and cultural structures through which violence is either realized or held in abeyance as a hegemonic impulse toward compulsory cohesion. Terena's proposal that "I can be what you are without ceasing to be who I am" thus resonates with a broadly shared—or, at least, a broadly and strategically articulated—Native belief that self and Other are inextricably bound, and that in order to achieve peace among human communities and between humankind and the natural world, indigenous knowledge must be "rescued from its status as a cultural artifact."[95]

Certainly, Flores's "rescue"—or the indigenous critique of dominant sovereignty—has long been carried out by other Native peoples around the world, regardless of any possible collaboration with nonindigenous partners and advocates.[96] Compared to their counterparts in South and Central America, for instance, indigenous scholars and activists in North America have established a secure foothold in the mainstream academy and civil society. Relatively new indigenous universities in Bolivia, Ecuador, Mexico, and Venezuela serve tens of thousands of students, and are promoting the value of indigenous knowledge among Native and non-Native populations alike.[97] Indigenous intellectuals and activists play a central if highly uneven role in mainstream politics in the Andes and Central America, one key instance of which has been the groundbreaking if fraught presidency of Evo Morales in Bolivia since 2005. Finally, over the last two decades, traditional indigenous knowledge has filtered into mainstream initiatives for sustainable development and ethically and ecologically responsible tourism across Africa, Asia, and the Pacific.[98] In Brazil, however, similar efforts to sustain traditional indigenous knowledge and ways of life have been comparatively anemic. Despite the tireless efforts of indigenous intellectuals, activists, and communities to promote their needs and interests, and to emphasize the relevance of their collective well-being to the long-term well-being of national society and the future of humankind, the dominant majority continues to relegate them to the political ghettos of entertainment, folklore, caricature, and a whitewashed colonial and national past.

In the face of their perpetual "inclusion through exclusion" in the national polity and, in particular, in state and local legislative bodies and the leadership of FUNAI, indigenous intellectuals and activists continue to work on behalf of their real and virtual communities and to emphasize the goals of having their languages, cultural practices, and traditional forms of knowledge treated respectfully and taken seriously by and in the society of the dominant majority. The Potiguara-descended writer and indigenous advocate Eliane Lima dos Santos (Eliane Potiguara), who founded the nongovernmental Grupo de Mulheres Indígenas (Group of Indigenous Women Network, or Rede GRUMIN) in 1979, and participated in the discussions that led up to the U.N. adoption of the Declaration on the Rights of Indigenous Peoples, has been at the forefront of this effort. Her work and that of other indigenous writers illustrates how creative cultural production—and in particular, creative writing—has become a vital mechanism through which Native Brazilians continue their uninterrupted struggle to enter mainstream political debates and influence the dominant national imaginary to their own benefit and on their own terms.

In her 2005 book *Metade cara, metade máscara*, Potiguara began her exploration of contemporary indigeneity with the story of her Potiguara grandmother, who migrated from Paraíba to Pernambuco, and then to Rio de Janeiro after her father was murdered in the 1920s by a family of English landholders.[99] Raped by a fellow servant and pregnant by age twelve, Maria de Lourdes raised three children in the Zona do Mangue near Rio's Praça XI, working "as a slave" in the city's open markets. Years later, when her eldest daughter met a similarly violent fate and went to work as a full-time maid, Maria de Lourdes became the primary caretaker of the young Eliane, who took up writing to escape from the painful stories of her grandmother and the lonely room where together they spent most of their days.[100]

Building on this distressing past, Potiguara guides her readers through a series of creative and critical writings, intercalating historical narrative with political commentary, and policy suggestions with short stories and poetry. A mythical indigenous couple, Cunhataí and Jurupiranga, appears at several junctures in the text as a reminder of the intricate ties between Native histories, cosmologies, and contemporary indigenous and indigenist politics. In a penultimate chapter titled "Combativeness and Resistance," Jurupiranga sets off in search of his beloved wife, who has been captured and enslaved by colonizers:

> He crossed rivers, mountains, valleys, and saw hundreds of peoples brought down by the war: entire villages destroyed; enslaved and crestfallen communities working for the Jesuits; Natives working in the farming of cotton, coffee, corn, rice, and millions of cadavers. . . . He saw Natives working in the mines of Potosí; the colonization due to tin, to gold, to silver, to coal, to marcasite, to sugar cane, to wood, and even to latex. He saw hundreds of peoples fall to the bayonets of the neo-Americans, English, Dutch, French, Spanish, Portuguese, and even the Brazilians. He understood that the American treaties between indigenous peoples and government were, in reality, more favorable to the latter. He crossed deserts in Mexican territory and entered Arizona. He collapsed. He forgot the sounds of his flute, the chords of his people, the rhythm of the drums. He traveled through the present, past, and future. He went hungry, grew calluses on his feet and hands, fell ill with the worst diseases of the invaders—tuberculosis, typhoid, malaria, scarlet fever, lunacy. . . . He saw the water of the planet polluted and wasted. He saw the biodiversity of the planet destroyed by the corrupt and the powerful. Across the centuries, Juripiranga, armed with his lance, fought the enemies, became a warrior without land, wandering and all alone. . . . He had but one objective: to persist with his conviction and his inner voice against the rulers; to find his community and rebuild it to last forever in peace and love.[101]

Thus Eliane Potiguara renders the post-Conquest indigenous experience in the Americas. Born of this mournful vision, however, is the protagonist's dream, which leads Jurupiranga and the reader away from a place of "difficulties, hunger, desperation, and illness" to one of harmony, fulfillment, hope, and strength:

> He dreamed he was in a large room full of varnished chairs and many Natives, including some of his own people, dressed in the odd clothes of foreigners. . . . He heard several warriors speak and be heard and respected. He heard several languages, indigenous and foreign. . . . He saw tables covered with maps of self-defined indigenous territories

and negotiations carried out to achieve indigenous peace. The white men in ties honored the decision of the Natives, because there were statutes, laws, international mechanisms, treaties, and articles in the Constitution that had been labored over by the Natives for centuries. . . . He saw the indigenous university, full of young people—future anthropologists, scientists, historians, journalists, and jurists—writers of their own history. He saw entire libraries full of books written by Natives and a quality of life never witnessed in his lifetime. Indigenous women were respected when they passed by the citadels on their way to the markets, or when they needed medical, educational, or legal resources. The elderly were venerated by all. Natives who lived outside their communities (descendants who so desired) were recognized by not only their people but society at large and reintegrated into their original communities by a legal mechanism approved in the Congress and the Senate by indigenous legislators. Indigenous judges succeeded in including indigenous peoples in all segments of society: in the media, in education, in health care, in the workplace, in the legislation of broader society. . . . He perceived the communion between the new and advanced technologies used by some Natives with traditional indigenous technologies; dialogue between the young and the old was a reality. . . . He dreamed of all the legends, songs, hymns; all the techniques of artisanship, cooking, agriculture; all the rules and ethics, life origins, spiritual principles; all the forgotten dreams of the shamans of all times, and the indigenous intellectual property encompassing the most noble biodiversity of nature. . . . Juripiranga . . . awoke. . . . Strong, reborn, he found . . . strength through the memories of his histories, his ancestors, and his culture, and managed to find the road from which he had departed five hundred years earlier. Like a divine wind and on the wings of light and love, he continued steadily into his village—*his indigenous nation*—remade in its entirety with the power of the *consciousness of the people*.[102]

And so, in Jurupiranga's dream, Potiguara can realize the claim of Marcos Terena and the many others who summon the day in which Brazil's indigenous peoples will be empowered vis-à-vis the dominant society in the realms of cultural practice, philosophy, education, law, and politics, not only without having to "cease being who they are" but, indeed, by strengthening a vision of indigeneity through which past and future, tradition and modernity, spirit and body, self and Other coexist in harmony and for the greater good of indigenous and nonindigenous peoples alike.

The reflections of these Native Brazilian writers on what it means to exist and know simultaneously from indigenous and nonindigenous perspectives point us toward the "new social and political reality" outlined in Alfred's critique of dominant sovereignty and give new meaning to the notion of "colonized thought" that in its distinct iterations sentences Native peoples, traditions, and philosophies unequivocally to the past.[103] While, as we have seen, Native Brazilians have contributed both willingly and under coercion to the "development" of their country for nearly two centuries, the dominant majority has never considered indigenous peoples *as such* to be compatible with the social, cultural, political, and economic necessities of a modern and "civilized" national society. As in the case of Belo Monte, the Brazilian state continues to foist "order and progress," both figuratively and literally, onto the lives and livelihoods of "her" Native peoples. Acutely aware of this undying past, indigenous writers, activists, and communities work toward a new political order against all odds, trying to make use of the "double" or "multiple" consciousness, the bi- or multilingualism, and the burden of "asymmetric knowledge"[104] that result from having to "be what one is" and "what others are" at the same time. But then, how to turn the "sense of always looking at one's self through the eyes of others, of measuring one's soul by the tape of a world that looks on in amused contempt and pity,"[105] into a source of inspiration, optimism, and empowerment, rather than a narrative of nostalgia, hopelessness, and defeat?

DISORDER AND BACKWARDNESS

When Marcos Terena and his fellow activists deployed their prophetic phrase in the 1970s to challenge the established truth that indigeneity and Brazilianness were fundamentally incompatible, and thus force a radical rethinking of national community, they were invoking not only the nebulous legacies of the colonial past but also half a century of lived experience with state-sponsored indigenist tutelage through the SPI.[106] Over decades of work punctuated by internal conflict, policy failure, administrative shortcomings, and moments of complete breakdown, the state's indigenist bureaucracy channeled the long-standing desire to transform "Indians" into something else—to make them civilized, acculturated, integrated, neo-Brazilian, non-Indian, tutees of the state, proto-Christians, proto-citizens, and so forth. The SPI's voluminous documentation reflects the sometimes coinciding, sometimes contradictory use of such expressions to address in juridical and scientific terms the processes and consequences of sociocultural change, whether real or imagined. The terms they chose to name the phenomenon, or that we might choose to try to understand it, however, matter less than the shared objective that they meant to communicate: to make of the "Indians" something fundamentally different from and "better" than what they were.

Throughout SPI and early FUNAI discourse, the state's indigenists posited this objective as a set of policy initiatives that would provide indigenous peoples with useful and productive lives, albeit lives whose purpose would never be of their own choosing. A 1947 film highlighting SPI accomplishments on the Guido Marlière indigenous post, located in the state of Minas Gerais, laid out the logic behind the contact, capture, and settlement of "itinerant" Indians who appeared as little more than vestiges of a foregone era.[107] "The nomad Indian in general does not build houses, but rustic shelters," the narrator explained. "His time passed, and the post brought him the innovation of the brick house, where he becomes accustomed to the new culture he is receiving. After the house, it's off to supervised work. The chosen seed grows well and makes for a profitable and abundant crop. This former Krenak Indian has survived to harvest and see for himself the fruit of this civilizing evolution."[108]

Responding in 2010 to criticism of his administration's Programa de Aceleração do Crescimento and allegations that its lynchpin—Amazonian "development"—would negatively impact indigenous, fishing, and riverbed communities, President Luis Inácio Lula da Silva appeared to have snagged a page from an old SPI playbook as he expressed his support for an improved and ostensibly less destructive plan: "We spent practically twenty years . . . ," he lamented, "prohibited from studying the viability of building the Belo Monte hydroelectric dam. Not from building the dam, but from conducting a study! . . . I saw in today's papers that there are lots of foreign NGOs arriving from various corners of the world, renting boats to head to Belém to try to keep us from building the dam. Now, obviously the project that was [originally] designed was modified. The lake is a third of what it was before, precisely so that we can give all the environmental guarantees and say to any citizen of the planet Earth that *no one cares more about taking care of the Amazon and our Indians than we do*."[109]

Lula's response to the indigenous and other protestors who remained unconvinced by this line of argument was that all remaining naysayers wished for something "disgraceful" to happen in the country so that they would be able to point fingers at the responsible government parties, including the president himself. This so-called blackout industry

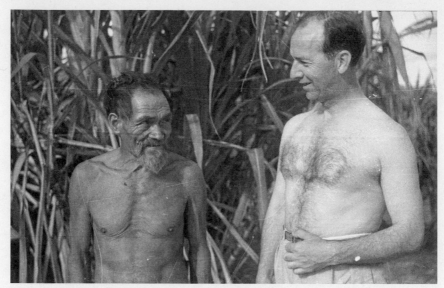

"Former Krenak Indian" with SPI director Modesto Donatini Dias da Cruz on the Guido Marliére (sic) Indigenous Post in Minas Gerais, 1946. Courtesy of the Museu do Índio/FUNAI Archive.

"Arrumamento do posto [Fixing up the post]": New and improved "civilized" housing on an SPI indigenous post in Mato Grosso, no date. Courtesy of the Museu do Índio/ FUNAI Archive.

(*indústria do apagão*), he ventured, hoped for a new and massive blackout (*apagão*) in order to excuse the massive power outages that had occurred across the country in 2001 as a consequence of then-president Fernando Henrique Cardoso's ineptitude. Nothing similar would happen on his watch, he insisted, and furthermore, Belo Monte was good for the local population, even if they were incapable of realizing it: "We foresee having to relocate [only] 16,000 people. We plan to build a model hydroelectric dam . . . to show that Brazil will keep on building hydroelectric dams; but above all, [to show] that Brazil will continue to prioritize the Brazilian people; to take care of *our Indians*; to take care of our rural producers; to take care of our riverbank residents. People will not be negatively affected. On the contrary, we want the dam to benefit those people [and] improve their quality of life."[110]

In a similar vein, and again reminiscent of early SPI discourse, the administration's PAC website highlighted the numerous benefits that the project's architects and advocates offered to local residents poised to lose not only their homes and their livelihood but an entire way of life: "Planning for the dam includes an urban enhancement plan for Altamira," one propaganda film comforted them. "[These are] investments that will benefit the city and its residents. Flood-prone areas will be treated and transformed into ecological parks and environmental preservation areas. . . . The city and its entire population will benefit. Altamira will have urban leisure areas for all of its residents. With the treatment of flood-prone areas, families who live in precarious conditions will be relocated to new neighborhoods *with suitable living conditions*."[111]

Organized opponents of Belo Monte answered the government's claims with a radically different interpretation of the project and its consequences, which they posed as a series of questions in an open letter to presidential candidates Dilma Rousseff and José Serra during the 2010 runoff elections: "Why build at a potential cost of up to 30 billion *reais* and with public funds . . . a dam that will only produce an average of 39 percent of its installed capacity? What justifies destroying the lives of more than 40,000 riverbank residents, small scale farmers, and indigenous peoples under the mistaken pretense that our lives are the price to be paid for the country's development? What kind of development exports energy and minerals while creating few jobs and destroying [the environment]? Are we lesser citizens, or do we deserve less respect than Brazilians from large cities or owners of large, electricity-intensive companies just because, far from the limelight of the media, we live on the river, from the river, and from that which our forests provide to us?"[112] We are left only to imagine,

The city of Altamira (Pará) "before and after" the anticipated construction of the Belo Monte hydroelectric dam in A usina hidroelétrica Belo Monte. *The informational video was released in 2011 by Norte Energia, S.A., a massive consortium of private and public enterprises that won the bid to construct and maintain the dam over thirty-five years. Reminiscent of early SPI discourse, it claims: "The families of Altamira now living in precarious conditions will have decent housing [moradias dignas] and locales with all of the urban infrastructure [now lacking]."*

of course, whether the "former Krenak Indian" of the Guido Marlière indigenous post and the other members of his newly settled "nomad community" might have posed similar questions to Rondon or his legions of indigenists who, armed only with the accouterments of "civilizing evolution," would swear their lives to the "Indian cause."[113] Regardless, the violence of compulsory Indian transformation through forced relocation and all of its intended and unintended consequences masquerades in both cases as a form of salvation—*the* salvation—for the very individuals and communities who would characterize the state's takeover of their lands and lives as perdition and calamitous loss.

Still emerging from the shadow of the Estado Novo in June 1946, the "father" of Brazilian indigenism sent a report of the Conselho Nacional pela Proteção dos Índios (National Council for the Protection of Indians, CNPI) regarding the "civilizing work [*trabalho civilizador*]" of the SPI to then-minister of agriculture Manoel Neto Campelo Junior. Rondon emphasized the critical nature of the state's indigenist mission with the words of one Senator Álvaro Maia, who had recently asserted to his fellow congressmen that "it [was] impossible to speak of democracy when there [were] a million *Brazilians* in the jungle needing to be defended and brought truly into nationality."[114] Although the number appears exaggerated for the period, Rondon's politicization of the language of national belonging was nonetheless significant, for it revealed, once again, the trappings of dominant sovereign thought—namely, as Deleuze and Guattari put it, that "sovereignty only reigns over what it is capable of internalizing, of appropriating locally."[115] If the Indians were technically Brazilian by dint of their presence inside Brazilian borders, they simultaneously occupied a political no man's land from which they could only be "included through exclusion." The jungle and its faceless "millions" would thus serve as a metaphor not only for the limits of the nation but also for the limits of civilization, and perhaps of humanity itself—that daunting threshold between the dark past of backwardness and underdevelopment and a promising future of order and progress.

Drawing on the work of *varguista* politician Luiz Simões Lopes, Rondon and the members of the CNPI offered Neto their blunt counsel: "All the efforts to transform the Indian into a citizen, to discipline him, to force him to work, to make him traverse in a short time the long centuries that separate the Stone Age from the Age of Radio, are useless."[116] Indeed, the state's indigenist task—"the incorporation of the Indian into the national communion [*comunhão nacional*]"—was never conceived as a simple, organic, or passive process. Rather, it would require trained professionals, goodwill, blood, sweat, tears, and perhaps most of all, capital. If the SPI had not already done more, argued a defensive Rondon, it was "because the resources furnished by the public treasury . . . ha[d] not allowed for the growth of the scope of its work on behalf of the large mass of indigenous populations . . . who await[ed] compliance in this civic duty by the Government of the Union."[117] Hence per ventriloquized Indian multitudes, apparently keen on their own colonization, the violence of sovereignty would produce, as it continues to produce, the conditions of its own necessity.

In 2010, President Lula da Silva turned the tables on the old tale of chronically scarce resources, instead articulating the discourse of inevitable progress in light of Brazil's newfound relative prosperity. To critics of the PAC he posed a challenge: "Instead of protesting, [why don't you] propose an alternative for using the 4 billion *reais* we have set aside to take care of social and environmental issues? Let's discuss how we're going to use those 4 billion to improve the lives of the river people, to improve the lives of the Indians, to improve the lives of the farmers."[118] Feast or famine, then, "progress" for the "Indians" remains fundamentally unchanged: a never-ending promise of a better life, but "better" always according to someone else's measure and due to someone else's efforts. Indeed, the primary complaint of indigenous leaders in the protests against Belo Monte has been their absolute exclusion from any meaningful dialogue, despite the administration's sponsorship of so-called discussion forums.[119]

When Darcy Ribeiro published *Os índios e a civilização* in 1970, at the height of the military dictatorship and during a particularly dark period for Brazil's indigenous peoples, he affirmed with irony that the "Indians" had not been successfully "de-Indianized" under the state's indigenist regime. Instead, as he put it, "the degree of ethnic transfiguration went from tribal Indian to generic Indian, and not from Indianness to Brazilianness."[120] On the one hand, then, he expressed some wishful thinking that the quality of indigeneity (or, in his words, of "being Indian") would not be undone through language learning and a change of clothes. On the other hand, he suggested, sustaining indigeneity meant that the "ethnically transfigured" individuals or groups at hand would never be unqualified Brazilians.

Thanks to the political, social, and cultural advocacy of indigenous scholars and organizations across the country, we can say forty years later that Ribeiro was right and wrong: Although the lives and ideas of most Native Brazilians doubtless exist in an inevitable state of postmodern flux and adaptation, the very notion of "generic Indianness" is clearly more expedient for state authorities and the dominant majority—and, more specifically, for their bureaucratic reification of Ramos's "hyper-real Indian"[121]—than it is now or can ever be for the cause of indigenous self-representation. Whereas many politicians, legislators, scientists, and citizens still dwell in the realm of "generic" and "hyperreal Indianness," indigenous peoples increasingly call into question the very use of the word *índio* to invoke or interpellate them, and continue working to give new life to traditional languages, belief systems, histories, and sociocultural practices, regardless of whether they are articulated in ancestral or local terms. In this sense, the intensification of interindigenous/intercommunal relations and indigenous/nonindigenous collaboration at national and international levels has served, quite to the contrary of dominant indigenist dogma, to strengthen the specific characteristics of Native peoples and organizations rather than to dilute or dissolve them.

The artists, activists, and theorists whose work I examine here have seldom had the opportunity to fulfill their alternative visions of sovereignty and justice in national or international arenas of politics or cultural production. Nonetheless, they have never ceased to offer, over many decades, a series of theoretical and practical proposals to transform the political and cultural processes and institutions by and through which they have been marginalized. On the one hand, they have contributed and appealed to supranational institutions like the United Nations and the International Labor Organization, whose backing they continue to seek to bolster their rights as "differentiated" citizens of nation-states. On the other hand, they have called on Native individuals and communities themselves to seek greater participation in a government from which they are almost entirely excluded; to reexamine and rewrite the past from indigenous perspectives and in indigenous languages; and to participate vigorously in national and international debates on a wide range of contentious issues, ranging from health care, education, and reproductive rights, to land distribution, development, and environmental protection.[122] In both cases, the political and the metaphysical once again go hand-in-hand with the expectation that, as Eliane Potiguara proposes, "the world can learn to build a new man and a new woman based on indigenous ethics and knowledge."[123] As she elaborates: "It is necessary to reevaluate the life stories of our ancient prophets without regard to ethnicity, nation, religion, or spiritual current, and to interpret their words in a new way, . . . by beginning to see in their prophecies the true paths for building the peace and ethics we all desire."[124]

Potiguara's proposal may seem rather conservative in light of the political, social, economic, and environmental challenges that we face collectively at the outset of the twenty-first century, but her call to reconsider the value of traditional indigenous knowledge to frame and address those challenges is, in fact, revolutionary. The task she presents is not to transform prophecies into policies, as if there were a simple correspondence between the two, but rather to reconsider the political from an indigenous perspective that values the reciprocity and mutual respect that inform nonhegemonic conceptions of sovereignty—to "think Indian," as the American Indian College Fund put it in defense of the simultaneous and indissoluble relationship between the "education of mind and spirit."[125] Potiguara's work thus resonates with the creative and political activism of Native communities across the Americas who impel us to understand that although "the Indian has not always has the opportunity to speak for him [or her]self,"[126] "indigenous ways of understanding the world are valuable and necessary for the survival of all people."[127]

In her 1998 book *Indigenism: Ethnic Politics in Brazil*, Alcida Ramos drew on years of fieldwork and political activism to analyze the relationship between national society and "its" Indians and reflected on her long engagement with the indigenous and indigenist actors whose lives and ideas helped to shape her own life and ideas in powerful ways. Lamenting the widespread tendency to associate Indianness with helplessness, and thus with the tropes and images of childhood, she wondered why "the Indian" was "so rarely the theme of serious adult writing in contemporary Brazil" and observed that the "light," "humorous," "candid," and "sweet" youth literature written by the likes of educational scholar Daniel Munduruku, whom she singled out, had done little—and in fact could only do little—to offset the customarily infantilizing portrayal of "Indians" by and in dominant society.[128] Ramos's line of query therefore implied, on the one hand, that by "serious" writing she meant something other than the ample body of "Indian-focused" travel literature, journalism, fiction, and science (or pseudoscience) that fed widespread ideas about Indianness from the colonial period to the end of the millennium, when her own book was published. On the other hand, her argument reveals how much the nature of indigenous representation itself has changed in the relatively short period that has since passed. Writing about and especially *by* indigenous peoples has grown so quickly and so extensively over the last decade through formal and informal communication channels that it is difficult even to begin to account for it all. From mainstream news outlets and nongovernmental associations, to a wide array of thematic and specialized listservs, web and video logs, digital archives, and social media, indigenous cultural production is challenging—despite all the familiar caveats about the lettered city and the digital divide—the entrenched essentialisms of traditional indigenist discourse on thousands and, soon, perhaps millions of new fronts.

Among the overwhelming number of sources that have become available to the general public in recent years, the foundational *Literatura indígena* listserv, created by Eliane Potiguara in June 2002, has been especially vital to the changing landscape of indigenous representation in Brazil. As the web portal explains:

> This network aims to unite indigenous writers and thinkers looking to exercise their human rights as reflected in . . . literature by focusing on diverse themes that we take to be a transformative force in our lives as indigenous peoples . . . —agents who mobilize opinion, generators of ideas, [and] champions of indigenous consciousness—a *national thinking* . . . devalued by the cultural imposition of [our] detractors. The network also aims . . . to foster exchange between national and international indigenous writers and . . . lovers of this literature who might not be indigenous. . . . The themes [addressed] are of the widest possible variety: traditional knowledge, intellectual property, indigenous rights, land rights, gender, biodiversity, health and reproductive rights, education, development and labor. . . . Afro-descended peoples, like resuscitated peoples [*povos ressurgidos*], descendants of fugitive slave communities [*quilombolas*], [and] indigenous peoples living outside traditional communities and in urban areas are all welcome . . . in this network [that collaborates] against the sociopolitical and racial system that oppresses us as indigenous peoples.[129]

For Potiguara, then, the "indigenous literatures" framework functions as a gateway to an array of political and cultural issues whose ultimate objective is to contribute a self-identified "Brazilian indigenous" perspective to a national and international dialogue about the historical and lived meanings of indigeneity. Indeed, in the years that I have participated in the group, rarely has the discussion been "literary" in any strict sense of the term. Most of the time, "indigenous literature" serves instead as a trope for the expression of an indigenous perspective about anything of import to self-identifying indigenous peoples and their allies.

The designation is not, however, without its critics and controversies. Olívio Jekupé, for instance, equates *indigenous literature* to any writing about "Indians," regardless of its proximity to lived indigenous experience or authorial "locus of enunciation." As he argues, *Native literature*, in contrast, is written from an indigenous perspective—a perspective he associates with those, like him, who self-identify as indigenous but also live inside an indigenous *aldeia*.[130] Paradoxically, Jekupé (meaning *mestiço*), who calls himself a "non-pure Indian [*índio não puro*]" and writes in Portuguese, collaborates with a bilingual fellow writer and friend to translate his work into Guarani. When I met with him in the *aldeia* Krukutu in August 2011, he expressed a good deal of frustration over the fact that some of the best-known indigenous writers, talented though they were, lived neither "like Indians" nor among other indigenous peoples. Thus, while some Native Brazilian writers articulate indigeneity as an origin— having been "born Indian," for instance, regardless of how or where ones lives the present, others associate indigeneity with the conscious choice to live as part of a physical indigenous community *as well as* a virtual one. My role, of course, is not to advocate for any one position in these debates but merely to place them in context. Discussions of who is more or less "Indian" and why are the flip side of Marcos Terena's calculated directive for indigenous peoples to embrace the capacity to explode old indigenist binaries by being like other and self at the same time and suggest, once again, that many self-identifying Natives may be no freer than anyone else from the quagmires of authenticity. The strategic embrace of "asymmetric knowledge" hence reveals itself not only as a basic methodology through which we might strive to think and to act when confronted with human difference, but also as the uneven and shaky ground on which we must try to stand in order to say or do anything useful at all.

POSTINDIGENISM

Despite the substantial, if sometimes conflict-ridden proliferation of indigenous self-representation, Alcida Ramos's 1998 observation that the depiction of "Indians" by non-Indians tends to infantilize them at every turn could not be more crucial than it is today.[1] The problem, however, is not, as she argued then, that such renderings have been directed primarily at children but, rather, that many of them, both scholarly and popular, *were* and *are* intended for general, adult audiences, and were and are taken by those audiences to be "authentic" or otherwise worthwhile representations of Brazilian "Indianness" by millions at home and abroad. So powerful has been the "authenticity" of such expressions that they have often succeeded, as we have seen repeatedly, in drowning out lived indigeneity—from the Terena Voluntários da Pátria in the late nineteenth century to the Kayapó opponents of the Belo Monte hydroelectric dam at the beginning of the twenty-first, with the lives of Inhanderu, Lyrio Arlindo do Valle, Kapêlituk, Diacuí Canualo Aiute, the Xavante on Xuxa's stage, numerous critics of SIVAM, and the Pataxó protestors of Brazil's quincentennial celebration all falling in between.[2]

This problem has been compounded by the old and common perception that indigenous knowledge is relevant mostly, if not exclusively, to itself. While non-Native scholarship has considered indigenous history and thought predominantly through the lenses of anthropology and ethnography, and while the popular culture of the dominant majority continues to manipulate "Indians" primarily as a source of entertainment and amusement, Native scholars, organizations, and communities have long argued that many of the social, political, cultural, and economic predicaments of our day can be addressed or resolved with the benefit of indigenous experience and knowledge regarding health and personal well-being, social relations, governance, the sacred, and the relationship between people, the Earth, and its resources.

As someone who has sought through writing to communicate indigenous histories, cultural practices, and philosophies to nonindigenous audiences, while at the same time formally studying Western philosophies and educational practices at the Universidade de São Paulo, Daniel Munduruku is particularly well-poised among the scholars and activists whose work I study here as an effective mediator among Native and non-Native philosophical and political traditions, approximating a figure that Dale Turner in the North American context has called the "word warrior." As progeny of and participants in diverse and sometimes contradictory traditions, word warriors are for Turner those individuals "who know . . . their tribal history while understanding that the survival of their people depends on knowing how to engage effectively in discourses that are mostly 'about' Indians, or 'for' Indians, and not determined by Indians."[3] They struggle with the double bind of having to work as part of the system in order to change it, as well as with the multiple challenges of "asymmetric knowledge," whose embrace I propose as one possible way out of a traditional and colonialist indigenist order.

Notwithstanding the substantial proliferation of indigenous literatures in which he has been a key protagonist, Munduruku has argued that the leaders of the Brazilian indigenous movement have sometimes "been heard" but only "rarely been read."[4] Even less frequently, he notes, have their ideas about politics, culture, history, philosophy, and spirituality served as the topic of nonethnographic intellectual inquiry or discussion by anyone other than indigenous peoples themselves. Olívio Jekupé has likewise observed that Native Brazilians are discriminated by "those who have never shared their knowledge; . . . those who consider themselves superior [and] do not know their place in the world . . . [or] their own roots."[5] By making young people one central focus of their work, Munduruku, Jekupé, and a generation of indigenous writers and activists along with them are living out their response to Ramos's critique by seeking to address this problem at its core.

Contemporary indigenous writing, educational campaigns, and political activism reflect the obvious but largely disregarded fact that children are fundamental to what Norberto Bobbio imagined as the "future of democracy"[6] and, as such, are vital members of the small but diverse audience with an unaffected interest in what Native peoples have to say. In other words, they tend not to assume that what it means to be and think "like an Indian" is readily accessible to them through old-school ethnography or the creative work of indigenist novelists, filmmakers, or hobbyists—an attitude that Munduruku described in his earliest chronicles as, "I knew it all along!"[7] Furthermore, if the implied readers of juvenile literature are also the adult mediators and purveyors of those texts,[8] parents and teachers who have never had an opportunity to hear an indigenous perspective on indigeneity (or anything else) certainly have much to learn from the contributions of writers like those discussed here. Indeed, in a dominant society where popular entertainment still serves, à la Xuxa, as a widely accepted palette on which to caricature indigenous peoples—to manipulate their images, stereotype their beliefs, and mock their social and cultural practices—the struggle to win over young hearts and minds is an indispensable component of the Brazilian indigenous movement.

Munduruku and Jekupé offer distinct and illustrative interpretations of their respective roles in this effort. Whereas Jekupé embraces the responsibility to set the record straight—to teach nonindigenous people what it is like to live as an indigenous person in an indigenous community; to cultivate appreciation for the diversity of indigenous experience; and to make sure, for example, that Guaranis are not taken for Xavantes, and vice versa[9]—Munduruku claims no exclusive privilege to a "true" or "authentic" story of indigeneity. Nor does he present his version of past or current events as corrective. Instead, he recognizes that the diverse contributions of self-identifying indigenous peoples to the ongoing construction of indigeneity are precisely to expose the *fact of its construction*, both social and historical, through an endless array of discourses that will always remain beyond the control of any one individual. Hence he seeks to add his voice to an already complex mix of voices, in hopes of fostering, alongside other collaborators, an open-hearted and productive discussion. "[These] . . . stories," he explains, " . . . uncover issues that are very present in peoples' daily lives: How do I see the Indian who arrives to my city? How does the Indian see the city where I live? Are they savages? Do they eat people? Do they have souls? I do not comment on these stories but let the reader arrive at his or her own conclusions. I have preferred, instead of analyzing them, to laugh with them, believing that whoever reads them will also laugh—about the situation, about me, and about him- or herself."[10] By positing the crisis of indigenous representation with an eye on our shared humanity, he suggests, we might begin to move forward in the task of fostering mutual understanding and respect.

One of the most popular forms of children's literature in Brazil, the Turma da Mônica comic series was created by artist Maurício de Sousa in the early 1970s and is now read by millions of children in Brazil and around the world in Portuguese, Spanish, English, and Mandarin. In this edition, one of the main characters, Papa-Capim—also the name of a bird, meaning "Grass Eater"—embarks on a series of "breathtaking adventures" alongside his human and animal friends. Papa-Capim is, according to Maurício de Sousa, "perfectly integrated into his tribe and nature" ("Personagem"). The caption to the published version of the image reads: "Quando indiozinhos e bichos se reúnem num Almanaque, o que não pode faltar [sic] são aventuras de tirar o fôlego! E tudo em meio a um cenário de matas, rios, e o que a natureza tem de mais belo! Venha você também apreciar essa beleza toda. [When little Indians and animals get together in an Almanaque, breathtaking adventures cannot be far behind! And everything (takes place) in a scenario (full) of forests, rivers, and the most beautiful facets of nature! Come along and witness all the beauty.]" From Almanaque Papa-Capim. Copyright © 2012 Maurício de Sousa Produções Ltda. All rights reserved.

Since Munduruku's authorial debut in the mid-nineties, he has completed a doctorate in education, penned over thirty books, and launched the Palavra de Índio publishing initiative to promote the creative work of other Native writers in Portuguese and several indigenous languages.[11] He has created multiple resources and networks for collaboration between indigenous and nonindigenous individuals and communities through education, and heads the Instituto Indígena Brasileiro para Propriedade Intelectual (Brazilian Indigenous Institute for Intellectual Property, or INBRAPI) in collaboration with Native political and spiritual leaders throughout the country. Each of these initiatives has at its core the desire to offer a counterpoint to dominant representations of "Indians" and "Indianness," and to cultivate exchange and seek out shared political ground among people who otherwise might never have an opportunity to meet or join forces. Like Eliane Potiguara, Lúcio Flores, Dale Turner, Taiaiake Alfred, Linda Tuhiwai Smith, and so many others, Munduruku posits the dissemination of indigenous ways of being in and knowing the world as meaningful not only to Native peoples, but also to the societies of the dominant majority whose ways of being and knowing continue to frame indigenous life in powerful and oftentimes inescapable ways.

The INBRAPI web portal explains:

The Traditional Knowledge of Brazilian indigenous peoples . . . is holistic and circular and does not distinguish between the Sacred and the Profane. This idea is represented through the *maracá*, an instrument for healing humanity, represented here as Occidental, rigid, compartmentalized knowledge that understands the human in isolation from nature—[as] a dominator capable of destroying everything. INBRAPI aims to . . . disseminate Holistic Knowledge through the sound of the *maracás* [and] the power of the herbs and dreams of our spiritual leaders—but also through the competence of its directors, collaborators, and partners. Accordingly, INBRAPI will seek new forms and methodologies to create laws that incorporate our holistic thinking into Occidental thinking in defense of the real interests of Brazilian indigenous communities."[12]

Seeking to influence the thought of the dominant majority, the directorship of INBRAPI has inverted the colonialist trajectory of power at work in the "civilizing mission" of twentieth-century indigenist discourse. If the future of Brazil's indigenous peoples is tied inextricably to the future of Occidental/dominant thinking, on the one hand, and the reformulation of Occidental/dominant law, on the other, then the work of the indigenous movement must be, of course, to understand and influence both. Anticipating the 2012 U.N. Conference on Sustainable Development (Rio+20), hosted in Brazil at the same time the Brazilian state continued to undermine the well-being of "its" own Native peoples, hundreds of Brazilian indigenous activists made this message the focus of their open letter at the Indigenous Social Forum held in Bertioga, São Paulo: *"[Our] traditional knowledge can bring about a better world.* . . . We reiterate . . . our right to participate in the Rio+20 Conference, not as a piece of folklore but as sovereign Indigenous Peoples. . . . Together with the nonindigenous, blacks, local communities, . . . academics, scientists, women, young people, and warriors, we want to open a dialogue about the Earth . . . for a World with quality of life.[13]

Although much work remains to educate nonindigenous peoples about Brazil's indigenous past, present, and future, and to offset the ever-popular lore of benevolent colonialism, racial democracy, and Indian grandmothers "caught with lassos,"[14] many indigenous scholars and teachers choose to prioritize first the educational needs of their own communities. This impetus has inspired national-level conferences aimed at improving the content and delivery of indigenous education and the intensified production of pedagogical materials in Native languages authored by or in collaboration with Native speakers of those languages.[15] Likewise, university-level programs offering specialized training in bilingual and intercultural pedagogies for indigenous teachers exist in at least nine states, and research centers for the study of indigenous languages, cultures, histories, and philosophies are expanding beyond the domain of state-backed indigenist institutions like FUNAI and the Museu do Índio.[16] Vital changes are taking place, for example, among Terena communities in Mato Grosso do Sul, where instruction in the Terena language is offered to Terena children and adolescents, as well as to Terena adults who may have never had an opportunity to read or write in their Native tongue.[17]

Notwithstanding such positive initiatives, the broader configuration of political, social, economic, and cultural power in which they take place reveals a steep road ahead. As a result of the intensified and institutionalized disempowerment of indigenous peoples and interests during the first decade of the twenty-first century, which culminates in state sponsorship of Belo Monte, it seems unlikely that a substantial number of nonindigenous politicians or citizens will in the near future embrace or even begin to consider the ideas and projects of indigenous intellectuals and communities seriously enough to assess their practical and theoretical implications for the future of national development policy, educational

INBRAPI
Instituto
Indígena
Brasileiro para
Propriedade
Intelectual

INBRAPI logotype representing the power of indigenous knowledge to influence Occidental knowledge and dominant society. Courtesy of the Instituto Indígena Brasileiro para Propriedade Intelectual (INBRAPI).

reform, environmental protection, governance, or international relations. Native Brazilians' efforts to counter the privatization of the indigenist bureaucracy and the deleterious effects of contemporary indigenist policy through intensified demands for land demarcation, ethnodevelopment, intercultural education, and other empowering social programs, as well as through heightened cultural activism and political participation at all levels of government indicate, indeed, that the struggle for indigenous self-representation has in some ways just begun. Nonetheless, the viral proliferation of indigenous political commentary and cultural production via the Internet in the form of journalism, fiction, film, video, blogging, and election campaigning (for example) continues to revolutionize the relationship between Native peoples and visual representation, on the one hand, and Native peoples and the written word, on the other.

The 2010 presidential and congressional elections provide a case in point. Precisely one century after Cândido Mariano da Silva Rondon founded the SPI to guide Native Brazilians out of Indianness and into the nation, sixteen indigenous candidates from across the country ran for national office, and more than thirty indigenous candidates ran for local and state office in Roraima, Amazonas, Acre, and Rondônia alone.[18] With limited resources, these candidates organized campaigns and promoted their candidacies to indigenous and nonindigenous constituencies alike through both traditional means and new media like Blogger, Orkut, Facebook, Twitter, and YouTube. Although indigenous uses of these resources raise new questions about "authenticity"—beginning with the observation that most Native Brazilian websites appear exclusively in Portuguese—they also reveal a desire for unmediated self-representation and activism that Rondon never could have imagined, and as self-appointed representative of Indian ideas and interests, might have hesitated to accept. The centennial of state-backed indigenism thus marked a radical transformation in the relationship between indigeneity and representation: Rather than indigenist actors' presenting ideas and images of indigeneity to suit their needs in accordance with the interests of a national society that could only include them through exclusion, self-identifying Natives made the Internet an additional canvas on which to envision new forms of horizontal collaboration with members of dominant society in accordance with overlapping indigenous and nonindigenous priorities and interests.

Upon declaring his official candidacy for state representative in the 2010 congressional elections, Marcos Terena redesigned his website by removing a banner photograph that depicted him wearing a T-shirt and several beaded necklaces and replaced it with another image that portrayed him in a collared dress shirt and blue blazer.[19] The original headline, "Orgulho pantaneiro" ("Pantaneiro Pride"), was removed and replaced with a map of Brazil adorned with flashing images of indigenous and nonindigenous men and women of all ages and the running tag line, "*Nós confiamos em você* [We trust in you]." For those, like me, who followed the blog before and after Terena's political candidacy, the new aesthetic read like a visual shortcut for a non-Native audience to that old idea that for so many still seems difficult to grasp or impossible to believe: "I can be what you are without ceasing to be who I am."

Rethinking how the representation of indigenous needs and interests works in local, national, and international politics, and reconfiguring the problematic relationship between indigeneity and dominant sovereignty, means more than Native peoples' being inserted or even inserting themselves into existing political structures and institutions—however crucial and challenging that feat continues to be. At the very least, it must also mean rethinking sovereignty in collaboration with indigenous peoples and not for them, while taking into account their interests, values, renderings of the past, and policy proposals with regard to development, education, social welfare, environmental protection, land tenure, governance, and freedom. As Marcos Terena suggested more than two decades ago, reforming politics and rethinking the political to the collective benefit of Native peoples means building and strengthening interindigenous connections and collaboration across national borders,

Marcos Terena participates in "Dialogue Days" during the United Nations Conference on Sustainable Development in Rio de Janeiro, 17 June 2012. Photo by Linh Do/Speak Your Mind. Reproduced with the permission of Marcos Terena.

as well as nationally, while at the same time restructuring the colonialist configurations of power that have shaped relations between Native and non-Native peoples since the Conquest. Seeking to explain his own political trajectory in the context of the Brazilian indigenous movement, he conceded: "After seeing so many of our brothers decimated over the course of four centuries, we discovered that we could not walk alone. It [was] necessary to discover allies for our cause and for the survival of our . . . peoples among the [then] 140 million [nonindigenous] members of Brazilian society."[20]

The population numbers have changed dramatically over the past two decades, but the urgency of forming such alliances across the dividing lines between indigenous and nonindigenous peoples, and among individuals and groups working within the parameters of other socially and historically formed notions of ethnicity, "race," class, and geography (for example), most certainly has not. Shared and increasing interest among indigenous and nonindigenous Brazilians in preventing the construction of the Belo Monte hydroelectric dam—because of the social and economic ills it will engender, the environmental destruction it will wreak, and the human rights it will violate—is surely the most significant example of our day. National and transnational opposition to the initiative articulates these issues as ultimately inseparable from one another, thus resonating with the traditional indigenous belief in the inexorable interconnectedness of all human experience, and an increasingly widespread questioning of dominant notions of progress.[21] "The hurt of one is the hurt of all," Phil Lane Jr. has long argued, "and the honor of one is the honor of all. . . . Unless justice animates all that we do in human and community work, what we are doing is not development."[22]

(top) Founder of the Movimento Indígenas em Ação (MIA), Ysani Kalapalo (fourth from the left) leads a demonstration against the Belo Monte hydroelectric dam in downtown São Paulo, 20 August 2011. Also pictured (from left to right): Yamuni Barbosa, Samantha Aweti Kalapalo, Mariana Aweti Kalapalo, Índia Tikuna Weena Miguel, Guayra Wassu, I. Wassu, and Tayla Kalapalo. Photo by the author; reproduced with the permission of Ysani Kalapalo.

(bottom) "We Are Xingu." Demonstration against the Belo Monte hydroelectric dam in downtown São Paulo, 20 August 2011. Photo by the author.

Reflecting on his many years of political activism and the culmination of that experience in his candidacy for public office, Marcos Terena expressed optimism about Native participation in the selection of Brazil's national self-government despite the growing improbability of success for his own bid: "An indigenous candidacy is an odd human feat, but one that manifests democracy—democracy that inspires us to throw off the discrimination that has until now placed us at the margins of the decisions that affect us, and that every four years gives us hope for a voice in a representative body like the National Congress."[23] That dozens of Native candidates chosen by mainstream political parties to defend mainstream political platforms sought in nationwide elections to represent indigenous interests in concert with the interests of their nonindigenous constituencies destabilizes the colonialist foundations of twentieth-century indigenism. The fact that they continue to work toward this goal in the wake of defeat, and the fact that at least part of the coalition against Belo Monte has come to articulate its opposition in resonance with Native conceptions of sovereignty, give us cautious hope that despite—and perhaps also, because of—the great challenges that together we face, a new political order may be on the horizon. If Jurupiranga has his way, it will be a postindigenist order in which indigeneity will be valued not only by indigenous peoples, and self-identification will nourish the terrain from which we all think and act, without constituting, at the same time, the only ends that we work to achieve, or the only dreams that we dare to dream.

FINAL DOCUMENT OF THE
CONFERENCE OF INDIGENOUS PEOPLES AND
ORGANIZATIONS OF BRAZIL

We arrived in the Pataxó community in the municipality of Santa Cruz Cabrália, Bahia, on 17 April 2000. We have fulfilled our promise to retrace the paths of the immense invasion of our territories, which has lasted for 500 years. We are more than 3,000 representatives, from 140 indigenous peoples throughout the country. We have traveled the lands, rivers, mountains, valleys, and plains once inhabited by our ancestors. We look with emotion on the regions where for more than 40,000 years indigenous peoples ruled and built their future. We look with emotion on the regions where indigenous peoples were defeated defending lands that were severed [first] by *bandeirantes*, adventurers, and miners, and later by roads, ranches, and businessmen, thirsty for land, profit, and power.

We retraced the path of struggle and pain in order to take history into our own hands and point, once again, toward a future worthy of all indigenous peoples. Here in this conference, we analyze Brazilian society in the 500 years of its history built on our territories. We confirm, more than ever before, that this society founded on invasion and the extermination of the peoples who lived here was built on slavery and the exploitation of black people and the popular sectors of society. It is an infamous and indignant history. The persecuted and exploited have maintained their dignity throughout these five centuries. Revolts, insurrections, political and social movements also marked our history, establishing a continuous line of resistance. For this reason, we have returned to recover this mark of the past in order to move toward the future, united with black and popular movements in building a broader alliance: Indigenous, Black, and Popular Resistance.

Principal demands and proposals:
What follows are the primary demands and proposals of indigenous peoples for the Brazilian state that have been highlighted in this conference.

1. Fulfillment of indigenous peoples' rights as guaranteed by the Constitution:
   a. . . . regularization and demarcation of all indigenous lands by the end of 2000;
   b. repeal of Decree 1.775/96 [regarding demarcation of indigenous territories];
   c. assurance and protection of indigenous lands;
   d. return of the territories claimed by various indigenous peoples all over Brazil;
   e. broadening the boundaries of the areas insufficient for life and growth of indigenous families;
   f. withdrawal of invaders from all demarcated lands; compensation and rehabilitation of degraded areas and rivers, such as the Rio San Francisco;
   g. recognition of resurgent peoples and their territories;
   h. protection against the invasion of the territories of isolated peoples;
   i. restructuring of municipalities established illegally in indigenous areas;
   j. respect for the right to the exclusive use of natural resources in indigenous areas with special attention to biopiracy;
   k. halting the construction of dams, waterways, railroads, highways, and pipelines under way, and compensation for damages caused by the projects that have already been completed.
2. support for [indigenous] self-sufficiency, including financial resources for agricultural and other projects for indigenous communities;
3. immediate adoption of Convention 169 of the International Labor Organization (ILO);
4. adoption of the Statute of Indigenous Peoples (PL 2.057/91), as approved by indigenous peoples and organizations, which is now making its way through Congress;
5. the end to all forms of discrimination, deportation, massacres, threats to leaders, violence, and impunity. Immediate investigation of all crimes committed against indigenous peoples in the past 20 years and punishment of the perpetrators. We demand respect for the cultures, traditions, languages, and religions of the various indigenous peoples of Brazil;
6. punishment at the discretion of the community of those responsible for the criminal sterilization of indigenous women;
7. that the true history of this country, including thousands of years of existence of indigenous peoples on this land, is recognized and taught in schools;
8. reform of the Indian agency by strengthening its relationship to the presidency through a Bureau of Indian Affairs; consultation with grassroots organizations regarding the choice of secretaries;
9. that the president of FUNAI be elected by indigenous people from different regions of Brazil;
10. that education serve indigenous struggle and strengthen our cultures;
11. guaranteed access for indigenous students to federal universities without entrance exams;

12. reform, expansion, and construction of indigenous schools and instruction at all levels; guaranteed indigenous teaching and vocational high school education;
13. oversight of the funds used for indigenous schools and the formation of an Indigenous Council;
14. that indigenous schooling and health care be considered a federal responsibility. We reject efforts at decentralization through state and municipal authorities;
15. the Arouca Law, establishing specialized health care for indigenous peoples, should be enforced;
16. strengthening and expansion of the active participation of communities and leaders in decision making with regard to public policies for indigenous peoples— and, in particular, the autonomy of Special Indigenous Sanitary Districts;
17. that health care consider and respect the culture of the people. Traditional medicine should be valued and enhanced;
18. specialized training and quality standards for indigenous teachers, health professionals, and others who work with indigenous communities;
19. elaboration of a specific policy for each major region of the country with the broad participation of indigenous peoples and all segments of society based on their knowledge and life projects;
20. forbidding the entry of military and civil police into indigenous areas without the permission of [indigenous] leaders and withdrawal of police forces already present;
21. termination of court proceedings opposing the demarcation of lands occupied by indigenous peoples.

We, the indigenous peoples of Brazil have come a long way in rebuilding our territories and communities. With this history firmly in our collective grasp, we are sure to break with the tragic past and move confidently toward the future. Despite the weight of the old story reflected in the ruling classes of this country—in its culture, its political and economic policies, and its state institutions—we have already have launched our battle cry and begun a new history—the great story of the "Next 500 years." Our indigenous struggle is a tribute to the many heroes who fell struggling over the course of five centuries. Our struggle is for our children and grandchildren: free people in a free land.

Coroa Vermelha, Porto Seguro, Bahia, 21 April 2000

NOTES

INTRODUCTION

1. The ethnically diverse Sioux peoples reside primarily not in the U.S. Southwest but in North and South Dakota, Nebraska, Minnesota, Montana, Manitoba, and Saskatchewan.

2. Sullivan and Massadas, "Brincar de índio." All translations are mine unless otherwise indicated. The performance described here is from 1989.

3. Xuxa refers to the men and boys as *índios*, never as Xavante.

4. Xuxa's music and performances have been marketed primarily for children. In the late eighties, she was highest-paid woman in Latin America and one of the wealthiest celebrities in the world. Two years after "Brincar de índio" hit the airwaves, another single from the LP on which it appeared (*Ilariê*) reached fifteenth place on the international music charts (*Billboard*). Four of the top ten best-selling Brazilian albums of all time are hers. Her television show (*O Xou da Xuxa*), translated into Spanish and exported throughout Latin America, became a regional success and had a short life in the English-speaking U.S. market. See Simpson, *Xuxa*.

5. Of course, countless personal (and thus political) factors, ranging from age, class, education, profession, and geography to ethnicity, religion, gender, and sexual orientation, mediate our perceptions of "Indianness," along with everything else. On such mediations see Hall and du Gay, "Encoding/Decoding."

6. P. Deloria, *Playing Indian*, 32–35, 185.

7. Ibid., 184.

8. Generally, I use the term *indigenism* to refer to the widest possible range of discourse about indigenous peoples and to *indigenists* as sources or practitioners of that discourse. Although *indigenism* is a discourse mostly *about* but not by indigenous peoples, some indigenous people do indeed call themselves *indigenists*. *Indigenism* should not be confused with *Indianism*, however, which in this study refers to two distinct phenomena: first and foremost, a romantic literary and cultural movement of the mid-to-late nineteenth century in Brazil (and elsewhere in Latin America); and second, the indigenous-led political movements that are now afoot in the Andes (especially Bolivia and Ecuador). For my purposes, both forms of *Indianism* are strains of the broader, inherently contradictory phenomenon of indigenist discourse. Although the term *indigenism* is now common in Brazil, it was not widely used until after the foundation of the Instituto Indigenista Interamericano (Interamerican Indigenist Institute) in Mexico in the 1940s. During the early years of Brazil's Serviço de Proteção aos Índios (founded in 1911), the common term to describe professionals

211

dedicated to the indigenous cause was *sertanista* (one who works in the *sertão* or "hinterlands").

9. See Ramos, *Indigenism*, 276.

10. On NGOs and development workers more generally, see also Postero, *Now We Are Citizens*, 164–188; Shah, *In the Shadows*; and Martínez Novo, *Who Defines Indigenous?*

11. Baudrillard, *Simulacros*, 13.

12. Darcy Ribeiro founded the Museu do Índio (Indian Museum) in 1953 while head of SPI's Educational Sector. The military government established FUNAI in 1967, after disbanding the SPI. I discuss these organizations in chapters 3 and 4.

13. Much of the debate regarding the question of subaltern "authenticity" in Latin America revolved around the case of Maya Quiché intellectual and activist Rigoberta Menchú Tum, whose 1983 *testimonio, Me llamo Rigoberta Menchú y así me nació la conciencia,* became for many people outside Guatemala emblematic of the indigenous plight during that country's long civil war. Menchú and her advocates were harshly criticized by anthropologist David Stoll (among others) for misrepresenting her life story and depicting the role and interests of Maya communities during the war as stemming primarily from a traditional and collective "indigenous identity." For different takes on "authenticity" as related to the case, see the essays in Gugelberger, *Real Thing*. Also see Arias, *Rigoberta Menchú Controversy*; Beverley, "What Happens When the Subaltern Speaks?"; Patai, "Whose Truth?"; Levinson, "Neopatriarchy"; Zimmerman, *Literature*; Menchú, *Rigoberta*; and Stoll, *Rigoberta Menchú*.

14. See Hale, "Does Multiculturalism Menace?"

15. Quijano and Wallerstein, "Americanity as a Concept," 549.

16. Viera wrote in a 1656 letter to Dom João IV of a gold-hunting expedition to the Pacajá River in which several hundred Pacajá and Tapirapé died from hunger and forced labor: "Sire, these are the only certain mines here. For the main and true purpose of the expedition was to capture Indians: to draw from their veins the red gold that has always been the mine of that state!" A. Viera, *Obras escolhidas*, 285. For commentary on the expedition, see Boxer, *Golden Age*, 277; and Hemming, *Red Gold*, 328.

17. Friedlander, *Being Indian*, 218. For an overview of this question in anthropology, see "Being Indian Revisited," chapter 9 of ibid.

18. This engagement developed through several media, including artisanship, the tourism industry, and literary and new media production. See Meisch, *Andean Entrepreneurs*; Verner, "Tourism"; Schiwy, *Indianizing*, 185–211; and Vídeo nas Aldeias. For recent work on indigenous political engagements in other national contexts, see Lucero, *Struggles*; Canessa, *Natives*; Postero, *Now We Are Citizens*; Warren and Jackson, *Indigenous Movements*; Becker, *Pachakutik*; Rappaport, *Intercultural Utopias*; Yashar, *Contesting Citizenship*; and Van Cott, *Friendly Liquidation*.

19. See n. 12. Though these efforts were not without impact, the Rousseff administration ultimately chose to replace one nonindigenous anthropologist (Márcio Meira) with another (Marta Azevedo). For recent indigenous and nonindigenous debates regarding this process, see the blogs of Marcos Terena, Juvenal Payayá, Mércio Gomes, and the Acampamento Revolucionário Indígena. Also see Guimarães, "Índios invadem sede da FUNAI," and related comments.

20. Revived from the period of military rule by the Lula administration in response to the national energy crisis of the Cardoso presidency, and continued by President Dilma Rousseff as part of the national development plan of the Workers' Party (Partido dos Trabalhadores, or PT), the highly contested dam will divert the flow of the Xingu River, flood indigenous lands, and destroy the livelihood of thousands who live on and off of the river. The designation "Belo Monte" attests to the historical amnesia of its proponents, as the same name was adopted by the antirepublican residents of Canudos who were infamously massacred by the Brazilian army in 1897. Canudos was rebuilt, only to be flooded by an artificial lake resulting from the Cocorocó Dam in 1967 (also during military rule). See Beebee, *Nation and Region*, 66–67; Levine, "Canudos"; and A. Johnson, *Sentencing Canudos*.

21. S. Guajajara, "Environmental Policy."

22. Clavero explains this problem as a consequence of (among other things), "indigenous peoples [living] among mestizo constitutions." *Geografía jurídica*, 13.

23. Lévi-Strauss, *Tristes Tropiques*, 140–41.

24. Taussig, *Shamanism*, xiii.

25. Questions of language and terminology are central to decolonization and pose particular challenges to scholars and activists seeking to think and work across national borders and languages. Words like *tribe* and *Indian*, which are frequently used by the Native peoples of North America, are often pejorative in their Portuguese- or Spanish-language equivalents, and particularly so in the Andes, Central America, and Mexico. In contrast, *Indian* in the North American context refers to more than 500 Native peoples of the continental United States but excludes Alaskan Eskimos and Native Hawaiians. On some of these uses in Brazil, see Ramos, *Indigenism*, 13–59.

26. Goodman's preference for "when" over "what" acknowledged, in a parallel fashion, the performative and referential nature of art. See Giovannelli, "Goodman's Aesthetics."

27. Canessa, "Who Is Indigenous?," 217–18.

28. Hall made the analogous argument that resignifying blackness meant fighting "the entire metaphorical structure of Christian thought." Hall and du Gay, "Old and New Identities," 11.

29. See, for example, Brandão's 1999 version of the Carta, rewritten for schoolchildren.

30. Caminha, "Carta," 68.

31. Ibid., 65–66.

32. Ibid., 71 (my emphasis).

33. Ciema, "O índio."

34. Caminha, "Carta," 73.

35. DaMatta, "For an Anthropology," 281.

36. On the *indio permitido*, see Hale, "Rethinking Indigenous Politics."

37. Humberto Mauro depicted this scene in his 1937 film *Descobrimento do Brasil*, which was partially funded by the Estado Novo and reissued in a restored, commemorative version for Brazil's quincentennial celebrations in 2000. On the Vargas-era version, see R. Gordon, "Recreating Caminha."

38. Caminha, "Carta," 63–64.

39. See Treece, *Exiles*; Sadlier, *Brazil Imagined*, 133; and Schwarcz, *O espectáculo*, 110–13.

40. See n. 8.

41. Cândido Mariano da Silva Rondon, a military engineer of Bororó descent, founded the SPI after his expeditions through northwestern Brazil in the late 1800s at the head of the Rondon Commission. See Teixeira da Fonseca, "A obra de proteção"; Diacon, *Stringing Together*; Garfield, *Indigenous Struggle*; and Souza Lima, *Um grande cerco*.

42. Said, *Orientalism*, 1; Marx, *Eighteenth Brumaire*, 145.

43. Spivak used this distinction in "Can the Subaltern Speak?" and elaborates on the difference between *Darstellung* (representation as "portrait") and *Vertretung* (representation as "proxy") in an interview with Sarah Harasym (Spivak, "Practical Politics," 108–9). See also Larsen, "Marxism."

44. See Shah, *In the Shadows*, 9–35; and Guha, *Dominance*, 60–94.

45. Beverley, *Subalternity*, 71.

46. See Walzer, *Thick and Thin*, xi.

47. For a more recent take on Xuxa's interest in indigenous peoples and issues, see her April 2012 hosting of Brô MCs (a Guarani-Kaiowá rap group from Mato Grosso do Sul) in celebration of the Semana do Índio (Indian Week), available on YouTube and the Globo TV website. For an interview with the group, see Mandrake, "Brô MCs."

48. The most recent show I have been able to trace is from 2006, in Chile. The show described here (http://www.youtube.com/watch?v=ba9JLbDrpWI) had more than 2.2 million hits as of mid-2012. Dozens of versions are available on the Rede Globo website (www.globo.com) and elsewhere.

49. The Lei Afonso Arinos, signed by President Getúlio Vargas in 1951, outlawed discrimination based on *raça* (race) and *cor* (color). The protection was expanded in 1985 by Law no. 7.437, which criminalized discrimination based on sex or civil status, and again in 1989 by Law no. 7.716, which included categories of ethnicity, religion, and national origin. After seven years of debate, a controversial Estatuto da Igualdade Racial (Statute for Racial Equality, Law no. 12.288) was passed by Congress and signed into law by President Luis Inácio Lula da Silva on 20 July 2010. This legislation was formulated initially to address the economic and social marginalization of indigenous as well as Afro-descended peoples but revised to include only a subset of the latter group, *negros*, which refers to self-identifying *pardos* and *pretos* (brown and black-skinned people). Unlike the original version, the 2010 statute included no provisions for "racial quotas" in institutions of higher education, public sector employment, or television programming. In April 2012, the Supremo Tribunal Federal (Supreme Court) upheld the constitutionality (but not the mandatory nature) of quota systems at public universities for black and Afro-descended students—systems that in many cases have been in place for several years.

50. Butler, *Gender Trouble*, 146.

51. Ibid., 148.

52. The Brazilian Institute for Public Opinion and Statistics (IBOPE) rating for the *novela* was the third highest for its time slot between 2000 and 2008. See Feltrin, "Ibope."

53. See my chapter 4.

54. Cavalcanti, "Brasil nunca pertenceu aos índios," 2.

55. On this issue, see my chapter 3; and Garfield, *Indigenous Struggle*, 141, 148–49.

56. These did not include the primary demand for indigenous leadership of FUNAI. See Barreto, letter to Márcio Meira, 15 June 2010.

57. I met with members of the AIR several days later, after their short-lived reoccupation of the site. See Devine Guzmán, "Writing Indigenous Activism "; and Acampamento Revolucionário Indígena blog.

58. The dam projects conceived in the mid-1970s were hotly contested by indigenous peoples, most notably the Kayapó, as well as by national and international environmental groups and celebrities. The Primeiro Encontro held in February 1989 drew more than 600 indigenous protestors to the city of Altamira (Pará), where Kayapó leader Tuíra famously brandished a machete in the face of Eletronorte representative José Antônio Muniz. In light of the political uproar, environmental concerns, and jeopardized funding, the project was shelved for reevaluation for over a decade. I discuss the revived project in chapter 5. See also Devine Guzmán, "Whence Amazonian Studies."

59. These are laid out in the five chapters of Title 2. Chapter 1, "Individual and Collective Rights and Duties," has seventy-eight clauses to guarantee equal treatment before the law and the "inviolability of the right to life, liberty, equality, security, and property."

60. Chapter 8 of Title 8, "Indians," explains the protection of indigenous social organization, customs, language, creeds, and traditions." Nonetheless, the 1973 Indian Statue would remain in place to ensure that indigenous peoples are deserving of special state protection because of their "relative incapability."

61. Garfield, *Indigenous Struggle*, 187–219.

62. He served in the Câmera dos Deputados (House of Representatives) from 1983 to 1986, representing Rio de Janeiro as a member of the Partido Democrático Trabalhista (Democratic Workers' Party, or PDT).

63. Otherwise known as the International War Crimes Tribunal. See Ramos, *Indigenism*, 104–18; and Garfield, *Indigenous Struggle*, 199–200.

64. Martins, "Um brasileiro," 201. He names the official as Van der Brook.

65. Ibid., 211–12.

66. Juruna, allegedly involved in bribery during his first term, was not reelected. See M. Gomes, *Indians*, 220–28; and Ramos, *Indigenism*, 104–18, 140. For more on Juruna's involvement in national politics, see Juruna, Hohlfelt, and Hoffman, *O gravador do Juruna*.

67. See Hoffman French, *Legalizing Identities*; McNally, "Indian Passion Play"; Ramos, "Hyperreal Indian"; and Warren, *Racial Revolutions*. On aboriginal tourism, see, for example, the cases of British Columbia (www.aboriginalbc.com); Australia http://www.aboriginaltourism.com.au); and Mexico (www.rita.com.mx). In Brazil, such tourism is growing, but it is not (yet) authorized or regulated by FUNAI.

68. Mariátegui, "El problema del indio," 221.

69. See n. 13. Other influential testimonial narratives from the second half of the twentieth century include those by Carolina Maria de Jesus (Brazil), Esteban Montejo (Cuba), Gregorio Condori Mamani (Peru), and Domitila Barrios de Chungara (Bolivia).

70. Compared to the highly visible indigenous movements in neighboring Bolivia and Ecuador, Peru's indigenous movement has been limited, in part, because many Quechua- and Aymara-speaking residents of the southern highlands choose not to identify with "Indianness" (or indigeneity) as a sociopolitical category or marker. The cultural, social, economic, and geographic considerations that factor into ethnic labels have led some scholars to claim that there are no *indios* in the Peruvian countryside but rather rural dwellers who identify as *campesinos*, *quechuas*, *runas* (Quechua for "people"), or simply Peruvians. For exceptions to this trend, see the work of the nongovernmental association CHIRAPAQ Centro de Culturas Indias (http://www.chirapaq. org.pe). On identification with indigeneity (or lack thereof) in Peru, see Castro-Klarén, "Posting Letters"; de la Cadena, *Indigenous Mestizos*; Degregori, "Ethnicity"; Devine Guzmán, "Indigenous Identity" and "Rimanakuy"; Lévano, "El indio"; M. E. García, *Making Indigenous Citizens*; Mazzotti, "Creole Agencies"; and Yashar, *Contesting Citizenship*. The Native peoples of the Peruvian Amazon, in contrast, have been highly organized in recent years, largely due to the heightened incursion of logging and mining interests into their territories. Their 2009 protests in Bagua led to armed conflict with authorities and several dozen deaths. In response, then-president Alan García warned that indigenous protestors would "lead [the country] to irrationality and primitive backwardness" ("President Alan García advierte"). See also the website of the Asociación Interétnica de Desarrollo de la Selva Peruana, http://www.aidesep.org.pe.

71. See Carvalho, Carvalho, and Carelli, *Vídeo nas Aldeias, 25 anos*. On mediation, see Corrêa, "Vídeo nas Aldeias." On other uses of film and video by indigenous peoples in Brazil and Latin America, see Ginsburg, "Parallax Effect"; Himpele, *Circuits*; Schiwy, *Indianizing*; and Stam, *Tropical Multiculturalism*. For a variety of indigenous perspectives on the technology debate, see the webpages of INBRAPI (http://www.inbrapi.org.br/), Daniel Munduruku (http://danielmunduruku.blogspot .com), Juvenal Payayá (http://juvenal.teodoro.blog.uol.com.br/), and Eliane Potiguara (http://www.elianepotiguara.org.br/), as well as Potiguara's edited collection, *Sol do pensamento*.

72. VNA became an independent nongovernmental organization in 2000.

73. Corrêa, "Vídeo nas Aldeias," 2.

74. This issue becomes more complex when we examine it across international borders. Consider the case of Native North America, where tribes and nations have the legal authority to determine blood quantum requirements for their members. While some, like the St. Croix Chippewa of Wisconsin and the Miccosukee Tribe of Indians of Florida, require "at least one-half Indian blood," others, like the Comanche Nation of Oklahoma and the Caddo Nation, require one-eighth or one-sixteenth, respectively. (These requirements are detailed on each community's webpage.)

75. Vizenor developed this term in the 1990s and has used it since to indicate Native capacity for something beyond "survival" and "resistance." As he put it in 2008, "Survivance is greater than the right of a survivable name. Survivance stories are renunciations of dominance, detractions, obtrusions, the unbearable sentiments of tragedy, and the legacy of victimry." See Vizenor, *Survivance*, 1, and *Manifest Manners*.

76. See S. Hall, "Old and New Identities" and "Ethnicity."

77. S. Hall, "Ethnicity," 349.

78. The phrase was misspelled on the cover of his 1967 book, *The Medium Is the Massage*. McLuhan liked the triple-entendre (message, massage, mass-age) and decided to keep it. See "Herbert Marshall McLuhan."

79. See McLuhan, *Gutenberg Galaxy*; and McLuhan and Fiore, *War and Peace*.

80. See "World Is a Global Village."

81. Schiwy, *Indianizing*, 210.

82. S. Hall, "Ethnicity," 349.

83. "Entrevista com Maria de Souza Delta."

84. See Borges, "El etnógrafo," which I discuss briefly in chapter 5.

85. See R. Ortiz, *A diversidade dos sotaques*.

86. See the discussions held at the Primeiro Encontro Nacional de Educação Indígena (First National Meeting on Indigenous Education), in Guarani-Bracuí, Rio de Janeiro, in March 2000 ("Primeiro Encontro Nacional de Educação Indígena"). For a more recent discussion, see the 2010 exchange between Cacique Tukumbó Dyeguaká (Robson Miguel) and Cacique Juvenal Payayá with regard to the former's self-nomination as candidate for the presidency of FUNAI. Disheartened by Payayá's lack of support, Miguel responded: "I should let you know right away that you don't even seem like an Indian, and if you are an Indian, I am your relative and I demand your sincerity and respect for my person because I DON'T LIKE INDIANS AGAINST INDIANS!" (original emphasis). See Miguel, Carta a Juvenal Payayá, 6 February 2010.

87. The most documented case in contemporary in Latin America is that of Bolivia, where President Evo Morales has been accused by detractors (especially political rival Felipe Quispe) of not being authentically indigenous. (On this question, see Canessa, "'Todos Somos Indígenas'"). In the United States, the debacle over Colorado University professor Ward Churchill evoked a statement on "wannabes" on behalf of the American Indian Movement (see the American Indian Movement Grand Governing Council and the website of the Ward Churchill Solidarity Network for opposing perspectives on this issue). For a broad overview of current international debates regarding indigeneity, see de la Cadena and Starn, *Indigenous Experience Today*; Maaka and Anderson, *Indigenous Experience*; and Brown and Sant, *Indigeneity*.

88. According to the state, official "racial" categories identified with African, European, and Asian descent are determined through skin color (*preto, pardo, branco, amarelo*), while indigenous heritage has a separate category (*indígena*). Inasmuch as African heritage becomes differentiated socially or politically in the present (through affirmative action programs, for example) it too becomes a source of contention. "Hyphenated" Brazilians (e.g., *ítalo-brasileiros, nipo-brasileiros, teuto-brasileiros*) also face social challenges related to their "liminal" status, but they are likewise identified by the state according to skin color. As the hyphen indicates, their Brazilianness is qualified, while that of *índios* tends to be suspect or denied. See Levine, *Brazilian Legacies*, 55–79; and Lesser, *Negotiating National Identity* and *Searching for Home Abroad*.

89. As I discuss in chapter 3, archival evidence suggests that this identification existed in some communities during the first decades of the twentieth century, if not earlier.

90. Flores, "Cultura e a ex-cultura," 30–31 (my emphasis).

91. See Vargas Llosa, *La utopía arcaica*.

92. Flores, "Cultura e a ex-cultura," 30–32.

93. On diversity within indigenous political and interest groups elsewhere in Latin America, see Canessa, *Who Is Indigenous?*; and Rappaport, *Intercultural Utopias*.

94. Payayá, "Reflexões indígenas," 39–40.

95. Munduruku, "A corrupção do conhecimento."

96. Ramos, "Commodification," 3.

97. Potiguara, "A informação," 8.

98. Ibid., 9.

99. Phil Deloria refers to the Native-European liaisons (Sommer's "foundational fictions" in the case of Latin America, as I discuss in chapter 2) that were common to the nineteenth-century literature of the region. See P. Deloria, *Playing Indian*, 185.

CHAPTER 1

1. The Canela are a Gê-speaking people whose village is located within the municipality of Barra do Corda. Their culture and history, along with those of other Eastern Timbira peoples, were studied by the Brazilian-nationalized German ethnographer Curt Nimuendajú in the 1940s and the Harvard Central Brazil Project in the 1960s. Anthropologist William Crocker has worked with the Canela since 1957. See Crocker, *Canela (Eastern Timbira)*; and Crocker and Crocker, *The Canela*.

2. Kapêlituk, "Ditado."

3. Getúlio Vargas declared the national Dia do Índio in 1943, following the first Interamerican Indigenist Congress in Pátzcuaro, México, in 1940. It is celebrated on 19 April to mark the day that the indigenous delegation joined the nonindigenous participants in that assembly. See Instituto Indigenista Interamericano, *Acta final*, 59.

4. Mohn, letter to Herbert Serpa, 6 April 1948.

5. Serpa, letter to Otto Mohn, May 1948. I have transcribed this and all other documents in their original form. In his published work, Crocker uses the spelling "Kaapêltùk" to refer, I believe, to the same person. It appears that the student who copied the dictation later became one of Crocker's closest informants.

6. Crocker mentions her in a much later account as the sister of another SPI teacher named Raimundo Ferreira Sobrinho ("Doca"). See Crocker, *Canela (Eastern Timbira)*, 43.

7. The school was named for Lieutenant Pedro Ribeiro Dantas, an indigenist inspector who was working as assistant to SPI founder Cândido Mariano da Silva Rondon in 1910, when the Third Regional Inspectorate was created. See A. Magalhães, *Impressões da Comissão Rondon*, 351–53.

8. All indigenous posts were meant to function according to the local population's degree of "civilization" or "assimilation." Other categories included Attraction Posts (to contact "un-pacified" tribes), Frontier Posts (for populations on the Bolivian border), and Ranching Posts (where livestock was raised for consumption and commerce). See Schultz and Vellozo, *Curt Nimuendajú*.

9. A. Cunha, *Entre os índios*, 179.

10. On my use of this terminology throughout the book, see the introduction.

11. Fulfilling Serpa's prophetic desire, "Raimundo Roberto" would go on to study Brazilian culture and the Portuguese language for two years with SPI functionaries in São Luis, later becoming a FUNAI employee and assuming the Canela chieftainship from 1987 to 1999. His "naming-uncle" (of maternal kinship), to whom Crocker refers as the "older Kaapêltùk," was a communal leader in the 1950s and an informant for ethnographer Curt Nimuendajú. Based on Crocker's account, I estimate that the younger Kaapêltùk ("Kaapêl," for short) was approximately sixteen when he copied the "Ditado."

12. The process of national independence began with the arrival of the Portuguese Crown in Brazil in 1808 and the elevation of Brazil to the status of the Portuguese Empire in 1815. Movement toward independence culminated in January 1822 with the Dia do Fico, when Pedro de Alcântra (Dom Pedro I) refused court orders to return to Lisbon. On 7 September of the same year he declared autonomy for the Império do Brasil—an independent monarchy that would remain in place until the formation of the First Republic (the República Federativa do Brasil) in 1889.

13. The first line of thought led to indigenous land reserves to safeguard people, and ethnographic museums and archives to safeguard ideas and objects: the Museu do Índio and Museu Nacional (Rio de Janeiro), the Museu do Ipiranga (São Paulo), and the Museu Paraense Emílio Goeldi (Belém). Associated with the second line of thought was the term *neo-brasileiro*, which I discuss in chapters 3 and 4. Although state-sponsored indigenism was predominantly secular, the conceptualization of its Native subject, as a legacy of colonial Iberia, was likely influenced by the racialized concept of *cristãos novos* or *neo-cristãos* (new Christians)—a concept that came to Brazil with the Inquisition. See Costigan, *Through Cracks in the Wall*; and Tucci Carneiro, *Preconceito*.

14. The 1973 Indian Statute (still on the books, as I discuss later in this chapter) was the first federal legislation to attempt a legal definition of Indianness.

15. See my introduction; and Sturm, *Becoming Indian*.

16. Genetic studies have become a bone of contention in public debates about quota policies in higher education and state employment. Critics argue that they are illogical and unfair because they fail to account for the high degree of miscegenation in Brazilian society or to recognize that biological analyses of "race" (i.e., genomics) have little to do with skin color. See BBC Brasil, "Especial"; and Pena and Bortolini, "Pode a genética." Proponents counter that genetic tests have little to do with lived experience, and that, as the former secretary of justice of São Paulo, Hédio Silva, put it, "No one asks for a genetic ID card to discriminate." See Glycerio, "Genética alimenta polêmica."

17. D. Turner, "Oral Traditions," 230. Although Turner refers to Canada and speaks primarily of indigenous peoples across North America, his portrayal of this paradox and conceptualization of Native intellectuals as "word warriors" is relevant to indigenous peoples in Brazil and Latin America, where dominant and subaltern notions of indigeneity are also tied to indigenous nationhood and land rights. On indigeneity and sovereignty, which I discuss in chapter 5, see Agamben, *Homo Sacer*; Alfred, *Peace, Power, Righteousness*; Barker, *Sovereignty Matters*; Deleuze and Guattari, *Thousand Plateaus*; Shaw, *Indigeneity and Political Theory*; Smith, Solinger, and Topik, *States and Sovereignty*; Tilley, "Role of the State"; and Van Cott, *Radical Democracy*. Also see Evans, Rueschemeyer, and Skocpal, *Bringing the State Back In*.

18. Prior to that date, beginning with the first census in 1872, they were either not counted or considered brown (*pardo*)—initially a default category for those not identifying as black, white, or yellow, and then an official category. IBGE, *Recenseamento*, xxi.

19. SPI, "Reportagem."

20. R. Williams, *Towards 2000*, 22.

21. The Native Brazilian population grew nationally by some 150% between 1991 and 2000 (from 294,131 to 734,127) and by just over 22% between 2000 and 2010 (from 734,127 to 896,917). As of early 2012, self-identified Natives (including those who identify simultaneously with another category of "color") comprise approximately 0.47% of the Brazilian population (190,732,694). Complete 2010 Census data and analysis tools are available at http://www.ibge.gov.br. See also n. 24.

22. Also known as the Brazilian Amazon, which comprises 59% of national territory and was established in 1966 by Article 2 of Law no. 5.173. The states of Acre, Amapá, Amazonas, Mato Grosso do Sul, Mato Grosso, Pará, Rondônia, Roraima, Tocantins, and parts of Maranhão and Goiás make up this diverse region, which according to the 2010 Census was home to more than 30 million people and some 17% of the national population (counting Maranhão and Goiás). See also nn. 21, 24.

23. See Warren, *Racial Revolutions*.

24. The 1991 Census only counted indigenous people living on FUNAI-sanctioned territories, resulting in a gross miscalculation. Following a regional trend spanning from the United States to Chile, the provision for self-identification led to a massive increase in Brazil's indigenous population. The final results of the 2010 Census, released as this manuscript went to press, included for the first time questions about community or tribal affiliation and languages spoken by indigenous respondents and identified a whopping 305 ethnicities and 274 indigenous languages across the country. These numbers are widely attributed to an increase in the population that self-identifies as indigenous rather than to a demographic increase, and they are hotly contested by guardians of authentic Indianness across the political spectrum. See IBGE, *Censo demográfico 2010*.

25. Up from 36.1% in 1950, 55.9% in 1970, 75.6% in 1970, and 81% in 2000. IBGE, *Tendências demográficas*, *Censo demográfico 2000*, and *Censo demográfico 2010*.

26. Over two decades in the making, the declaration was endorsed by 143 countries. Eleven countries abstained, and four—the United States, Canada, Australia, and New Zealand—opposed. These countries reversed their opposition in 2009 and 2010. See the declaration and related news at www.un.org.

27. See Sommer, *Foundational Fictions*, 138–71; Brookshaw, *Race and Color*; Driver, *Indian in Brazilian Literature*; and Treece, *Exiles*.

28. Iracema is the protagonist of Alencar's 1865 novel by the same name. Peri is the Native hero of *O guarany*, originally published through *folhetins* (newspaper chronicles), and then as a novel (1857), before being adapted into an Italian opera by composer Antônio Carlos Gomes in 1870. "A confederação dos tamoios," the best-known epic poem of Domingos José Gonçalves de Magalhães, was based on an alliance of indigenous peoples living on the southeast coast (now the states of São Paulo and Rio de Janeiro), who fought together against the Portuguese during the mid-sixteenth

century. *The Last Tamoio* (1883), a well-known painting by Rodolfo Amoedo, depicts a dead indigenous man lying on the beach.

29. See, for example, "São antropófagos os boca negra," *O Globo*, 30 June 1948; "Viu os índios comer o seu companheiro," *O Radical*, 2 August 1948; "O matador do tenente Fernando: Dois outros estavam sendo engordados para rosbife," *Diário da Noite*, 2 August 1948; "Morto a flechadas um trabalhador pelos temíveis índios gaviões," *Folha da Tarde*, 19 November 1952; and "'Os brancos são um povo mau e devem ser mortos,'" *O Globo*, 4 July 1952.

30. Land demarcation has been a highly polemical question for indigenous and nonindigenous peoples alike, but interest in the issue on behalf of non-Natives has come primarily from legislators, those occupying contested lands, and those whose livelihood has been directly affected by the demarcation process. Reporting on this issue skyrocketed beginning in the early 1930s, both in the popular press and the *Diário do Congresso Nacional*.

31. In 1550, Carlos V of Spain convened a group of theologians and legal scholars to study the question of whether force could be used against "Indians" to facilitate their conversion to Christianity. Although a 1537 papal bull had already determined that the Natives were rational beings, Sepúlveda questioned this finding and cited Aristotle's notion of natural slavery to characterize them as "uncivilized," "barbarian," and "inhuman," and argued in favor of the use of force. See Sepúlveda, *Tratado*, 153. Las Casas countered by deconstructing the notion of "barbarism" and arguing, instead, on behalf of what he considered the "civilizations" of indigenous peoples. On these debates, see Hanke, *Aristotle*; Losada, "Controversy"; and Keen, "Legacy."

32. The issues of mortuary cannibalism and infanticide, for example, inspire impassioned debates among those who would represent modern-day Natives as victimizers and their "defenders," who claim that such practices have always been grossly misunderstood and misrepresented. For opposing views on these controversies, see Conklin, *Consuming Grief*; and the Hakani Project (http://hakani.org/en/default.asp).

33. On the Coordenação das Organizações Indígenas da Amazônia Brasileira, see my introduction.

34. S. Guajajara, "Environmental Policy."

35. The comparative role of blackness in the dominant imaginary is, I argue, the opposite. Although survey numbers vary widely, the 2010 Census found that 7.6% of Brazilians self-identified as black (*preto*) and 43.1% as brown (*pardo*), while just 0.47% self-identified as indigenous. Despite growing political identification with Afro-Brazilianness and the powerful legacies of African cultural forms in language, music, dance, and cuisine (for example), the notion of blackness, per se, has not been a preferred marker of Brazilianness among the dominant majority. On the contrary, influential Afro-Brazilians and popular cultural forms and practices of African origin have typically been "whitened" in dominant discourse. As Livio Sansone puts it, such manipulations stem from the common assumption that "a basic incompatibility exists between being black and social advantage" (*Blackness*, 2). His skepticism regarding the "intrinsic . . . emancipating possibility in political mobilization around ethnic identity and race" leads him to suggest that it is more productive for scholars and activists to

prioritize "ethnitization" (a process) over "ethnicity" (a thing). See ibid., 2–19; S. dos Santos, "Who Is Black?"; Hoffman French, *Legalizing Identities*; and *Casa de Cultura*.

36. See Coutinho, Paulin, and Medeiros, "A farra." On constructed authenticity and "posttraditional" indigeneity, see Hoffman French, *Legalizing Identities*; and Warren, *Racial Revolutions*.

37. Although recent examples abound, perhaps the most infamous act of anti-indigenous violence was committed against the Pataxó Hãhãhãe activist Galdino Jesus dos Santos, burned alive in 1997 as he slept on a park bench in Brasília, where he had arrived to defend the rights of his community to occupy the Caramuru-Paraguaçu indigenous territory in Bahia.

38. Or *negros*, which, per the 2010 Estatuto da Igualdade Racial, indicates those individuals self-identifying as *pretos* and *pardos* (black and brown-skinned people) according to national census categories.

39. Although the demarcation of indigenous territories guaranteed by the 1988 Constitution was to be completed in five years, it remains incomplete and, in many cases, contested by nonindigenous individuals and groups with competing land claims. As of late 2011, the Instituto Socioambiental identified 603 "terras indígenas" (TIs) comprising 1,095,841 square kilometers (some 13% of national territory). FUNAI reported a slightly greater number of TIs (611) and indicated that 123 of these were "under study." See Instituto Socioambiental, "Terras indígenas"; and FUNAI, "As terras indígenas."

40. Although the debate over quotas for Afro-descended students in institutions of higher education has somewhat eclipsed the debate over similar policies for indigenous students, the question at the heart of the debates is the same: namely, the legality of "favorable" discrimination based on ethnoracial self-identification. The controversial measure was removed from the Estatuto da Igualdade Racial (which became law in 2010, after years of congressional debate), but dozens of universities use quota systems as part of the admissions process. In late 2010, the Legislative Assembly of Maranhão overturned Governor Roseana Sarney's veto of a quota system for *negros* and *indígenas* at the Universidade Estadual do Maranhão, and the Universidade Federal do Rio de Janeiro established quotas for public school students (rather than students of color) (see Franco, "Acesso 2011"). The constitutionality of racial quotas was upheld by Brazil's Supremo Tribunal Federal in April 2012. The question of "differentiated education," in contrast, is particular to indigenous students and communities, for it involves not only access to educational institutions but also the content of the education and the language(s) in which it will be delivered and received.

41. Newmanezinho, comment on Liana Melo.

42. See, for example, the "Manifesto of 113 Anti-racist Citizens against Racial Laws" that circulated throughout the country, receiving criticism and praise for its stand against affirmative action measures, especially in higher education. Signed by "intellectuals, union members, business owners, and social activists," including public figures like Caetano Veloso, João Ubaldo Ribeiro, Lya Luft, and Ruth Cardoso, the manifesto argued that the postemancipation "one drop rule" at the heart of U.S. racial determinism and segregation was "the inspiration of racial quota laws in Brazil." (This "rule" held that anyone with a drop of "black blood" was black, regardless of physical appearance.)

43. "Câmera aprova projeto."

44. See Contreiras, *AI-5*. Interestingly, reports announcing the Indian Statue during the first half of 1973 also referred to increasing media censorship, particularly with reference to indigenous matters. During the same interview in which then FUNAI president Bandeira de Melo referred to heighted indigenous "protection," he blamed the national press for the international community's increased negative attention to Brazil's indigenous question: "The Indian is still headline news, at home and abroad, and that means our press must be more responsible, because by publishing untrue or distorted news, they provide other countries with the opportunity to attack not just FUNAI, but also Brazil." The general went on to describe new measures to curtail and control media access to indigenous areas and preselect "two or three" journalists to report on the construction of the Transamazonian Highway and "attraction efforts" in the Perimetral Norte ("Funai garante").

45. Ramos, *Indigenism*, 249.

46. Warren, *Racial Revolutions*, 5–33.

47. Hoffman French, *Legalizing Identities*, 69.

48. Per the 1973 legislation, much of the state's power would be executed with regard to economic matters, nullifying, for example, the financial transactions of "Indians" who had acted without the assistance of the "competent tutorial organ."

49. Nineteenth-century antecedents are the subject of chapter 2. On the history of colonial legislation, see Carneiro da Cunha, *Legislação indigenista*; *História dos índios*; and *Os direitos dos índios*.

50. See *Diário Oficial*, quoted in Ministério de Agricultura, "Legislação." The 2002 Civil Code (Law no. 10.406), in contrast, specifies the exceptionalism of the indigenous condition in the context of the relative incapacity of other groups. Per Chapter 1, Article 4: "Deemed incapable with regard to certain acts, or in the manner of exercising them are: I—those older than sixteen and younger than eighteen years old; II—habitual drunks, drug addicts, and those who, due to mental deficiency, have impaired judgment; III—exceptional people with incomplete mental development; IV—Prodigals. . . . The Indians' capacity will be regulated by special legislation." See the website of the Presidência da República: http://www.planalto.gov.br/ccivil_03/LEIS/2002/L10406.htm.

51. Ministério de Agricultura, "Legislação."

52. Ibid.

53. Article 2 of Decreto-Lei no. 5.484 of 27 June 1928 established four categories according to which different categories of "Indians" would receive different types of state assistance. These were: (1) *índios nomades* (nomadic Indians); (2) *índios arranchados* or *aldeados* (settled Indians); (3) *povoações indígenas* (indigenous communities); and (4) *centros agrícolas* (agricultural centers). The referent of the third category would remain, in practice, indistinguishable from the second, while the final category reflected, above all, the indigenist desire for a productive future of indigenous agricultural labor. See SPI, "Sobre a classificação dos índios"; and Schultz and Vellozo, *Curt Nimuendajú*.

54. Brazil has had eight national constitutions—one as an independent monarchy (1824) and seven as a republic (1891, 1934, 1937, 1946, 1967, 1969, and 1988).

55. I discuss this transfer and the logic of national security in chapter 5.

56. Decree-Law no. 24.700 of 12 July 1934.

57. SPI, "Projeto de regulação."

58. I discuss the posts further in chapters 3 and 4.

59. See D. Ribeiro, *Os índios*; Hemming, *Die If You Must*; M. Gomes; *Indians*; and Souza Lima, *Um grande cerco*.

60. Founder of Peru's Socialist Party, Mariátegui argued in the 1920s that the *problema del índio* was, above all, one of land use and ownership. See my introduction; and Mariátegui, *Siete ensayos*, 20–30.

61. Law no. 245 of 1950. Malcher based his arguments on Article 216 of the 1946 Constitution: "Indigenous peoples have the nontransferrable right to hold the lands on which they find themselves permanently situated."

62. The Dawes or General Allotment Act was enacted in 1887 and remained in place until 1934. Complete legislation is available through the U.S. National Archives: http://www.archives.gov/education/lessons/fed-indian-policy/.

63. Malcher, "Senhor Ministro," 2.

64. Ibid., 3.

65. In March 2009, the Supremo Tribunal Federal ruled ten-to-one in favor of maintaining the Raposa Serra do Sol reserve comprising northern Roraima as contiguous territory for the exclusive use of the approximately 20,000 Ingaricõ, Macuxi, Patamona, Taurepang, and Wapichana whose traditional lands are located there. Controversially, the ruling required the expulsion of resident, nonindigenous rice farmers who challenged the demarcation by FUNAI—a process initiated in the late 1970s and ratified only in April 2005. See FUNAI, "TI–Raposa Serra do Sol–Roraima."

66. ADRIANO, comment on "Exército."

67. Elizeu, comment on "Exército."

68. In Brazil, the Vídeo nas Aldeias initiative has been producing indigenous film since 1986 (http://www.videonasaldeas.com.br). Also see the work of the GRUMIN; Rede de Comunicação Indígena (http://grumin.blogspot.com); and the Núcleo de Escritores Indígenas of the Instituto Indígena Brasileiro para Propriedade Intelectual (INBRAPI) (http://escritoresindigenas.blogspot.com). These sites represent a tiny sampling of the many collaborative political and creative efforts of indigenous intellectuals and activists under way across the country, several of which I discuss in detail in chapter 5.

69. Brasileiro Trabalhador, comment on "Exército" (original emphasis).

70. "Os americanos tinham razão!!," comment on "Exército."

71. Von Ihering was a naturalized Brazilian citizen, though he returned to his native Germany as an elderly man and died there. He made this argument, which I discuss further in chapter 2, in a 1911 edition of the *Revista do Museu Paulista*.

72. LALÁ, comment on "Exército."

73. *Constituição da República Federativa do Brasil de 1988*, "Preâmbulo."

74. Brubaker, *Ethnicity*, 10.

75. Friedlander, *Being Indian*, 157–80.

76. Brubaker, *Ethnicity*, 29.

77. See Pena and Bortolina, "Pode a genética."

78. In 2008, the Instituto Brasileiro de Geografia e Estatística (IBGE), in collaboration with the World Bank, published a study of data gathered between 2000 and 2003 showing that in nearly 33% of Brazilian municipalities, more than half of the population was living in poverty. The percentages varied dramatically according to region (for example, over 77% of northeastern municipalities demonstrated more than 50% poverty, compared to less than 1% in the South). See IBGE, "IBGE lança mapa de pobreza e desigualdade."

79. Hoffman French, *Legalizing Identities*, 43–76.

80. Ibid., 70. On the comparative processes of "legalizing" indigenous and black identities in her case studies, see ibid., introduction and chapter 5.

81. Ibid., 69–76.

82. Ibid., 69.

83. In addition to Hoffman French, *Legalizing Identities*, see Clifton, *Being and Becoming Indian*; Maybury-Lewis, "Becoming Indian"; Sturm, *Becoming Indian*; and Peterson and Brown, *New Peoples*.

84. This is not to say that there were not deep ideological and political divides among different schools of indigenist practitioners and scholars, a subject I address in chapter 4.

85. V. Vasconcelos, "Assistência aos índios."

86. Freyre wrote not of "racial democracy" per se but of the possibility of a racialized "social democratization" of Brazilian society (*Casa grande e senzala*, xiii).

87. My emphasis. Freyre shares this distinction with Darcy Ribeiro, whose work I discuss throughout the book and highlight in chapter 4.

88. See Article 5 of Law no. 3.044, which created the Dia do Mestiço in Amazonas state on 21 March 2006 (*Diário Oficial do Estado de Amazonas*). Nação Mestiça, an NGO established in 2001 in Manaus, is dedicated to "the valorization of the process of miscegenation (mixture) between the diverse ethnic groups that gave origin to the Brazilian nationality, to the promotion and defense of the *parda-mestiça* identity, and to the recognition of *pardos-mestiços* as the progeny of the ancestral peoples from which they are descended." See http://www.nacaomestica.org.

89. The controversial law (12.288), which instituted affirmative action measures for self-identifying Afro-descendants (*negros*), was authored by then-deputado and later senator Paulo Paim in 2005, passed by the Câmara de Deputados in modified form in September 2009, and passed by the Senate with further modifications in July 2010. Key among the modifications was the elimination of a controversial quota system in education, civil service, and the entertainment industry (although the constitutionality of racial quota initiatives was upheld by the Supremo Tribunal Federal in 2012). The Nação Mestiça movement (along with other detractors) further opposed the proposed subsumption of *preto* (black) and *pardo* (brown) as census categories for "color or race" into the category *negro* per the provisions of Article 1, Section 4. The organization argues that this classification denies the mixed nature (particularly, the European, indigenous, and other non-African ancestry) of brown-skinned and *mestiça* peoples. According to its website, Nação Mestiça accepts donations to help ensure "that Brazil is

not divided up into races [*para que o Brasil não se divida em raças*]." The 2010 Statute of Racial Equality included no provisions for indigenous peoples.

90. *Caboclo* typically refers to people of mixed white and indigenous descent, especially those residing in the North and Northeast. Nação Mestiça's position is grounded in the belief that *pardos* (brown-skinned people), characterized as *negros* and Afro-Brazilians under the Estatuto da Igualdade Racial, are fundamentally distinct from *pretos* (blacks) and should not be subsumed under the categories "*negro*" or "*Afro-brasileiro*." The underlying message is that *pardos* or *mestiços* from the North, in particular, are descended mostly from whites and indigenous peoples and not from whites and blacks. The group contends: "*Mestiço* is not a race, it's a mixture. A brown-skinned person is not Indian but *caboclo*. A brown-skinned person is not white, but *mulato*. A brown-skinned person is not black but *cafuzo* (black and Indian). A brown-skinned person is not yellow but *mestiço* and Brazilian. He's a citizen and demands respect." See Nação Mestiça.

91. On the relationship between indigenous movements and sovereignty in the Hobbesian tradition, see Shaw, *Indigeneity and Political Theory* (discussed in my chapter 5): "A reconstitution of the political that addresses the historical violences of sovereignty . . . must happen in a context of understanding them not as givens, but as complex social, economic, political, and material productions" (212). In the case of Brazil, I would add to the list of critical "productions" the realm of culture, broadly conceived, without which it is impossible to understand the construction of indigeneity or the meanings that it holds across the country (or indeed, across the Americas). The flows between political and cultural production are undeniable yet difficult to trace. On the one hand, the primary actors in these two spheres (those with the authority to legislate and the power to make their voices heard) have often blurred the lines between fact and fiction through their own simultaneous participation in politics, journalism, and the arts. On the other hand, cultural production with regard to indigeneity is always inherently political in nature. The debate over Horace's dictum on the purpose of art ("to instruct and to delight") is long and complex in Latin America (and therefore in Latin American studies), marked by the assumed or imposed moral imperative for artists to engage the political as well as by the questions of who is best suited to do so, and from where. Punctuated by a 1968 exchange between Julio Cortázar and José María Arguedas and a later critique of Arguedas by Mario Vargas Llosa (*La utopía arcaica*), this discussion has caused much ink to flow, and I am unable to retrace all of its intricacies here. In addition to these debates, see the Latin American Subaltern Studies group as well as the work of Hugo Achugar, John Beverley, Sara Castro-Klarén, Jean Franco, Efraín Kristal, Walter Mignolo, Mabel Moraña, Alberto Moreiras, Neil Larsen, Julio Ramos, Ileana Rodríguez, Doris Sommer, George Yúdice, and Marc Zimmerman, much of which I discuss in this book.

92. See Degler, *Neither Black nor White*; and Eidelberg, "Race, Labour."

93. S. Hall, "Identity and Difference," 348–49.

94. See my chapter 5 and the work of André Baniwa, Marcos Terena, Olívio Jekupé, Ailton Krenak, Ysani Kalapalo, Davi Kopenawa Yanomami, and Eliane Potiguara discussed therein.

95. Prado, "André Baniwa."

96. Butler, *Gender Trouble*, 25. She draws on Nietzsche: "There is no 'being' behind the doing, effecting, becoming; the 'doer' is merely a fiction added to the deed—the deed is everything." Nietzsche, *On the Genealogy of Morals*, 45.

97. Markun, "Entrevista com Davi Kopenawa Yanomami."

98. Ibid.

99. Agamben, *Homo Sacer*, 88.

100. Agamben proposed this idea in relation to "whatever singularities," through which he imagined the possibility of community without an affirmation of singular or collective identities, or otherwise "representable condition[s] of belonging." Agamben, *Coming Community*, 85–87.

101. The relationship between indigeneity and sovereignty is the focus of my chapter 5.

102. Alcoff, "Who's Afraid of Identity Politics?," 321. In his 1970 essay "Ideology and Ideological State Apparatuses," Louis Althusser, drawing on Lacan, explained the process through which "pre-ideological" beings were produced as subjects by external ideological discourse(s) as "interpellation."

103. Alcoff, "Who's Afraid of Identity Politics?," 323.

104. Ibid., 334.

105. Ibid., 340.

106. Maybury-Lewis, "Becoming Indian," 220–21.

107. Ramos, *Indigenism*, 81.

108. Extermination campaigns also occurred in Brazil in the late nineteenth and early twentieth centuries, though not clearly as official state policy. See my chapter 2; Foreman, *Indian Removal*; Navarro Florida, "Un país sin indios"; Prucha, *Documents*; and Vidart, *El mundo de los charrúas*.

109. See Dhaliwal, "Can the Subaltern Vote?"; Trend, "Democracy's Crisis"; and Van Cott, *Radical Democracy*.

110. The influential ideas of Walter Mignolo, for instance, have been put forth by many as pertaining to the first category and criticized by others for romanticizing non-European thought rather than engaging with it. Critic Pheng Cheah complains: "One would need to look at true heterogeneity of the outside and the complex and multifarious technologies that fabricate these various outsides, not just at the level of a racist rhetoric of exclusion, but at the most concrete level of the production of the bodily needs and interests of subjects claiming alterity." Also see Alcoff, "Mignolo's Epistemology"; and Lund, "Barbarian Theorizing." Freya Schiwy, in contrast, builds on Mignolo's work to formulate a "sustained engagement" with indigenous media in the Andes that "explore[s] an understanding of decolonization articulated from subalternized perspectives." See her *Indianizing*, 24. A growing archive of decolonial scholarship is available through the Worlds and Knowledge Otherwise Forum—a web dossier run by an editorial collective of mainly U.S.-based scholars. See http://www.jhfc.duke.edu /wko/about.php.

111. Almeida Vaz, "Discurso," 43–44.

112. Stoll, *Rigoberta Menchú*, 247.

113. Menchú, *Rigoberta*, 189.

114. See Van Cott, *From Movements to Parties*; and Yashar, *Contesting Citizenship*.

115. The movement began in the Andes but spread throughout Latin America, including to Brazil, to a limited degree. For an overview of the movement's early years, see López and Küper, "La educación intercultural bilingüe"; and Godenzzi, "Investigaciones."

116. See Pratt, *Imperial Eyes* and "Planetarity."

117. The term *transculturation* was used by Cuban anthropologist Fernando Ortiz in his *Contrapunteo cubano del tabaco y el azúcar* (1940) and referred to processes of miscegenation (*mestizaje* or *mestiçagem*) that could not be understood through the unidirectional notion of acculturation. Ortiz theorized the modification of dominant culture through its exposure to and contamination by subaltern ones—a concept that would later be taken up by critics Ángel Rama in *Transculturación narrativa en América Latina* and Antonio Cornejo Polar in his theorization of heterogeneity (*Escribir en el aire*; "Indigenismo and Heterogeneous Literatures"; and "Mestizaje, transculturación, heterogeneidad").

118. On heterogeneity, see the works of Cornejo Polar. On hybridity, see García Canclini's *Culturas híbridas* and Yúdice's introductory essay to García Canclini's *Consumers and Citizens*.

119. For diverse takes on interculturality, see n. 115 as well as de la Cadena, "Production"; Godenzzi, *Educación e interculturalidad*; Mato, "Interculturalidad"; Walsh, *Interculturalidad, Estado, sociedad*; and Zúñiga, "Educación en quechua." Also see the *Manual of Intercultural Education* and other intercultural resources from Europe and Latin America in the digital archive of the Federación de ONG de Desarrollo de la Comunidad de Madrid (FONGDCAM): http://www.fongdgcam.org.

120. See Algot, *Educación intercultural*; L. E. López, *Educación bilingüe intercultural*; Moya, *Desde el aula*; and Zúñiga, "Educación en quechua."

121. Lozano Vallejo, *Interculturalidad*, 35.

122. Godenzzi, "Política," 1. For information on how the concept has been implemented in various parts of the region, see http://www.funai.gov.br/ultimas/informa tivos/CGE/Documento_Referenciais_CONEEI.pdf (Brazil); http://www.minedu.gob .pe/dineibir/deib/index.php (Peru); and http://www.mineduc.gob.gt/default.asp?secci on=573 (Guatemala).

123. Chakrabarty, *Provincializing Europe*, 28.

124. See Lopes da Silva and Grupioni, *A temática indígena*.

125. Examples can also be found in the implementation of EBI in the Andes, Mexico, and Guatemala, where, in my experience, parents are sometimes critical of their children's having to learn to read and write an indigenous language rather than a "useful" and "modern" one. The prospect of literacy in an indigenous language is not *necessarily* perceived as a liberating practice and in fact is sometimes considered a burden that imposes a notion of indigeneity in which those implicated do not see (or wish to see) themselves represented. EBI advocates tend to characterize this view, in turn, as the internalization of anti-indigenous discrimination. For a discussion of the Peruvian and Bolivian contexts, see García, *Making Indigenous Citizens*; and Luykx, *The Citizen Factory*, respectively. A second example of the problem can also be drawn from Bolivia, where diverging groups of self-identifying indigenous Bolivians continue to vie, at times with violence, for the cultural capital of "authenticity." Since 2005, this question

has divided supporters of President Evo Morales (who self-identifies as Aymara) from his detractors, including the well-known writer and activist Felipe Quispe and the so-called Ponchos Rojos. Representatives of the latter group accuse Morales of being a racial huckster and deny his legitimacy to represent Native Quechua, Aymara, Guarani, and Amazonian populations, politically or otherwise.

126. Freire, *Pedagogía del oprimido*.

127. Freire's best known work refers not to race, ethnicity, or skin color but to class categories and other expressions of socioeconomic subalternity. For his ideas and his work, rooted in the Christian Marxist tradition, he was imprisoned by the Brazilian dictatorship in 1964 and forced into exile. He returned to Brazil some fifteen years later.

128. Freire and Araújo Freire, *Pedagogia da tolerância*, 23–120.

129. Ibid., 85.

130. Ibid., 23.

131. A. Hall, "Enhancing," 341.

132. See Ramos, "Commodification."

133. Sônia Guajajara associates these conditions with ethnodevelopment as theorized by Rodolfo Stavenhagen in the 1970s. Against the notion that development ought to be constrained by ethnicity or limited to an "endogenous dimension" (Pieterse, *Development Theory*, 74), she argues that the broadly shared goal of "national progress" is compatible with interculturality and the future of indigeneity. See Guajajara, "Environmental Policy"; Cerqueira, "A luta"; and Melo, "Cartas a Dilma e Serra."

134. Freire and Araújo Freire, *Pedagogia da tolerância*, 24.

135. Dias de Paula, "O caso."

136. Ibid., 181–82.

137. See the Encontro Nacional de Educação Indígena, Guarani-Bracuí, and the public debates over the radical restructuring of FUNAI beginning in 2010 (Acampamento Revolucionário Indígena blog and Devine Guzmán, "Writing Indigenous Activism").

138. One of the most successful initiatives for the development and consolidation of a "differentiated" indigenous education has taken place among the Pataxó with the collaboration of the Ministry of Education and Culture, FUNAI, and the School of Education of the Federal University of Bahia, in addition to the National Association of Indigenist Action (ANAI), dozens of indigenous teachers, and more than 2,000 indigenous students. See Profesores de Pataxó, *Uma história*, 64.

CHAPTER 2

1. Itiberê da Cunha, "Il guarany," 250.

2. On Alencar's novel, see Sommer, *Foundational Fictions*, 138–71. On differences between the novel and the opera, see Volpe, "Remaking the Brazilian Myth," 179–94.

3. In the novel, the evil adventurers are Italian rather than Spanish, and the year is 1607. Volpe asserts that both dates "lack historical meaning and operate within the mythical 'center' proposed by the novel" (182); and in his intellectual autobiography, *Como e porque sou romancista*, Alencar makes no argument to the contrary. However,

given that the libretto was coauthored by Italians Carlo d'Omerville and Antonio Scalvini for a predominantly Italian audience, these changes were likely strategic: 1607 falls between the 1595 prohibition of Indian slavery by Felipe II and the 1609 founding of the first Spanish Jesuit missionaries near the Paranapanema River. In keeping with the shifting villainization from the Italians to the Spanish, 1560 follows the Peace of Cateau-Cambrésis between England, France, and Spain that consolidated the Spanish control over Italy into the eighteenth century.

4. The tale also represents an inversion of what historian Phil Deloria calls the "wilderness marriage"—the hemispheric myth of indigenous-European union in which the sacrificial figure is typically the indigenous female, as in the case of Malinche, Pocahontas, or Alencar's best-known protagonist, Iracema, whom I discuss in chapter 4.

5. Fontainha, "Prefácio,"78.

6. Later the Universidade Federal do Rio de Janeiro. The conference was transferred to Rio from Montevideo in the planning stages to coincide with the centenary of Gomes's birth and was projected to cost 100 *contos de réis* (approximately US$8,568). Due to "various motives beyond [their] control," however, the planners canceled the conference and promised to reschedule. As far as I have discerned, the event never materialized.

7. H. Viera, "O romance," 39–40.

8. Ibid., 39.

9. Leaders of Brazil's first provisional government headed by Deodoro Fonseca invited Gomes to rewrite the *hino nacional*. He declined out of loyalty to his friend and sponsor Pedro II. See Augusto, *As penas*, 82.

10. Gomes moved to Rio in 1860 to further music studies begun with his father. His successful compositions (including two operas) brought him to the attention of Pedro II, who sent him to Milan on a music scholarship in 1863. Gomes made his life in Italy but often visited Brazil. He relocated to Belém in 1895, months before his death.

11. A disclaimer at the end of the index credits the drawings to Iris Pereira. The captions read, "Ornamental motif of the extinct Indians of the Ilha do Marajó/Ilha Goanany/Ilha Coary," etc.

12. See M. de Andrade, "Fosca"; Goés, *Carlos Gomes*; A. C. Gomes, letters to Francisco Manoel, Manoel José de Souza Guimarães, Ítala Gomes Vaz de Carvalho, and Theodoro Teixeira Gomes; and Imbassahy, "Carlos Gomes."

13. On the contemporary discourse of racial improvement, see L. Schwarcz, *O espectáculo*; and S. A. dos Santos, "Historical Roots."

14. Vianna, *Mystery of Samba*, 41.

15. On the racialization of *brasilidade* under Vargas, see Weinstein, "Racializing Regional Difference"; and D. Williams, *Culture Wars in Brazil*.

16. A popular term customarily indicating mixed European and indigenous descent.

17. See Goés, *Carlos Gomes*; and Fonseca, *O selvagem*. Controversy remains over the ways he has been racialized outside Brazil. Drawing on nineteenth-century French sources and a 1941 *Negro History Bulletin* article that identified Gomes as a "man of color," U.S.-based Jamaican historian J. A. Rogers included him in his 1947 book, *The World's Great Men of Color*. Updated by historian and Africana studies pioneer John Henrik Clarke, the book was republished in 1996 by Simon and Shuster as "a

comprehensive account of the great black personalities of world history." Though Rogers's study and Clarke's edition mention Gomes's "Negro," "Indian," and "Caucasian" ancestry, subsequent publications citing the volume reduce Gomes to "black," which, when translated back into Portuguese as *negro*, inaccurately represents a man identified during his lifetime as *branco, caboclo*, or of mixed mulatto heritage.

18. Fontainha, "Prefácio," 78.

19. As he wrote from Bahia to his friend Manoel José de Souza Guimarães on 12 August 1895: "I will not take with me any nostalgia for the world or for the Government of the Republic that has treated me with such injustice. I only regret not being able to destroy everything written with such enthusiasm by my hand for the benefit of national art." A. C. Gomes, letter to Manoel José de Souza Guimarães, 3 November 1864.

20. Nogueira, "Música e política," 244–49.

21. I discuss this rhetoric and policy in chapters 3 and 4. See also Garfield, *Indigenous Struggle*, chaps. 1–3; and D. Williams, *Culture Wars in Brazil*, chap. 5.

22. Treece, *Exiles*, 3.

23. Sommer, *Foundational Fictions*, 166. On the precolonial indigenous population, see D. Ribeiro, *Os índios*, 284–93; Hemming, *Red Gold*; and M. Gomes, *Indians*, 33–34.

24. See Treece, *Exiles*, chaps. 3 and 4; as well as Brookshaw, *Race and Color*; Carneiro da Cunha, "Política indigenista"; Hemming, *Die If You Must*; D. Ribeiro, *Os índios*; L. Schwarcz, *O espectáculo*; and Souza Lima, *Um grande cerco*.

25. DaMatta, "For an Anthropology," 281.

26. See Volpe, "Remaking the Brazilian Myth," 179–94. Citing Mário de Andrade's 1939 essay on Brazilian music, she argues that "scholars have long been reluctant to acknowledge the nationalist significance" of *Il guarany*—an assertion with which, as I explain here, I disagree.

27. Goés, *Carlos Gomes*, 129.

28. Casa Ricordi became the largest music publisher in southern Europe in the mid-nineteenth century, and it is today the largest music publisher in Italy. See Casa Ricordi, *Ricordi & C.*

29. Goés, *Carlos Gomes*, 129.

30. "*O guarany* de Carlos Gomes," 1.

31. E. Gordon, "New Opera House," 49.

32. Theatro Lyrico Fluminense, "Opera italiana," 6.

33. Terena and Morin, *Saberes globais*, 44.

34. The Aimoré or *selvagens* of *Il guarany* were advertised alongside "good Indians," the Portuguese, and other foreign "adventurers," and likewise showcased in the performance. While the fictionalized European role in the early colonial period was based on a (nebulous) historical encounter, however, the Aimoré representation stemmed from historical misunderstanding. Some contemporary indigenous scholars argue that the label was a distortion of *embaré*—a term used by the Tupi of the northeastern coast to refer generically to "inferior" peoples of the forest (see Tavares Coelho, "Genocídio e resgate," 196). *Il guarany* and *O guarany* thus reinforced an ethnic misidentification grounded in linguistic barriers that have yet to be overcome. Tellingly, the term *Aimoré* also appeared in early SPI documentation (see "Relatório ao Ministro da Guerra"). A

century later, the *Dicionário Aurélio* defines *aimoré* as "an indigenous person of the tribe of the Aimoré; bellicose Botocudo Indians who during the sixteenth and seventeenth centuries occupied . . . the states of Bahia and Espírito Santo."

35. Theatro Lyrico Fluminense, "Opera italiana," 6.

36. See advertisements in the *Jornal do Commercio* during the week of 12 December 1870.

37. The *folhetim* was a novella published in parts on a daily or weekly basis. A regular component of major papers, it often appeared on the front page.

38. Said, *Culture and Imperialism*, 111. Verdi's Indian-themed operas, *Alzira* (1845) and *La forza del destino* (1862, based on the duke of Rivas's 1835 drama), referred to Peru and were important (but not necessarily successful) antecedents to *Il guarany*.

39. In his 1908 treatise *Porque me ufano do meu país*, Afonso Celso offered eleven "motives for Brazil's superiority," including "excellence of the elements that contributed to the formation of the national type—the American savage; the black African, and the Portuguese" (chap. 16). Summarizing the indigenous contribution to the "Brazilian race," he concluded: "Without the exaggeration of fantasy, we find in the history of *our Indians* sublime traits. . . . Even the government of the metropolis recognized officially the superiority of the Brazilian indigenous peoples [in the] Charter of 4 April 1755." However, Celso considered Indians "strange" and emphasized the superiority of past indigeneity in terms of its proximity to European culture and whiteness: "João Francisco Lisboa establishes a curious parallel between the customs of the Brazilian savages and those of the ancient Germans immortalized by Tacitus. . . . The Coroado [Indians] . . . live in small communities. . . . They are almost Caucasian in type [and] among them are handsome, virile specimens and beautiful women. The Canoeiro [Indians] of the Amazon speak of a mysterious race of albinos who only appear at night. . . . The Mundurucu [Indians are] tall, strong, muscular, [and] light-skinned" (chap. 17).

40. The opera played in London (1872); Santiago (1873); Buenos Aires (1874); Vienna and Stockholm (1875); Brussels, Barcelona, Warsaw, and Montevideo (1876); Havana, St. Petersburg, and Moscow (1879); Nice (1880); and New York (1884). See Goés, *Carlos Gomes*, 136. All these performances occurred after the March 1870 debut in Milan and the December 1870 run in Rio de Janeiro.

41. Taunay, *Reminiscências*, 87.

42. See Hulme, *Colonial Encounters*, 112. As I argue in chapters 1 and 5, the extreme violence of this ongoing encounter has been particularly evident in disputes over protected indigenous territories.

43. "[O êxito] depende da continuidade na acção que deve ser sempre ejercida, sob pena de malogro e perda total da conquista já realisada pela mesma pessoa . . . já conhecid[a] . . . [por eles], graças á extrema acuiuade physica e moral do índio, no sentido do bem ou do mal [*sic*]" ("Relatório ao Ministro da Guerra," 3). On SPI discourse as progressive, see Urban, "Semiotics."

44. Harasowska, *Morphophonemic Variability*, 26.

45. Brazil's declaration of war came on 27 January 1865, but the conflicts preceding it dated to before Uruguayan independence in 1828 and stemmed from unresolved border disputes between Argentina, Brazil, Paraguay, and Uruguay. When in September 1864 Brazilian troops marched on Montevideo, ousted Uruguayan president Atanasio

Aguirre, and installed a regime friendly to Brazil, Paraguay retaliated in support of Uruguayan sovereignty. In November 1864, Paraguayan forces captured a Brazilian steamer as it passed through Asunción on its way up the Paraguay River. One month later, they invaded Brazil's western border. See Barman, *Citizen Emperor*, 198–202.

46. Von Versen wrote in 1913: "It's not even worth mentioning the help of the Oriental Republic . . . [and] the Argentine Republic never maintained more than a minimal number of troops on the battlefield. The entire burden of the war and none of its advantages fell on Brazil. Only Brazil sustained the fight with energy until the end, providing war material, money, and soldiers." See Von Versen, "História da guerra do Paraguai e episódios," 98. These allegations notwithstanding, some 10,000 Uruguayans lost their lives in the war.

47. Fatalities on all sides have been the subject of debate, though there are more studies of the Paraguayan demographics than of the other cases. Scheina places Paraguayan casualties at 300,000 and Brazilian casualties at around 100,000 (*Latin America's Wars*, 331). Regarding the Paraguyan population, Whigham and Potthast estimate a loss of 60% to 70%, Kleinpenning 43% to 51%, and Reber 8% to 18%. See also Burton, *Letters*; and Doratioto, *O conflito* and "História e ideologia."

48. José Ricardo Pires de Almeida's *O coração e a espada* ran contemporaneously with *Il guarany* in Milan (see *Jornal do Commercio*, 18 March 1870). Also published in 1870 were the plays *O voluntário*, by Bernardo Taveira Júnior, and *Os voluntários da honra*, by Tomás Antônio Espiuca. Patriotic poetry included Antônio José dos Santos Neves's "Homenagem aos heróis brasileiros" and Manuel de Sousa Garcia's "O triunfo das armas brasileiras." Unlike *Il guarany* and *O guarany*, none of these works now holds a particularly important place in the history of Brazilian letters.

49. See "Lambaré kuatia ñe'ê," 2; and "Los camba," 4.

50. The first "Guarani Republic," which traversed the borders of present-day Brazil, Argentina, Paraguay, and Uruguay, was founded in the seventeenth century by Jesuit missionaries and lasted for nearly 150 years, until the order was expelled from South America in 1767. For a variety of interpretations of the republic and its legacies, see Gadelha, *Missões guarani*. On the racialization, see the wartime publications of *Cabichuí*, *El Centinela*, and *Cacique Lambaré*; Amaral de Toral, "A participação," 287–88; A. Johnson, "Cara Feia"; Sarmiento, *Las escuelas*, 321–323; and M. Sastre, "El Mamboretá."

51. "Kuatia veve," 3.

52. Later the visconde de Taunay, he was a writer and army officer who went to Matto Grosso province during the war and, like Carlos Gomes, remained loyal to the monarch after the 1889 declaration of the Republic.

53. The score was mostly plagiarized, as I explain later.

54. The volume was originally published as *La retraite de Laguna* (1872) and today remains little known outside of Brazil,

55. See Taunay, *A retirada da Laguna*, 20, 32, 50, 55, 59, 71, 73. These categorizations pepper the historiography on the war despite the fact that, as Amaral de Toral points out, African and Afro-descended slaves were also sold into the Paraguayan fighting forces (see Amaral de Toral, "A participação," 89–90). Paradoxically, slavery had been abolished in Paraguay by the time the slaveholding Brazilians won the war.

López's chief opponent, Cirilo Antonio Rivarola, signed a decree marking the "first year of freedom of the Paraguayan Republic" on 2 October 1869—five months before López's death and his own ascendancy to the presidency.

56. "The *Cabichuí* is . . . a soldier. . . . On the journalism scene, [it] is inspired by love of the fatherland to . . . fight for the idea that has roused the whole Republic and seeks a positive outcome in the war of the free against the slaves. . . . It is pure Guarani, and . . . will never be able to abandon without great suffering the delicious idiom of its fathers. See "A nuestros lectores," *El Cabichuí* 1 (my translation of the Spanish version by W. Lustig).

57. *Rejistro Oficial del Gobierno Provisorio*, 5–8, 10.

58. An 1867 article in *El Cabichuí* read: "They say that there are still teachers of yesteryear who don't want to know anything written in our language. . . . In the school of today there is no longer a whip for those who speak in Guarani [or] . . . a 'list for those who have spoken in Guarani.' That's over. . . . There is now no reason to disrespect our own language" ("Tata piriri"; my translation of the Spanish version by W. Lustig).

59. *Rejistro Oficial*, 73.

60. "Volunteers of the Fatherland" was for many a euphemism considering that National Guardsman could purchase slaves to serve as their proxies, and slaveowners received compensation for sending their slaves to the front lines. Male slaves considered "property" of the nation were promised freedom in exchange for service, though often it was not granted. See Amaral de Toral, "A participação"; Barman, *Citizen Emperor*, 211; Prata de Sousa, *Escravidão*; and Viotti da Costa, *Da senzala à colônia*, 446, 461–62.

61. See August–December 1870 in *Jornal do Commercio*, *Diário do Rio de Janeiro*, *Correio Paulistano*, *Diário Popular*, *O Paiz*, and *O Fluminense*.

62. Romero, *Machado de Assis*, 172–73.

63. The commander was Princess Isabel's French-born husband, the Count d'Eu, otherwise known as Louis Philippe Marie Ferdinand Gaston d'Orléans. Barman notes that Rebouças witnessed the event on 29 April 1870 and wrote of it in his diary. See Barman, *Citizen Emperor*, 230.

64. "To Brazil, on the occasion of its celebration for the splendid and excellent victory of its arms in Paraguay."

65. "Glory to you, Brazil, O mighty Empire. Glory to your defender, Pedro II. Glory to the heroes who gave you eternal honor."

66. Between 1884 and 1939, 1,412,263 Italian farmworkers immigrated, mostly to the state of São Paulo. Some 1,204,394 Portuguese immigrated during the same period, mostly to Rio de Janeiro. See S. A. dos Santos, "Historical Roots," 69; IBGE, "Imigração no Brasil por nacionalidade," and "A imigração no Brasil nos períodos anuais (1820–1975)."

67. "Manifesto republicano de 1870."

68. All men who self-identified as doctors, lawyers, engineers, and "capitalists."

69. Sodré, *História da imprensa*, 211.

70. For differing views, see Barman, *Citizen Emperor*, 241; Boehrer, *Da monarquia*, 47; and Sodré, *História da imprensa*, 212.

71. For titles published in Amazonas, Pará, Piauí, Paraíba, Pernambuco, Alagoas, Bahia, São Paulo, Minas Gerais, Paraná, and Rio Grande do Sul, see Sodré, *História da imprensa*, 212–13.

72. See *Colleção das leis ... de 1871*, 6, 7, 42, 147, 318–19; *Colleção das leis ... de 1872*, 102–3; and *Colleção das leis ... de 1873*, 138, 315.

73. Law no. 2040, also known as the Lei do Ventre Livre (Law of the Free Womb).

74. Article 1 read: "The children of slave mothers born in the Empire from the date of this law shall be considered free" (*Colleção das leis ... de 1871*, 147).

75. Barman, *Citizen Emperor*, 250.

76. The rule (*regimento*) of 1758 under the (relatively) "pro-Indian" government of the marquês de Pombal, which recognized the freedom of indigenous peoples and limited missionary influence over them, had already established the position of Indian director. However, widespread abuse of indigenous peoples under that regime led to its dissolution in 1798. See Melatti, *Índios do Brasil*, 250–51.

77. Melatti, *Índios e criadores*.

78. Law no. 601 (Lei de Terras).

79. Decree no. 1318.

80. For different interpretations of the impact of this law, see Carneiro da Cunha, "Política indigenista," 145; Hoffman French, *Legalizing Identities*, 24; Holston, *Insurgent Citizenship*, 71–74; M. Gomes, *Indians*, 72–73; and Melatti, *Índios do Brasil*, 41, 251, 274.

81. The Carta, from the Prince Regent to Pedro Maria Xavier de Ataide e Mello (governor of the *capitania* of Minas Gerais between 1803 and 1810), justified war on any "tyrannical" Indians (and specifically the Botocudo) who would not live under the protection and "sweet yoke [*o suave jugo*]" of the law. Carneiro da Cunha argues that the legislation implied permanent land rights for the communities against whom "just war" had not been declared. "So much so," she states, "that in 1819, the Crown reverse[d] the concession of a *seismaria* located inside Valença, *aldeia* of the Coroado Indians, and reaffirm[ed] fundamental principles: the lands of the *aldeias* are inalienable and cannot be considered empty [*devolutas*]." See Carneiro da Cunha, "Política indigenista," 141. As Holston points out, however, the Carta Régia reveals an unequivocal desire for the "restoration" of land control by the Crown through whatever means necessary. It hints at no Indian policy other than expedient de-Indianization by the sword or under the cross. See Holston, *Insurgent Citizenship*, 324.

82. On the debate, see Holston, *Insurgent Citizenship*, 71–74, 324.

83. Carta Régia de 2 de Dezembro de 1808.

84. Carneiro da Cunha, "Política indigenista,"145.

85. See also Bittencourt and Ladeira, *A história*, 75–76; and my chapters 3 and 4.

86. "The measurement of all terrains pertaining to each of the [Indian] communities will . . . determine the exact area of those who are in control of the Indians and their descendants and of the occupants and tenants, but also . . . discern those which, being wrongly occupied or in abandon, must revert to the domain of the State." See the "Instrucções expedidas ao Engenheiro Luiz José da Silva para proceder nos extinctos aldeamentos da Província de Pernambuco," given by the Secretária de Estado dos

Negócios da Agricultura, Commercio e Obras Públicas, Directoria da Agricultura on 8 July 1875. *Colleção das decisões*, 223.

87. *Colleção das decisões*, 229.

88. Jourdon, *Atlas histórico*, n.p.

89. For exceptions to this erasure, see Bittencourt and Ladeira, *A história*; Ferreira Vargas, *A construção*; M. Gomes, *Indians*, 41; and Schmuziger Carvalho, "Chaco," 468–70.

90. M. Gomes, *Indians*, 40–41.

91. Bittencourt and Ladeira, *A história*, 78.

92. Ibid., 78–79.

93. Ibid., 79.

94. Ibid., 78.

95. Personal communication, May 2010.

96. Portions of the text were rewritten, edited, and published along with indigenous-language glossaries and other short essays for a posthumous book called *Entre os nossos índios*.

97. Located west of Campo Grande and east of Corumbá, the city of Miranda (originally Mondego) was named for Governor General Caetano Pinto de Miranda in 1835 and destroyed by the Paraguayans during the war.

98. Taunay, *Scenas*, 73.

99. Ibid., 108.

100. Ibid., 111. The Portuguese orthography of indigenous names always represents a distortion and varies drastically in the literature and throughout Taunay's writing. I maintain original spelling in all cases to reveal these discrepancies and because the question of who has the authority to determine the "proper" spelling of the names constitutes a substantial debate that will remain unresolved in these pages.

101. See Pratt, *Imperial Eyes*. Although Taunay states that much has been written on his topic, his most frequent reference is Léry, whose 1578 *Histoire d'un voyage fait en la terre du Brésil*, written among the Tupinambá, is cited several times (115, 120, 121).

102. Taunay, *Scenas*, 112.

103. Ibid., 113.

104. Ibid.

105. Ibid., 114.

106. He mentions her in memoirs penned between 1890 and 1899 and recently reedited by Sérgio Medeiros. See Taunay, *Memórias*, 269–70, 277. Later critics found in Antônia the inspiration for two fictional characters: Inocência, from the 1872 novel by the same name; and the protagonist of the 1874 novel *Ierecê a Guaná*. See Cândido, *Formação da literatura*; Campos, "Ierecê e Iracema"; and Sá, "Índia romântica."

107. Taunay, *Scenas*, 114, 183.

108. Taunay, *Entre os nossos índios*, 51–52, 66.

109. In the twentieth century, Guaycurú peoples referred to as Kadiwéu, Kaduveo, Caduveo, Kadivéu, and Kadiveo would be the subject of much ethnographic interest, including that of Claude Lévi-Strauss and Darcy Ribeiro, who lived among the Kadiwéu in the 1930s and 1940s, respectively.

110. A *cudinho* was "a man who acts like a woman" or the "abominable" figure of the *berdache* noted by European soldiers, priests, and adventurers beginning in the sixteenth century. See Trexler, *Sex and Conquest*.

111. Taunay, *Entre os nossos índios*, 53–59, 61–62, 66, 69.

112. Ibid., 52–61, 64–65, 69. Taunay was amused that Natives referred customarily to the Brazilians as *portuguezes* and to the Paraguayans as *castelhanos*. See Taunay, *Scenas*, 127.

113. Taunay, *Entre os nossos índios*, 70.

114. Taunay, *Scenas*, 86.

115. Ibid., 109.

116. Ibid., 68, 105.

117. Ibid., 184.

118. Ibid., 117, 123–24.

119. Ibid., 123.

120. Ibid., 172–73. Captain Antônio Florêncio Pereira do Lago, an adjunct to the commission of engineers, accompanied him on the trip.

121. Ibid., 174–75 (my emphasis).

122. See *Jornal do Commercio*, 3 April 1870, 9 December 1870, and 13 December 1870; and *O Fluminense*, 22 September 1889, 25 September 1889, 29 September 1889, and 2 October 1889.

123. See n. 3.

124. Alencar, *Como e porque sou romancista*, 27.

125. Alencar denied the influence of James Fenimore Cooper alleged by his critics: "My writings are as similar to those of the illustrious American novelist as the lowlands of Ceará are to the margins of the Delaware River." Alencar, *Como e porque sou romancista*, 26.

126. Ibid., 21.

127. Alencar wrote years later that he had been especially influenced by Chateaubriand, Vigny, Dumas *père*, Balzac, and Hugo.

128. Alencar, *O guarany*, 14.

129. Taunay, *Reminiscências*, 85–86.

130. I discuss this tendency in chapter 3 with regard to the role of "Indians" in protecting the Amazon from real and imagined foreign takeover.

131. See the correspondence between the emperor and Arthur de Gobineau during the decade preceding emancipation in Raeders, *Dom Pedro II*, 318–45.

132. A vast literature examines this issue, which I address here only as it relates to my argument. On the use of Brazil by international scientists of race, see Stepan, *Picturing Tropical Nature*. On the participation of Brazilian intellectuals and politicians (including abolitionist Joaquim Nabuco) in the debates, see S. A. dos Santos, "Historical Roots." On the history of racial politics and the racialization of national discourse, see S. A. dos Santos, "A formação"; L. Schwarcz, *O espetáculo*; Skidmore, *Black into White*; and Azevedo, *Onda negra*.

133. Harvard-based Agassiz traveled to Brazil after the outbreak of the Paraguayan War at the head the Thayer Expedition, looking for evidence of an Ice Age in the tropics and seeking to refute the theories of Charles Darwin. Son of a Christian minister,

Agassiz considered transmutation theory a "scientific mistake" and dedicated his professional life to figuring out "how God created the earth." Although he opposed slavery in the United States and Brazil, Agassiz was a polygenist who believed "races" comprised "separately . . . created human species." Supported by Pedro II, he established a human laboratory in Manaus where he cataloged "mixed-race" peoples and determined that "the Indian impresse[d] his mark more deeply upon his progeny than the other races" (Agassiz and Agassiz, *Journey in Brazil*, 529–32). Agassiz's ideas gained a foothold among the *carioca* elite, who congregated in the capital to hear him deliver public lectures in French. See Robinson, *Runner of the Mountaintops*, 251.

134. Gobineau's *Essai sur l'inégalité des races humaines* (*The Inequality of Human Races*) (1853–55) predated Darwin's *On the Origin of Species* by four years. In it, Gobineau condemned the "union of the races" and argued that racial mixture "raised the small" while "lowering the great" to produce an undesirable end (209). Hence his grim outlook for Brazil: "Peoples degenerate only in consequence of the various admixtures of blood which they undergo. . . . There is no greater curse than such disorder, for however bad it may have made the present state of things, it promises still worse for the future" (209–11). In correspondence with Pedro II over the thirteen years that followed his happy departure from Brazil in 1869, the count encouraged his friend to "grace the providence" of his nation with hardworking, Catholic, German immigrants to offset its mixed-race inferiority (see Raeders, *Dom Pedro II*, 22). As the republican and abolitionist movements gained momentum, he observed with "alarm" and "disgust" the "crazed," "foolish" masses who dared to opine about rights and justice (320–33).

135. The reference, reflected in an 1895 painting by Spaniard Modesto Brocos called *Redenção de Cam* (*Redemption of Ham*) originated in the Old Testament. In Genesis 9:20–27, Noah cursed his grandson (Canaan) to servitude for his son Ham's sin of seeing "the nakedness of his father" (Noah). In doing so, however, Noah made no reference to skin color or to "race." Edith Sanders argued that the association with dark skin came later, in the Babylonian Talmud of the sixth century, and that "the notion of the Negro-Hamite was generally accepted by the year 1600" (522). The association was henceforth used to justify slavery. From the eighteenth century onward, racial theorists in Europe and the Americas related the Biblical story in their deliberations (sometimes "scientific") over whether humans of different "races" derived from the same origin and thus pertained to the same species (monogenism); or whether they derived from different origins and constituted distinct species (polygenism). These debates took on increasing importance in the mid-nineteenth century with the 1859 publication of *On the Origin of Species* by Charles Darwin (a monogenist) and the growth of abolitionist movements throughout the Americas. In light of its entrenched institution of slavery and high degree of "interracial" mixing, Brazil was a hotbed for such research and debate by Brazilians and foreigners alike.

136. Goés suggests that Carlos Gomes originally rejected Taunay's suggestion to produce a second Indianist opera but changed his mind after receiving his friend's proposed script for *Lo schiavo*, which was adapted and translated (contentiously) by Italian Rodolfo Paravicini. He also points out that Taunay's "original" was almost entirely plagiarized from Alexandre Dumas's *I Danicheff* and Gonçalves de Magalhaes's "A

confederação dos tamoios." Having been sued by a librettist in Italy prior to the opera's scheduled debut in Bologna, Gomes arrived in Brazil in a legal quagmire and severe debt. He was only able to stage the piece thanks to the intervention and financial support of the royal family. See Goés, *Carlos Gomes*, 352, 375–76.

137. Theatro Lyrico Brazileiro, *O escravo*, 11–19, 20–33, 43–47.

138. Ibid., 25–26.

139. "A fé de um rei"—a play on the well-known phrase of Portuguese historian Pêro de Magalhães Gândavo, who claimed in the sixteenth century that "Indian language" must have lacked the letters F, R, and L since, to his horror, the Indians had no *fé, rei*, or *lei* (faith, king, or law).

140. Theatro Lyrico Brazileiro, *O escravo*, 46–47.

141. That the piece was set in 1557, he argued, made no sense, because by 1555 the French had already invaded the Bay of Guanabara to join forces with the Tamoyos against the Portuguese. French "invaders" were expelled from Brazil in 1567, two years after the founding of Rio de Janeiro, by Estácio de Sá.

142. Granadaliso, "Diversões," 2–3.

143. Bicudo, "Viva Carlos Gomes," 2.

144. "De pele trocada."

145. The phrase (quoted in Goés, *Carlos Gomes*, 371) belongs to Domingos José Gonçalves de Magalhães, whose 1856 poem "A confederação dos tamoios" was attacked by Alencar but defended by the emperor. On the debates, see Castello, *Polêmica*; and Sá, *Rainforest Literatures*, 122–23.

146. Goés, *Carlos Gomes*, 374.

147. Bicudo, "Viva Carlos Gomes," 3.

148. Gomes Vaz de Carvalho, *A vida de Carlos Gomes*, 190; Itiberê da Cunha, "Lo schiavo," 299; Marques, "A volta," 11.

149. Quoted in Wisnik, *O coro dos contrários*, 71.

150. O. de Andrade, "Manifesto antropófago," 3.

151. Ibid.

152. In the 1550s, French colonists in Rio de Janeiro brought part of a Tupinambá community to Rouen and placed them in a residence built in honor of Henry II and Catherine de Medici. There the "Indians" were observed by curious onlookers, including Michel de Montaigne (see Stam, *Tropical Multiculturalism*, 248). Nearly three decades later, drawing on that experience and the captivity memoirs of Hans Staden, Montaigne penned "On Cannibals," where he questioned the meaning of savagery in the context of the Inquisition: "While we quite rightly judge [the cannibals'] faults, we are blind to our own. . . . It is more barbaric . . . to tear apart through torture and pain a living body which can still feel . . . as we have . . . seen in recent times . . . among neighbors and fellow citizens . . . under the pretext of piety and religion."

153. The statement is also a play on words, as *preguiça* means sloth in Portuguese and *ai* means sloth in Old Tupi (*Dicionário Aurélio*).

154. M. de Andrade, *Macunaíma*, 31–32.

155. Ibid., 201.

156. Ibid., 206.

157. Ibid., 210.

158. See H. de Campos, "Da razão antropofágica"; T. P. Ancona Lopez, *Macunaíma*; Sá, *Rainforest Literatures*; and Wasserman, *Exotic Nations*.

159. See M. de Andrade, *Macunaíma*, 217, 225, 233; and "Dossiê Macunaíma."

160. M. de Andrade, *Macunaíma*, 225.

161. Sá argues, for instance, that studies prior to her own "refused" to engage the "indigenous sources" on which *Macunaíma* was based. By "indigenous sources," she refers primarily to renderings of Taurepang (Pemon) narratives collected by German ethnographer Theodor Koch-Grünberg in 1911 and published in 1924 as *Vom Roroima zum Orinoco*. Sá does not seem to account, however, for the fact that the narratives were transcribed and filtered through multiple layers of language—from Portuguese, Pemon, and Arekuna, to German, Spanish, English, and back to Portuguese—before Andrade's readers would be able to have access to them. She acknowledges the negative attitude of the German scientist toward his subjects but nonetheless likens his version of their narratives to "indigenous knowledge." Perhaps the transcriptions that Andrade "plagiarized" represented narratives shared among Pemon people, but perhaps the informants were people whom Sá (and others) calls "tricksters" (68), who used "lies," guile, and "secrets" to invent, embellish, or otherwise manipulate their tales. Whatever the case may be, to pose the question is to acknowledge that, in the end, Koch-Grünberg's renderings of Pemon discourse are German sources, not indigenous ones. See Sá, *Rainforest Literatures*, 3–33.

162. Tuhiwai Smith, *Decolonizing Methodologies*, 22, 36.

163. See Moreiras's adaptation of Taussig's term in *Exhaustion of Difference*, 195.

164. Goés, *Carlos Gomes*, 110.

165. An Afro-indigenous mythological "prankster" invoked in folklore and popular culture.

166. M. de Andrade, *Macunaíma*, 210.

167. DaMatta, "For an Anthropology," 275.

168. From García Márquez's 1982 Nobel acceptance speech, "La soledad de América Latina": "The interpretation of our reality through patterns not our own serves only to make us ever more unknown, ever less free, ever more solitary."

169. M. de Andrade, *Macunaíma*, 144–45.

170. Ibid., 151. Andrade was more charitable in his 1928 *Ensaio sobre a música brasileira*: "Carlos Gomes can make us proud beyond the limits of the period and rightly we must place him among the best composers of the nineteenth century" (21).

171. Approximately US$3.2 million, as the historical rates vary in the literature. I take the rate of $1,600 per ten *contos de réis* from a 1900 edition of the *Monthly Bulletin of the Bureau of the American Republics*. On the history of the theater see Monteiro, *Teatro Amazonas*.

172. Brooke, "Opera Is Ready."

173. Weinstein, "Racializing Regional Difference."

174. In the Southeast, for example, *paraíba* and *baiano* (Paraíban and Bahian) are still used to refer pejoratively to Northeasterners (especially migrants), regardless of their origin. The terms are often invoked to connote phenotype.

175. Weinstein, *Amazon Rubber Boom*, 192–93.

176. Historian Greg Grandin writes that by the time Henry Ford founded his ill-fated Fordlândia about halfway between Belém and Manaus, rubber traders had "exhausted" their supply of Native workers and replaced them with *sertanejos* brought in by "boatloads" from the arid Northeast (see G. Grandin, *Fordlândia*, 30–31). There is also evidence, however, to suggest that rubber barons of the second boom (during the 1940s) relied heavily on a local indigenous and *caboclo* workforce. Of course, the "purity" of Native Amazonian peoples was by then frequently called into question by outsiders. Even the official documentation of the SPI refers to locals as *acaboclados*. See also Barbosa Rodrigues, *Rio Jauapery*, 128; Galeano, *Las venas abiertas*, 116–121; Oliveira Junior, "Bilhete da Guanabara"; and my chapter 3.

177. Rocha Freire published a list of 192 "branch tribes" (*tribus-tronco*) from the (incomplete) local census conducted by the SPI's First Regional Inspectorate in 1919 under the leadership of Bento de Lemos. See his *O SPI na Amazônia*, 23–27. The number of distinct peoples living in the international Amazon today is more than twice that. See OTCA, *Tierras*, 184.

178. In his writing, Barbosa Rodrigues refers to the Native groups as Jaupery and Waimiri (see Barbosa Rodrigues, *Rio Jauapery*). The ideas of Domingo Faustino Sarmiento (Pedro II's close friend) had circulated in Brazil since the mid-nineteenth century. See Calmon, *História de Dom Pedro II*, 403–8.

179. Barbosa Rodrigues, *Rio Jauapery*, 197.

180. Quoted in ibid., 186.

181. *Revista do Museu Paulista*, 215. For his "scientific" take on Brazilian Indians, see also von Ihering, *Anthropology* and "El hombre prehistórico."

182. See the dossier of letters (by Falcão and others) and related documents in Barbosa Rodriques, *Rio Jauapery*, 179–241.

183. *O Paiz*, XXVII.

184. See Carlos Gomes, letters to Manoel José Souza de Guimarães, 9 and 13 November 1889.

185. *O Paiz*, XXVII (my emphasis).

186. He referred to the joyful torture and mass murder of Native slaves performing extractive labor in the Peruvian Amazon during the late nineteenth and early twentieth centuries, recently fictionalized in *El sueño del celta*, Mario Vargas Llosa's historical novel based on the life of Roger Casement. See part 1 of Taussig's *Shamanism* on the Putumayo affair and the Peruvian Amazon Company.

187. H. White, "Historical Emplotment," 46–53.

188. Barbosa Rodrigues, *Rio Jauapery*, 10; H. White, "Historical Emplotment," 52.

189. I discuss potential meanings of this "survival" in chapter 5.

190. Barbosa Rodrigues, *Rio Jauapery*, 10–26; *O Paiz*, XXVII.

191. *O Paiz*, XXVII (my emphasis).

192. "Hunting Indians."

193. Ibid. Though imperial officials dismissed the charges, raids and "Indian hunting" would persist into the twenty-first century, often reportedly facilitated by the negligence, complicity, or outright support of state officials. See, for example, Barbosa Rodrigues, *Rio Jauapery*; "Defendendo seus irmãos"; Hemming, *Die If You Must*; D. Price, *Before the Bulldozer*; and, more recently, Caufield, "Lost Tribe"; and Survival

International, "Gunmen Destroy Indigenous Camp." For a comparison of indigenous and nonindigenous interpretations of state-sponsored "pacification" during the early twentieth century, see Urban, "Interpretations of Inter-cultural Contact," and Coelho dos Santos, *Índios e brancos no sul do Brasil*.

194. Da Costa, "Indian Hunting."

195. In conjunction with his sponsorship of Carlos Gomes's second Indianist opera and its opening in Rio de Janeiro, Dom Pedro II received a small group of Carabú visitors at the Imperial Palace and heard their unspecified requests (*pedidos*) with "great attention." The emperor requested that a Carabú-Portuguese glossary be compiled with the collaboration of the Carabú visitors. It appeared on the front page of *O Paiz* on 29 September 1898—less than two months shy of the declaration of the First Republic.

196. I refer to the 1910 establishment of the SPI, which I examine in chapters 3 and 4.

CHAPTER 3

1. The name of the "author" might relate to the Normans, who conquered territories from Hastings to Syria from the eleventh to the early thirteenth century. Historian David Nicolle attributes to them military prowess, ruthlessness, "business sense," and "appreciation for money." Nicolle, *Normans*, 4. Or perhaps, as Alex Martin has suggested to me, the name was intended to invoke the imperialist Nor(th)man.

2. Ambassador Rubens Antônio Barbosa attributed the fabrication to retired military personnel and an anonymous webpage called "Brasil, ame-o ou deixe-o" ("Brazil, Love It or Leave It")—a slogan associated with the 1964–85 dictatorship. Paulo Roberto de Almeida (minister-counselor of the Brazilian embassy in Washington between 1999 and 2003), who documented the circulation of the message by university professors, members of Congress, and thousands of outraged citizens, condemned the uncritical embrace of ultranationalism by the intellectual Left that had once opposed the manipulation of that rhetoric by the military dictatorship. As a result, critics across the political spectrum accused him of backing U.S imperialism. See www.pralmeida.org.

3. See Treece, *Exiles*; Béhague, "Indianism"; and "Querem comer nossas matas."

4. Slater, *Entangled Edens*, 3–16.

5. For the context of Bush's comment, see "Transcript: Presidential Debate."

6. That is, as so-called Voluntários da Pátria. See my chapter 2; Berthold, *History of the Telephone and Telegraph*; Summerhill, *Order against Progress*; Weinstein, *Amazon Rubber Boom*; and G. Grandin, *Fordlândia*.

7. Souza Lima, *Um grande cerco*.

8. Giddens, *Consequences of Modernity*, 18.

9. Though the March to the West began officially in 1940, the 1933 founding of Goiânia and the establishment of the Departamento Nacional de Estradas de Rodagem (National Department of Roads, or DNER) at the beginning of the Estado Novo were important antecedents. "Fifty Years in Five" was a multipronged, accelerated program for national development.

10. These officials included indigenist Raimundo Vasconcelos Aboim, National Museum director Heloisa Alberto Tôrres, *sertanista* Orlando Villas-Bôas, and ethnologist Darcy Ribeiro. The park changed names twice and is now Terra Indígena do Xingu. For debates over the territory and name changes, see Pires Menezes, *Parque*; and Garfield, "Nationalist Environment."

11. "Ante-projecto de lei de 1952"; quoted in Pires Menezes, *Parque*, 344–45.

12. Pires Menezes, *Parque*, 299–316.

13. Early "Indian schooling" adhered to a nineteenth-century principle that rural instruction had to be technical, as education for leisure (*educação para o ócio*) would impede national development. See Romanelli, *História da educação*, 44–45. Peruvian politician González Prada thus railed famously against "enlightened minds and starving bellies." González Prada, "Nuestros indios," 212.

14. See my chapter 5.

15. See Berry, "Myth of the Vanishing Indian"; Ramos, "Hyperreal Indian"; and my introduction and chapter 1.

16. I refer to José Martí's 1891 manifesto of pan–Latin Americanism, "Nuestra América."

17. SIVAM was the infrastructure-implementation phase of the Sistema de Proteção da Amazônia (Amazonian Protection System, or SIPAM). The transfer took place in April 2006. See Grupo Schahin, "Inauguração do projeto"; Raytheon, "SIVAM"; and http://www.sipam.gov.br/.

18. Raytheon, "SIVAM."

19. Brazilian territory is divided into four Centros Integrados de Defesa Aérea e Controle de Tráfego Aéreo (Integrated Air Traffic Control and Air Defense Centers, or CINDACTAs). CINDACTA I (Brasília, Rio, São Paulo, Belo Horizonte) dates to 1973. CINDACTA IV covers the Amazon and began functioning with SIVAM technology in 2006. See Bonalume Neto, "Depois de 15 anos"; and Departamento de Controle do Espaço Aéreo, "Unidades."

20. The chief of protocol, Júlio César Gomes dos Santos; the Air Force minister, Brigadier General Mauro Gandra; the head of the Federal Police's Centro de Dados Operacionais (Operations Center, or CDO), Mário Oliveira; and the director of the Instituto Nacional de Colonização e Reforma Agrária (National Institute for Colonization and Agrarian Reform, or INCRA), Francisco Grazziano. The judicial body that oversees public financing (Tribunal de Contas da União) concluded that the contracts in the case were legal, while the CPI found evidence of bribery and "influence trafficking." See Taylor and Buranelli, "Ending Up in Pizza," 73–74; Hynds, "Administration"; and Ramos, *Indigenism*, 240–41.

21. Comissão, "Histórico."

22. The governmental website documented financing as follows: U.S. Export-Import Bank, 73.3%; Raytheon, 17%; Exportkreditnämnden, 6%; and Vendor's Trust, 3.4%.

23. Lima, "SIVAM," 5.

24. Lima, phone interview.

25. Comissão, "Sivamzinho."

26. Affected cities included Altamira (Pará) (the city to be partially displaced by Belo Monte), Barcelos (Amazonas), Cachimbo (Pará), Carauari (Amazonas), Conceição do Araguaia (Pará), Cruzeiro do Sul (Acre), Eirunepé (Amazonas), Guajará-Mirim (Rondônia), Imperatriz (Maranhão), Jacareacanga (Pará), Manicoré (Amazonas), Marabá (Pará), Porto Esperidião (Mato Grosso), Porto Trombetas (Pará), Santarém (Pará), São Félix do Araguaia (Mato Grosso), São Félix do Xingu (Pará), São Gabriel da Cachoeira (Amazonas), Sinop (Mato Grosso), Tabatinga (Amazonas), Tefé (Amazonas), Tiriós (Pará), and Vilhena (Rondônia). See Lima, "SIVAM," 17; and Comissão, "Revista."

27. Lima, "SIVAM," 4–17; Comissão, "Uma legião."

28. Comissão, "Sivamzinho."

29. Rumors circulated that SIVAM satellite technology would target untapped mineral wealth in particular. See Lima, "SIVAM"; "Pintura de Vivi Castro"; and Rohter, "Deep in Brazil." This discourse has been invigorated over the years by the likes of Peter Wittcoff, a U.S. Navy officer who proposed in 1999 that "SIVAM might benefit U.S. national security interests in Latin America," and Williard Price, who half a decade earlier argued that Amazonia was the world's breadbasket. See Wittcoff, "Amazon Surveillance System," xix–xx; and W. Price, *Amazing Amazon*, 6.

30. Medeiros, "Sob os olhos do SIVAM," 46.

31. See Anderson, *Imagined Communities*. Abolition in 1888 heightened the need for rural workers and spawned intense immigration when the government conceded unoccupied lands to new settler colonies. Vargas established immigration quotas before banning immigration entirely in 1932. The ban was lifted in 1934, and the 1937 Constitution limited newcomers annually to 2% of each existing immigrant population. See Diégues, *Etnias*, 123–32; and Lesser, *Negotiating National Identity*.

32. See my introduction, n. 20.

33. On the origin and operation of the SPI, see Diacon, *Stringing Together*; Garfield, *Indigenous Struggle*; Hemming, *Die If You Must*; and Souza Lima, *Um grande cerco*.

34. The statement was a directive for indigenists to sacrifice themselves, if necessary, to save indigenous lives.

35. The posts were grouped under nine *inspetorias* in Manaus, Belém, São Luis, Recife, Campo Grande, Cuiabá, Curitiba, Goiânia, and Porto Velho and functioned (at least in theory) according to local needs. Attraction posts contacted "unpacified" tribes. Frontier posts served populations in Acre, which was once Bolivian territory, had three short lives as an independent Republic, became part of Brazil in 1904, and gained statehood in 1962. Residents of ranching posts raised livestock for consumption and commerce. Finally, literacy and nationalization posts facilitated the economic integration of people in "advanced stages of de-Indianization." See Schultz and Vellozo, *Curt Nimuendajú*.

36. "Integrando o índio."

37. Ibid.

38. As Berthold explained in 1922, foreign shareholders financed Brazil's communication lines with North America, Europe, and Western Africa before Brazilians at opposite ends of the country could communicate with one another by telegraph. Indeed, European (primarily British) investment dominated transportation, utilities,

and manufacturing from the first half of the nineteenth century until World War I, when U.S. investment took over. By 1950, Skidmore maintains, nearly 40% of Brazil's export earnings would go to debt service. See Geiger, *General*, 29; and Skidmore, *Politics of Military Rule*, 12.

39. Vargas lost to Júlio Prestes in the 1930 presidential elections to succeed Washington Luís. With the backing of the anti-establishment Aliança Liberal and disgruntled military, Vargas's supporters removed Luís in late October, before the legal transfer of power could occur. Vargas assumed the presidency days later and remained in office until the end of the Estado Novo. He returned to the presidency in 1951 after being elected democratically and served until his suicide in 1954. On Rondon's relationship with the first Vargas regime and the impact of the 1930s financial crisis on the SPI, see Hemming, *Die If You Must*, 210–11.

40. G. Vargas, "Decreto 24.715."

41. Schultz and Vellozo, *Curt Nimuendajú*.

42. The first term referred to the Amazon rainforest; the second echoed the title of Euclides da Cunha's famous account of the Canudos War.

43. Schultz and Vellozo, *Curt Nimuendajú*.

44. Ibid.

45. As of 2005, there were still 15 Kaingang living in Icatu (founded as an indigenous post in 1919) and 28,830 throughout Brazil. See Veiga and Rocha d'Angelis, "Terra Indígena Icatu."

46. The 1973 Indian Statute kept this practice in place. The 2002 Civil Code specified the exceptionalism of the indigenous condition in the context of the "relative incapacity" of adolescents, drug addicts, the mentally handicapped, and the financially insolvent. Article 4 of Chapter 1 states simply that "the Indians' capacity will be regulated by special legislation." See Presidência da República (www.planalto.gov.br /ccivil_03/LEIS/2002/L10406.htm); and FUNAI (www.funai.gov.br/quem/legislacao /estatuto_indio.html). Also see M. Gomes, *Indians*, 82–89; Hoffman French, *Legalizing Identities*, 66–70; Ramos, *Indigenism*, 15–24; and my chapter 1.

47. See Bolívar's 1815 "Carta de Jamaica." Following Bolívar, ideologues of American independence including Andrés Bello, José Enrique Rodó, Franz Tamayo, José Carlos Mariátegui, José Vasconcelos Calderón, and Ernesto "Che" Guevara referred to the region's "infancy" and the need to bring it to "maturity" through education. Guevara wrote of postrevolutionary Cuba: "Society as a whole must be converted into a giant school. . . . We are still in diapers" (Guevara, "El hombre y el socialismo," 11).

48. Serpa, "RES NOSTRA" (my emphasis).

49. Renato Inácio da Silva posited the struggle over Amazonian riches as a Cold War conflict, asserting that Brazil was "coveted by two wolves prowling through the entire world." Avaricious explorers hailed from many countries, but North Americans were the most egregious: "They aim to take everything, including atomic minerals! . . . They took an aerial photographs of the region in 1965 . . . as if we Brazilians were living in 1500!" R. da Silva, *Amazônia*, 333–34.

50. Golbery's *Planejamento estratégico* (1955) and *Geopolítica do Brasil* (1967) were among the most influential pieces of Cold War geopolitical doctrine in the region. Therein, the controversial National Intelligence Service director and presidential

advisor argued for the conquest of national space, border control, and strategic but not subservient collaboration with the United States.

51. See Szmrecsányi and Ramos, "O papel das políticas governamentais," 228.

52. Souza Lima, *Um grande cerco*, 131.

53. Foucault, *History of Sexuality*, 140.

54. Instituto Indigenista Interamericano, *Acta*, 23. Due to budgetary constraints, Brazil did not ratify the early III Convention and became a signatory only in 1953. Nonetheless, Edgard Roque Pinto participated in the 1940 meeting and Rondon corresponded regularly with his regional counterparts, including Manuel Gamio, director of the Instituto Indigenista Interamericano, and John Collier, representative of the U.S. Bureau of Indian Affairs. See Oliveira Junior, "Bilhete"; "Primeiro Congresso"; Gamio, letter; and Rondon, letter to John Collier, 28 January 1947.

55. Now affiliated with the Organization of American States and headquartered in Mexico, the Instituto Indigenista Interamericano supports collaborative indigenist policy to promote regional development.

56. The Ilha do Bananal was then located in northern Goiás and now is in Tocantins, which gained statehood in 1988.

57. Rondon, "O índio é a maior preciosidade."

58. Darcy Ribeiro identified this dependency as an early stage of "ethnic transfiguration," which would transform "tribal Indians" into "generic Indians" but never "de-Indianize" them. See D. Ribeiro, *Os índios*, 241–54.

59. "Civilização para os índios."

60. "Defendendo seus irmãos."

61. Studied famously by Michael Taussig, the reports written by Roger Casement in the early 1910s have long been the subject of controversy. The Irish-born British consul who documented horrifying abuse of indigenous rubber workers by the British-run Peruvian Amazon Company was later "uncovered" as a homosexual and a pedophile, accused of treason for his support for Irish revolution, and executed. The source of the supposedly autobiographical writings that revealed his sexuality and alleged victimization of minors has been hotly debated ever since. See Taussig, *Shamanism*; Goodman, *Devil and Mr. Casement*; and Vargas Llosa's 2010 novel, *El sueño del celta*.

62. "Defendendo seus irmãos."

63. The military regime established the commission to discredit the SPI further and found it complicit in rape, torture, murder, and genocide. See Hemming, *Die If You Must*, 227–34.

64. "Memorial do Sr. Lyrio Arlindo do Valle."

65. Ibid.

66. Ibid.

67. The current FUNAI president, Marta Maria do Amaral Azevedo (a nonindigenous anthropologist), replaced her embattled predecessor, Márcio Augusto Freitas de Meira (also a nonindigenous anthropologist), in April 2012. For years, indigenous activists had campaigned vigorously for Meira's removal and the establishment of a new Ministry of Indigenous Affairs to be run by indigenous people. They succeeded in the first effort but failed in the second and third.

68. The Potiguara warrior immortalized by José de Alencar in *Iracema* fought alongside the Portuguese against the Dutch during the early seventeenth century.

69. "Memorial do Sr. Lyrio Arlindo do Valle."

70. Ibid.

71. The document, also studied by Seth Garfield ("Roots," 765–68) is typewritten on Ministry of Agriculture letterhead and titled "Memorial do Sr. Lyrio Arlindo do Valle, diretamente ao Sr. Dr. Getúlio Dorneles Vargas [*sic*]." It is dated September 1945 but has an October distribution date and contains many errors and spelling inconsistencies, including in the author's first name. Although Valle claimed to have written the letter, SPI employees may have typed (or retyped) it. At best, his enthusiasm for Vargas's policies offers some insight into the ambiguous nature of "neo-Brazilian" thought. At worst, it is yet another instance of the indigenist appropriation of indigenous voice and subjectivity.

72. The *Dicionário Aurélio* explains that Alexander von Humboldt and Aimé Goujaud Bonpland used *hylea* (from the Greek *hylaîa*, "of the forest") to refer to the Amazon during the late eighteenth and early nineteenth centuries. (This is not the oft-cited 1952 UNESCO study of race led by Charles Wagley, Thales Azevedo, Roger Bastide, Florestan Fernández, Luiz de Aguiar Costa Pinto, and Renée Ribeiro in Bahia, São Paulo, Rio de Janeiro, and Pernambuco. On that study, see Chor, *UNESCO*; D. Ribeiro, *Confissões*; and my chapter 4.)

73. For a brief biography of Mishkin, see Wagley, "Bernard Mishkin." A model of international collaboration in the spirit of postwar diplomacy, the IIHA established headquarters in Rio de Janeiro before moving to the Amazon. Although staffed with Brazilian scientists and led by CNPI member and National Museum director Heloisa Alberto Tôrres, nationalists accused the organization of marginalizing national science and contributing to the "territorial disintegration" of the country. See *Diário do Congresso Nacional*.

74. "Civilização para os índios."

75. Mishkin, "Fundamental Education: Interim Report," 4–5.

76. Ibid., 3.

77. Ibid., 2.

78. Mishkin, "Fundamental Education: Second Interim Report," 28.

79. Mishkin, "Problems of Fundamental Education," 3.

80. Mishkin, "Fundamental Education: Second Interim Report," 28.

81. Ibid., 9.

82. In 1967, the year the SPI was dissolved, reports by Angelina da Silva Vicente on Indigenous Post Capitão Vitorino, for example, documented lessons on the national anthem, Independence Day, "respecting the flag," voting, and elections. On SPI education, see also my chapter 1; and Devine Guzmán, "Indians and Ailing National Culture." On indigenous citizenship before and after the 1988 Constitution, see Ramos, *Indigenism*, 89–118.

83. Anthropologist David Price's research with documents secured through the Freedom of Information Act places Mishkin in Brazil during the late 1940s as an employee of the Nesco Company and as a business partner of Abraham Brothman (a

target of McCarthyism). They mention neither his consulting work for UNESCO nor the documents examined here. Accusations regarding Mishkin's political activities remain inconclusive (Price claims his requests for CIA documentation were ignored) and warrant further study (which I take up in an ongoing project).

84. Mishkin, "Good Neighbors," 510–13.

85. Ibid., 515.

86. Four years later, Mishkin died in Germany of a "sudden heart attack" at the age of forty-one, having given up a lectureship at Brandeis University to pursue an international air travel business (the Flying Tigers). His manuscript on Peru was never finished, and knowledge about the work he did there is limited. Having moved between academia, the military, consulting, and entrepreneurship, Mishkin's career was inconsistent and erratic. See Wagley, "Bernard Mishkin," 1034.

87. Giddens, *Consequences of Modernity*, 1–54.

88. Ibid., 39.

89. Ibid., 19.

90. As I mention in the introduction and discuss in chapter 5, the Programa de Aceleração do Crescimento (PAC) revived dictatorship-era plans to build "Belo Monte," the world's third-largest hydroelectric dam, now under way in Pará. See also Devine Guzmán, "Writing Indigenous Activism," "Whence Amazonian Studies," and "Subalternidade e soberania."

91. Giddens explains disembedding as the "lifting out of social relations from local contexts of interaction and their restructuring across indefinite spans of time-space." Giddens, *Consequences of Modernity*, 21.

92. As Antônio Torres puts it, "o índio é o povo." See Torres, "Entrevista com Luis Pimentel," 11; and my chapter 4.

93. On the legal structure of the international Amazon, see the Amazon Cooperation Treaty Organization: http://www.otca.info/portal/.

94. BR-080 cut off some 8,000 of the 22,000 square kilometers originally dedicated to the park. See Callado, "O parque," 10.

95. Ibid.

96. Ibid., 11.

97. *Nossos índios*.

98. Quoted in "O Serviço de Proteção aos Índios."

99. Ibid.

CHAPTER 4

1. See O. de Andrade, "Manifesto antropófago"; Campos, "Da razão antropofágica"; R. Johnson, "Tupy or Not Tupy"; and my chapter 2.

2. On scientific racism in late-nineteenth-century Brazil, see L. Schwarcz, *O espectáculo*; Maciel, "A Eugenia"; and my chapter 2.

3. Precursors and contributors to these paradigms who have particularly influenced my study include J. Vasconcelos, *La raza cósmica*; Freyre, *Casa grande e senzala*; Ortiz, *Contrapunteo cubano del tabaco y el azúcar*; Arguedas, *Los rios profundos*, "No soy," and *El zorro de arriba*; D. Ribeiro, *Os índios*, *As Américas e a civilização*, and *O povo*

brasileiro; Cornejo Polar, *Escribir en el aire* and *Los universos narrativos*; Rama, *Ciudad letrada* and *Transculturación narrativa*; R. White, *Middle Ground*; Lienhard, *La voz y su huella*; García Canclini, *Culturas híbridas*; Vargas Llosa, *La utopía arcaica*; Godenzzi, *Educación e interculturalidad*; Mignolo, *Darker Side*; Beverley, *Subalternity*; de la Cadena, *Indigenous Mestizos* and "Are Mestizos Hybrids?"; Moreiras, *Exhaustion of Difference*; Yúdice, *Expediency of Culture*; Rappaport, *Intercultural Utopias*; and Walsh, "Interculturalidad, colonialidad y educación." See also my chapter 1.

4. On the national-popular, see Moreiras, *Exhaustion of Difference*, 162–83, 264–300.

5. In addition to my comments on the 2010 Census in chapter 1, see IBGE, *Censo demográfico 2010*; and Instituto Socioambiental, "Povos indígenas no Brasil."

6. Das et al., *Remaking a World*, 5.

7. *Gaúcho* or *gaúcha* is an informal term that refers to a man or woman from Rio Grande do Sul.

8. During the early to mid-twentieth century, the term *sertanista*, derived from *sertão* (backlands), referred to young men who worked as explorers, adventurers, and "Indian tamers" in rural areas of the interior. The SPI existed alongside the FBC but was given no new role to play in the project of westward expansion, likely because of its growing reputation for corruption. Maybury-Lewis noted: "Significantly, the Villas-Bôas brothers, who . . . became famous as the protectors of Indians and the creators of the Xingu National Park, worked for the Central Brazil Foundation and not for the SPI." See Maybury-Lewis, "Becoming Indian," 221.

9. A. Cunha, *Entre os índios*, 178.

10. Indigenist hero Leonardo Villas-Bôas, for instance, was accused of having improper relationships with indigenous women that year. See "Tentação nas selvas" and "Da civilização às selvas!"

11. Indigenous peoples shared this status with orphans and the mentally impaired. Ramos elaborates: "Indians were inserted in the 1916 Civil Code as objects of guardianship to last until they became adapted to national society. They remained as orphans until 1928 when the Indian Protection Service . . . took over their guardianship from the judge of orphans." See Ramos, *Indigenism*, 18; and my chapters 1 and 2.

12. On the SPI under the War Ministry, see Souza Lima, *Um grande cerco*, 266–85; and my chapter 3.

13. A. Cunha, *Entre os índios*, 186.

14. Ibid.

15. Ibid., 188.

16. Chateaubriand, who owned several newspapers, had personal and professional ties with numerous members of the governing administration. For a detailed account of his influence on Brazilian media and politics during and after the Vargas period, see Morais, *Chatô*.

17. "O homem branco."

18. D. Ribeiro, *Os índios*, 212.

19. On 3 July 1951, Vargas signed the Afonso Arinos Law (no. 1.390) outlawing racial discrimination. On racial discrimination against other groups during the Vargas regime, see O. da Cunha, "Sua alma"; Dávila, *Diploma of Whiteness*; Lesser, *Negotiating*

National Identity; Maio, "Qual anti-semitismo?"; Seyferth, "Os imigrantes"; and D. Williams, *Culture Wars in Brazil*.

20. See Souza Lima, *Um grande cerco*, 286–305. For an analysis of how the expansion initiative affected state "Indian policy" and the Xavante, in particular, see Garfield, *Indigenous Struggle*. On Vargas and nation-building, also see M. Gomes, *Indians*; and Pandolfi, *Repensando*.

21. Rocha Freire, "Indigenismo," 200.

22. Like the FBC, this administrative body was established under the Vargas administration.

23. On changes in SPI goals and policies in this regard, see D. Ribeiro, *Os índios* and *Confissões*; Souza Lima, *Um grande cerco*; and Devine Guzmán, "Our Indians."

24. The language barrier was one of the primary justifications for the SPI's refusal to permit the marriage. In the Twelfth Report of the CNPI Acts, seven prominent ethnographers explained their opposition. Heloisa Alberto Tôrres, who voted with the majority against the union, argued: "(5) The Indian Diacuí does not know how to speak any language other than her indigenous language. (6) The Indian Diacuí does not understand any language other than her own. (7) Ayres Câmara Cunha does not speak Kalapalo. (8) There is no Kalapalo-Portuguese translator among those who accompanied Diacuí to Rio de Janeiro. (9) There is no known person in Rio de Janeiro who speaks Kalapalo." Echoing Darcy Ribeiro's distinction between more and less acculturated Indians, Tôrres added: "If that indigenous woman were capable of understanding the obligations they want her to take on before men and God, she would be ashamed to see a portrait of herself completely naked passed around from hand to hand." See CNPI, "Relatório No. 12."

25. Ibid.

26. Ibid. The weight of Ribeiro's convictions must be considered alongside the fact that he, too, had sexual relations with indigenous women. Years later, he revealed: "I was taught not to screw Indians, . . . [but] spent months with [them] and figured out a way to have one. . . . I didn't do the Urubú-Kaapor women, because I was working with the Kaapor, but I did Tembé women—some relatively decadent Indian women around there." See D. Ribeiro, *Mestiço*, 36–37, and *Confissões*, 167–80.

27. Seven members sat on the council: José da Gama Malcher, president of the SPI; General Júlio Caetano Horta Barbosa, president of the CNPI; Heloisa Alberto Tôrres, director of the National Museum; General Boaneges Lopes de Souza; Coronel Amilcar Botelho de Magalhães, and Professors Guilherme de Almeida and Boaventura Ribeiro da Cunha. Only Boaventura voted in favor of the wedding. See A. Cunha, *Entre os índios*, 210.

28. "Os índios não terão com quem casar."

29. Anderson, *Imagined Communities*.

30. On Alencar, see also my chapter 2.

31. Although an admirer of José de Alencar and an occasional contributor to the Indianist movement, Machado de Assis objected to the predominance of the "indigenous theme" in national literature. In 1873 he asserted that "Brazilian civilization is neither linked to nor influenced by the Indian element; this is sufficient reason not to search among the defeated tribes for the titles of our literary personality." See Machado

de Assis, "Notícia," 802. Two years later, abolitionist Joaquim Nabuco punctuated the criticism of the "Indianization" of national identity in an extended debate with Alencar that appeared in *O Globo*. "We're Brazilians," he insisted, "not Guaranis." See Cotinho, *A polêmica*, 191.

32. See Brookshaw, *Race and Color*; Driver, *Indian in Brazilian Literature*; and Sommer, *Foundational Fictions*.

33. Treece, *Exiles*, 139. The association is correct, but the attribution is not, as I explain in chapters 1 and 5.

34. Alencar's *O guarany*, which appeared in the *Diário do Rio de Janeiro* in 1856, reversed the archetypal gender roles of the colonial encounter to unite "white virgin" Ceci and former Indian-slave Peri in an idealized union that would survive violent conflict and inspire Peri's embrace of Christianity. See Treece, *Exiles*, 180–93; and my chapter 2. On the history of the *folhetim*, see Tinhorão, *O romance*; and Meyer, *Folhetim*.

35. While the SPI garnered support for its decision from the CNPI and centers of anthropological expertise throughout the country, including the National Museum and the Universities of São Paulo and Brasília, Cleofas authorized Aiute's visit to Rio de Janeiro. He was the godfather or sponsor (*padrinho*) of her civil wedding, while Chateaubriand was godfather of the religious ceremony that followed. See Rocha Freire, "Indigenismo," 263–65.

36. See "Delírio indescritível no aeroporto."

37. Gurgel, "Abençoada," 13.

38. "Diacuí está feliz"; "Às 3 horas da tarde"; "Inspiração para a nova moda feminina."

39. "Unidos perante a lei."

40. Gurgel, "Abençoada," 12.

41. The cause of death was not immediately indicated, but Cunha later claimed that she died from hemorrhaging when the placenta did not detach during labor. See A. Cunha, *Entre os índios*, 243–44.

42. Famous among them was English coronel Percy Fawcett, who disappeared in 1925 with his two-man expedition to find the gold-laden, lost city of "Z." Obsessed with the missing explorers, the Brazilian and international media speculated for decades about their death at the hands of the Kalapalo or other "fierce Indians" nearby. See A. Cunha, *Entre os índios*, 236–37; "Strange Case"; and Grann, *Lost City*.

43. On the death and funeral rituals among the Kalapalo, see Basso, *Kalapalo*, 56–60, and *Musical View*, 105.

44. Writes Basso: "The Kalapalo consider marriage between two brother-sister pairs . . . a highly desirable practice, because the powerful sibling relationship can be continued in the same household throughout marriage. . . . Such marriages are . . . fortuitous arrangements. . . . They usually depend upon the death or divorce of at least one prior spouse." See Basso, *Kalapalo*, 88.

45. Basso describes a ten-day seclusion period, while Cunha claimed it was a month. See Basso, *Musical View*, 106–8; and A. Cunha, *Entre os índios*, 246.

46. On Kalapalo naming, see Basso, *Kalapalo*, 85–87. On Diacuizinha, see A. Cunha, *Entre os índios*, 247–48. The child was raised by her grandmother, aunt, and uncle (Cunha's brother, Arnóbio) in Uruguaiana. Although she reportedly wanted to be a teacher, Diacuizinha ceased her studies to work at her uncle's acrylic factory and

prepare for her marriage to a merchant and former taxi driver named José Antônio Dutra. In 1973, her father reported plans to visit Kuluene and relay news of the marriage to the Kalapalo, but I have not been able to confirm that visit or to contact Diacuizinha myself. Ysani Kalapalo, a distant relative of Diacuí Canualo Aiute, maintains that Diacuizinha never visited her extended family in Xingu (conversation with the author, São Paulo, 20 August 2011).

47. "O viúvo da Diacuí."

48. Cunha discusses his childhood in Rio Grande do Sul; life as an FBC *sertanista*; encounters with the Kalapalo prior to his relationship with Aiute; married life in Xingu; and specific events surrounding his wife's death. He went on to publish other books, including *Além de Mato Grosso*, *História da índia Diacuí*, *Nas selvas de Xingu*, and *O mistério do explorador Fawcett*, all of which demonstrated the commercial value of the "Indian adventures" recounted in his writing.

49. In A. Cunha, *Nas selvas*, 11.

50. A. Cunha, *Entre os índios*, 174.

51. Ibid., 207–8.

52. As he put it: "The question 'to marry or not to marry' became a tremendous polemic that made everyone extremely emotional. . . . The passion of the arguments was equally intense from the *racists* and those who sought the union of the two races." A. Cunha, *Nas selvas*, 207.

53. A. Cunha, *Entre os índios*, 179.

54. Prominent proponents of the marriage included Assis Chateaubriand, Getúlio Vargas, and SPI founder Cândido Rondon.

55. A. Cunha, *Entre os índios*, 205.

56. Vargas was reportedly unable to visit due to illness. Ibid.

57. D. Williams, *Culture Wars in Brazil*, 82–88.

58. Ciema, "O índio."

59. See my chapter 3.

60. "Getúlio vai amparar."

61. A. Cunha, *Entre os índios*, 224, 227, 243.

62. Gurgel, "Abençoada," 14.

63. The question was reportedly translated by Professor Boaventura Ribeiro da Cunha (the only CNPI member who voted in favor of the marriage), though SPI documentation suggests there were no bilingual Kalapalo speakers in Rio de Janeiro at the time of her visit. See n. 24.

64. French ambassador to Brazil from 1869 to 1870, Gobineau infamously characterized Brazil as a "desert inhabited by scoundrels with a fearfully ugly, half-bred population of vitiated blood and spirit." See Maciel, "A Eugenia," 124, and my chapter 2.

65. "Serviço de Proteção aos Índios: Sucursal."

66. On the UNESCO study and its leaders, see chapter 3, n. 72.

67. D. Ribeiro, *Confissões*, 190–91.

68. See n. 19.

69. On "export culture" under the Estado Novo, see D. Williams, *Culture Wars in Brazil*, 214–18.

70. D. Ribeiro, *Os índios*, 241–503.

71. See Ramos, *Indigenism*, 249; and my chapters 1 and 5.

72. Gaúdio, "Proteção."

73. "Getúlio vai amparar."

74. "A nossa opinião."

75. On this dichotomy, see my chapter 2; and Ramos, *Indigenism*, 292.

76. I refer to Jean Baudrillard's development of the notion with regard to ethnography and the proliferation of images that are progressively removed in "stages" from the objects they represent. See Baudrillard, *Simulacros*, 13–15; Ramos, *Indigenism*, 275; and my introduction.

77. Compare, for instance, official and unofficial reports on the 6 June 2012 ceremony at the Palácio do Planalto, commemorating President Dilma Rousseff's approval of seven demarcated indigenous territories. Whereas FUNAI touted the administration's commitment to indigenous issues on the eve of the U.N. Conference on Sustainable Development, rights activist Sônia Guajajara spoke critically on behalf of the indigenous movement and questioned, among other things, why she and her cohort had been asked to appear at the event "in adornment [*paramentados*]." See "O que os índios disseram" and "Presidenta Dilma assina decreto da PNGATI."

78. The Movimento dos Trabalhadores Rurais sem Terra (Landless Workers' Movement, or MST) is a national social organization that has worked for the redistribution of unoccupied and unproductive lands since the early 1980s. *Sem terras* have often been at odds with indigenous land interests, as well as with those of large-scale landholders (see http://www.mst.org.br/).

79. The Final Document of the Conference of Indigenous Peoples and Organizations of Brazil (see Appendix 1) was signed on 21 April 2000 in Coroa Vermelha (Porto Seguro, Bahia).

80. *Uga! Uga!* aired in Brazil during the run-up to the quincentenary and elsewhere in South America beginning in September 2003. The *novela* depicted the life of a young man lost in the wilderness as a child and raised by "Indians." Eventually making his way to "civilization," the protagonist turns out to be heir to the massive estate of his biological grandfather. Struggling to learn Portuguese and make his way in dominant society, the blue-eyed "Indian" is torn between gratitude to his indigenous community and affection for his newfound family members. Caught between an Indian past and a civilized present, he accomplishes what nonindigenous intellectuals have fantasized about for over a century: the feat of being white and Indian at the very same time.

81. "Índio quer respeito," 11.

82. The complete film is available at www.videonasaldeias.org.br or http://www.youtube.com/watch?v=1h4arulGnFM (accessed 7 June 2012).

83. Das et al., *Remaking a World*, 5.

84. I refer, of course, to the famous testimonial gesture of Rigoberta Menchú Tum and the voluminous debate spawned by her testimony and its critics in the Latin American(ist) academy. See my introduction and chapter 1.

85. Das et al., *Remaking a World*, 5.

CHAPTER 5

1. Mead, *People and Places*, 88.
2. Tuhiwai Smith, *Decolonizing Methodologies*, 11.
3. Minh-Ha, *Woman, Native, Other*, 59.
4. For an introduction to related debates in the field of Latin American studies, see, for example, Beverley, "What Happens When the Subaltern Speaks?" and *Subalternity*; Patai, "Whose Truth?"; Moreiras, *Exhaustion of Difference* and "Freedom from Transculturation"; Sommer, "Rigoberta's Secrets"; and Stoll, *Rigoberta Menchú*.
5. See NAFPS website.
6. See Luttrell, "'Good Enough' Methods"; and Scheper-Hughes, *Death without Weeping*, 23–28.
7. Refusing to turn over the precious secret of the "red men" to his academic advisors, the protagonist of Borges's "El etnógrafo" repudiates Western scientific knowledge as useless and renounces anthropological research altogether. He opts instead to marry, then divorce, and ends up working as a librarian at Yale. On this story, see Avelar, *Letter of Violence*, 51–63.
8. The community is named for Alfredo Maria Adriano d'Escragnolle Taunay (the viscount of Taunay), whose work and writing I examine in chapter 2.
9. Alcida Ramos goes so far as to divide the country's indigenist and indigenous history into BC and AC—before and after the constitution. See Ramos, "Brasil no século XXI"; and my chapter 1.
10. The first was Xavante Mário Juruna, who in 1982 was elected to the same office from the state of Rio de Janeiro (see my introduction). In the 2010 elections, sixteen indigenous candidates (all men) ran for state and federal office in Acre, Amazonas, Bahia, Mato Grosso, Mato Grosso do Sul, Roraima, São Paulo, and Tocantins, as well as for district office in the Federal District of Brasília. None was successful.
11. I discuss the work of SPI founder Cândido Mariano da Silva Rondon in chapters 3 and 4, and nineteenth-century antecedents to the SPI in chapter 2. On Rondonian indigenism, see also Souza Lima, *Um grande cerco*; Garfield, *Indigenous Struggle*; Hemming, *Die If You Must*; and M. Gomes, *O índio na história* and *Indians*.
12. Nationally visible leaders of the contemporary movement include (in alphabetical order by first name) Ailton Krenak, Arão da Providência Guajajara, Azelene Kaingang, Daniel Munduruku, Eliane Potiguara, Ely Macuxi, Florêncio Almeida Vaz Filho, Graça Graúna, Juvenal Payayá, Lúcia Fernanda Kaingang, Lúcio Flores, Lúcio Xavante, Mário Xavante, Megaron Txucarramãe, Olívio Jekupé, Paulo Baltazar, Raoni Metuktire, Sônia Bone Guajajara, and Ysani Kalapalo (among many others).
13. For different perspectives on this notion from Brazil, the Americas, and the Pacific, see Barnhardt and Kawagly, "Indigenous Knowledge Systems"; V. Deloria, "Philosophy"; Menchú, *Rigoberta*; Munduruku, *Coisas de índio*; Potiguara, *Metade cara*; Tuhiwai Smith, *Decolonizing Methodologies*; and D. Turner, "Oral Traditions." Intellectuals in Latin and Latino/a America, indigenous and otherwise, have long aimed to describe and theorize from "within" the epistemological and political positions of those for whom traditional forms of knowledge and dominant (or Western) knowledge overlap. Classic examples include Anzaldúa, *Borderlands*; Arguedas, *El zorro, Los ríos*

profundos, and "Yo no soy un aculturado"; Kusch, *Indigenous and Popular Thinking*; Mignolo, *Local Histories*; and D. Ribeiro, *Maíra*.

14. Provedello, "Marcos Terena."

15. Terena and Feijó, *O índio aviador*, 5–11, 51–69; Terena, "Vôo do índio."

16. Terena, "Vôo de índio." On the Indian Statute, see my introduction and chapter 1.

17. In addition to founding the UNI and the *Voz indígena* radio program (the first indigenous radio program in Brazil), Terena helped articulate indigenous rights in the 1988 Brazilian Constitution and coordinated the World Conference of Indigenous People on Territory, Environment, and Development during the 1992 Rio Earth Summit. He was a spokesperson for the U.N. Working Group on Indigenous Peoples and participated in drafting the U.N. Declaration on the Rights of Indigenous Peoples. In June 2012, he led indigenous participation in the U.N. Conference on Sustainable Development (Rio+20), and he continues to serve as a consultant to the United Nations on international indigenous issues.

18. Terena, "Vôo do índio."

19. See Agamben, *Homo Sacer*, 18, and *State of Exception*, 2–31.

20. See my chapter 4.

21. Chapter 8 of the Constitution, "Dos índios," is dedicated to indigenous rights and related matters. See my introduction and chapter 1.

22. Thus historian John French's apt metaphor for this discrepancy with regard to workers' rights: "Drowning in Laws, but Starving (for Justice?)." Souza Lima and Hemming point to a similar paradox regarding the treatment of indigenous peoples under the framework of state protection. See Souza Lima, *Um grande cerco*; and Hemming, *Die If You Must*.

23. The November 2011 murder of Guarani-Kaiowá leader Nísio Gomes over a land dispute in Mato Grosso do Sul is one recent example.

24. U.N. Human Rights Council, "Report by the Special Rapporteur," 31–36.

25. The name, stolen from the Kayapó people, who have opposed the project for decades, was changed after the 1989 Encontro dos Povos Indígenas do Xingu, which led to the cancelation of international financing and forced the regime to table its initiative. See Fearnside, "Dams in the Amazon"; Santos, Andrade, and Wright, *Hydroelectric Dams*; and Devine Guzmán, "Whence Amazonian Studies."

26. On the environmental and social effects of the project and those of other hydroelectric dam projects in the region, see Kozloff, *No Rain*, 148–52.

27. Relatively recent initiatives like Pontos de Cultura, a Ministry of Culture program that has supported local cultural production since 2004, may provide a counterpoint (or a hiatus) to the state's central role in the long-term destruction and disappearance of indigenous peoples, cultures, and languages. Considering the state's historic failure to protect indigenous lands (a failure that culminates in Belo Monte), and the ongoing dismantlement and privatization of the indigenist bureaucracy, however, this support is for indigenous peoples a material and political palliative.

28. See Cerqueira, "A luta."

29. Nicaragua during the 1980s provides one well-known case (see Dennis, "Miskito-Sandinista Conflict"), but other examples abound across the region. On Bolivia, see Mignolo, "Communal and Decolonial." For a recent instance in Peru, consider the

abysmal record of Alan García's 2006–11 APRA administration with Native Amazonian communities (Hearn, "Bagua Movement"). On the "Indian policies" of his first presidency (1985–90), see Devine Guzmán, "Rimanakuy."

30. See the government's web portal at http://www.brasil.gov.br/pac.

31. Tuhiwai Smith, *Decolonizing Methodologies*, 30.

32. Cerqueira, "A luta."

33. On the double bind, see the conclusion to Shaw, *Indigeneity and Political Theory*; D. Turner, "Oral Traditions"; and V. Deloria, "Philosophy and the Tribal Peoples."

34. D. Turner, "Oral Traditions," 231–32.

35. Mignolo, "When Speaking Was Not Good Enough."

36. See Rama, *La ciudad letrada*; and Chasteen, introduction to *Lettered City*, xiv.

37. Fanon, *Black Skin*, 112. See also S. Hall, "Ethnicity," 22.

38. Alfred, *Heeding the Voices*, 1.

39. Agamben, *Homo Sacer*, 187.

40. On "sense of presence," see Vizenor, *Survivance*; and my introduction.

41. Reynaga Burgoa, *Ideología y raza*, 5.

42. "I wanted to build a bridge between Marxism and the Indian multitudes. Colonial fidelity to European dogma impeded me from doing so. It also showed me that the Indian and Marxism were not divorced, as I had believed, but that they were never together. . . . My effort to dislodge the hate of the Indian from the revolution was censored as a dangerous deviation from the truth coined over a century ago by two Germans who knew nothing about the Andes." Reynaga Burgoa, *Tawantinsuyu*, 334–36.

43. Reynaga Burgoa, *Ideología y raza*, 71–78, and *Reconstruyamos*, 33–43.

44. Tuhiwai Smith, *Decolonizing Methodologies*, 108.

45. Lane, *Fourth Way*, 8, 38.

46. Indigenous peoples and nations throughout the Americas expressed their solidarity with Mapuche hunger strikers who in mid-2010 protested for land rights and respectful dialogue with the Chilean government. During the same period, members of the Lakota Nation in North America and self-identified Mapuches, Quechuas, Aymaras, and Mayas from South and Central America visited Brasília to show support for the Acampamento Revolucionário Indígena, whose participants demonstrated for more than six months against the privatization of state services to indigenous communities and against the nonindigenous leadership of FUNAI (see "Acampamento"). Interindigenous collaboration to link Native social movements and literary and cultural production has also produced scholarly initiatives among Aymara, Kichwa, Mapuche, Maya, Quechua, and nonindigenous scholars from Bolivia, Brazil, Chile, Colombia, Ecuador, Mexico, Peru, and the United States (Emilio del Valle Escalante and Luis Cárcamo-Huechante, personal communication). Each collaboration builds on networks established by indigenous and nonindigenous educators working throughout the region in bilingual intercultural education (EBI) since the early 1970s. This initiative was formalized through the Latin American Congress on Bilingual Intercultural Education, which began in 1995 and was held for the ninth time in 2010 with participation of scholars from across the Americas, including Brazil and the United States (see "América Latina").

47. The meanings of sovereignty in the European tradition have of course changed over time, ranging from the power to represent God during the late Middle Ages, to the birth of the modern state system after the 1648 Peace of Westphalia, to the eighteenth- and nineteenth-century will to self-governance and self-determination of peoples ruled through representative democracy and under constitutional law. With regard to the treatment of Native peoples, however, leaders of nation-states have used the concept mostly as a tool of neocolonization and neocolonialism. Within indigenous political discourses, in contrast, sovereignty takes on a different set of meanings to invoke tools and strategies for territorial demarcation and a host of social, political, cultural, and economic rights. Alfred, for instance, refers to the reformulation of sovereignty among Mohawks as "a flexible sharing of resources and responsibilities in the act of maintaining the distinctiveness of each community" (*Heeding the Voices*, 102). For other contemporary Native views on sovereignty, see, for example, Barker, *Sovereignty Matters*; Tuhiwai Smith, *Decolonizing Methodologies*, 19–34; Pataxó et al., "Manifesto"; and D. Turner, *This Is Not a Peace Pipe*, 57–70.

48. On the theoretical relationship between dominant (nonindigenous) concepts of sovereignty and indigeneity beginning in the mid-seventeenth century, see Shaw, *Indigeneity and Political Theory*.

49. In 1515, Ferdinand of Spain used the papal bull as the basis of the *Requerimiento*, which claimed the Church was "Ruler of the Whole World" and ordered "idolatrous Indians" to acknowledge its precepts or face the consequences: "We shall take you and your wives and children and shall make slaves of them . . . and we shall take away your goods, and shall do all the harm and damage that we can, as [we do] to vassals who do not obey" (quoted in Anaya, *Indigenous Peoples*, 228, n. 20).

50. See Correia de Oliveira Andrade, *Tordesilhas*; and Graça Moura, *Tordesilhas*.

51. Piecemeal apologies have been offered in recent years, including John Paul II's plea for the forgiveness of sins committed against Native (and other) peoples during the 2000 "purification of memory" initiative. See Amstutz, *Healing of Nations*, 74.

52. See Anaya, *Indigenous Peoples*, 9–38; and Newcomb, *Pagans*, for an elaboration of these arguments.

53. Quoted in Anaya, *Indigenous Peoples*, 14, 15.

54. Ibid., 15.

55. See Max Weber's classic essay, "Politics as a Vocation."

56. Ibid., 123.

57. Deleuze and Guattari, *Thousand Plateaus*, 448. See also Shaw, *Indigeneity and Political Theory*, 167–68.

58. Deleuze and Guattari, *Thousand Plateaus*, 430.

59. On "productions of sovereignty," see Shaw, *Indigeneity and Political Theory*, 168–69.

60. See Souza Lima, *Um grande cerco*.

61. Shaw, *Indigeneity and Political Theory*, 212.

62. Shaw offers this disclaimer: "I do not wish to speak on behalf of Indigenous peoples, or in the interests of extending (our) justice to them, both of which . . . are essentially demeaning and disempowering. . . . Nor am I interested in 'them'—their

worlds, cosmologies, modes of social and political interaction, and so on. Although such an interest has an important place, . . . that place is not here. I am interested in 'us': in how our modes of understanding, practices of knowing and acting, structures of social and political organization, establish and reflect political possibilities, in how these spaces are always both enabling and constraining for Indigenous peoples . . . and in how they might be critically reformulated" (ibid., 6). Shaw's use of "us" and "them" in this passage removes self-identifying indigenous peoples from her projected audience, sidestepping both the social and historical construction of indigeneity and the fragile contingency of its meanings across time and space. In keeping with the dominant indigenist discourses of the nineteenth and most of the twentieth century, the easy divide between "us" and "them" also overlooks the millions of individuals and communities who occupy the ontological and epistemological frontiers between indigenous and nonindigenous worlds.

63. Ibid., 212.

64. Although Shaw's declaration of "noninterest" may reflect practical concerns regarding the scope of her book and its implied readership, it seems at cross-purposes with her claim that indigenous politics is important to all politics, and in particular, to her efforts to "rethink indigeneity." In her final chapter, she considers English-speaking and writing indigenous academics but overlooks (or chooses to omit) the possibility that their theories and politics might in fact be connected to their "worlds, cosmologies, [and] modes of social and political interaction." Her observation that "we must be willing not merely to adapt existing systems, but to participate in rethinking the ontological and epistemological grounding of them" (*Indigeneity and Political Theory*, 202) is confounding if "we" indeed have no interest in "them." How then, one wonders, to begin to rethink this grounding without returning Native peoples to the status of "our" perpetually silenced and colonized objects of study?

65. See Tuhiwai Smith, *Decolonizing Methodologies*.

66. Beverley, "What Happens When the Subaltern Speaks?," 81–82.

67. Political commentators including President Lula made this argument in 2010 after Hollywood actress Sigourney Weaver and Canadian director James Cameron of *Avatar* fame visited Xingu to support indigenous and other opposition to Belo Monte. For diverse opinions regarding their visit, see Baretto Motta, "James Cameron"; Lula da Silva, Opening Address; M. Leitão, "Avatar"; and Salm, "Avatar II."

68. See the writings of Lyrio Arlindo da Valle in my chapter 3.

69. The protest took place in front of the Ministry of Justice during the first half of 2010. See Devine Guzmán, "Writing Indigenous Activism" and "Subalternidade e soberania."

70. This is not, of course, meant as a generalization, since many Native peoples indeed do self-identify as U.S. or Canadian citizens despite the fact that they or their ancestors have been treated like foreigners or immigrants by their respective governments. See, for instance, Daynes, "George Washington," 21; and D. Weber, *Foreigners in Their Native Land*.

71. This understanding of sovereignty constitutes what the executive director of the National Congress of American Indians, Jacqueline Johnson, calls "the nearest and dearest, No. 1 issue in Indian Country." See Kamb, "Bush's Comment." Some Mohawks

living in communities that straddle the U.S.-Canadian border, for instance, repudiate identification as U.S. or Canadian citizens. Until the end of the twentieth century, they could travel between the two countries under the 1794 Jay Treaty, to which the United States is signatory. After 9/11, however, this freedom became circumscribed to the point that in summer 2010, an Akwesasne Mohawk hockey team backed out of a world championship tournament because the British government refused to accept Akwesasne passports. Insistence on Western notions of sovereignty vis-à-vis nonindigenous governments and societies does not mean, of course, that sovereignty within or among Native communities is necessarily conceived in the same way. See Barker, "For Whom Sovereignty Matters"; and Alfred, "Sovereignty."

72. Including, most notably, ILO Convention 169 of 1989 and the U.N. Declaration on the Rights of Indigenous Peoples of 2007.

73. This was the slogan of the Lula da Silva administration.

74. I refer to Deleuze and Guattari's explanation in *Thousand Plateaus*: "It is the flow of naked labor that makes the people, just as it is the flow of Capital that makes the land and its industrial base. In short, the nation is the very operation of a collective subjectification, to which the modern State corresponds as a process of subjection. It is in the form of the nation-state, with all its possible variations, that the State becomes the model of realization for the capitalist axiomatic" (504).

75. See Bhabha, *Location of Culture*, 49–50; EZLN, *Documentos*, 263, 380; and Yúdice, *Expediency of Culture*, 96–108.

76. Alfred, "Sovereignty," 33.

77. Article 46 reads: "Nothing in this Declaration may be interpreted as implying for any State, people, group or person any right to engage in any activity or to perform any act contrary to the Charter of the United Nations or construed as authorizing or encouraging any action which would dismember or impair, totally or in part, the territorial integrity or political unity of sovereign and independent States."

78. Including Articles 8, 10, 25–30, and 31.

79. Alfred, "Sovereignty," 46.

80. Shaw, *Indigeneity and Political Theory*, 168–69.

81. Alfred, "Sovereignty," 46.

82. Mariátegui, *Siete ensayos*, 20–31.

83. AIR, "Quem somos."

84. On "posttraditional Indians," see Warren, *Racial Revolutions*.

85. Munduruku, *Coisas de índio*, 86–89.

86. See also Flores, *Adoradores do sol*, 25–26.

87. Jekupé, *Irandu*, 30.

88. D. Turner, "Oral Traditions," 230.

89. On this question, see Menchú's *Rigoberta*, for example, or, more recently, Rappaport's *Intercultural Utopias*.

90. Flores, *Adoradores do sol*, 15.

91. Ibid., 15–16.

92. Ibid., 39.

93. Ibid., 40.

94. Alfred, "Sovereignty," 48.

95. Ibid., 49.

96. In Bolivia, thinkers like Fausto Reinaga and Felipe Quispe transformed this critique into an outright rejection of *mestizaje* that calls for the "Indianization" of non-Indians and dominant strains of political thought (including Marxism). See Quispe Huanca, *El indio en escena* and *Tupak Katari vive e vuelve—carajo*; Quispe Huanca and Confederación Sindical Única de Trabajadores Campesinos de Bolivia, "Pachakuti educativo"; and Reinaga, *La revolución india*. Several contemporary scholars refer to the indigenous adaptation of nonindigenous sociocultural practices and technologies in accordance with a critique of dominant sovereignty. See Canessa, "'Todos Somos Indígenas'" and "Who Is Indigenous?"; Sanjinés, *Mestizaje Upside Down*; and Schiwy, *Indianizing*.

97. For instance, the administration of Bolivian president Evo Morales created three indigenous universities in 2008: Universidad Tupac Katari (Aymara); Universidad Casimiro Huanca (Quechua), and Universidad Apiaguaiki Tupa (Guarani); (http://ves.minedu.gob.bo/ves/index.php?ID=unibol). The Universidad Intercultural de las Nacionalidades y Pueblos Indígenas "Amawtay Wasi" was founded in Ecuador in 2004 (http://www.amawtaywasi.edu.ec/). The Universidad Autónoma Indígena de México was founded in the early 1980s and formalized in 2001 (http://www.uaim.edu.mx/). The initiative to found the Universidad Indígena de Venezuela began in the 1970s and was realized in 2001 during the second term of President Hugo Chavez (http://www.causamerindia.com/uit/).

98. See Butler and Hinch, *Tourism*.

99. Potiguara, *Metade cara*, 24–26.

100. Ibid., 26–28.

101. Ibid., 127–28.

102. Ibid., 128–30 (original emphasis).

103. The practitioners and critics of this scholarship are too many to account for here comprehensively. Taiaiake Alfred, José María Arguedas, Dipesh Chakrabarty, Frantz Fanon, Ranajit Guha, Paulo Freire, Rigoberta Menchú Tum, Walter Mignolo, Aníbal Quijano, Felipe Quispe, Darcy Ribeiro, Edward Said, Linda Tuhiwai Smith, Gayatri Spivak, Dale Turner, Gerald Vizenor, and Catherine Walsh are, alongside the indigenous intellectuals, writers, and activists whose work I consider in these pages, some of the scholars who have most influenced my thinking on colonialism and coloniality.

104. I use this term to refer to the flip side of what Dipesh Chakrabarty famously called the "asymmetric ignorance" of colonizers vis-à-vis their colonial subjects. See Chakrabarty, *Provincializing Europe*, 28.

105. Du Bois, *Souls of Black Folk*, 9.

106. On the formation and work of the SPI, see my chapters 3 and 4.

107. The post was named for the French soldier Guido Thomaz Marlière, namesake of the town of Marliéria (Minas Gerais), who landed in Brazil in 1807. Imprisoned that year as a suspected envoy of Napoléon Bonaparte, he was found not guilty and released. Appointed *diretor geral dos índios* in São João Batista do Presídio and São Manoel do Pomba in 1814, he made (per his biographers) a long career out of "pacifying and settling ferocious Indians." See Oilam, *Marlière o civilizador*.

108. See Forthmann, *Guido Marliére* [*sic*].

109. Lula da Silva, Opening Address (my emphasis).

110. "Café com o presidente" (my emphasis). For additional context on the president's statement, see "Lula defende."

111. *AHE Belo Monte* (my emphasis).

112. Melo, "Cartas a Dilma e Serra."

113. As I discuss in chapters 3 and 4, the motto of the SPI was "Die if necessary, but never kill [*Morrer se preciso for, matar nunca*]."

114. Rondon, "Exposição," 4.

115. Deleuze and Guattari, *Thousand Plateaus*, 360.

116. Rondon, "Exposição," 5.

117. Ibid.

118. "Discurso do Presidente Lula."

119. Melo, "Cartas a Dilma e Serra"; Cerqueira, "A luta"; Kayapó, Kayapó, and Juruna, "Nós, indígenas." The administration contends that indigenous peoples are represented by FUNAI, which has never been led by a Native person. In 2011, the government fired several employees (including Kayapó leader Megaron Txucurramãe) for their opposition to Belo Monte.

120. D. Ribeiro, *Os índios*, 503.

121. See Ramos, "Hyperreal Indian," and *Indigenism*, 153–71; and my introduction.

122. See Potiguara, *Metade cara*, 48–58; INBRAPI web page; Potiguara, *Literatura indígena* (web page); Professores de Pataxó, *Uma história*; and Troncarelli, Kaiabi, and Instituto Socioambiental, *Brasil e África*.

123. Potiguara, "A informação," 9.

124. Potiguara, *Metade cara*, 84.

125. American Indian College Fund, "Think Indian."

126. Flores, *Adoradores do sol*, 8.

127. D. Turner, "Oral Traditions," 237.

128. Ramos, *Indigenism*, 22.

129. See Potiguara, *Literatura indígena* (my italics).

130. Interview with the author, Aldeia Krukutu, 21 August 2011.

EPILOGUE

1. See Ramos, *Indigenism*; and my chapter 5.

2. On the Terena Voluntários da Pátria, see my chapter 2. On Lyrio Arlindo do Valle and SIVAM, see my chapter 3. On Diacuí Canualo Aiute and Pataxó protests of the Brazilian quincentennial, see my chapter 4. On Xuxa and the Xavante, see my introduction.

3. D. Turner, "Oral Traditions," 238.

4. Munduruku, "Visões de ontem," 17.

5. Jekupé, *Tekoa*, 27.

6. Bobbio, *Future of Democracy*, 23–43.

7. Munduruku, *Histórias de índio*, 34–35.

8. Nodelman, *Hidden Adult*, 206–208.

9. Interview with the author, Aldeia Krukutu, 21 August 2011. See also Jekupé, *Tekoa* and *Literatura*.

10. Munduruku, *Histórias de índio*, 9.

11. Information on published titles is available at the Editora Palavra de Índio website: http://www.danielmunduruku.com.br/editora.html.

12. INBRAPI, "Nosso símbolo: nosso pensar."

13. See "Carta de Bertioga" and the official Rio+20 website: http://www.uncsd2012.0rg/about.html.

14. On the circulation of ideas about Native peoples in nonindigenous classrooms and curricula, see A. Lopes da Silva and Grupioni, *A temática indígena*.

15. On such initiatives across Brazil, see Nincao, "Kóho Yoko Hovôvo"; "Primeiro Encontro Nacional de Educação Indígena"; Professores de Pataxó, *Uma história*; and Troncarelli, Kaiabi, and Instituto Socioambiental, *Brasil e África*.

16. As of late 2011, such programs are in place at the Universidade Federal de Roraima (UFRR); Universidade Federal de Minas Gerais (UFMG); Universidade Federal do Amazonas (UFAM); Universidade Federal do Tocantins (UFT); Universidade Federal de Campina Grande (UFCG); Universidade Federal da Bahia (UFBA); Universidade Estadual do Mato Grosso (UNEMAT); Universidade Estadual de Londrina (UEL); Universidade Estadual do Amazonas (UEA); Universidade Estadual da Bahia (UNEB); Universidade Estadual do Mato Grosso do Sul (UEMS); and Universidade Estadual do Oeste do Paraná (UNIOESTE). See Rede, "Conheça a REDE."

17. Recent initiatives also exist to offer classes in indigenous languages to nonindigenous students, teachers, and researchers (Paulo Baltazar, personal communication; "Base de Estudos Indígenas").

18. See "Indígenas querem representação."

19. Photographs of Terena wearing more traditional dress continued to appear on the website along with blog entries, visitors' notes, music, and a glossary of indigenous expressions.

20. Terena, "Vôo do índio."

21. And yet the problem of popular perception and media representation remains. The day following the 20 August 2011 manifestation against Belo Monte in São Paulo, the print version of the *Folha de São Paulo* included not a word about the protest. Instead, it highlighted a new Globo TV reality show called *Expedição Xingu*, in which eight (nonindigenous) university students would "leave the comforts of the city" and head to the forest, suffering various hardships of the 1950s and otherwise following in the footsteps of the Villas-Bôas brothers. Their adventure "even included participating in indigenous celebrations and fighting with them [*sic*]." See Castro Torres, "Jovens refazem expedição."

22. Lane, "Indigenous Guiding Principles."

23. Terena, "Uma candidatura indígena."

BIBLIOGRAPHY

NEWSPAPERS AND MAGAZINES

Agência Brasil
The Americas
Aquidauna News
Brazil Herald
El Cabichuí
Cacique Lambaré
Careta
Correio da Manhã
Correio da Noite
Correio do Povo
Correio Paulistano
O Cruzeiro
Cuadernos Mexicanos
O Dia
O Diário
Diário Carioca
Diário da Noite
Diário da Tarde (Manaus)
Diário da Tarde (Rio de
   Janeiro)
Diário de Exécutivo
Diário de Notícias
Diário do Congresso
   Nacional
Diário do Povo
Diário Oficial
Diário Trabalhista
A Época
O Estado
Estado de Minas
O Estado de São Paulo

Folha Carioca
Folha da Manhã (Recife)
Folha da Manhã (São
   Paulo)
Folha da Noite
Folha da Tarde
Folha de Minas
Folha de São Paulo
Folha do Meio Ambiente
Fon Fon
A Gazeta
Gazeta de Notícias
Gazeta do Povo
O Globo
Harper's
A Hora
O Imparcial
O Jornal
Jornal de Brasília
Jornal do Brasil
Jornal do Commercio
Life
Luta Democrática
A Manhã
Marcha
Monthly Bulletin of
   the Bureau of the
   American Republics
Mundial
O Mundo
The Nation

Negro History Bulletin
New York Daily News
New York Times
A Noite
A Noite Ilustrada
A Notícia
O Paiz
A Palavra
O Pasquim
O Popular
Pukara
O Radical
Revista Agronotícias
Revista Brasileira de
   Estudos Pedagógicos
Revista Brasileira de
   Música
Revista Bundas
Revista da Semana
Revista Época
Revista Illustrada
O Tempo
A Tribuna
Tribuna de Imprensa
Tribuna de Minas
Última Hora
A União
Veja
A Voz Trabalhista

Acampamento Revolucionário Indígena (AIR). http://
acampamentorevolucionarioindigena.blogspot.com (10 June 2012).

———. "Carta aberta ao povo brasileiro." 7 June 2010. http://
acampamentorevolucionarioindigena.blogspot.com/2010/06/carta-aberta-ao
-povo-brasileiro.html (10 June 2012).

———. "Quem somos." http://acampamentorevolucionarioindigena.blogspot.
com/2010/03/quem-somos.html (10 June 2012).

Achugar, Hugo. "Historias paralelas/Historias ejemplares." *Revista de crítica literaria
latinoamericana* 36 (1992): 49–71.

"Adjudication des travaux d'amélioration du port de Manaos." *Monthly Bulletin of the
Bureau of the American Republics* (January–June 1900): 373.

ADRIANO. Comment on "Exército deve 'pedir licença' para atuar em reserva, diz
líder." *Terra*, 29 April 2009.

Agamben, Giorgio. *Coming Community*. Translated by Michael Hardt. Minneapolis:
University of Minnesota Press, 1993.

———. *Homo Sacer*. Stanford, Calif.: Stanford University Press, 1998.

———. *State of Exception*. Chicago: University of Chicago Press, 2005.

Agassiz, Louis, and Elizabeth Cabot Cary Agassiz. *A Journey in Brazil*. Boston: Fields,
Osgood, 1871.

Agostini, Angelo. *Revista Illustrada*, 31 July 1884.

———. *A vida fluminense*, 11 June 1870.

AHE Belo Monte. Programa de Aceleração do Crescimento–PAC; Eletronorte;
Eletrobrás; Ministério de Minas e Energia. 2009. Video. 10 June 2012.

Alcoff, Linda Martín. "Mignolo's Epistemology of Coloniality." *New Centennial Review*
7, no. 3 (2007): 79–101.

———. "Who's Afraid of Identity Politics?" In *Reclaiming Identity: Realist Theory
and the Predicament of Postmodernism*, edited by Paula M. L. Moya and Michael
R. Hames-Garcia, 312–44. Berkeley: University of California Press, 2000.

Alencar, José M. de. *Como e porque sou romancista*. Rio de Janeiro: G. Leuzinger &
Filhos, 1883.

———. *O guarany*. São Paulo: Ateliê, 1999.

———. *Iracema*. 2nd ed. São Paulo: Cultrix, 1969.

Alfred, Gerald R. (Taiaiake). *Heeding the Voices of Our Ancestors*. Oxford: Oxford
University Press, 1995.

———. *Peace, Power, Righteousness*. Oxford: Oxford University Press, 2009.

———. "Sovereignty." In *Sovereignty Matters*, edited by Joanne Barker, 33–50.
Lincoln: University of Nebraska Press, 2005.

Algot, Bergli, ed. *Educación intercultural*. Yarinacocha, Peru: Instituto Lingüístico de
Verano, 1995.

Aliedo. "Cartoon." *Jornal do Brasil*, 22 April 2000, 8.

Almanaque Papa-Capim & Turma da Mônica, no. 5 (12 April 2012). Rio de Janeiro:
Maurício de Sousa Editora/Panini Comics.

Almeida Vaz, Florêncio. "Discurso de resistência indígena." In *Sol do pensamento*, edited by Eliane Potiguara, 42–44. São Paulo: Inbrapi/Grumin, 2005.

Althusser, Louis. *Ideología y el estado*. Mexico City: Siglo XXI, 1978.

———. "Ideology and Ideological State Apparatuses." In *Lenin and Philosophy and Other Essays*, translated by Ben Brewster, 127–86. New York: Monthly Review Press, 1971.

Alto, Herve do. "I Am the Bad Conscience of Evo Morales: Interview with Felipe Quispe." *International Viewpoint*, December 2005. http://www.international viewpoint.org/spip.php?article937 (10 June 2012).

Alvez Filho, Manuel. "Libretos em libro." *Jornal da UNICAMP* 1, no. 7 (2007): 12.

Amaral de Toral. "A participação dos negros escravos na guerra do Paraguai." *Estudos Avançados* 9, no. 24 (1995): 287–96.

"América Latina: Convocan IX Congreso de Educación Intercultural Bilingüe." *Servindi*, 27 May 2012. http://servindi.org/actualidad/26252 (11 June 2012).

American Indian College Fund. "Think Indian." 2008. http://www.collegefund.org /content/think_indian (12 June 2011).

"Os americanos tinham razão!! [*sic*]." Comment on "Exército deve 'pedir licença' para atuar em reserva, diz líder." *Terra*, 29 April 2009.

Amstutz, Mark R. *The Healing of Nations: The Promise and Limits of Political Forgiveness*. Lanham, Md.: Rowman and Littlefield, 2005.

Anaya, S. James. *Indigenous Peoples in International Law*. Oxford: Oxford University Press, 2004.

Anderson, Benedict. *Imagined Communities: Reflections on the Origen and Spread of Nationalism*. London: Verso, 1991.

Andrade, Mario de. *Ensaio sobre a música brasileira*. 3rd ed. São Paulo: Vila Rica; Brasília: INL, 1972.

———. "Fosca." *Revista Brasileira de Música* 3, no. 2 (1936): 251–63.

———. *Macunaíma: O herói sem nenhum caráter*. Edited by Têle Porto Ancona Lopez and Tatiana Longo Figueiredo. Rio de Janeiro: Agir, 2008.

Andrade, Oswald de. "Manifesto antropófago." *Revista de Antropofagia* 1, no. 1 (1928): 3, 7.

Andrews, Jean. "Carlos Gomes' *II Guarany*: The Frontiers of Miscegenation in Nineteenth-Century Grand Opera." *Portuguese Studies* 16 (2000): 26–42.

"Ante-projeto de lei de 1952." In *Parque Indígena do Xingu*, by Maria Lucia Pires Menezes, 333–45. Campinas: UNICAMP, 2000.

Anzaldúa, Gloria. *Borderlands/La Frontera*. 3rd ed. San Francisco: Aunt Lute, 2007.

Apaza, Juan. "Seguir el sendero de Tupak Katari: La verdadera tarea de los Ponchos Rojos." *Pukara* 26 (2008). http://www.periodicopukara.com/pasados/pukara-26 -articulo-del-mes.php (10 June 2012).

Aquézolo Castro, M., ed. *La polémica del indigenismo*. Lima: Mosca Azul, 1976.

Arguedas, José María. "No soy un aculturado." Discurso Inca Garcilaso de la Vega. Lima, October 1968. In *El zorro de arriba y el zorro de abajo*, 13–14. Lima: Horizonte, 1988 [1970].

————. *Los ríos profundos*. Madrid: Cátedra, 1995 [1958].

————. *El zorro de arriba y el zorro de abajo*. Lima: Horizonte, 1988 [1970].

Arias, Arturo. *Taking Their Word: Literature and the Signs of Central America*. Minneapolis: University of Minnesota Press, 2007.

————, ed. *The Rigoberta Menchú Controversy*. Minneapolis: University of Minnesota Press, 2001.

"Às 3 horas da tarde, o casamento de Diacuí." *Gazeta de Notícias*, 29 November 1952, 1, 7.

Aufderheide, Patricia. "True Confessions: The Inquisition and Social Attitudes in Brazil at the Turn of the XVII Century." *Luso-Brazilian Review* 10, no. 2 (1973): 208–40.

Augusto, Sérgio. *As penas do ofício: Ensaios de jornalismo cultural*. Rio de Janeiro: Agir, 2006.

Avelar, Idelber. *The Letter of Violence: Essays on Narrative, Ethics, and Politics*. New York: Palgrave, 2004.

Azevedo, Célia Maria Marinho. *Onda negra, medo branco: O negro no imaginário das elites—século XIX*. Rio de Janeiro: Paz e Terra, 1987.

Back, Sylvio. *Índio do Brasil*. VHS. Rio de Janeiro: Sagres Vídeo, 1995.

Balibar, Etienne, and Immanuel Wallerstein. *Race, Nation, Class: Ambiguous Identities*, translated by Chris Turner. London: Verso, 1991.

Bandeira Mello, Manoel Silvino. "Relatório ao Illmo. Sr. Tenente-Coronel Alencarliense Ferandes da Costa." 16 January 1930. SEDOC/MI. Microfilm 380.

Barbosa Rodrigues, João. *Rio Jauapery: A pacificação dos Crichanás*. Rio de Janeiro: Imprensa Nacional, 1885.

Barceló, Raquel, María Ana Portal, and Martha Judith Sánchez, eds. *Diversidad étnica y conflicto en América Latina*. Mexico City: Universidad Nacional Autónoma, 1995.

Baretto Motta, Sérgio. "James Cameron almeja exterminar futuro do Brasil." *Monitor Mercantil Digital*, 29 March 2010.

Barker, Joanne. "For Whom Sovereignty Matters." In *Sovereignty Matters*, edited by Joanne Barker, 1–31. Lincoln: University of Nebraska Press, 2005.

Barker, Joanne, ed. *Sovereignty Matters*. Lincoln: University of Nebraska Press, 2005.

Barman, Roderick J. *Citizen Emperor: Pedro II and the Making of Brazil, 1825–1891*. Stanford, Calif.: Stanford University Press, 1999.

Barnhardt, Ray, and Angayuqaq Oscar Kawagley. "Indigenous Knowledge Systems and Alaska Native Ways of Knowing." *Anthropology and Education Quarterly* 36, no. 1 (2005): 8–23.

Barreto, Luiz Paulo. Letter to Márcio Meira, 15 June 2010. Memorandum no. 1375. Ministério da Justiça. Gabinete do Ministro—Divisão de Documentação. http://www.monitormercantil.com.br/mostranoticia.php?id=76825 (10 June 2012).

Barth, Frederick. *Ethnic Groups and Boundaries*. London: Allen and Unwin, 1963.

"Base de Estudos Indígenas será inaugurada hoje na UFMS." *Aquidauna News*, 11 August 2010. http://www.aquidauananews.com/0,0,00,2615-161840-BASE+DE

+ESTUDOS+INDIGENAS+SERA+INAUGURADA+HOJE+NA+UFMS.htm (10 June 2012).

Basso, Ellen. *The Kalapalo Indians of Central Brazil*. New York: Holt, Rinehart and Winston, 1973.

———. *A Musical View of the Universe: Kalapalo Myth and Ritual Performaces*. Philadelphia: University of Pennsylvania Press, 1985.

Bastos de Ávila, João. *Questões de antropologia brasileira*. Rio de Janeiro: Civilização Brasileira, 1935.

Baudrillard, Jean. *Simulacros e simulação*. Lisbon: Relógio d'Água, 1991.

BBC Brasil. "Especial: Raízes afro-brasileiras." 31 August 2007. http://www.bbc.co .uk/portuguese/noticias/cluster/2007/05/070427_raizesafrobrasileiras.shtml (10 June 2012).

Becker, Marc. *Pachakutik: Indigenous Movements and Electoral Politics in Ecuador*. Lanham, Md.: Rowman & Littlefield, 2011.

Beebee, Thomas O. *Nation and Region in Modern American and European Fiction*. West Lafayette, Ind.: Purdue University Press, 2008.

Béhague, Gerard. "Indianism in Latin American Art-Music Composition of the 1920s to 1940s." *Latin American Music Review* 27, no. 1 (2006): 28–37.

Benjamin, Walter. "The Work of Art in the Age of Mechanical Reproduction." In *Illuminations*, edited by Hannah Arendt, 217–51. New York: Schocken, 2007.

Bergamaschi, G. "Al Brasile." *Jornal do Commercio*, 29 April 1870, 1.

Berry, Brewton. "The Myth of the Vanishing Indian." *Phylon* 21, no. 1 (1960): 51–57.

Berthold, Victor M. *History of the Telephone and Telegraph in Brazil*. New York: n.p., 1922.

Beverley, John. "The Dilemma of Subaltern Studies at Duke." *Nepantla* 1, no. 1 (2000): 33–44.

———. "The Real Thing." In *The Real Thing*, edited by Georg M. Gugelberger, 266–86. Durham, N.C.: Duke University Press, 1996.

———. *Subalternity and Representation: Arguments in Cultural Theory*. Durham, N.C.: Duke University Press, 1999.

———. "What Happens When the Subaltern Speaks? Rigoberta Menchú, Multiculturalism, and the 'Presumption of Equal Worth.'" In *The Rigoberta Menchú Controversy*, edited by Arturo Arias, 219–36. Minneapolis: University of Minnesota Press, 2001.

Bhabha, Homi. *The Location of Culture*. New York: Routledge, 1994.

———, ed. *Nation and Narration*. New York: Routledge, 1990.

Bicudo, Fernando. "Viva Carlos Gomes, Viva o Brasil!!!" In *O escravo. Drama lírico em quatro atos*, by Alfredo d'Escragnolle and Rodolfo Paravicini, 2–4. Maranhão: Governo do Estado do Maranhão, 1988.

Bittencourt, Circe Maria Fernandes, and Maria Elisa Ladeira. *A história do povo terena*. Brasília: Ministério de Educação, 2000.

Bobbio, Norberto. *The Future of Democracy*. Edited by Richard Bellamy and translated by Roger Griffen. Minneapolis: University of Minnesota Press, 1987.

Boehrer, George. *Da monarquia à República*. Rio de Janeiro: Ministério de Educação e Cultura, 1954.

Bonalume Neto, Ricardo. "Depois de 15 anos, Sivam deve ser concluído." *Folha de São Paulo*, 12 June 2005. http://www1.folha.uol.com.br/folha/brasil/ult96u69614 .shtml (10 June 2012).

Borges, Jorge Luis. "El etnógrafo." In *Prosa completa*, 2:355–57. Barcelona: Bruguera, 1980.

Bourdieu, Pierre. *Language and Symbolic Power*. Edited by John B. Thompson and translated by Gino Raymond and Matthew Adamson. Cambridge: Harvard University Press, 1991.

Boxer, Charles Ralph. *The Golden Age of Brazil: Growing Pains of a Colonial Society, 1695–1750*. New York: St. Martin's, 1995.

Brandão, Antônio de Padua. *Carta de Pêro Vaz de Caminha pra crianças*. São Paulo: Stúdio Nobel, 1999.

Brasileiro Trabalhador. Comment on "Exército deve 'pedir licença' para atuar em reserva, diz líder." *Terra*, 29 April 2009.

Brice, William, and Silvia de M. Figueroa. "Charles Hartt, Louis Agassiz, and the Controversy over Pleistocene Glaciation in Brazil." *History of Science* 39 (2001): 161–84.

Brígido, Carolina, and Jailton de Carvalho. "STF decide pela demarcação em terra contínua." *BSB: Estação da Notícia*, 19 March 2009. http://www.estacaodanoticia .com/index/comentarios/id/13772 (10 June 2012).

Brooke, James. "Opera Is Ready for a Comeback in the Amazon." *New York Times*, 16 January 1990, C16.

Brookshaw, David. *Race and Color in Brazilian Literature*. Metuchen, N.J.: Scarecrow, 1986.

Brotherston, Gordon. *Book of the Fourth World: Reading the Native Americas through Their Literature*. Cambridge: Cambridge University Press, 1992.

———. "Debate: Regarding the Evidence in *Me llamo Rigoberta Menchú*." *Journal of Latin American Studies* 6, no. 1 (1997): 93–102.

Brown, James, and Patricia Sant, eds. *Indigeneity: Construction and Re/Presentation*. Commack, N.Y.: Nova Science, 1999.

Brubaker, Rogers. *Ethnicity without Groups*. Cambridge: Harvard University Press, 2006.

Bueno, Raul. "Sujeto heterogéneo y migrante." In *Antonio Cornejo Polar y los estudios culturales*, edited by Friedhelm Schmidt-Welle, 173–94. Pittsburgh: Serie Críticas, 2002.

Bueno, Silveira. *Vocabulário tupi-guarani-português*. São Paulo: Brasilivros,1982.

Burton, Richard Francis. *Letters from the Battle Fields of Paraguay*. London: Tinsley Bros., 1870.

Butler, Judith. *Gender Trouble: Feminism and the Subversion of Identity*. New York, Routledge, 1990.

Butler, Richard, and Thomas Hinch. *Tourism and Indigenous Peoples: Issues and Implications*. Oxford: Butterworth Heinemann, 2007.

"Café com o presidente." *Empresa Brasil de Comunicação*. Brasília. 26 April 2010. http://historico.cafe.ebc.com.br/cafe/programas/o-custo-da-energia-gerada-por -uma-hidreletrica-e-a-mais-barata-afirma-lula (10 June 2012).

Callado, Antônio. "O parque decapitado." In *Nossos índios, nossos mortos*, edited by Edilson Martins, 9–11. Rio de Janeiro: Codecri, 1982.

———. *Quarup*. Rio de Janeiro: Civilização Brasileira, 1973.

Calmon, Pedro. *História de Dom Pedro II*. Rio de Janeiro: J. Olympico, 1975.

Calvo, Beatriz, and Laura Donnadieu Aguado. *Una educación ¿indígena, bilingüe y bicultural?* Mexico City: Centro de Investigaciones y Estudios Superiores en Antropología Social, 1992.

"Câmera aprova projeto sobre os direitos dos índios." *O Globo*, 6 April 1973, 6.

Caminha, Pero Vaz de. "Carta a D. Manuel." In *Livro do Centenário (1500–1900)*, edited by J. de Barros Raja Gabaglia, 1:63–73. Rio de Janeiro: Imprensa Nacional, 1900.

Campos, Haroldo de. "Da razão antropofágica: Diálogo e diferença na cultura brasileira." *Boletín Bibliográfico* 44 (1983): 107–21.

———. "Ierecê e Iracema: Do verismo etnográfico à magia verbal." In *Ierecê a Guaná*, by Alfredo d'Escragnolle Taunay. Edited by Sérgio Luiz Medeiros, 145–72. São Paulo: Iluminuras, 2000.

———. "The Rule of Anthropophagy: Europe under the Sign of Devoration." *Latin American Literature Review* 14, no. 27 (1986): 42–60.

Cândido, Antônio. *Formação da literatura brasileira*. Belo Horizonte: Editorial Itatiaia, 1981.

Canessa, Andrew. "'Todos Somos Indígenas': Towards a New Language of National Political Identity." *Bulletin of Latin American Research* 25, no. 2 (2006): 241–63.

———. "Who Is Indigenous? Self-Identification, Indigeneity, and Claims to Justice in Contemporary Bolivia." *Urban Anthropology* 36, no. 3 (2007): 195–237.

———, ed. *Natives Making Nation: Gender, Indigeneity, and the State in the Andes*. Tuscon: University of Arizona Press, 2005.

Capacla, Marta Valleria, ed. *O debate sobre a educação indígena no Brasil, 1975–1995*. Brasília: Grupo de Educação Indígena/USP, 1995.

Cardoso, André. "Carlos Gomes e sua última obra lírica." In *Colombo: Poema vocal-sinfônico em quatro partes*, edited by Inácio de Nonno. Rio de Janeiro: Universidade Federal do Rio de Janeiro, 2004.

Carey-Webb, Allen, and Stephen Benz, eds. *Teaching and Testimony: Rigoberta Menchú the North American Classroom*. Albany: SUNY Press, 1996.

"Carlos Gomes." *Fon Fon*, 18 July 1936, 39–40.

Carlos Gomez, A. [*sic*]. *Il Guarany: Grand Opera in Four Acts*. San Francisco: Francis, Valentine, 1884.

Carneiro da Cunha, Manuela. *Os direitos dos índios*. São Paulo: Brasiliense, 1987.

———. *Legislação indigenista do Século XIX*. Vol. 11. São Paulo: EDUSP e Comissão Pró-Índio de São Paulo, 1993.

———. "Política indigenista no século XIX." In *História dos índios do Brasil*, edited by M. Carneiro da Cunha, 133–54. São Paulo: Companhia das Letras, 1992.

———, ed. *História dos índios do Brasil*. São Paulo: Companhia das Letras, 1992.

Carta ao diretor do SPI sobre o "Dia do Índio." 1948. SEDOC/MI. Microfilm 335.

"Carta de Bertioga." Open letter signed by 250 Native activists representing twenty-one peoples at the Fórum Social Indígena in Bertioga, São Paulo, 21 April 2012.

Carta Régia de 2 de Dezembro de 1808. *Colleção das leis do Brazil de 1808*. Rio de Janeiro: Imprensa Nacional, 1891. 171–74.

Carvalho, Ana, Ernesto I. Carvalho, and Vincent Carelli, eds. *Vídeo nas Aldeias, 25 anos: 1986–2011*. São Paulo: Vídeo nas Aldeias, 2011.

Casa de Cultura da Mulher Negra, 15 January 2001. http://www.casadeculturadamulhernegra.org.br/ (10 June 2012).

Casa Ricordi. *Ricordi & C.*, January 2011. http://www.ricordicompany.com/ (10 June 2012).

Castello, José Aderaldo, ed. *Polêmica sobre "A confederação dos tamoios."* São Paulo: Universidade de São Paulo, 1953.

Castro-Klarén, Sara. *Escritura, transgresión y sujeto en la literatura latinoamericana*. Mexico City: Premia, 1989.

———. "Posting Letters: Writing in the Andes and the Paradoxes of the Postcolonial Debate." In *Coloniality at Large*, edited by Mabel Moraña, Enrique Dussel, and Carlos Jáugregui, 130–57. Durham, N.C.: Duke University Press, 2008.

Castro Torres, Iuri de. "Jovens refazem expedição dos irmãos Villas Bôas." *Folha de São Paulo*, 21 August 2011, E3.

Caufield, Philip. "Lost Tribe in Brazilian Amazon Missing after Suspected Drug Traffikers Raid Jungle." *New York Daily News*, 9 August 2011. http://articles.nydailynews.com/2011-08-09/news/29887709_1_indian-tribe-indian-affairs-traffickers (10 June 2012).

Cavalcanti, Sandra. "Brasil nunca pertenceu aos índios." *Jornal do Brasil*, 21 April 2000, 9.

Celso, Afonso. *Porque me ufano do meu país*. Rio de Janeiro: Laemert, 1908.

"Centenary of Gomes: Brazil Observes Day as National Holiday in Composer's Honor." *New York Times*, 12 July 1936.

Cerqueira, Cleymenne. "A luta não é só contra Belo Monte." *Conselho Indigenista Missionário*, 10 August 2010. http://www.cimi.org.br/site/pt-br/?system=news&action=read&id=4864 (10 June 2012).

Chakrabarty, Dipesh. "Postcoloniality and the Artifice of History." *Representations* 37 (Winter 1992): 1–26.

———. *Provincializing Europe: Postcolonial Thought and Historical Difference*. Princeton, N.J.: Princeton University Press, 2000.

Chasteen, John C. *Americanos: Latin America's Struggle for Independence*. New York: Oxford University Press, 2008.

———. Introduction to *The Lettered City*, by Ángel Rama. Edited and translated by John C. Chasteen, vii–xiv. Durham, N.C.: Duke University Press, 1996.

Cheah, Pheng. "The Limits of Thinking in Decolonial Strategies." Townsend Center for the Humanities, University of California at Berkeley, November 2006. http://townsendcenter.berkeley.edu/article10.shtml (15 June 2012).Chiodi, Francisco, ed. *La educación indígena en América Latina*. Vols. 1–2. Quito: MEC-GTZ, 1990.

Ciema, Anselmo M. "O índio, esse esquecido." *Diário do Povo*, 5 December 1952.

"Civilização para os índios da Amazônia." *A Noite*, 12 June 1947.

Clavero, Bartolomé. *Geografía jurídica de América Latina: Pueblos indígenas entre constituciones mestizas*. Mexico City: Siglo XXI, 2008.

Clifton, J. *Being and Becoming Indian: Biographical Studies of North American Frontiers*. Chicago: Dorsey, 1989.

Coelho dos Santos, Sílvio. *Índios e brancos no sul do Brasil: A dramática experiência dos Xokleng*. Florianópolis: EDEME, 1973.

Cohen, Anthony Paul. *Self-Consciousness: An Alternative Anthropology of Identity*. London: Routledge, 1994.

Cojtí Cuxil, Demetrio. Interview with author, Guatemala City, 1 August 1998.

———. *Ri Maya' moloj pa iximulew/El movimiento maya en Guatemala*. Guatemala City: CHOLSAMAQ, 1997.

Colleção das decisões de governo do Império do Brasil de 1875. Vol. 38. Rio de Janeiro: Typographia Nacional, 1876.

Colleção das leis do Império do Brasil de 1871. Vol. 31. Rio de Janeiro: Typographia Nacional, 1871.

Colleção das leis do Império do Brasil de 1872. Rio de Janeiro: Typographia Nacional, 1872.

Colleção das leis do Império do Brasil de 1873. Vol. 32. Rio de Janeiro: Typographia Nacional, 1873.

Comissão para Coordenação do Projeto do Sistema de Vigilância da Amazônia. "Hino Nacional." 2006. http://www.sivam.gov.br/AMAZONIA/sivam12.htm (15 August 2008).

———. "Histórico." 2006. http://www.sivam.gov.br/PROJETO/hist1.htm (15 August 2008).

———. "Uma legião de Sivamzinhos." 2006. http://www.sivam.gov.br/AMAZONIA /sivam3.htm (15 August 2008).

———. "Revista." 2006. http://www.sivam.gov.br/AMAZONIA/revista1.htm (15 August 2008).

———. "Sivamzinho." 2006. http://www.sivam.gov.br/AMAZONIA/sivam1.htm (15 August 2008).

Conklin, Beth. "Body Paint, Feathers, and VCRs." *American Ethnologist* 24, no. 4 (1997): 711–37.

———. *Consuming Grief: Compassionate Cannibalism in an Amazonian Society*. Austin: University of Texas Press, 2001.

Conselho Nacional pela Proteção aos Índios (CNPI). "Relatório No. 12." 1952. SEDOC/MI. Microfilm 281.

Constituição da República Federativa do Brasil de 1988. http://www.planalto.gov.br /ccivil_03/constituicao/constitui%C3%A7ao.htm (11 June 2012).

Contreiras, Hélio. *AI-5: A opressão no Brasil*. Rio de Janeiro: Record, 2005.

Coordenação das Organizações Indígenas da Amazônia Brasileira (COIAB). 15 January 2011. http://www.coiab.com.br/ (11 June 2012).

Cornejo Polar, Antonio. *Escribir en el aire: Ensayo sobre la heterogeneidad sociocultural en las literaturas andinas*. Lima: Horizonte, 1994.

———. "Una heterogeneidad no dialéctica." *Revista Iberoamericana* 62, nos. 176–77 (1996): 837–84.

———. "*Indigenismo* and Heterogeneous Literatures: Their Dual Socio-Cultural Logic." *Journal of Latin American Cultural Studies* 7, no. 1 (1998): 15–27.

————. "Mestizaje, transculturación, heterogeneidad." *Revista de crítica literaria latinoamericana* 21, no. 42 (1995): 368–71.

————. *Los universos narrativos de José María Arguedas*. Lima: Horizonte, 1997.

Coronado, Jorge. *The Andes Imagined: Indigenismo, Society, and Modernity*. Pittsburgh: University of Pittsburgh Press, 2009.

Corrêa, Mari. "Vídeo nas Aldeias no olhar do outro." Vídeo nas Aldeias. 2006. http://www.videonasaldeias.org.br/2009/biblioteca.php?c=18 (11 June 2012).

Corrêa, Mariza. *Historia da antropologia no Brasil*. São Paulo: Vértice, 1987.

Correia de Oliveira Andrade, Manuel. *Tordesilhas: Um marco geopolítico*. Recife: Fundação Joaquim Nabuco, 1997.

Costa, Angyone. *Indiologia*. Rio de Janeiro: Ministério da Guerra, 1943.

Costigan, Lúcia Helena. *Through Cracks in the Wall: Modern Inquisitions and New Christian Letrados in the Iberian Atlantic World*. Leiden: Brill, 2010.

Cotinho, A., ed. *A polêmica Alencar-Nabuco*. Rio de Janeiro: Tempo Brasileiro, 1965.

Coutinho, Leonardo, Igor Paulin, and Júlia de Medeiros. "A farra da antropologia oportunista." *Veja*, 5 May 2010. http://veja.abril.com.br/050510/farra-antropologia-oportunista-p-154.shtml (11 June 2012).

Crocker, William H. *The Canela (Eastern Timbera), 1: An Ethnographic Introduction*. Washington, D.C.: Smithsonian, 1990.

Crocker, William H., and Jean G. Crocker. *Kinship, Ritual, and Sex in an Amazonian Tribe*. Belmont, Calif.: Wadsworth, 2003.

Cummings, S. M., and Stella Tamayo. *Language and Education in Latin America*. New York: World Bank, 1994.

Cunha, Ayres Câmara. *Além de Mato Grosso*. São Paulo: Clube do Livro, 1974.

————. *Entre os índios do Xingu: A verdadeira história de Diacuí*. São Paulo: Livraria Exposição do Livro, 1960 [1953].

————. *História da índia Diacuí: Seu casamento e sua morte*. São Paulo: Clube do Livro, 1976.

————. *O mistério do explorador Fawcett: Expedição à serra dos Gradaús*. São Paulo: Clube do Livro, 1984.

————. *Nas selvas do Xingu*. São Paulo: Clube do Livro, 1969.

Cunha, Edgar Teodoro da. "Cinema e imaginação." Ph.D. diss., Universidade de São Paulo, 1999.

Cunha, Olívia Maria Gomes da. "Sua alma em sua palma." In *Repensando o Estado Novo*, edited by Dulce Pandolfi, 257–88. Rio de Janeiro: Fundação Getúlio Vargas, 1999.

"Da civilização às selvas! Uma índia ibaraporé de amores com um funcionário do Departamento Federal de Segurança Pública!" *Diário do Povo*, 14 November 1952.

Da Costa, August J. "Indian Hunting in Brazil." *New York Times*, 29 July 1888.

DaMatta, Roberto. "For an Anthropology of the Brazilian Tradition, or 'A Virtude Está no Meio.'" In *The Brazilian Puzzle: Culture on the Borderlands of the Western World*, edited by David J. Hess and Roberto DaMatta, 270–92. New York: Colombia University Press, 1995.

"Darcy Ribeiro, a utopia do intelectual indignado." *Folha de São Paulo*, 1 October 1983, 43.

Das, Veena, Arthur Kleinman, Margaret Lock, Mamphela Ramphele, and Pamela Reynolds, eds. *Remaking a World: Violence, Social Suffering, and Recovery.* Berkeley: University of California Press, 2001.

da Silva, Luiz Inácio (Lula). Opening Address. 21º Congresso do Aço. São Paulo, 14 March 2010. http://www.youtube.com/watch?v=uT4tM-JyzkE (11 June 2012).

da Silva, Renato Ignácio. *Amazônia: Paraíso e inferno.* São Paulo: Quatro Artes, 1970.

Dávila, Jerry. *Diploma of Whiteness: Race and Social Policy in Brazil, 1917–1945.* Durham, N.C.: Duke University Press, 2003.

Davis, Shelton. H. *Victims of the Miracle.* Cambridge: Cambridge University Press, 2009 [1977].

Daynes, Byron W. "George Washington: Reluctant Occupant, Uncertain Model for the Presidency." In *George Washington and the Origins of the American Presidency,* edited by Mark J. Roznell, William D. Pederson, and Frank J. Williams. Westport, Conn.: Praeger, 2000.

"Defendendo seus irmãos de raça." *A Noite,* 27 February 1931, 8.

Degler, Carl N. *Neither Black nor White: Slavery and Race Relations in Brazil and the United States.* Madison: University of Wisconsin Press, 1971.

Degregori, Carlos Iván. "Ethnicity and Democratic Governability in Latin America." In *Fault Lines of Democracy in Post-transition Latin America,* edited by Felipe Agüero and Jeffrey Stark, 203–34. Miami: University of Miami/North-South Center Press, 1998.

de la Cadena, Marisol. "Are Mestizos Hybrids?" *Journal of Latin American Studies* 37, no. 2 (2005): 259–84.

———. *Indigenous Mestizos: The Politics of Race and Culture in Cuzco, Peru, 1919–1991.* Durham, N.C.: Duke University Press, 2000.

———. "Las mujeres son más indias." In *Detrás de la puerta: Hombres y mujeres en el Perú de hoy,* edited by Patricia Ruiz Bravo and Liuba Kogan, 181–202. Lima: Pontífica Universidad Católica, 1986.

———. "The Production of Other Knowledges and Its Tensions: From Andeanist Anthropology to *Interculturalidad?*" In *World Anthropologies: Disciplinary Transformations within Systems of Power,* edited by Gustavo Lins Ribeiro and Arturo Escobar, 201–24. Oxford: Berg, 2006.

de la Cadena, Marisol, and Orin Starn, eds. *Indigenous Experience Today.* Oxford: Berg, 2007.

De Lerma, Dominique-Rene. "Black Composers in Europe: A Works List." *Black Music Research Journal* 10, no. 2 (1990): 275–334.

Deleuze, Gilles, and Félix Guattari. *A Thousand Plateaus: Capitalism and Schizophrenia.* Translated by Brian Massumi. Minneapolis: University of Minnesota Press, 1987.

"Delírio indescritível no aeroporto: Diacuí no Rio—A multidão rompeu os cordões de isolamento." *Diário da Noite,* 15 November 1952, 1.

Deloria, Phil. *Playing Indian.* New Haven, Conn.: Yale University Press, 1999.

Deloria, Vine, Jr. "Philosophy and the Tribal Peoples." In *American Indian Thought,* edited by Anne Waters, 3–14. New York: Blackwell, 2005.

Del Valle Escalante, Emilio. *Maya Nationalisms and Postcolonial Challenges in Guatemala: Coloniality, Modernity and Identity Politics.* Santa Fe, N.M.: School for Advanced Research Press, 2009.

Dennis, Philip. "The Miskito-Sandinista Conflict in Nicaragua in the 1980s." *Latin American Research Review* 28, no. 3 (1993): 214–34.

Departamento de Controle do Espaço Aéreo. "Unidades." http://www.decea.gov.br/unidades/ (11 June 2012).

"De pele trocada." *Veja na História: República, 20 Nov. 1889.* September 1989. http://veja.abril.com.br/historia/republica/opera-lo-schiavo-carlos-gomes.shtml (11 June 2012).

Devine Guzmán, Tracy. "Diacuí Killed Iracema: Indigenism, Nationalism and the Struggle for Brazilianness." *Bulletin of Latin American Research* 24, no. 1 (2005): 91–120.

———. "Indians and Ailing National Culture in Brazil under Vargas." *Journal of the Southeastern Council of Latin American Studies* 35 (2003): 61–71.

———. "Indigenous Identity and Identification in Peru." *Journal of Latin American Cultural Studies* 8, no. 1 (1999): 63–74.

———. "Legacies of the Indianist Imagination and the Failures of Indigenist Politics." Ph.D. diss., Duke University, 2002.

———. "Writing Indigenous Activism in Brazil: Belo Monte and the Acampamento Indígena Revolucionário." *A Contracorriente* 10, no. 1 (2012): 280–309.

———. "Our Indians in Our America: Anti-imperialist Imperialism and the Construction of Brazilian Modernity." *Latin American Research Review* 45, no. 3 (2010): 35–62.

———. "Rimanakuy '86 and Other Fictions of National Dialogue in Peru." *Latin Americanist* 53, no. 1 (2009): 75–97.

———. "Subalternidade e soberania: Auto-representação indígena e a reformulação da política nacional." *América Latina em Movimiento*, 22 November 2011. http://alainet.org/active/51026&lang=es.

———. "Subalternidade hegemônica: Darcy Ribeiro e a virtude da contradição." *Cadernos de Estudos Culturais* 3, no. 5 (2011): 139–55.

———. "Whence Amazonian Studies." *LASA Forum* 43, no. 1 (2012): 24–27.

Dhaliwal, Amarpal. "Can the Subaltern Vote?" In *Radical Democracy: Identity, Citizenship, and the State*, edited by David Trend, 42–61. New York: Routledge, 1996.

Diacon, Todd. *Stringing Together a Nation: Cândido Mariano da Silva Rondon and the Construction of a Modern Brazil, 1906–1930.* Durham, N.C.: Duke University Press, 2004.

"Diacuí está feliz e Aires [*sic*] aborrecido." *Folha de São Paulo*, 19 November 1952.

Diário do Congresso Nacional. December 1949 and June 1951.

Diário Oficial. Section 1, July 1948.

Dias de Paula, Eunice. "O caso tapirapé: Uma escola indígena frente às políticas públicas." *Tellus* 8, no. 14 (2008): 171–83.

Diégues Júnior, Manuel. *Etnias e culturas no Brasil.* Rio de Janeiro: Biblioteca do Exército, 1980.

"Discurso do Presidente Lula no ato por Belo Monte." *International Rivers*, 21 June 2010. http://www.internationalrivers.org/pt-br/node/4293 (11 June 2012).

Domingues, Ângela. *Quando os índios eram vassalos*. Lisbon: Comissão Nacional para as Comemorações dos Descobrimentos Portugueses, 2000.

Do Nascimento, Abdias, and Elisa Larkin Nascimento. "Reflections of an Afro-Brazilian." *Journal of Negro History* 64, no. 3 (1979): 274–82.

Doratioto, Francisco. *O conflito com Paraguai: A grande guerra do Brasil*. São Paulo: Ática, 1996.

———. "História e ideologia: A produção brasileira sobre a guerra do Paraguai." *Nuevo Mundo, Mundos Nuevos*, 13 January 2009, 2–10.

"Dossiê Macunaíma." In *Macunaíma: O herói sem nenhum caráter*, by Oswald de Andrade. Edited by Têle Porto Ancona Lopez and Tatiana Longo Figueiredo, 215–37. Rio de Janeiro: Agir, 2008.

Driver, David Miller. *The Indian in Brazilian Literature*. New York: Hispanic Institute in the United States, 1942.

Duarte, Patrícia. "Funai diz que negociações com índios que estavam acampados em Brasília se esgotaram." *O Globo*, 10 July 2010. http://oglobo.globo.com/politica/funai-diz-negociacoes-com-indios-que-estavam-acampados-em-brasilia-se-esgotaram-2981313 (11 June 2012).

Du Bois, W. E. B. *The Souls of Black Folk*. 3rd ed. Chicago: AC McClurg, 1903.

"Editorial: Después de la ilusión, la reflexión." *Pukara* 34 (2008). http://www.periodicopukara.com/pasados/pukara-34-editorial-del-mes.php (11 June 2012).

Eidelberg, P. G. "Race, Labour, and the Mestizo Escape Hatch in Colonial Latin America. *South African Historical Journal* 19, no. 1 (1987): 159–66.

Ejercito Zapatista de Liberación Nacional (EZLN). *Documentos y comunicados*. Mexico City: Era, 2003.

Elizeu, José. Comment on "Exército deve 'pedir licença' para atuar em reserva, diz líder." *Terra*, 29 April 2009.

"Empleo de las lenguas vernáculas en la enseñanza." Paris: UNESCO, 1954.

"Entrevista com Maria de Souza Delta." 10 February 2000. Video. SEDOC/MI.

Evans, Peter E., Dietrich Rueschemeyer, and Theda Skocpal, eds. *Bringing the State Back In*. Cambridge: Cambridge University Press, 1985.

"Exército deve 'pedir licença' para atuar em reserva, diz líder." *Terra*, 29 April 2009. http://noticias.terra.com.br/brasil/noticias/0,OI3733092-EI306,00-Exercito+deve+pedir+licenca+para+atuar+em+reserva+diz+lider.html (12 June 2012).

"Falemos um pouco dos donos da Nossa Terra." *O Paiz*, 1 November 1955.

Fanon, Frantz. *Black Skin, White Masks*. Translated by Richard Philcox. New York: Grove, 2008.Fearnside, Philip M. "Dams in the Amazon." *Environmental Management* 20, no. 10 (2006): 1–13.

Feltrin, Ricardo. "Ibope de novelas desaba na Globo." *UOL*, 18 September 2008. http://noticias.uol.com.br/ooops/ultnot/2008/09/18/ult2548u604.jhtm (11 June 12).

Fernandes, Millôr. Cartoon. *Revista Bundas*, 18 April 2000, 9.

Ferreira Vargas, Vera. "A construção do território terena (1870–1966)." M.A. thesis, Universidade Federal de Mato Grosso do Sul, 2003.

"Filha de Diacuí casa-se no Sul." *Jornal do Brasil*, 29 September 1973, 13.

Flores, Lúcio Paiva. *Adoradores do sol*. Petrópolis: Vozes, 2003.

———. "Cultura e a ex-cultura." In *Sol do pensamento*, edited by Eliane Potiguara, 30–32. São Paulo: Inbrapi/Grumin, 2005.

Fonseca, Rubem. *O selvagem da ópera*. São Paulo: Companhia das Letras, 1994.

Fontainha, Guilherme. "Prefácio." *Revista Brasileira de Música* 3, no. 2 (1936): 78–82.

Foreman, Grant. *Indian Removal*. Norman: University of Oklahoma Press, 1932.

Forthmann, Heinz, dir. *Guido Marliére: Um posto indígena de nacionalização*. Film. Seção de Estudos do Serviço de Proteção aos Índios, 1947.

Foucault, Michel. *Em defesa da sociedade*. Translated by M. E. Galvão. São Paulo: Martins Fontes, 1999.

———. *The History of Sexuality*. New York: Vintage, 1990.

———. *Power/Knowledge: Selected Interviews and Other Writings, 1972–1977*. New York: Random House, 1977.

Franco, Bruno. "Acesso 2011: 20% das vagas para rede pública." *Jornal da UFRJ*, 19 August 2010. http://www.ufrj.br/mostraNoticia.php?noticia=10345_Acesso—% -das-vagas-para-rede-publica.html (12 June 2012).

Frankl, Viktor E. *Man's Search for Meaning*. 4th ed. Boston: Beacon, 2000.

Freire, Paulo. *Pedagogía del oprimido*. Lima: Saldaña, 1995.

———. *Pedagogy of Hope*. New York: Continuum, 1994.

Freire, Paulo, and Ana Maria Araújo Freire. *Pedagogia da tolerância*. São Paulo, UNESP, 2005.

French, John D. "Drowning in Laws but Starving (for Justice?)" *Political Power and Social Theory* 12 (1998): 181–218.

———. "The Missteps of Anti-imperialist Reason." Durham, N.C.: Duke and UNC Program in Latin American Studies, 1999.

Freyre, Gilberto. *Casa grande e senzala*. 16th ed. Rio de Janeiro: José Olympio, 1973 [1933].

Friedlander, Judith. *Being Indian in Hueyapan*. 2nd ed. New York: Macmillan, 2006.

"Funai garante que a cultura do silvícola será preservada." *O Globo*, 6 April 1973, 6.

Fundação Nacional do Índio (FUNAI). "As terras indígenas." http://www.funai.gov .br/ (12 June 2012).

———. "TI–Raposa Serra do Sol–Roraima." http://www.funai.gov.br (12 June 2012).

Gadelha, Regina Maria A. F., ed. *Missões guarani: Impacto na sociedade contemporânea*. Madrid: Universidad Pontífica de Comillas, 1999.

Galeano, Eduardo. *Las venas abiertas de América Latina*. Mexico City: Siglo XXI, 2006.

Galvão, Jean. Cartoon. *Revista Bundas*, 25 April 2000.

Gamio, Manuel. Letters to Cândido Mariano da Silva Rondon, 17 January and 24 April 1946. SEDOC/MI.

García, José Uriel. *El nuevo indio*. Cusco: H. G. Rozas Sucesores, 1930.

———. "Problemas de sociología peruana." *Cuadernos Mexicanos* 9, no. 2 (1950): 147–79.

García, Maria Elena. *Making Indigenous Citizens: Identities, Education and Multicultural Development in Peru*. Stanford, Calif.: Stanford University Press, 2005.

García Canclini, Néstor. *Culturas híbridas: Estrategias para entrar y salir de la modernidad*. Mexico City: Grijalbo, 1990.

García Márquez, Gabriel. "La soledad de América Latina." Nobel lecture, 8 December 1982. http://www.nobelprize.org/nobel_prizes/literature/laureates/1982/marquez-lecture-sp.html (12 June 2012).

García Mérou, Martín. *El Brasil intelectual*. Buenos Aires: Didot, 1900.

Garfield, Seth. *Indigenous Struggle at the Heart of Brazil*. Durham, N.C.: Duke University Press, 2001.

———. "A Nationalist Environment: Indians, Nature, and the Construction of the Xingu National Park in Brazil." *Luso-Brazilian Review* 41, no. 1 (2004): 139–67.

———. "The Roots of a Plant That Today Is Brazil: Indians and the Nation-State under the Brazilian Estado Novo." *Journal of Latin American Studies* 29 (1997): 747–68.

Garmendia, José I. *Recuerdos de la Guerra del Paraguay*. Buenos Aires: Jacobo Peuser, 1883.

Gaúdio, María Luiza. "Proteção aos índios." *O Tempo*, 16 December 1952, 8.

Geiger, Theodore. *General Electric Company in Brazil*. New York: Arno, 1976.

Gelles, Paul. "Testimonio, Ethnography and Processes of Authorship." *Anthropology Newsletter* 39, no. 3 (1998): 16–17.

"Getúlio vai amparar a filha de Diacuí." *Gazeta de Noticias*, 15 August 1953, 14.

Giddens, Anthony. *The Consequences of Modernity*. Stanford, Calif.: Stanford University Press, 1990.

Ginsburg, Faye. "The Parallax Effect: The Impact of Aboriginal Media on Ethnographic Film." *Visual Anthropology Review* 11, no. 2 (1995): 64–76.

Giovannelli, A. "Goodman's Aesthetics." In *The Stanford Encyclopedia of Philosophy*, edited by Edward N. Zalta. http://plato.stanford.edu/archives/fa112008/entries/goodman-aesthetics/ (12 June 2012).

Glycerio, Carolina. "Genética alimenta polêmica sobre raças no Brasil." *BBC Brasil*, 28 May 2007. http://www.bbc.co.uk/portuguese/reporterbbc/story/2007/05/070523_dna_polemica_raca_cg.shtml (12 June 2012).

Gobineau, Arthur de. *The Inequality of the Human Races*. Translated by Adrian Collins. New York: G. P. Putnam's Sons, 1915.

Godenzzi, Juan Carlos. Interviews with author, Lima, 6 August 1997 and 13 May 1999.

———. "Investigaciones sobre educación bilingüe en Perú y Bolivia: 1980–1990." *Revista Andina* 16, no. 2 (1990): 481–506.

———. "Política y estrategias para el desarrollo de la educación bilingüe intercultural." Lima: EBI Sector of the Peruvian Ministry of Education, 1997.

———, ed. *Educación e interculturalidad en los Andes y la Amazonia*. Cusco: Centro de Estudios Regionales Andinos "Bartolomé de Las Casas," 1996.

———, ed. *Revista Andina* 28 (1996).

Goés, Marcus. *Carlos Gomes: A força indômita*. Belém: SECULT, 1996.

Gomes, Ângela de Castro. *Vargas e a crise dos anos 50*. Rio de Janeiro: Relume-Dumaráz, 1994.

Gomes, Antônio Carlos. Letter to Francisco Manoel, 3 November 1864. *Revista Brasileira de Música* 3, no. 2 (1936): 329–30.

———. Letters to Manoel José de Souza Guimarães, 3 November 1864, 9 November 1889, 13 November 1889, 3 June 1892, 12 July 1895, and 12 August 1895. *Revista Brasileira de Música* 3, no. 2 (1936): 358–66.

———. Letters to Ítala Gomes Vaz de Carvalho, 10 August 1863, 6 November 1893, and 20 May 1895. *Revista Brasileira de Música* 3, no. 2 (1936): 344–47.

———. Letters to Theodoro Teixeira Gomes, 29 July 1880, 16 June 1892, 18 March 1893, and 17 July 1895. *Revista Brasileira de Música* 3 no. 2 (1936): 347–57.

Gomes, Mércio. *Blog do Mércio: Índios, Antropologia, Cultura*. http://merciogomes.blogspot.com/ (12 June 2012).

———. *O índio na história*. Petrópolis: Vozes, 2002.

———. *The Indians and Brazil*. Translated by J. W. Moon. Gainesville: University Press of Florida, 2000.

Gomes Vaz de Carvalho, Ítala. *A vida de Carlos Gomes*. Rio de Janeiro: A Noite, 1937.

Gonçalves Dias, Antônio. *Poesia e prosa completas*. Edited by Alexei Bueno. Rio de Janeiro: Nova Aguilar, 1998.

González Prada, Manuel. "Nuestros indios." In *Free Pages and Hard Times*. New York: Oxford, 2002 [1904].

Goodman, Jordan. *The Devil and Mr. Casement: One Man's Battle for Human Rights in South America's Heart of Darkness*. New York: Farrar, Straus and Giroux, 2009.

Gordon, Eric. "A New Opera House: An Investigation of Elite Values in Mid-Nineteenth-Century Rio de Janeiro." *Anuario* 5 (1969): 49–66.

Gordon, Richard. "Recreating Caminha: The Earnest Adaptation of Brazil's Letter of Discovery in Humberto Mauro's *Descobrimento do Brasil* (1937)." *Modern Langauge Notes* 120, no. 2 (2005): 408–36.

Graça Moura, Vasco. *Tordesilhas: A partilha do mundo*. Lisbon: Comissão Nacional para as Comemorações dos Descobrimentos Portugueses, 1994.

Granadaliso, Oscar. "Diversões: Theatro Companhia Lyrica Italiana—*Lo schiavo*." *O Paiz*, 29 September 1880, 2–3.

Grandin, Greg. *Fordlândia: The Rise and Fall of Henry Ford's Forgotten Jungle City*. New York: Picador, 2009.

Grandin, Paul. "He Said, She Said." *Anthropology Newsletter* 4 (1998): 52.

Grann, David. *The Lost City of Z: A Tale of Deadly Obsession in the Amazon*. New York: Doubleday, 2009.

"Os gringos querem nos tomar a Amazônia." *Revista Bundas*, 31 October 2000, front cover.

Grupo Schahin. "Inauguração do projeto SIVAM, motivo de orgulho para a Schahin." August 2002. http://www.schahin.com.br/schahin/br/noticias.asp?pag_atual=18&secao=&cod_secao=&cod_assunto=3&assunto=Destaques&mes=&ano= (12 June 2012).

Guajajara, Sônia Bone. "Environmental Policy, Social Movements, and Science for the Brazilian Amazon: Special Address." University of Chicago, 5 November 2009. http://amazonia.uchicago.edu/en/special-address.shtml (12 June 2012).

"*O Guarany* de Carlos Gomes." *Correio Paulistano*, 21 April 1870, 1.

Guevara, Ernesto. "El hombre y el socialismo en Cuba." *Marcha*, 12 March 1965, 11.

Gugelberger, Georg M. *The Real Thing: Testimonial Discourse and Latin America.* Durham, N.C.: Duke University Press, 1996.

Guha, Ranajit. *A Subaltern Studies Reader, 1986–1995.* Minneapolis: University of Minnesota Press, 1997.

————. *Dominance without Hegemony: History and Power in Colonial India.* Cambridge: Harvard University Press, 1998.

Guimarães, Larissa. "Índios invadem sede da FUNAI e 'empossam' presidente indígena." *Folha.com*, 6 May 2010. http://www1.folha.uol.com.br/poder/741289 -indios-invadem-sede-da-funai-e-empossam-presidente-indigena.shtml (12 June 2012).

Gurgel, Romildo. "Abençoada por Deus: O casamento da índia com o branco." *O Cruzeiro*, 13 December 1952, 8–16.

Guzmán, Leila Silva Reque. Conversations with the author. 1999–2008.

Guzmán Bockler, Carlos. *Colonialismo y revolución.* Mexico City: Siglo XXI, 1975.

Hale, Charles. "Does Multiculturalism Menace?" *Journal of Latin American Studies* 34, no. 3 (2002): 485–524.

————. "Rethinking Indigenous Politics in the Era of the 'Indio Permitido.'" *NACLA* 38, no. 2 (2004): 16–20.

Hall, Anthony. "Enhancing Social Capital: Productive Conservation and Traditional Knowledge in the Brazilian Rain Forest." In *Human Impacts on Amazonia,* edited by Darrell Addison Posey and Michael J. Balick, 328–45. New York: Columbia University Press, 2006.

Hall, Stuart. "Ethnicity: Identity and Difference." *Radical America* 23, no. 4 (1989): 9–20.

————. "Old and New Identities, Old and New Ethnicities." In *Culture, Globalization, and the World System: Contemporary Conditions for the Representation of Identity,* edited by Anthony D. King, 41–68. Minneapolis: University of Minnesota Press, 1997.

Hall, Stuart, and Paul du Gay, eds. "Encoding/Decoding." In *Culture Media Language,* edited by Stuart Hall, Dorothy Hobson, Andrew Love, and Paul Willis, 128–38. London: Hutchinson, 1980.

————. *Questions of Cultural Identity.* London: Sage, 1996.

————. "Who Needs Identity?" In *Questions of Cultural Identity,* edited by Stuart Hall and Paul du Gay, 1–17. London: Sage, 1996.

Hanke, Lewis. *Aristotle and the American Indians.* Bloomington: Indiana University Press, 1970.

Harasowska, Marta. *Morphophonemic Variability, Productivity, and Change.* Berlin: Mouton de Gruyter, 1998.

Hearn, Kelly. "The Bagua Movement." *The Nation*, 13 July 2009. www.thenation.com /article/bagua-movement (12 June 2012).

Hemming, John. *Die If You Must: Brazilian Indians in the Twentieth Century*. London: Macmillan, 2003.

———. *Red Gold: The Conquest of the Brazilian Indians*. Cambridge: Harvard University Press, 1978.

¿He vivido en vano? Mesa redonda sobre Todas las sangres–23 de junio de 1965. Lima: Instituto de Estudios Peruanos, 1985.

Himpele, Jeff. *Circuits of Culture: Media, Politics, and Indigenous Identity in the Andes*. Minneapolis: University of Minnesota Press, 2007.

"Historia." *Voz do Brasil*. Radiobrás, 15 January 2009. http://www.ebcservicos.ebc .com.br/programas/a-voz-do-brasil/historia (12 June 2012).

Hoffman French, Jan. *Legalizing Identities: Becoming Black or Indian in Brazil's Northeast*. Chapel Hill: University of North Carolina Press, 2009.

Holston, James. *Insurgent Citizenship: Disjunctions of Democracy and Modernity in Brazil*. Princeton, N.J.: Princeton University Press, 2008.

"O homem branco quer casar-se com índia kalapalo." *Diário da Noite*, 4 October 1952, 1.

Hulme, Peter. *Colonial Encounters: Europe and the Native Caribbean, 1492–1797*. London: Routledge, 1992.

"Hunting Indians in Brazil." *New York Times*, 25 July 1888.

Hynds, Patricia. "Administration of President Fernando Henrique Cardoso Rocked by SIVAM Scandal." *Latin American Political Affairs* 5, no. 47 (1995). http://ladb .unm.edu/notisur/1995/12/08-055844 (12 June 2012).

Imbassahy, Arthur. "Carlos Gomes: Alguns traços episódicos do homem e do artista." *Revista Brasileira de Música* 3, no. 2 (1936): 104–16.

"Indígenas exigem reunião com ministro da Justiça para desocupação de área na Esplanada." *O Globo*, 1 June 2010. http://extra.globo.com/noticias/brasil /indigenas-exigem-reuniao-com-ministro-da-justica-para-desocupacao-de -area-na-esplanada-136260.html (12 June 2012).

"Indígenas querem representação no legislativo." *Jornal de Brasília*, 28 July 2010. http://www.jornaldebrasilia.com.br/site/noticia.php?id=290968 (12 June 2012).

"Índio quer respeito: Comissão protesta contra novela *Uga! Uga!* da Globo." *Jornal do Brasil*, 11 November 2000, 11.

"Os índios não terão com quem casar." *Folha da Tarde*, 11 October 1952.

"Ingressam os índios nas escolas agrícolas brasileiras." *O Globo*, 3 April 1947, 2.

"Inspiração para a nova moda feminina brasileira." *Diário da Noite*, 29 October 1952, 17.

Instituto Brasileiro de Geografia e Estatística (IBGE). *Censo demográfico 2000*. Rio de Janeiro: IBGE, 2003. http://www.ibge.gov.br/home/estatistica/populacao /censo2000/default.shtm (12 June 2012).

———. *Censo demográfico 2010*. Rio de Janeiro: IBGE, 2010. http://www.ibge.gov .br/censo2010/ (12 June 2012).

———. "IBGE lança mapa de pobreza e desigualdade 2003." 18 December 2008. http://www.ibge.gov.br/home/presidencia/noticias/noticia_visualiza.php?id _noticia=1293&id_pagina=1 (12 June 2012).

———. "A imigração no Brasil nos períodos anuais (1820–1975)." 20 May 2010. http://www.ibge.gov.br/brasi1500/tabelas/imigracao_brasil.htm (12 June 2012).

———. "Imigração no Brasil por nacionalidade." http://www.ibge.gov.br/brasi1500 /tabelas/imigracao_nacionalidade_45a54.htm (12 June 2012).

———. *Recenseamento geral do Brasil (1 setembro de 1940)*. Rio de Janeiro: Serviço Gráfico do IBGE, 1950.

———. *Tendências demográficas: Uma análise dos resultados da sinopse preliminar do censo demográfico 2000*. Rio de Janeiro: IBGE, 2001.

Instituto Indígena Brasileiro para Propriedade Intelectual (INBRAPI). 15 January 2011. http://www.inbrapi.org.br/ (12 June 2012).

———."Nosso símbolo: nosso pensar." http://www.inbrapi.org.br/index. php?option=com_content&view=article&id=46&Itemid=53 (12 June 2012).

Instituto Indigenista Interamericano. *Acta final del primer Congreso Indigenista Interamericano*. Pátzcuaro, Mexico: Instituto Indigenista Interamericano, 1940.

Instituto Socioambiental. "Povos indígenas no Brasil." http://pib.socioambiental.org /pt. (15 June 2012).

———. "Terras indígenas no Brasil." http://www.socioambiental.org/inst/pub/detalhe _down_html?codigo=10102 (12 June 2012).

"Instrução militar para os índios brasileiros!" *O Radical*, 30 March 1940, 1.

"Integrando o índio na civilização." *O Paiz*, 20 May 1925.

Itiberê da Cunha, João. "Il guarany: Algumas palavras sobre a ópera." *Revista Brasileira de Música* 3, no. 2 (1936): 247–50.

———. "Lo schiavo." *Revista Brasileira de Música* 3, no. 2 (1936): 293–99.

Jabor. Arnaldo. "Nosso coração está cada vez mais frio." *O Estado de São Paulo*, 27 April 2004, caderno 2.

Jameson, Fredric. *The Political Unconscious*. London: Routledge, 2002.

———. "Third-World Literature in the Era of Multinational Capitalism." *Social Text* 15 (1986): 65–88.

Jekupé, Olívio. *Iarandu: O cão falante*. São Paulo: Peirópolis, 2006.

———. *Literatura escrita pelos povos indígenas*. São Paulo: Scortecci, 2009.

———. *Tekoa: Conhecendo uma aldeia indígena*. São Paulo: Global, 2011.

Johnson, Adriana Michele Campos. "Cara Feia al Enemigo: The Paraguayan War and the War of the Triple Alliance." *Colorado Review of Hispanic Studies* 4 (2006): 169–85.

———. *Sentencing Canudos: Subalternity in the Backlands of Brazil*. Pittsburgh: University of Pittsburgh Press, 2010.

Johnson, Randal. "Tupy or Not Tupy." In *Modern Latin American Fiction*, edited by John King, 41–59. London: Faber and Faber, 1987.

Jourdon, E. C. *Atlas histórico da guerra do Paraguay*. Rio de Janeiro: Rensburg, 1871.

Juruna, Mário, Antônio Hohlfeldt, and Assis Hoffman. *O gravador do Juruna*. Porto Alegre: Mercado Aberto, 1982.

Kamati Kayapó, Bet, Raoni Kayapó, and Yakareti Juruna, "Nós, indígenas do Xingu, não queremos Belo Monte." Coordenação das Organizações Indígenas da

Amazônia Brasileira (COAIB). 23 April 2010. http://www.coiab.com.br/coiab.php
?dest=show&back=index&id=468&tipo=E (12 June 2012).

Kamb, Louis. "Bush's Comment on Tribal Sovereignty Creates a Buzz." *Seattle Post-Intelligencer*, 13 August 2004. http://www.seattlepi.com/local/article/Bush-s
-comment-on-tribal-sovereignty-creates-a-1151615.php (12 June 2012).

Kapêlituk, Raimundo Roberto. "Bandeira do Brasil." 1948. SEDOC/MI. Microfilm
289.

———. "Ditado." 1948. SEDOC/MI. Microfilm 289.

Keen, Benjamin. "The Legacy of Bartolomé de Las Casas." *Ibero-Americana Pragensia*
11 (1977): 57–67.

Kleinpenning, Jan M. G. "Strong Reservations about 'New Insights into the
Demographics of the Paraguayan War.'" *Latin American Research Review* 37, no. 2
(2002): 137–42.

Kozloff, Nikolas. *No Rain in the Amazon: How South America's Climate Change
Affects the Entire Planet*. New York: Macmillan, 2010.

Krupat, Arnold. *Ethnocriticism: Ethnography, History, Literature*. Berkeley:
University of California Press, 1992.

"Kuatia veve." *Cacique Lambaré*, 24 July 1867, 3.

Kusch, Rodolfo. *Indigenous and Popular Thinking in America*. Translated by María
Lugones and Joshua Price. Durham, N.C.: Duke University Press, 2010.

Laclau, Ernesto. "Power and Representation." In *Politics, Theory, and Contemporary
Culture*, edited by Mark Poster, 277–96. New York: Columbia University Press,
1993.

Lailson. Cartoon. *Revista Bundas* 2 May 2000, 30.

LALÁ. Comment on "Exército deve 'pedir licença' para atuar em reserva, diz líder."
Terra, 29 April 2009.

"Lambaré kuatia ñe'ê." *Cacique Lambaré*, 24 July 1867, 2.

"Lances empolgantes do romance que nasce na selva: A nudez inocente de Diacuí."
Diário da Noite, 22 October 1952.

Lane, Phil, Jr. *The Fourth Way: An Indigenous Contribution for Building Sustainable
and Harmonious Prosperity in the Americas*. Seattle: Four Worlds International
Institute, 2006.

———. "Indigenous Guiding Principles for Building a Sustainable and Harmonious
World." Four Worlds International Institute, 10 December 2011. http://www.fwii
.net/profiles/blogs/indigenous-guiding-principles-for-building-a-sustainable-and
-harm (15 June 2012).

Larsen, Neil. *Determinations*. New York: Verso, 2001.

———. "Marxism, Postcolonialism, and the *Eighteenth Brumaire*." In *Marxism,
Modernity, and Postcolonial Studies*, edited by Crystal Bartolovich and Neil
Lazarus, 204–20. Cambridge: Cambridge University Press, 2002.

———. *Reading North by South*. Minneapolis: University of Minnesota Press, 1995.

Le Clézio, J. M. G. *Índio branco*. Lisbon: Fenda, 1989.

Lei N° 601 de 18 de setembro de 1850 (Lei de Terras).

Lei N° 1.390 de 3 de julho de 1951 (Lei Afonso Arinos).

Lei N° 2040 de 28 de setembro de 1871 (Lei do Ventre Livre).

Leitão, Miriam. "Avatar de Belo Monte." *O Globo*, 24 June 2010. http://oglobo.globo
.com/economia/miriam/posts/2010/06/24/avatar-de-belo-monte-302747.asp (12
June 2012).

Lesser, Jeffrey. *Negotiating National Identity: Immigrants, Minorities, and the
Struggle for Ethnicity in Brazil*. Durham, N.C.: Duke University Press, 1999.

———, ed. *Searching for Home Abroad: Japanese Brazilians and Transnationalism*.
Durham, N.C.: Duke University Press, 2003.

Lévano, César. "El indio no existe: Entrevista exclusiva con el antropólogo William
Stein." *Revista Agronoticias*, September 1996.

Lévi-Strauss, Claude. *Tristes Tropiques*. Translated by John Russell. New York:
Criterion, 1961.

Levine, Robert M. *Brazilian Legacies*. New York: M. E. Sharpe, 1997.

———. "Canudos in the National Context." *The Americas* 48, no. 2 (1991): 207–22.

Levino, José Carlos. "A política indigenista no Brasil, 1940–1960." 1981. Doc. 79/
MIPE3317. SEDOC/MI.

Levinson, Brett. "Neopatriarchy and After: *I, Rigoberta Menchú* as Allegory of Death."
Journal of Latin American Cultural Studies 5, no. 1 (1996): 33–50.

Lhullier dos Santos, Yolanda. *Imagem do índio: O selvagem americano na visão do
homem branco*. São Paulo: Instituição Brasileira de Difusão Cultural, 2000.

Lienhard, Martin. *Cultura popular andina y forma novelesca*. Lima:
Latinoamericana, 1981.

———. *La voz y su huella*. Lima: Horizonte, 1992.

Lima, Eucy da Silva. Phone interview with author, 8 August 2008.

———. "SIVAM mostra a sua cara." Unpublished manuscript. Rio de Janeiro, 1998.

Lobato Azevedo, Ana L. "Índios de tela." Ph.D. diss., Universidade de São Paulo,
2000.

Lopes da Silva, Aracy, and Luís D. B. Grupioni, eds. *A temática indígena na escola:
Novos subsidios para professores de 1º e 2º graus*. Brasília: Ministério de Educação
e Cultura, 1995.

López, Luis Enrique, ed. *Educación bilingüe intercultural*. Lima: Fomciencias, 1991.

López, Luis Enrique, and W. Küper. "La educación intercultural bilingüe en América
Latina." *Revista Iberoamericana de Educación* (May–August 1999): 17–84.

Lopez, Têle Porto Ancona. *Macunaíma: A margem e o texto*. São Paulo: HUCITEC,
1974.

López Albújar, Enrique. "Sobre la psicología del indio." *Amauta* 4 (1926): 1–2. In *La
polémica del indigenismo*, edited by Manuel Aquézolo Castro, 15–31. Lima: Mosca
Azul, 1976.

Losada, Ángel. "Controversy between Sepúlveda and Las Casas." *Bartolomé de Las
Casas in History*, edited by Juan Friede and Benjamin Keen, 279–309. DeKalb:
Northern Illinois University Press, 1971.

"Los camba." *Cacique Lambaré*, 24 July 1867, 4.

Lozano Vallejo, Ruth, ed. *Interculturalidad: Desafío e proceso en construcción*. Lima:
Servicios en Comunicación Intercultural, 2005.

Lucero, José Antonio. *Struggles of Voice: The Politics of Indigenous Representation in
the Andes*. Pittsburgh: University of Pittsburgh Press, 2008.

"Lula defende construção da usina de Belo Monte." *G1*, 26 April 2010. http://g1.globo
.com/economia-e-negocios/noticia/2010/04/lula-defende-construcao-da-usina
-de-belo-monte.html (12 June 2012).

Lund, Joshua. "Barbarian Theorizing and the Limits of Latin American
Exceptionalism." *Cultural Critique* 47 (2001): 54–90.

Lurie, Edward. "Louis Agassiz and the Races of Man." *History of Science Society* 45,
no. 2 (1954): 227–42.

Lustig, Wolf. *Repertorio de la revista paraguaya "Cacique Lambaré" (1867/68)*.
Seminario de Románicas–Universidad de Maguncia. 2005. http://www.staff.uni
-mainz.de/lustig/guarani/welcome.html (12 June 2012).

Luttrell, Wendy. "'Good Enough' Methods for Ethnographic Research." *Harvard
Educational Review* 70, no. 4 (2000): 499–523.

Luykx, Aurolyn. *The Citizen Factory: Schooling and Cultural Production in Bolivia*.
Albany: SUNY Press, 1999.

Maaka, Roger, and Chris Anderson, eds. *The Indigenous Experience: Global
Perspectives*. Toronto: Canadian Scholars, 2006.

Maciel, Maria Eunice de S. "A Eugenia no Brasil." *Anos 90* 11 (1999): 121–43.

Machado de Assis. "Notícia da atual literatura brasileira, instinto de nacionalidade."
In *Obra completa*, edited by Afrânio Coutinho, 3:801–4. Rio de Janeiro: J. Aguilar,
1962.

Machado, Maria Helena P. T. *Brazil through the Eyes of William James*. Cambridge:
Harvard University Press, 2006.

Maestri, Mário. "A guerra contra o Paraguai: História e historiografia." *Estudios
Históricos* 2 (2009): 1–29.

Magalhães, Amilcar Armando Botelho de. *Impressões da Comissão Rondon*. 5th ed.
Recife: Brasiliana, 1942.

Magalhães, Basílio de. *Em defeza do índio e das fazendas nacionais: Discursos na
Câmara a 28 de novembro, 19, 28 e 30 de dezembro de 1924*. Rio de Janeiro:
Typographia do Jornal do Commercio, de Rodrigues & C., 1925.

Maio, Marcos Chor. "Qual anti-semitismo? Relativizando a questão judaica no Brasil
dos anos 30." In *Repensando o Estado Novo*, edited by Dulce Pandolfi, 229–56. Rio
de Janeiro: Fundação Getúlio Vargas, 1999.

———. "UNESCO and the Study of Race Relations in Brazil." *Latin American
Research Review* 36, no. 2 (2001): 118–36.

Malinowski, Bronislaw. *Um diário no sentido estrito do termo*. Rio de Janeiro:
Record, 1997.

Malcher, José Maria da Gama. "Senhor Ministro." 22 May 1951. Doc. 2.072/51.
SEDOC/MI.

Mandrake. "Brô MCs: 1° grupo de rap indígena." *Portal Rap Nacional*, 5 July 2010.
http://www.rapnacional.com.br/2010/index.php/noticias/bro-mc%C2%B4s
-1%C2%BA-grupo-de-rap-indigena/ (12 June 2012).

"Manifesto: Cento e treze cidadãos anti-racistas contra as leis raciais." Open letter to
President of the Supremo Tribunal Federal, Gilmar Mendes. *Revista Época*, 21
April 2008. http://revistaepoca.globo.com/Revista/Epoca/0,EDR83466-6014,00
.html (12 June 2012).

"Manifesto de Porto Seguro." In *Uma história de resistência Pataxó*, edited by Professores de Pataxó do Extremo Sul da Bahia, 65–68. Salvador: ANAI, CESE, and MEC, 2007.

"Manifesto republicano de 1870." *Cadernos ASLEGIS* 37 (2009): 42–60.

Marcos, Subcomandante. *El sueño zapatista*. Mexico City: Plaza Ijanés, 1997.

Mariátegui, José Carlos. "Intermezzo polémico." *Mundial* 350 (25 February 1927). In *La polémica del indigenismo*, edited by Manuel Aquézolo Castro, 73–77. Lima: Mosca Azul, 1976.

———. "El problema del indio." In *Siete ensayos de interpretación de la realidad peruana*, edited by Elizabeth Garrels, 20–30. Caracas: Biblioteca Ayacucho, 1979 [1928].

———. *Siete ensayos de interpretación de la realidad peruana*. Edited by Elizabeth Garrels. Caracas: Biblioteca Ayacucho, 1979 [1928].

———. *Temas de educación*. Edited by Sandro Mariátegui. Lima: Amauta, 1970.

Markun, Paulo. "Entrevista com Davi Kopenawa Yanomami." 5 October 1998. *Roda Viva–TV Cultura*. http://www.rodaviva.fapesp.br/materia_busca/42/%EDndio/entrevistados/davi_yanomami_1998.htm (12 June 2012).

Marques, Clóvis. "A volta do Filho Maduro." In *O escravo: Drama lírico em quatro atos*, by Alfredo d'Escragnolle and Rodolfo Paravicini, 6–12. Maranhão: Governo do Estado do Maranhão, 1988.

Martínez Novo, Carmen. *Who Defines Indigenous?: Identities, Development, Intellectuals, and the State in Northern Mexico*. New Brunswick, N.J.: Rutgers University Press, 2006.

Martins, Edilson. "Antropologia ou, a teoria do Bombardeio de Berlim." Interview with Darcy Ribeiro. *Encontros com a civilização* 12 (1979): 81–100.

———. "Um brasileiro chamado Juruna." *O Pasquim*, 4 December 1977. In *Nossos índios, nossos mortos*, by Edilson Martins, 201–15. Rio de Janeiro: Codecri, 1982.

———. *Nossos índios, nossos mortos*. Rio de Janeiro: Codecri, 1982.

Marx, Karl. *The Eighteenth Brumaire of Louis Bonaparte*. Translated by Daniel De Leon. Chicago: Charles H. Kerr, 1913.

Mato, Daniel. "Interculturalidad, produccíon de conocimientos y prácticas socioeducativas." *Revista ALCEU* 6, no. 11 (2005): 120–38.

———. "Not 'Studying the Subaltern,' but Studying *with* 'Subaltern' Social Groups." *Nepantla* 1, no. 3 (2000) 479–502.

Maybury-Lewis, David. "Becoming Indian in Lowland South America." In *Nation States and Indians in Lowland South America*, edited by Greg Urban and Joel Sherzer, 207–35. Austin: University of Texas Press, 1991.

Mazzotti, José Antonio. "Creole Agencies and the (Post)Colonial Debate in Spanish America." In *Coloniality at Large*, edited by Mabel Moraña, Enrique Dussel, and Carlos Jáugregui, 77–110. Durham, N.C.: Duke University Press, 2008.

McLuhan, Marshall. *The Gutenberg Galaxy*. London: Routledge & Kegan Paul, 1962.

McLuhan, Marshall, and Quentin Fiore. *War and Peace in the Global Village*. New York: McGraw-Hill, 1968.

McLuhan, Marshall, Quentin Fiore, and Jerome Agel. *The Medium Is the Massage: An Inventory of Effects*. New York: Random House, 1967.

McNally, Michael D. "The Indian Passion Play: Contesting the Real Indian in Song of Hiawatha Pageants." *American Quarterly* 58, no. 1 (2006): 105–13.

Mead, Margaret. *People and Places*. Cleveland: World, 1959.

Measuring Worth, 15 January 2011. http://www.measuringworth.com/ (12 June 2012).

Medeiros, Alexandre. "Sob os olhos do SIVAM." *Revista Época*, 30 May 1998. http://epoca.globo.com/edic/19980601/soci1.htm (12 June 2012).

Meisch, Lynn A. *Andean Entrepreneurs: Otavalo Merchants and Musicians in the Global Arena*. Austin: University of Texas Press, 2002.

Melatti, Júlio Cezar. *Índios do Brasil*. São Paulo: Editora da Universidade de São Paulo, 2007.

———. *Índios e criadores: A situação dos Craôs na área pastoril do Tocantins*. Rio de Janeiro: Instituto de Ciências Sociais da UFRJ, 1967.

Melo, Antônia. "Cartas a Dilma e Serra pedem posicionamento sobre Belo Monte." Open letter to presidential candidates Dilma Rousseff and José Serra, 26 October 2012. *Movimento Xingu Vivo para Sempre*. http://www.xinguvivo.org.br/2010/10/27/cartas-a-dilma-e-serra-pedem-posicionamento-sobre-belo-monte/ (12 June 2012).

Melo, Liana. "Mineração em terra indígena só com aval dos índios." O blog verde. *O Globo*, 9 April 2009. http://oglobo.globo.com/blogs/blogverde/posts/2009/04/19/mineracao-em-terra-indigena-so-com-aval-dos-indios-178549.asp (12 June 2012).

"Memorial do Sr. Lyrio Arlindo do Valle, diretamente ao Sr. Dr. Getúlio Dorneles Vargas." September 1945. MI/SEDOC.

Menchú, Rigoberta. *Rigoberta: La nieta de los mayas*. Mexico City: Aguilar, 1998.

———. *Me llamo Rigoberta Menchú y así me nació la conciencia*. Edited by Elizabeth Burgos. Mexico City: Siglo XXI, 1983.

Meyer, Marlyse. *Folhetim: Uma história*. São Paulo: Companhia das Letras, 1996.

Michaelsen, Scott, and David E. Johnson, eds. *Border Theory: The Limits of Cultural Politics*. Minneapolis: University of Minnesota Press, 1997.

Mignolo, Walter D. "The Communal and the Decolonial." In *Rethinking Intellectuals in Latin America*, edited by Mabel Moraña, 245–63. Madrid: Iberoamericana, 2010.

———. *The Darker Side of the Renaissance: Literacy, Territoriality, and Colonization*. Ann Arbor: University of Michigan Press, 1995.

———. "Globalization, Civilization Processes, and the Relocation of Languages and Cultures." In *The Cultures of Globalization*, edited by Fredric Jameson and Masao Miyoshi, 32–53. Durham, N.C.: Duke University Press, 1998.

———. *Local Histories/Global Designs: Coloniality, Subaltern Knowledges, and Border Thinking*. Princeton, N.J.: Princeton University Press, 2000.

———. "When Speaking Was Not Good Enough: Illiterates, Barbarians, Savages, and Cannibals." In *Amerindian Images and the Legacy of Columbus*, edited by Rene Jara and Nicholas Spadaccini, 312–45. Minneapolis: University of Minneapolis Press, 1992.

Mignolo, Walter, and Elizabeth Hill Boone, eds. *Writing without Words*. Durham, N.C.: Duke University Press, 1994.

Miguel, Robson. Carta a Juvenal Payayá. *Blog de Juvenal Payayá*, 6 February 2010. http://juvenal.teodoro.blog.uol.com.br/arch2010-05-30_2010-06-05. html#2010_06-03_10_00_27-9811273-0 (12 June 2012).

Miles, Robert. *Racism after Race Relations*. London: Routledge, 1993.

Ministério de Agricultura. "Legislação." 1920. SEDOC/MI. Microfilm 380.

Minh-Ha, Trinh. *Woman, Native, Other: Writing Postcoloniality and Feminism*. Bloomington: Indiana University Press, 1989.

Mishkin, Bernard. "Fundamental Education: Interim Report on Fundamental Education in the Hylean Amazon." Paris: UNESCO, 1947.

———. "Fundamental Education: Second Interim Report on Fundamental Education in the Hylean Amazon." Paris: UNESCO, 1947.

———. "Good Neighbors." *The Nation*, 26 November 1947. 510–15.

———. "Problems of Fundamental Education in the Amazon Area." Mexico City: UNESCO, 1947.

Mohn, Otto Ernesto. Letter to Herbert Serpa, 6 April 1948. SEDOC/MI. Microfilm 289.

Monteiro, Mário Ypiranga. *Teatro Amazonas*. Manaus: Valer Editora, 2003.

Morais, Fernando. *Chatô: O rei do Brasil*. São Paulo: Companhia das Letras, 1994.

Moreiras, Alberto. "The Aura of Testimonio." In *The Real Thing*, edited by Georg Gugelburger, 192–224. Durham, N.C.: Duke University Press, 1996.

———. *The Exhaustion of Difference*. Durham, N.C.: Duke University Press, 2001.

———. "Freedom from Transculturation: A Response to Priscilla Archibald." *Social Text* 25, no. 4 (2007): 115–22.

———. "A Second Look: On Brotherson re Levinson and Testimonio Criticism." *Journal of Latin American Cultural Studies* 6, no. 2 (1997): 227–32.

Mota, Carlos Guilherme. "Cultura e política no Estado Novo (1937–1945)." In *Encontros com a civilização brasileira*. Rio de Janeiro: Civilização Brasileira, 1979.

Moura Pessoa, Maria Alice. "Aplicação dos 'testes ABC' em crianças terenas e caiuás de Matto Grosso." *Revista Brasileira de Estudos Pedagógicos* 3, no. 8 (1945): 191–207.

Moya, Ruth. *Desde el aula bilingüe*. Chimaltenango: Editorial Sabq'e, 1996.

Munduruku, Daniel. *Coisas de índio*. São Paulo: Callis, 2003.

———. "A corrupção do conhecimento ancestral dos povos indígenas." In *Sol do pensamento*, edited by Eliane Potiguara, 20–24. São Paulo: Inbrapi/Grumin, 2005.

———. *DM projetos especiais: O blog de Daniel Munduruku*. http://daniel munduruku.blogspot.com/ (12 June 2012).

———. *Histórias de índio*. São Paulo: Companhia das Letras, 1997.

———. *Meu vô Apolinário*. São Paulo: Studio Nobel, 2001.

———. *Todas as coisas são pequenas*. São Paulo: ARX, 2008.

———. "Visões de ontem." In *Metade cara, metade máscara*, by Eliane Potiguara, 15–20. São Paulo: Global, 2004.

———. *Você lembra, pai?* São Paulo: Global, 2003.

Muñoz M., Jairo. "Identidad étnica y educación." *Pueblo indígenas y educación* 7 (1988): 7–12.

"Na cidade maravilhosa, a mais bela kalapalo." *A Época*, 16 November 1952, 2.

Navarro Florida, Pedro. "Un país sin indios: La imagen de la Pampa y la Patagonia en la geografía del naciente estado argentino." *Scripta Nova* 51 (1999). http://www.ub.edu/geocrit/sn-51.htm (12 June 2012).

New Age Frauds and Plastic Shamans (NAFPS). http://newagefraud.org/ (12 June 2012).

Newcomb, Steven T. *Pagans in the Promised Land*. Golden, Colo.: Fulcrum, 2008.

Newmanezinho. Comment on Liana Melo. "Mineração em terra indígena só com aval dos índios." O blog verde, *O Globo*, 9 April 2009. http://oglobo.globo.com/servicos/blog/comentarios.asp?cod_Post=178549 (11 June 2011).

Nicolle, David. *The Normans*. Oxford: Osprey, 1987.

Nietzsche, Friedrich. *On the Genealogy of Morals*. Translated by Walter Kaufmann. New York: Vintage, 1969.

Niezen, Richard. *The Origins of Indigenism: Human Rights and the Politics of Identity*. Berkeley: University of California Press, 2003.

Nincao, Onilda Sanches. "Kóho Yoko Hovôvo/O Tuiuiú e o Sapo." Ph.D. diss., Universidade Estatual de Campinas, 2008.

Nodelman, Perry. *The Hidden Adult: Defining Children's Literature*. Baltimore: Johns Hopkins University Press, 2008.

Nogueira, Lenita W. M. "Música e política: O caso de Carlos Gomes." *Anais da ANPPOM* (2005): 243–49.

———. "O progresso e a produção musical de Carlos Gomes entre 1879 e 1885." *OPUS* 10 (2004): 37–46.

Nossa, Leonêncio. "O grande inimigo é a falta de assistência aos índios." *O Estado de São Paulo*, 4 February 2004, 8.

"A nossa opinião: Diacuí matou Iracema." *Diário Carioca*, 23 November 1952, 4.

"A nuestros lectores." *El Cabichuí*, 13 May 1867, 1.

Oilam, José. *Marlière o civilizador*. Belo Horizonte: Itatiaia, 1958.

Oliveira Junior, A. S. "Bilhete da Guanabara." *A Época*, 14 April 1947.

Ong, Walter J. *Orality and Literacy*. New York: Methuen, 1982.

O Paiz, 6 March 1911.

Organización del Tratado de Cooperación Amazónica (OTCA). *Tierras y áreas indígenas en la Amazonía*. Lima: OTCA, 1997.

Orico, Osvaldo. "Looping the Loop: Carlos Gomes e o Pará." *Careta*, 11 July 1936, 15–17.

Ortiz, Fernando. *Contrapunteo cubano del tabaco y el azúcar*. Barcelona: Ariel, 1940.

Ortiz, Renato. *A diversidade dos sotaques*. São Paulo: Brasiliense, 2008.

Pandolfi, Dulce. *Repensando o Estado Novo*. Rio de Janeiro: Fundação Getúlio Vargas, 1999.

Patai, Daphne. "Whose Truth?" In *The Rigoberta Menchú Controversy*, edited by Arturo Arias, 270–87. Minneapolis: University of Minnesota Press, 2001.

Payayá, Juvenal. *Blog de Juvenal Payayá*, 22 July 2006. http://juvenal.teodoro.blog.uol.com.br/ (12 June 2012).

———. "Reflexões indígenas sobre direito e propiedade." In *Sol do pensamento*, edited by Eliane Potiguara, 37–41. São Paulo: Inbrapi/Grumin, 2005.

Pena, Sérgio D. J., and Maria Cátira Bortolini. "Pode a genética definir quem deve se beneficiar das cotas universitárias e demais ações afirmativas?" *Estudos Avançados* 18, no. 50 (2004): 31–50.

"Personagem—Papa-Capim." Portal Turma da Mônica. http://www.monica.com.br /index.htm (15 July 2012).

Pessoa, Igor. "Todas as tribos." *Carta Capital*, 8 November 2000, 20–29.

Peterson, Jacqueline, and Jennifer Brown, eds. *The New Peoples: Being and Becoming Métis in North America*. Lincoln: University of Nebraska Press, 1985.

Pieterse, Jan Nederveen. *Development Theory*. Thousand Oaks, Calif.: Sage, 2009.

"Pintura de Vivi Castro brinca com Obama e Lula." *Abril*, 21 February 2009. http:// www.abril.com.br/blog/carnaval-2009/2009/02/pintura-vivi-castro-brinca-com -obama-lula/ (12 June 2012).

Pires Menezes, Maria Lucia. *Parque Indígena do Xingu*. Campinas: UNICAMP, 1999.

Plank, David N. *The Means of Our Salvation: Public Education in Brazil, 1930–95*. Boulder, Colo.: Westview, 1996.

Poole, Deborah. *Vision, Race and Modernity: A Visual Economy of the Andean Image World*. Princeton, N.J.: Princeton University Press, 1997.

Portugal Mollinedo, Pedro. "Evo Morales en el ejército del poder." *Pukara* 16 (2007). http://www.periodicopukara.com/pasados/pukara-16-articulo-del-mes.php (12 June 2012).

Postero, Nancy. *Now We Are Citizens: Indigenous Politics in Post-Multicultural Bolivia*. Stanford, Calif.: Stanford University Press, 2006.

Potiguara, Eliane. *GRUMIN/Rede de Comunicação Indígena*, 31 October 2006. http://elianepotiguara.org.br/noticias/ (12 June 2012).

———. "A informação para o desenvolvimento indígena não está em nossas mãos." In *Sol do pensamento*, edited by Eliana Potiguara, 7–10. São Paulo: Inbrapi/Grumin, 2005.

———. *Literatura indígena: Um pensamento brasileiro* (web page), 2005. http:// www.elianepotiguara.org.br/ (12 June 2012).

———. *Literatura indígena* (listserv), 21 June 2002. http://br.groups.yahoo.com /group/literaturaindigena/ (12 June 2012).

———. *Metade cara, metade máscara*. São Paulo: Global, 2004.

———, ed. *Sol do pensamento*. São Paulo: Inbrapi/Grumin. 2005.

"Povos indígenas no Brasil." *Instituto Socioambiental*, 30 January 2011. http://pib .socioambiental.org/pt (12 June 2012).

Pozzi-Escot, Inés. "Un testimonio de fe." *Pueblo indígenas y educación* 17 (1991): 114–20.

Prada, Manuel Gonzáles. *Pájinas libres*. Lima: Thesis, 1966 [1894].

Prado, Thays. "André Baniwa e o novo índio brasileiro." *Planeta sustentável*, 17 April 2009. http://planetasustentavel.abril.com.br/noticia/desenvolvimento/conteudo _450216.shtml (12 June 2012).

"Presidente Alan García advierte a nativos." *Peru.com*, 5 June 2009. http://www .peru.com/noticias/portada20090605/37781/Presidente-Alan-Garcia-advierte -a-nativos-Ya-esta-bueno-de-protestas (12 June 2012).

"Presidenta Dilma assina decreto da PNGATI e homologa sete terras indígenas."
FUNAI, 5 June 2012. http://www.funai.gov.br/ultimas/noticias/2012/06_jun
/20120605_03.html (12 June 2012).

"Primeiro Encontro Nacional de Educação Indígena." Guarani-Bracuí, Rio de Janeiro.
March 2000. Video. SEDOC/MI.

Prata de Sousa, Jorge. *Escravidão ou morte: Os escravos brasileiros na guerra do
Paraguai*. Rio de Janeiro: Mauad, 1996.

Pratt, Mary Louise. *Imperial Eyes: Travel Writing and Transculturation*. London:
Routledge, 1992.

———. "Planetarity." In *Intercultural Dialogue*, edited by Mary Louise Pratt, Ronald
G. Manley, and Susan Bassnett, 10–31. London: British Council, 2004.

Price, David. *Before the Bulldozer: The Nambiquara Indians and the World Bank*.
Washington, D.C.: Seven Locks, 1989.

Price, Williard. *The Amazing Amazon*. London: William Heinemann, 1952.

"Primeiro Congresso Inter-americano de Indianistas." *Correio da Manhã*, 2 October
1939.

Professores de Pataxó do Extremo Sul da Bahia. *Uma história de resistência pataxó*.
Salvador: ANAI, CESE, MEC, 2007.

Programa de Aceleração do Crescimento (PAC). Portal Brasil. http://www.brasil.gov
.br/pac (12 June 2012).

Provedello, Maysa. "Marcos Terena: Em busca de reconhecimento." *Desafios do
Desenvolvimiento* 8 (2004). http://www.ipea.gov.br/desafios/index.php?option
=com_content&view=article&id=1318:entrevistas-materias&Itemid=41 (12 June
2012).

Prucha, Francis. *Documents of United States Indian Policy*. Lincoln: University of
Nebraska Press, 1975.

Pulitano, Elvira. *Toward a Native American Critical Theory*. Lincoln: University of
Nebraska Press, 2003.

"O que os índios disseram a Dilma Rousseff." *Minuto*, 6 June 2012. http://dominuto
.com.br/o-que-os-indios-disseram-a-dilma-rousseff/ (12 June 2012).

"Querem comer nossas matas." *Revista Bundas*, 23 May 2000, cover.

Rabelo, Genival. *Ocupação da Amazônia*. Rio de Janeiro: Gernasa, 1968.

Rama, Ángel. *La ciudad letrada*. Hanover, N.H.: Del Norte, 1984.

———. *Transculturación narrativa en América Latina*. Mexico City: Siglo XXI,
1982.

Ramos, Alcida. "Brasil no século XXI." Paper presented at BRASA Conference,
Brasília, 22 July 2010.

———. "The Commodification of the Indian." *Série Antropologia* 281 (2000): 2–17.

———. "The Hyperreal Indian." *Critique of Anthropology* 14, no. 2 (1994): 153–71.

———. *Indigenism: Ethnic Politics in Brazil*. Madison: University of Wisconsin
Press, 1999.

———. "The Indigenous Movement in Brazil." *Cultural Survival* 21, no. 2 (1997):
50–53.

———. *Sanumá Memories: Yanomami Ethnography in Times of Crisis*. Madison:
University of Wisconsin Press, 1995.

Rappaport, Joanne. *Intercultural Utopias: Public Intellectuals, Cultural Experimentation, and Ethnic Pluralism in Colombia*. Durham, N.C.: Duke University Press, 2005.

Raytheon Corporation. "SIVAM Presentation," Massachusetts Institute of Technology, November 2002. http://web.mit.edu/12.000/www/m2006/kvh/sivam.html (12 June 2012).

Raeders, Georges. *Dom Pedro II e o conde de Gobineau*. São Paulo: Nacional, 1938.

Rede Brasileira de Instituições de Ensino Superior com Programas e Projetos para Povos Indígenas no Brasil (REDE). "Conheça a REDE." 1 January 2011. http://redesestudantesindigenas.unemat.br/htm/home.php (12 June 2012).

Reichmann, Rebecca. *Race in Contemporary Brazil: From Indifference to Inequality*. University Park: Pennsylvania State University Press, 1999.

Reinaga, Fausto. *La revolución india*. La Paz: Partido Indio de Bolivia (PIB), 1969.

Reis, João José. *Slave Rebellion in Brazil*. Translated by Arthur Brakel. Baltimore: John Hopkins University Press, 1993.

Rejistro Oficial del Gobierno Provisorio. 1869 and 1870. Asunsión: Imprenta de *El Pueblo*, 1871.

Relatório de pesquisas. SEDOC/MI. Microfilm 335.

Reynaga Burgoa, Ramiro. *Ideología y raza en América Latina*. La Paz: Ediciones Futuro Bolivia, 1972.

———. *Reconstruyamos nuestro cerebro*. Chukiawu-Kullasuyu [Bolivia]: Sataña Ph'ajsi, 1979.

———. *Tawantinsuyu: Cinco siglos de guerra queswaymara contra España*. La Paz: Centro de Coordinación y Promoción Campesina Mink'a, 1978.

Ribeiro, Berta G. *O índio na cultura brasileira*. Rio de Janeiro: União Brasileira Desenvolvimento Económico (UNIBRADE), 1987.

Ribeiro, Darcy. *As Américas e a civilização*. Rio de Janeiro: Civilização Brasileira, 1970.

———. *Arte plumária dos índios kaapor*. Rio de Janeiro: Gráfica Seikel, 1957.

———. *O Brasil como problema*. Rio de Janeiro: Francisco Alves, 1995.

———. "Carta à diretoria do SPI." Rio de Janeiro: SPI, 1995. In *Parque Indígena do Xingu*, by Maria Lúcia Pires Menezes. Campinas: UNICAMP, 1995. 97–107.

———. *Confissões*. São Paulo: Companhia das Letras, 1997.

———. *Diários índios*. São Paulo: Schwarcz, 1996.

———. *Os índios e a civilização*. São Paulo: Companhia das Letras, 1996 [1970].

———. *Maíra*. São Paulo: Círculo do Livro, n.d.

———. *Mestiço é que é bom!* Rio de Janeiro: Revan, 1996.

———. "Notas críticas sobre a atuação do SPI junto aos índios no sul de Mato Grosso." 1 January 1950. SEDOC/MI. Microfilm 381.

———. *O povo brasileiro*. São Paulo: Companhia das Letras, 1995.

Quijano, Aníbal, and Immanuel Wallerstein. "Americanity as a Concept, or the Americas in the Modern World System." *International Social Science Journal* 134 (1992): 549–57.

Quispe Huanca, Felipe. *El indio en escena*. La Paz: Ediciones Pachakuti, 1999.

———. *Tupak Katari vive y vuelve—carajo*. 2d ed. Bolivia: Ediciones Ofensiva Roja, 1990.

Quispe Huanca, Felipe, and Confederación Sindical Única de Trabajadores Campesinos de Bolivia. "Pachakuti educativo: Propuesta de la CSUTCB al II Congreso Nacional de Educación, basada en el modelo de ayllu." Qullasuyo [Bolivia]: Confederación Sindical Única de Trabajadores Campesinos de Bolivia, 2005.

Riviere, Peter. *The Forgotten Frontier: Rancher of North Brazil*. New York: Holt, Rinehart & Wilson, 1972.

Robinson, Mabel Louise. *Runner of the Mountaintops: The Life of Louis Agassiz*. New York: Random House, 1939.

Rocha Freire, Carlos Agosto da. "Indigenismo e antropologia: O CNPI na gestão Rondon (1935–1955)." Ph.D. diss., Universidade Federal do Rio de Janeiro, 1990.

———. *O SPI na Amazônia*. Rio de Janeiro: Museu do Índio, 2007.

Rogers, Joel Augustus. *World's Great Men of Color*. Vol. 2. Introduction and commentary by John Henrik Clarke. New York: Simon and Schuster, 1996.

Rohter, Larry. "Deep in Brazil, a Flight of Paranoid Fancy." *New York Times*, 23 June 2002. http://www.nytimes.com/2002/06/23/weekinreview/ideas-trends-deep-in -brazil-a-flight-of-paranoid-fancy.html?pagewanted=all&src=pm (12 June 2012).

Romanelli, Otaíza de Oliveira. *História da educação no Brasil*. Petrópolis: Vozes, 1999.

Romero, Sylvio. *Machado de Assis: Estudo comparativo de litteratura brasileira*. Rio de Janeiro: Laemmert, 1897.

Rondon, Cândido Mariano da Silva. "Exposição que acompanha o ofício n. 306, de 7/VI/1946" (Report to Minister of Agriculture Manoel Neto Campelo Junior from the Conselho Nacional de Proteção aos Índios, CNPI). 1946. SEDOC/MI. Microfilm 380.

———. "O índio é a maior preciosidade que encontramos na Marcha para o Oeste." *O Radical*, 4 September 1940, 5.

———. Letter to John Collier, 28 January 1947. SEDOC/MI. Microfilm 359.

"Rondon favorável ao casamento do branco com a índia Dacuí [*sic*]." *O Jornal*, 17 October 1952, 8.

Sá, Lúcia. "Índia romântica, brancos realistas." In *Ierecê a guaná*, by Alfredo d'Escragnolle Taunay. Edited by Sérgio Luiz Medeiros, 133–43. São Paulo: Iluminuras, 2000.

———. *Rainforest Literatures: Amazonian Texts and Latin American Culture*. Minneapolis: University of Minnesota Press, 2004.

Sadlier, Darlene. *Brazil Imagined: 1500 to the Present*. Austin: University of Texas Press, 2008.

Said, Edward W. *Culture and Imperialism*. New York: Vintage, 1994.

———. *Orientalism*. Random House: New York, 1978.

Salina, Nilton. "Arco e flecha, só para pose diante das câmeras." *O Estado de São Paulo*, 23 April 2004, A4.

Salm, Rodolfo. "Avatar II: A luta contra Belo Monte." *Portal Ecodebate*, 11 April 2010. http://www.ecodebate.com.br/2010/04/11/uhe-belo-monte-avatar-ii-a-luta -contra-belo-monte-artigo-de-rodolfo-salm/ (12 June 2012).

Sánchez, Luis Alberto. "Batiburrillo indigenista." *Mundial* 349 (18 February 1927). In *La polémica del indigenismo*, edited by Manuel Aquézolo Castro, 69–73. Lima: Mosca Azul, 1976.

Sanders, Edith R. "The Hamitic Hypothesis: Its Origin and Functions in Time Perspective." *Journal of African History* 10 (1969): 521–32.

Sanjinés, Javier. *Mestizaje Upside Down: Aesthetic Politics in Modern Bolivia*. Pittsburgh: University of Pittsburgh Press, 2004.

Sansone, Livio. *Blackness without Ethnicity: Constructing Race in Brazil*. New York: Palgrave, 2003.

Santos, Leinad A. O., Lúcia M. M. Andrade, and Robin Wright. *Hydroelectric Dams on Brazil's Xingu River and Indigenous Peoples*. Cambridge: Cultural Survival, 1990.

Santos, Sales Augusto dos. "A formação do mercado de trabalho livre em São Paulo: Tensões raciais e marginalização social." M.A. thesis, Universidade de Brasília, 1997.

———. "Historical Roots of the Whitening of Brazil." *Latin American Perspectives* 29, no. 1 (2002): 61–82.

———. "Who Is Black in Brazil?" *Latin American Perspectives* 33, no. 4 (2006): 30–48.

Sarmiento, Domingo Faustino. *Las escuelas: Base de la prosperidad de la república en los Estados Unidos*. New York: n.p., 1866.

———. *Facundo: Civilización y barbarie*. Barcelona: Planeta, 1986 [1845].

Scheina, Robert L. *Latin America's Wars*. Dulles, Va.: Brassey's, 2003.

Scheper-Hughes, Nancy. *Death without Weeping: The Violence of Everyday Life in Brazil*. Berkeley: University of California Press, 1992.

Schiwy, Freya. *Indianizing Film: Decolonization, the Andes, and the Question of Technology*. New Brunswick, N.J.: Rutgers University Press, 2009.

Schmuziger Carvalho, Silvia M. "Chaco: Encruzilhada de povos e 'melting pot' cultural." In *História dos índios no Brasil*, edited by Manuela Carneiro da Cunha, 457–74. São Paulo: Companhia das Letras, 1992.

Schultz, Harold, and Nilo Oliveira Vellozo, dirs. *Curt Nimuendajú e Icatú: Dois postos indígenas de nacionalização*. Film. Seção de Estudos do SPI, 1942.

Schwarcz, Lilia Moritz. *O espectáculo das raças: Cientistas, instituicoes e questao racial no Brasil, 1870–1930*. São Paulo: Companhia das Letras, 1993.

Schwarz, Roberto. *Misplaced Ideas: Essays on Brazilian Culture*. New York: Verso, 1992.

Schwartz, Jorge, ed. *Las vanguardias latinoamericanas*. Madrid: Cátedra, 1991.

Semali, Ladislaus, and Joe L. Kincheloe, eds. *What Is Indigenous Knowledge?* New York: Routledge, 1999.

Sepúlveda, Juan Ginés de. *Tratado sobre las justas causas de la guerra contra los indios*. Mexico City: Fondo de Cultura Económica, 1987.

Serpa, Herbert. Letter to Otto Mohn, May 1948. SEDOC/MI. Microfilm 289.

———. "RES NOSTRA–O Dia do Índio." *Correio da Noite*, 22 April 1944.

———. "Saudação." Ministério de Agricultura, 19 April 1945. SEDOC/MI.

Serviço de Proteção aos Índios (SPI). "Projeto de regulação." 1935. SEDOC/MI. Microfilm 380.

———. "Relatório ao Ministro da Guerra." 1911. SEDOC/MI.

———. "Reportagem para a Bulletin of the International American Institute." 1933. SEDOC/MI.

———. "Sobre a classificação dos índios." n.d. SEDOC/MI. Microfilm 380.

"O Serviço de Proteção aos Índios." *Jornal do Brasil*, 18 September 1929.

"Serviço de Proteção aos Índios: Sucursal nativa do racismo!" *Tribuna de Minas*, 4 November 1952.

Seyferth, Giralda. "Os imigrantes e a campanha de nacionalização do Estado Novo." In *Repensando o Estado Novo*, edited by Dulce Pandolfi, 199–228. Rio de Janeiro: Fundação Getúlio Vargas, 1999.

Shah, Alpa. *In the Shadows of the State: Indigenous Politics, Environmentalism, and Insurgency in Jharkhand, India*. Durham, N.C.: Duke University Press, 2010.

Shaw, Karena. *Indigeneity and Political Theory: Sovereignty and the Limits of the Political*. New York: Routledge, 2008.

Sierra Camacho, María Teresa. *La lucha por los derechos indígenas en el Brasil actual*. Mexico City: Centro de Investigaciones y Estudios Superiores en Antropología Social (CIESAS), 1993.

Simon, Iumna Maria. "Esteticismo e participação." *Novos Estudos* 26 (1990): 120–40.

Simpson, Amelia. *Xuxa: The Mega-marketing of Gender, Race, and Modernity*. Philadelphia: Temple University Press, 1993.

Skidmore, Thomas. *Black into White: Race and Nationality in Brazilian Thought*. Oxford: Oxford University Press, 1974.

———. *The Politics of Military Rule in Brazil*. Oxford: Oxford University Press, 1988.

Slater, Candace. *Entangled Edens: Visions of the Amazon*. Berkeley: University of California Press, 2002.

Smith, Carol, ed. *Guatemalan Indians and the State*. Austin: University of Texas Press, 1990.

Smith, David C., and Harold W. Borns Jr. "Louis Agassiz, the Great Deluge, and Early Maine Geology." *Northeastern Naturalist* 7, no. 2 (2000): 157–77.

Smith, David, Dorothy Solinger, and Steven C. Topik, eds. *States and Sovereignty in the Global Economy*. New York: Routledge, 1999.

"Sobre as causas determinantes da diminuição das populações indígenas do Brasil." 1945. SEDOC/MI. Microfilm 340.

Sodré, Nelson Werneck. *História da imprensa no Brasil*. Rio de Janeiro: Mauad, 1999.

Sommer, Doris. *Foundational Fictions: The National Romances of Latin America*. Berkeley: University of California Press, 1991.

———. *Proceed with Caution When Engaged with Minority Writing in the Americas*. Cambridge: Harvard University Press, 1999.

———. "Rigoberta's Secrets." *Latin American Perspectives* 18, no. 3 (1991): 32–50.

Souza Lima, Antonio Carlos de. *Um grande cerco de paz: Poder tutelar, indianidade e formação do estado no Brasil*. Petrópolis: Vozes, 1995.

————. "On Indigenism and Nationality in Brazil." In *Nation-States and Indians in Latin America*, edited by Greg Urban and Joel Sherzer, 236–57. Austin: University of Texas Press, 1991.

Spivak, Gayatri Chakravorty. "Can the Subaltern Speak?" In *Marxism and the Interpretation of Culture*, edited by Cary Nelson and Lawrence Grossberg, 271–313. Urbana: University of Illinois Press, 1988.

————. "Practical Politics of the Open End." In *The Postcolonial Critic*, edited by Sarah Harasym. New York: Routledge, 1990.

Stam, Robert. *Tropical Multiculturalism: A Comparative History of Race in Brazilian Cinema and Culture*. Durham, N.C.: Duke University Press, 1997.

Stepan, Nancy Leys. *The Hour of Eugenics: Race, Gender, and Nation in Latin America*. Ithaca, N.Y.: Cornell University Press, 1991.

————. *Picturing Tropical Nature*. Ithaca, N.Y.: Cornell University Press, 2001.

Stoll, David. *Rigoberta Menchú and the Story of All Poor Guatemalans*. Boulder, Colo.: Westview, 1999.

"The Strange Case of Colonel Fawcett." *Life*, 30 April 1951. 95–103.

Sturm, Circe. *Becoming Indian: The Struggle over Cherokee Identity in the Twenty-First Century*. Santa Fe, N.M.: School for Advanced Research Press, 2011.

Sullivan, Michael, and Paulo Massadas. 1988. "Brincar de índio." Recorded by Xuxa. On *Xou da Xuxa 3* (CD). Som Livre.

Summerhill, William. *Order against Progress: Government, Foreign Investment, and Railroads in Brazil, 1854–1913*. Stanford, Calif.: Stanford University Press, 2007.

Survival International. "Gunmen Destroy Indigenous Camp." 23 August 2011. http://www.survivalinternational.org/news/7622 (12 June 2012).

Szmrecsányi, Tamás, and Pedro Ramos. "O papel das políticas governamentais na modernização da agricultura brasileira." In *História econômica do Brasil contemporáneo*, edited by Tamás Szmrecsányi and Wilson Suzigan, 227–49. São Paulo: Hucitec, 2002.

Tagore, Rabindranath. Poem 60. In *Gitanjali*. Wellesley, Mass.: 2000.

Tamayo Herrera, José. *Historia del indigenismo cuzqueño, siglos XVI–XX*. Lima: Instituto Nacional de Cultura, 1980.

"Tata piriri." *Cacique Lambaré*, 22 August 1867, 4.

Taunay, Alfredo d'Escragnolle. *Entre os nossos índios*. São Paulo: Melhoramentos, 1931.

————. *Memórias*. Edited by Sérgio Medeiros. São Paulo: Iluminuras, 2004.

————. *Reminiscências*. 2nd ed. São Paulo: Companhia Melhoramentos de S. Paulo, 1923.

————. *A retirada da Laguna*. São Paulo: Ediouro, n.d. [1874].

————. *Scenas de viagem: A campanha de Matto Grosso*. São Paulo: Globo, 1923.

Taunay, Alfredo d'Escragnolle, and Rodolfo Paravicini. *O escravo: Drama lírico em quatro atos*. Maranhão: Governo do Estado do Maranhão, 1988.

Taussig, Michael. *Shamanism, Colonialism, and the Wild Man: A Study in Terror and Healing*. Chicago: University of Chicago Press, 1987.

Tavares Coelho, Marco Antônio. "Genocídio e resgate dos Botocudos: Entrevista com Ailton Krenak." *Estudos Avançados* 23, no. 65 (2009): 193–204.

Taylor, Matthew, and Vinícius Buranelli. "Ending Up in Pizza." *Latin American Politics and Society* 49, no. 1 (2007): 59–87.

Teixeira, Anísio. *Educação não é privilégio*. São Paulo: Nacional, 1977.

Teixeira da Fonseca Vasconcelos, Vicente de Pablo. "A obra de proteção ao indígena no Brasil." *América Indígena* 1, no. 1 (1940): 21–28.

"Tentação nas selvas." *O Globo*, 26 September 1952, 1.

Terena, M. Marcos. "Uma candidatura indígena." *Facebook*, 15 September 2010.

———. "M. Marcos Terena." 2010. http://marcosterena.blogspot.com/ (12 June 2012).

———. "Traditional Kuarup Rituals of Alto Xingú, Pantanal, and Southwest Brazil." In *Historic Cities and Sacred Sites*, edited by Ismail Serageldin, Ephim Shluger, and Joan Martin-Brown. Washington, D.C.: World Bank, 2001.

———. "Vôo do índio" (letter to journalist Zózimo Barroso from 26 July 1990). *Folha do Meio Ambiente*, 26 April 2007. http://www.folhadomeio.com.br/publix/fma /folha/2007/04/carta_terena176.html (12 June 2012).

Terena, M. Marcos, and Ateneia Feijó. *O índio aviador*. São Paulo: Moderna, 1995.

Terena, M. Marcos, and Edgar Morin. *Saberes globais e saberes locais*. Rio de Janeiro: Garamond, 2000.

Theatro Lyrico. "O guarany." *Jornal do Commercio*, 19 December 1870.

Theatro Lyrico Brazileiro. *O escravo: Drama lyrico em 4 actos*. Rio de Janeiro: Nuno da Graça, 1889.

Theatro Lyrico Fluminense. "Opera italiana: *Il guarany*." *Jornal do Commercio*, 29 November 1870.

Tilley, Virginia Q. "The Role of the State in Ethnic Conflict: A Constructivist Reassessment." In *Constructivism and Comparative Politics*, edited by Daniel M. Green, 151–74. New York: M. E.Sharpe, Inc., 2002.

Tinhorão, José Ramos. *O romance em folhetins no Brasil (1830 à atualidade)*. São Paulo: Duas Cidades, 1994.

Torres, Antônio. "Entrevista com Luis Pimentel." *Revista Bundas*, 9 May 2000, 6–11.

"Transcript: Presidential Debate, Winston-Salem, N.C." *Washington Post*, 11 October 2000. http://www.washingtonpost.com/wp-srv/onpolitics/elections/debatetext 101100.htm (1 October 2012).

Treece, David. *Exiles, Allies, Rebels: Brazil's Indianist Movement, Indigenist Politics, and the Imperial Nation-State*. Westport, Conn.: Greenwood, 2000.

Trend, David. "Democracy's Crisis of Meaning." In *Radical Democracy: Identity, Citizenship, and the State*, edited by David Trend, 7–18. New York: Routledge, 1996.

Trexler, Richard. *Sex and Conquest: Gendered Violence, Political Order, and the European Conquest of the Americas*. Ithaca, N.Y.: Cornell University Press, 1999.

Troncarelli, Maria Cristina, Kaomi Suyá Kaiabi, and Instituto Socioambiental. *Brasil e África: Uma visão xinguana da formação do povo brasileiro*. São Paulo: Instituto Socioambiental (ISA), 1999.

Tucci Carneiro, Maria Luiza. *Preconceito racial em Portugal e Brasil-Colônia*. São Paulo: Perspectiva, 2005.

Tuhiwai Smith, Linda. *Decolonizing Methodologies: Research and Indigenous Peoples*. London: Zed, 1999.

Turner, Dale. "Oral Traditions and the Politics of (Mis)Recognition." In *American Indian Thought*, edited by Anne Waters, 229–38. Malden, Mass.: Blackwell, 2004.

———. *This Is Not a Peace Pipe: Towards a Critical Indigenous Philosophy*. Toronto: University of Toronto Press, 2006.

Turner, Terence. "Representing, Resisting, Rethinking: Essays on the Contextualization of Ethnographic Knowledge." In *Colonial Situations*, edited by George W. Stocking Jr., 285–313. Madison: University of Wisconsin Press, 1991.

"Unidos perante a lei Diacuí e Aires da Cunha." *A Hora*, 28 November 1952.

U.N. Human Rights Council. "Report by Special Rapporteur on the Situation of Human Rights and Fundamental Freedoms of Indigenous Peoples, James Anaya." 15th session, Agenda item 3, 15 September 2010.

Urban, Greg. "Interpretations of Inter-cultural Contact: The Shokleng and Brazilian National Society, 1914–1916." *Ethnohistory* 32, no. 3 (1985): 224–44.

———. "The Semiotics of State-Indian Linguistic Relationships." In *Nation-States and Indians in Latin America*, edited by Greg Urban and Joel Sherzer, 307–30. Austin: University of Texas Press, 1991.

Uriel García, J. "Problemas de sociología peruana." *Cuadernos Mexicanos* 9, no. 2 (1950): 147–79.

A usina hidroelétrica Belo Monte. Film. Norte Energia, 2011. http://www.youtube.com/watch?v=U6VNKvL1cMQ (10 June 2012).

U.S. State Department. "The 'U.S. Takeover of the Amazon Forest' Myth." 7 July 2005. http://www.america.gov/st/pubsenglish/2005/July/20050707124835atlahtneve10.1665003.html (12 June 2012).

Valcarcél, Luis E. *Memorias*. Lima: Instituto de Estudios Peruanos, 1981.

———. *Ruta cultural del Perú*. Mexico City: Fondo de Cultura Económica, 1945.

———. *Tempestad en los Andes*. Lima: Minerva, 1927.

Valiente, Teresa. "Doce años de PEEB-P." *Pueblo Indígenas y Educación* 18 (1991): 17–20.

Van Cott, Donna Lee. *The Friendly Liquidation of the Past: The Politics of Diversity in Latin America*. Pittsburgh: University of Pittsburgh Press, 2000.

———. *From Movements to Parties in Latin America: The Evolution of Ethnic Politics*. Cambridge: Cambridge University Press, 2007.

———. *Radical Democracy in the Andes*. Cambridge: Cambridge University Press, 2008.

Vargas, Getúlio. "Decreto 24.715." *Diário Oficial*, 12 July 1934.

Vargas Llosa, Mario. "Questions of Conquest." *Harper's*, December 1990: 45–53.

———. *El sueño del celta*. New York: Alfaguara, 2010.

———. *La utopía arcaica: José María Arguedas y las ficciones del indigenismo*. Mexico City: Fondo de Cultura Económica, 1996.

Vasconcelos, José. *La raza cósmica/The Cosmic Race*. Edited by Robert Reid-Pharr and translated by Didier T. Jaén. Baltimore: Johns Hopkins University Press, 1997 [1925].

Vasconcelos, Vicente de Paulo T. F. "Assistência aos índios." *Revista do Serviço Público* 3, no. 2 (1939). In "Sobre as causas determinantes da diminuição das populações indígenas do Brasil." 1945. SEDOC/MI. Microfilm 340.

Vattel, Emmerich de. *The Law of Nations*. Edited by Joseph Chitty. Philadelphia: T. and J. W. Johnson, 1883.

Veiga, Juracilda, and Wilmar Rocha d'Angelis. "Terra Indígena Icatu." *Portal Kaingang*. 2005. http://www.portalkaingang.org/index_icatu.htm (12 June 2012).

"A verdadeira catequese." *Correio da Manhã*, 4 April 1947, 4.

Verner, Dorte. "Tourism and Indigenous Peoples." *En Breve* 144 (2009): 1–4.

Vianna, Hermano. *The Mystery of Samba: Popular Music and National Identity in Brazil*. Translated by John Charles Chasteen. Chapel Hill: University of North Carolina Press, 1990.

Vicente, Angelina da Silva. "Escola Indígena Capitão Vitorino: Programa da festa em comemoração do Dia do Índio." 1965. SEDOC/MI.

———. "Relatórios da Atividade da Escola Indígena Capitão Vitorino, 1°–4° ano." 1965. SEDOC/MI.

Vidart, Daniel D., ed. *El mundo de los charrúas*. Montevideo: Banda Oriental, 1996.

Viera, Antônio. *Obras escolhidas*. Lisbon: Sá da Costa, 1951–54.

Viera, Hermes. "O romance de Carlos Gomes." *Fon Fon*, 18 July 1936, 16–17.

Viotti da Costa, Emília. *Da senzala à colônia*. São Paulo: Universidade Estadual Paulista (UNESP), 1997.

"O viúvo da Diacuí não aconselha casamento entre branco e índia." *O Globo*, 5 December 1960.

Viveiros de Castro, Eduardo. *From the Enemy's Point of View: Humanity and Divinity in an Amazonian Society*. Translated by Catherine V. Howard. Chicago: University of Chicago Press, 1992.

———. *The Inconsistency of the Indian Soul: The Encounter of Catholics and Cannibals in Sixteenth-Century Brazil*. Translated by Gregory Duff Morton. Chicago: Prickly Paradigm Press, 2011.

Vizenor, Gerald. *Manifest Manners: Narratives on Postindian Survivance*. Lincoln: University of Nebraska Press, 1999.

———. *Survivance: Narratives of Native Presence*. Lincoln: University of Nebraska Press, 2008.

Volpe, Maria Alice. "Remaking the Brazilian Myth of National Foundation: *Il Guarany*." *Latin American Music Review* 23, no. 2 (2002): 179–94.

von Ihering, Herman. The Anthropology of the State of São Paulo, Brazil. São Paulo: Duprat, 1904.

———. "El hombre prehistórico del Brasil." *Historia* 1, no. 1 (1903): 161–70.

———. "A questão dos índios no Brasil." *Revista do Museu Paulista* 8 (1911): 132–33.

———. *Revista do Museu Paulista*. Vol 6. São Paulo: Typographia do Diário Oficial, 1904.

Von Versen, Maximilian. *História da guerra do Paraguai*. São Paulo: Itatiaia, 1976 [1913].

———. "História da guerra do Paraguai e episódios de viagem na América do Sul." *Revista do Instituto Histórico e Geográfico Brasileiro* 76, pt. 2 (1914): 5–270.

Wade, Peter. *Race and Ethnicity in Latin America*. New York: Pluto, 1997.

Wagley, Charles. "Bernard Mishkin, 1913–1954." *American Anthropologist* 57, no. 5 (1995): 1033–35.

Walsh, Catherine. "Interculturalidad, colonialidad y educación." *Revista Educación y Pedagogía* 19, no. 48 (2007): 25–35.

———. *Interculturalidad, Estado, sociedad*. Quito: Universidad Andina Simón Bolívar (UASB), 2009.

———. "Post-coloniality in Ecuador." In *Coloniality at Large*, edited by Mabel Moraña, Enrique Dussel, and Carlos Jáugregui, 506–18. Durham, N.C.: Duke University Press, 2008.

Walzer, Michael. *Thick and Thin: Moral Argument at Home and Abroad*. Notre Dame, Ind.: University of Notre Dame Press, 1994.

Warren, Jonathan W. *Racial Revolutions: Antiracism and Indian Resurgence in Brazil*. Durham, N.C.: Duke University Press, 2001.

Warren, Kay B., and Jean Elizabeth Jackson. *Indigenous Movements, Self-Representation, and the State in Latin America*. Austin: University of Texas Press, 2002.

Wasserman, Renata R. Mautner. *Exotic Nations: Literature and Cultural Identity in the United States and Brazil, 1830–1930*. Ithaca, N.Y.: Cornell University Press, 1994.

Weber, David J. *Foreigners in Their Native Land: Historical Roots of the Mexican Americans*. Albuquerque: University of New Mexico Press, 2003.

Weber, Max. "Politics as a Vocation." In *From Max Weber: Essays in Sociology*, edited by H. H. Gerth and C. Wright Mills, 77–128. New York: Oxford University Press, 1946.

Weinstein, Barbara. *The Amazon Rubber Boom, 1850–1920*. Stanford, Calif.: Stanford University Press, 1983.

———. "Racializing Regional Difference." In *Race and Nation in Modern Latin America*, edited by Nancy Appelbaum, 237–62. Chapel Hill: University of North Carolina Press, 2003.

Whigham, Thomas, and Barbara Potthast. "Refining the Numbers: A Response to Reber and Kleinpenning." *Latin American Research Review* 37, no. 3 (2002): 143–48.

White, Clarence Cameron. "Antonio Carlos Gomes." *Negro History Bulletin* 4, no. 5 (February 1941): 104, 110.

White, Hayden. "The Politics of Historical Interpretation: Discipline and De-sublimation." *Critical Inquiry* 9 (1982): 113–37.

———. "Historical Emplotment and the Problem of Truth." In *Probing the Limits of Representation*, edited by Saul Friedlader, 37–53. Cambridge: Harvard University Press, 1992.

White, Richard. *The Middle Ground: Indians, Empires, and Republics in the Great Lakes Region, 1650–1815*. Cambridge: Cambridge University Press, 1991.

Williams, Daryle. *Culture Wars in Brazil: The First Vargas Regime, 1930–1945*. Durham, N.C.: Duke University Press, 2001.

Williams, Raymond. *Towards 2000*. London: Chatto & Windus, 1983.

Wisnik, José Miguel. *O coro dos contrários: A música em torno da Semana de 22*. São Paulo: Duas Cidades, 1977.

Wittcoff, Peter. "Amazon Surveillance System (SIVAM): U.S. and Brazilian Cooperation." M.A. thesis, Navy Postgraduate School, 1999.

"World Is a Global Village." *Explorations*, 18 May 1960. Guest: Marshall McLuhan. Hosts: Alan Miller and John O'Leary. Canadian Broadcasting Corporation. http:// www.cbc.ca/archives/categories/arts-entertainment/media/marshall-mcluhan -the-man-and-his-message/world-is-a-global-village.html (12 June 2012).

Yanomami, David. "Descobrindo o descobrimento." In *A outra margem do Ocidente*, edited by Adauto Novaes and Mino Funarte. Rio de Janeiro: Companhia das Letras, 1999.

Yashar, Deborah. *Contesting Citizenship in Latin America*. Cambridge: Cambridge University Press, 2005.

Yúdice, George. *The Expediency of Culture: Uses of Culture in the Global Era*. Durham, N.C.: Duke University Press, 2003.

———. "Postmodernity and Transnational Capitalism." In *Consumers and Citizens: Globalizationand Multicultural Conflicts*, by Nestor Canclini, ix–xxviii. Minneapolis: University of Minnesota Press, 2001.

Zavala, Iris. "La ética de la violencia: Identidad y silencio en 1494." *Revista Iberoamericana* 170–71 (1995): 13–26.

Zimmerman, Marc. *Literature and Resistance in Guatemalan Literature*. Athens: Ohio University Center for International Studies, 1995.

Zúñiga, Madeleine. "Educación en quechua y castellano en Ayacucho." In *Educación en poblaciones indígenas*. Santiago: Ansión Zuñiga y Cueva, 1987.

———. *Educación, escuelas y culturas indígenas de América Latina*. Vols. 1–2. Quito: Abya-Yala, 1986.

INDEX

Carneiro da Cunha, Manuela, 81, 223 (n. 49), 235 (n. 81)

Carta Régia of 2 December 1808, 81, 235 (n. 81)

Casa grande e senzala (Freyre), 49, 121. *See also* Freyre, Gilberto

Casa Ricordi, 69. *See also* Italy: Milan; Opera

Casement, Roger, 241 (n. 186), 246 (n. 61)

Cassino Fluminense, 92

Catherine de Medici, 239 (n. 152)

Catholic Church, 39, 170, 221 (n. 31), 257 (n. 47). *See also* Christianity; Christians

Cavalcante, José Bezerra, 129–30

Cavalcante, Sandra, 16

Ceará, 89, 123, 237 (n. 125)

Ceci (from *Il guarany*/*O guarany*), 63, 90, 99, 251 (n. 34)

Celso, Afonso, 71, 232 (n. 39)

Census, 23, 37, 38, 220 (nn. 18, 21, 22, 24)

Central America, 180, 213 (n. 25), 256 (n. 46). *See also* Guatemala

Chakrabarty, Dipesh, 58, 260 (nn. 103–4). *See also* "Asymmetric ignorance"

Chané, 84, 85

Chateaubriand, Assis, 134, 138, 139, 249 (n. 16), 251 (n. 35), 252 (n. 54)

Chateaubriand, François-René, 87, 237 (n. 127)

Chavez, Hugo, 260 (n. 97)

Cheah, Pheng, 227 (n. 110)

Childhood, 150, 192. *See also* Children; Education

Children: nonindigenous, 1, 2, 3, 55, 105, 116; and entertainment, 1–5, 211 (n. 4); indigenous, 2, 3, 27, 29, 32, 55, 60, 67, 85, 102, 103, 116, 117, 125, 126, 166, 200, 209, 257 (n. 49); figures of, 76, 95, 112, 117, 138, 145, 198, 253 (n. 80); and slavery, 78, 235 (n. 74), 257 (n. 49); and literature, 195, 197, 198, 199, 213 (n. 29); and democracy,

196. *See also* Childhood; Diacuizinha; Education

Chile, 170, 220 (n. 24), 256 (n. 46)

CHIRAPAQ Centro de Culturas Indígenas, 216 (n. 70)

Chooronó [*sic*], 67, 84, 85

Christianity, 89, 94, 179, 221 (n. 31), 251 (n. 34). *See also* Catholic Church; Christians

Christians, 10, 29, 94, 101, 184, 219 (n. 13). *See also* Catholic Church; Christianity

CINDACTAs (Centros Integrados de Defesa Aérea e Controle de Tráfego Aéreo), 243 (n. 19)

"Cinqüenta anos em cinco," 109, 242 (n. 9). *See also* "Development"

Citizenship: and national belonging, 18, 226 (n. 90); and perceptions of "Indianness," 28, 35, 46, 112, 119, 122, 184; neo-, 36, 144, 148, 164, 172, 175; and sovereignty, 36, 168, 172, 174; of indigenous peoples, 41, 42, 47, 51, 61, 68, 122, 126, 160, 164, 185, 187, 189, 191, 200, 247 (n. 82), 258 (n. 70); and interculturality, 57; and republicanism, 78; and Dom Pedro II, 82; and *Lo schiavo*, 93; and Vargas period, 136, 143, 144, 148. *See also* Belonging; Identity: national; "Neo-Brazilians"

Civil Code of 1916, 42, 43, 117, 249 (n. 11)

Civil Code of 2002, 223 (n. 50), 245 (n. 46)

"Civilization": Brazilian, 32, 39, 42, 43, 44, 80, 81, 84, 87, 98, 99, 101, 117, 122, 123, 124, 143, 144, 145, 146, 148, 149, 150, 164, 171, 172, 184, 189, 218 (n. 8), 250 (n. 31), 253 (n. 80); and "barbarity," 87, 99, 100, 101, 102, 116, 139, 140, 146, 221 (n. 31); European, 97, 98, 139

"Civilizing mission," 60, 114, 189, 199

Cleofas, João, 139, 251 (n. 35)

Coelho, Nicolau, 11

Cold War, 245 (nn. 49, 50)

Expedição Xingu (television program), 262 (n. 21)

Extermination of indigenous peoples, 44, 53, 100–101, 133, 207, 227 (n. 108). *See also* Genocide; Violence: anti-indigenous

Falcão, João do Rego Barros, Colonel, 100

Fanon, Franz, 168

Farias, Genésio, 83

Farming, 44, 129, 182, 187, 190, 224 (n. 65). *See also* Agricultural work and technologies

Fawcett, Percy, 251 (n. 42), 252 (n. 48)

Ferdinand (king of Spain), 257 (n. 47)

Ferreira Sobrinho, Raimundo ("Doca"), 218 (n. 6)

"Fifty Years in Five," 109, 242 (n. 9). *See also* "Development"

Figueiredo Commission, 122, 246 (n. 63)

Filho, João Café, 109, 144

Filippo, Filippe, 69

FINRAF (Former International Reserve of Amazon Forest [*sic*]), 105–11, 127, 128. *See also* SIVAM; Sivamzinho

First Regional Inspectorate, 241 (n. 177)

First Republic, 41, 42, 65, 67, 77, 84, 91, 93, 106, 114, 219 (n. 12)

Flor dos Campos, 140. *See also* Aiute, Diacuí Canualo

Flores, Lúcio Paiva, 25–26, 179, 180, 199

Folha da Tarde, 138

Folha de São Paulo, 262 (n. 21)

Folhetim, 70, 139, 232 (n. 37), 251 (n. 34)

Fonseca, Deodoro, 230 (n. 9)

Fonseca, Jurandy Marcos da, 163

Fontainha, Guilherme, 65, 67

Ford, Henry, 241 (n. 176)

Fordlândia, 241 (n. 176)

Foreign investment in Brazil, 111, 114–15, 119, 126, 243 (n. 22), 244–45 (n. 38)

Foucault, Michel, 119

Frankl, Viktor, 168

Freedom, 78, 82, 85, 97, 170, 202, 209, 234 (n. 60), 259 (n. 71)

Freedom of Information Act, 247 (n. 83)

Freire, Paulo, 58–60, 229 (n. 127), 260 (n. 103)

French, John, 255 (n. 22)

Freyre, Gilberto, 49, 67, 121, 136, 139, 147, 225 (n. 86)

Friedlander, Judith, 47

Fundação Brasil Central (FBC), 134, 135, 136, 249 (n. 8), 250 (n. 22), 252 (n. 48)

Fundação Nacional do Índio (FUNAI): leadership of, 6, 11, 14, 15, 24, 177, 181, 208, 215 (n. 56), 217 (n. 86), 246 (n. 67), 256 (n. 46), 261 (n. 119); and Decree 7.056/09, 16, 174, 229 (n. 137); and Mário Juruna, 17; founding of, 32, 117, 212 (n. 12); and determination of "Indianness," 42, 45, 48; critiques of, 53, 129, 149; and indigenous-state relations, 61, 129, 130, 185, 200, 253 (n. 77); and Marcos Terena, 163–64; and tourism, 215 (n. 67); and Kapêlituk (Raimundo Roberto), 219 (n. 11); and national census, 220 (n. 24); and land, 222 (n. 39), 224 (n. 65); and media, 223 (n. 44); and education, 229 (n. 138); and Belo Monte hydroelectric dam, 261 (n. 119)

Galvão, Eduardo, 134

Gamio, Manuel, 246 (n. 54)

Gândavo, Pêro de Magalhães, 239

García, Alan, 216 (n. 70), 255 (n. 256)

García Canclini, Néstor, 228 (n. 118)

García Márquez, Gabriel, 96

Garfield, Seth, 17, 247 (n. 71), 250 (n. 20)

Gaúcho/gaúcha, 133, 146, 249 (n. 7)

General Allotment Act. *See* Dawes Act

Genocide, 101, 102, 103, 122, 246 (n. 63)

Geopolitics, 118

Gericke, William, 141

Hucksterism, 40, 161, 177, 229 (n. 125)
Humanity, 25, 28, 76, 105, 108, 114, 189, 197, 199
Hybridity, 56, 132, 160, 228 (n. 117)
Hydroelectric dams, 6, 17, 18, 27, 128, 165, 166, 185, 187, 188, 195, 203, 204, 208, 213 (n. 20), 215 (n. 58), 248 (n. 90), 255 (n. 26). *See also* Belo Monte hydroelectric dam
Hylean Amazon, 124, 247 (n. 71)
"Hyperreal Indian," 4, 155, 191. *See also* Baudrillard, Jean; Ramos, Alcida Rita; Simulacrum

Ibarê (from *Lo schiavo*), 91, 92, 94
Icatu indigenous post, 117, 245 (n. 45)
I Danicheff (Dumas), 238 (n. 136)
Identity, 14, 20, 48, 50, 52, 54, 133, 156, 221 (n. 35), 225 (n. 88); national, 4, 24, 49–50, 57, 107, 139, 148, 152, 160, 251 (n. 31); indigenous, 14, 47, 133, 156, 160, 212 (n. 13); politics of, 19, 36, 149, 152, 157, 170; as tautology, 157
Ilára (from *Lo schiavo*), 91
Ilha do Bananal, 121, 246 (n. 56)
Immigration, 77, 91, 98, 234 (n. 66), 238 (n. 134), 244 (n. 31)
Imperialism, 105–30 passim, 132, 160, 169, 242 (n. 2)
Imperial Order of the Rose, 93, 150
Import-substitution industrialization, 119
Independence of Brazil, 35, 98, 107, 219 (n. 12)
"Indian Day," 31, 117, 218 (n. 3), 219 (n. 14)
Indianism: popularity of, 12, 65–71, 90–93, 138–39, 144–45, 150–51, 156–57, 192; legacies of, 38, 72, 89, 131, 138, 144–45, 156; relation to indigenous peoples, 67, 68, 89, 138–39, 144–45, 150–51; and physical traits, 86, 89, 150–51; critiques of, 94,

95, 96, 97; and Brazilian indigenous movement, 162; meanings of, 211 (n. 8); versus indigenism, 211 (n. 8)
Indianismo. See Indianism
Indianist movement. *See* Indianism
"Indianization," 251 (n. 31), 260 (n. 96)
"Indianness": appropriation of, 2–5, 6, 9, 15, 16, 29, 32, 37, 40, 46, 68, 72, 96, 132, 149, 152; performance or construction of, 2–5, 13, 43, 193, 194, 211 (n. 5); definitions of, 8, 9, 31, 42, 43, 44, 47, 49, 149, 160, 213 (n. 25), 216 (n. 70), 219 (n. 14); and power, 10, 58, 117, 152, 156, 192; legitimate or "authorized," 11, 14, 164; transformation of, 11, 34, 36, 49, 132, 136, 159, 164, 190–91, 201; desire for, 11, 72, 132, 144, 149; as related to "Brazilian-ness," 12, 16, 17, 28, 35, 36, 38, 39, 60, 67, 68, 72, 97, 131, 132, 138, 149, 152, 157, 195; versus indigeneity, 14, 20, 24, 28, 29, 33, 37, 38, 40, 49, 55, 60, 68, 72, 95; representations of, 14, 25, 29, 35, 39, 72, 79, 89, 90, 156, 199, 201; and authenticity, 19, 46, 48, 81, 164, 220 (n. 24); and nationalism, 29, 38, 55, 65, 68, 77, 79, 107; test for, 42, 45, 177; in Americas, 120; and geography, 129
"Indian policy," 72, 80, 107, 145, 235 (nn. 76, 81), 250 (n. 20). *See also* Indigenist policy
"Indian problem." *See* "Indian question"
Indian Protection Service. *See* Serviço de Proteção aos Índios
"Indian question": meaning of, 3, 35–37, 58, 101; and representations of difference, 14, 28; and indigenous activism, 21; current relevance of, 27–28; and land, according to José Carlos Mariátegui, 44, 176, 224 (n. 60); and sovereignty, 51, 173; and Indianism, 90; and indigenous survival, 102–3; and economic productivity, 114; and

environment, 116; failures to "resolve," 144, 152; public debates over, 135–53 passim

Indian Statute of 1973 (Estatuto do Índio), 41, 48, 49, 163, 164, 219 (n. 14), 223 (nn. 44, 48), 245 (n. 46), 255 (n. 16)

Indies, 97

Indigeneity: official and dominant renderings of, 3, 30, 34, 37, 38, 39, 48, 149, 170, 173, 190, 232 (n. 39), 258 (nn. 62, 64); versus "Indianness," 8, 24, 28, 29, 37, 46, 47, 48, 60, 152, 173; lived experience of, 8, 40, 47, 55–56, 163, 164, 193, 195; reclaiming, 9, 48–49, 54, 73, 163, 202, 205; and representation, 12–19, 46, 48, 89, 95–96, 156, 167, 170, 202, 205; and authenticity, 20, 42, 45, 48, 50–53, 163, 197, 222 (n. 36); indigenous renderings of, 20–28, 30, 35, 36, 46, 47, 48, 54, 55, 61, 73, 163, 170, 173, 178, 181, 183, 194, 197, 202, 226 (n. 91); and sovereignty, 28, 36, 159–202 passim, 219 (n. 17), 257 (n. 48); and Brazilianness, 28, 47, 95–96, 117, 131, 152, 168, 174, 184, 190; attempts at erasure of, 29, 135; and terminology, 34–35, 37, 41, 42, 43, 47, 72, 73, 121, 173, 191, 213 (n. 25), 236 (nn. 100, 109); heterogeneity of, 36, 52, 55–56, 152, 157; and politics, 36, 161, 178, 205, 226 (n. 91); contingency of, 37, 39, 46, 47, 55–56; and law, 40–44, 46, 47, 48; and interculturality, 56–58, 229 (n. 133); management of, 133–53 passim; and power, 156, 160, 169, 170. *See also* "Indianness"

Indigenism, 30, 114, 195–205 passim, 211 (n. 8). *See also* Fundação Nacional do Índio; "Indian policy"; Indigenist bureaucracy; Indigenist discourse; Indigenist policy; Indigenous posts; Indigenous "protection"; Serviço de Proteção aos Índios

Indigenismo. See Indigenism

Indigenist bureaucracy, 4, 32, 39, 48, 53, 133–53 passim, 164, 184, 201, 202, 255 (n. 27). *See also* Indigenism; Indigenist discourse; Indigenist policy

Indigenist Council of Roraima, 45

Indigenist discourse, 7, 19, 36, 55, 72, 108, 156, 167, 191, 192, 193, 194, 196, 199, 205, 211 (n. 8). *See also* Indigenism; Indigenist bureaucracy; Indigenist policy

Indigenist movement. *See* Indigenism

Indigenist policy, 29, 31, 34, 35, 42, 48, 49, 51, 114, 124, 128, 156, 164, 165, 177, 184, 201, 209, 244 (n. 34); and *caso* Diacuí, 133–53, 156–57. *See also* Indigenism; Indigenist bureaucracy; Indigenist discourse

Indigenous and nonindigenous collaboration, 15, 27, 176, 191, 202, 204, 205, 207, 209. *See also* Transnationalism

Indigenous knowledge, 26, 27, 59, 60, 159–205 passim. *See also* Activism: indigenous; Indigenous writers; *and under specific authors, activists, and intellectuals*

Indigenous movements in Americas, 56, 169, 170, 173, 178, 199–200, 207, 211 (n. 8), 216 (n. 70), 226 (n. 91), 256 (n. 46). *See also* Acampamento Revolucionário Indígena; Activism: indigenous; Brazilian indigenous movement; Indigenous writers; Transnationalism

Indigenous posts, 31, 32, 114–22 passim, 129–30; categorization of, 44, 218 (n. 8), 244 (n. 34). *See also under specific posts*

Indigenous "protection," 29, 35, 43, 90, 109, 112, 117, 118, 121, 122, 123, 125, 129, 137, 142, 150, 169, 172. *See also* Fundação Nacional do Índio; Indigenist policy; Rondon, Cândido Mariano da Silva; Serviço de Proteção aos Índios

Indigenous Social Forum (Bertioga, São Paulo), 200

Indigenous writers, 30, 35, 167, 168, 180, 181, 183, 184, 192–94, 196, 197, 199, 260 (n. 103). *See also* Activism; Intellectuals: indigenous; *and under specific authors*

Inhanderu (Mário Cardoso), 122, 123, 124, 195

Inquisition, 219 (n. 13), 239 (n. 152)

Inspetoria Especial de Fronteiras, 115

Instituto Brasileiro de Desenvolvimento Florestal (IBDF), 129

Instituto Brasileiro de Geografia e Estatística (IBGE), 225 (n. 78), 234 (n. 66). *See also* Census

Instituto Indígena Brasileiro para Propriedade Intelectual (INBRAPI), 27, 199, 201 (ill.), 224 (n. 68). *See also* Activism; Brazilian indigenous movement; Indigenous writers; Munduruku, Daniel

Instituto Indigenista Interamericano, 120, 121, 218 (n. 3), 246 (nn. 54–55). *See also* Pátzcuaro

Instituto Internacional da Hiléia Amazônica (IIHA), 124, 247 (n. 73)

Intellectual property, 27, 167, 183, 193, 199, 201, 216 (n. 71), 224 (n. 68); and biopiracy, 209

Intellectuals, 35, 55, 66, 68, 69, 100, 136, 147, 174, 222 (n. 42), 237 (n. 132), 253 (n. 80), 254 (n. 13); indigenous, 35, 60, 163, 166–67, 168, 172, 173, 174, 175, 176, 177, 180, 181, 191–205 passim, 219 (n. 17), 224 (n. 68). *See also* Activism; Indigenous writers; *and under specific authors and intellectuals*

Inter-American Indigenist Conference, 120

Inter catera of 1493, 170–71

Interculturality, 31, 56–61, 132, 160, 201, 228 (n. 119). *See also* Bilingual Intercultural Education

Interindigenous relations, 191, 202, 256 (n. 46). *See also* Activism; Transnationalism

International Labor Organization, 175, 191, 208, 259 (n. 72)

Internet: indigenous uses of, 15, 16, 20, 27, 45, 201, 202; and FINRAF, 105–8. *See also* Activism; Blogging

Interpellation, 51, 52, 72, 109, 110, 117, 132, 168, 191, 227 (n. 102)

Iracema (Alencar), 138, 139, 148, 150, 151, 152, 157, 230 (n. 4), 247 (n. 68). *See also* Aiute, Diacuí Canualo; Alencar, José de

Isabel, Imperial Princess of Brazil, 78, 91

Italians: and opera, 63, 68, 69, 70, 71, 72, 73, 92, 100, 220 (n. 28), 230 (n. 4), 238 (n. 136); and immigration to Brazil, 77, 78, 98, 234 (n. 66); racial prejudices of, 93; and fiction, 229 (n. 2)

Italy, 91, 92, 97, 230 (nn. 3, 10), 231 (n. 28), 239 (n. 136); Milan, 63, 65, 68, 69, 70, 71, 74, 77, 88, 92, 93, 230 (nn. 3, 10), 232 (n. 40), 233 (n. 48), 234 (nn. 64, 65, 66)

Jacaré Beach, 100

Jaupery, 241 (n. 178)

Jay Treaty of 1794, 259 (n. 71)

Jekupé, Olívio, 178, 179, 193, 194, 196, 197, 254 (n. 12)

Jesuits, 5, 101, 182, 230 (n. 3), 233 (n. 50)

John Paul II (pope), 257 (n. 47)

Jornal do Brasil, 155

Jourdon, E. C., 82

Journalism: representation of "Indians" and indigenous peoples, 15, 16, 29, 31, 65, 69, 99, 124, 192, 221 (n. 30); and Mário Juruna, 17; and social identification, 73; and Paraguayan War, 74, 76, 234 (n. 56); and republican movement, 78; and critiques of "Indian problem," 101, 102, 103, 129, 130; and

SIVAM, 111; and *caso* Diacuí, 133–57; and indigenous activism, 154–55, 183, 201, 226 (n. 91); and Marcos Terena, 163; and censorship regarding indigenous issues, 223 (n. 44). *See also* Chateaubriand, Assis; Media; Republican movement; *and under specific publications*

Juruna, Mário (Mário Dzururá), 17, 18 (ill.), 20, 215 (n. 66), 254 (n. 10)

Jurupiranga (from *Metade cara, metade máscara*), 182, 183, 205

Justice: minister and Ministry of Justice, 16; social, 20, 48, 156, 157, 164, 170, 255 (n. 22); and indigenous policy, 43, 53, 126, 172, 257 (n. 62); indigenous visions of, 55, 191, 203; "racial," 150; and affirmative action, 219 (n. 16); and treatment of Carlos Gomes, 219 (n. 16), 231 (n. 19); and Arthur de Gobineau, 238 (n. 134)

"Just war," 81, 171, 235 (n. 81)

Kaingang, 9, 101, 103, 116, 165–66, 245 (n. 45)

Kaingang, Kretã, 165–66

Kalapalo, 29; and *caso* Diacuí, 133–53, 156–57, 251 (n. 42), 252 (n. 48); and funeral rites, 141, 251 (n. 43); and marriage, 141, 251 (n. 43); language, 145, 250 (n. 24), 252 (n. 63); and naming, 251 (n. 46), 252 (n. 48). *See also* Aiute, Diacuí Canualo; Cunha, Ayres Câmara

Kalapalo, Ysani, 204 (ill.), 226 (n. 94), 252 (n. 46), 254 (n. 12)

Kapêlituk (Raimundo Roberto), 31, 32, 33, 34 (ill.), 35, 38, 60, 120, 195, 218 (n. 5), 219 (n. 11)

Karajá, 120, 121

Kararâo, 165. *See also* Belo Monte hydroelectric dam; Kayapó

Kayapó, 195, 215 (n. 58), 255 (n. 25), 261 (n. 119)

Kayapó, Tuíra, 215 (n. 58)

Kichwa, 170, 256 (n. 46)

Kinship ties, 141, 171, 219 (n. 11)

Koch-Grünberg, Theodor, 96, 240 (n. 161)

Kopenawa, Davi, 51

Krenak, 185, 186, 189

Krenak, Ailton, 226 (n. 94), 254 (n. 12)

Krukutu (São Paulo), 194

Kubitschek, Juscelino, 109

Kuluene, 134, 135, 141, 145, 251 (n. 46). *See also* Aiute, Diacuí Canualo; Cunha, Ayres Câmara; Kalapalo

Kúmatse (cacique of Kalapalo people), 141

Laiana, 67, 84, 85, 87

Lakota, 170, 256 (n. 46)

Land: indigenous uses of, 2, 40, 45, 46, 55, 82, 112, 170, 176, 177, 178, 182, 202, 208, 219; demarcation of, 4, 39, 45, 201, 208, 219 (n. 13), 221 (n. 30); loss of, 5, 41, 81, 82; dominant uses of, 10, 11, 45, 67, 81, 82, 101, 109, 123, 147, 170, 207, 235 (n. 81); disputes over, 11, 41, 44, 48, 101, 163, 168, 174, 176, 177, 191, 207, 209, 222 (n. 39), 224 (n. 60), 253 (n. 78), 255 (n. 23); land rights, 17, 20, 48, 167, 193, 219 (n. 17), 256 (n. 46). *See also* Belo Monte hydroelectric dam; "Indian question"; Indigenous posts; Territories; *and under specific places*

Land Law (Lei de Terras), 81–82, 235 (nn. 78–81, 83, 86)

Land of the True Cross (Terra da Vera Cruz), 11

Lane, Phil, Jr., 169, 203

Language/languages: interpretations and meanings of, 8, 15, 37, 213 (n. 25), 221 (n. 35), 240 (n. 161); indigenous uses of, 9, 13, 137–38, 167, 191, 202, 208, 228 (n. 125); Portuguese as foreign, 31, 32, 85, 219 (n. 11), 222 (n. 40); indigenous, 40, 75, 76, 200,

314 / *Index*

215 (n. 60), 236 (n. 96), 239 (n. 139), 262 (n. 17); and definitions of indigeneity, 43, 50, 144, 190; European, 71; racist, 74; structure of, 74; dominant uses of, 101, 163, 234 (n. 58), 240 (n. 161); language barriers, 137, 250 (n. 24). *See also* Indigeneity: and terminology *and under specific languages*

Latin American Subaltern Studies Group, 226 (n. 91), 254 (n. 4)

Law: and racism, 14, 136, 164–65, 214 (n. 49), 222 (n. 42), 249 (n. 19); and Brazilian rights, 15, 215 (n. 59); and indigenous rights, 36, 40–45, 46, 47, 49, 51, 57, 80, 103, 199, 222 (n. 50), 224 (n. 56); international, 36, 47, 170–71; and miscegenation, 49, 225 (n. 88); and education, 57, 222 (n. 40), 225 (n. 88); and slavery, 78–79, 235 (nn. 73, 74); and "civilization," 79, 80, 81; and land, 81, 220 (n. 22), 224 (n. 61), 235 (nn. 72, 76, 78, 80, 81); and indigenous "protection," 103; law enforcement, 110; indigenous appeals to and navigations of, 154, 163, 175, 178, 183, 199; versus justice, 164, 255 (n. 22); and indigenous health care, 209; and affirmative action, 214 (n. 49), 222 (n. 40), 225 (n. 88); and Amazon, 220; "Indians'" lack of, 238 (n. 139); and sovereignty, 257 (n. 47). *See also* Constitution of 1988; Estatuto da Igualdade Racial; Indian Statute of 1973; International Labor Organization; Justice; Land Law; Lei Áurea; Statute of Indigenous Peoples

Law of the Free Womb (Lei do Ventre Livre). *See* Lei Rio Branco

Legal Amazon, xxii (ill.), 38, 220 (n. 22)

Lei Áurea, 91, 103

Lei Rio Branco, 78, 235 (nn. 73, 74)

Lemos, Bento de, 241 (n. 177)

Léry, Jean de, 84, 236 (n. 101)

"Lettered city," 168, 193

Lévi-Strauss, Claude, 7, 236 (n. 109)

Literatura indígena list-serv, 193. *See also* Potiguara, Eliane

Literatura Nativa, 193. *See also* Jekupé, Olívio

Literature: and images of indigenous peoples, 38, 39, 67–68, 71, 88–91, 95–98, 128, 131, 135, 138–39, 142–43, 145, 148–52, 157, 220 (n. 28), 229 (nn. 2–3), 241 (n. 186); Indianist, 67–68, 71–72, 88–91, 138–39, 142, 145, 148–52, 157, 218 (n. 99), 220 (n. 28), 229 (nn. 2, 3), 237 (n. 125); and *folhetim*, 70 (n. 139), 232 (n. 37), 251 (n. 34); by indigenous peoples, 192–205 passim; children's and juvenile, 196–99; debates over, 250 (n. 31). *See also* Indianism; Indigenous writers; *and under specific authors and works*

Luís, Washington Pereira de Sousa, 245 (n. 39)

"Lula" da Silva, Luiz Inácio, 16, 165, 185, 187, 190, 213 (n. 20), 258 (n. 67), 259 (n. 73)

Machado de Assis, Joaquim Maria, 139, 250 (n. 31)

Macunaíma (M. de Andrade), 95–98, 240 (n. 161). See also *Modernismo*

Maia, Álvaro, 189

Malcher, José Maria da Gama, 44, 134, 224 (n. 61), 250 (n. 27)

Malinche, 230 (n. 4)

Manaus, 98, 99, 100, 225 (n. 88), 238 (n. 133), 241 (n. 176), 244 (n. 35)

"Manifesto antropófago" (O. de Andrade), 94, 95

"Manifesto of 113 Anti-Racist Citizens against Racial Laws," 222 (n. 42). *See also* Affirmative action; Law: and racism; Estatuto da Igualdade Racial

Manuel I (king of Portugal), 11

Peace of Cateau-Cambrésis, 230 (n. 3)

Pedro I (emperor of Brazil), 219 (n. 12)

Pedro II (emperor of Brazil): and Antônio Carlos Gomes, 64, 67, 70, 71, 230 (n. 10); and Paraguayan War, 74, 76, 82; expulsion from Brazil, 77; critique of and end of empire, 78; and indigenous peoples, 80, 82, 104, 239 (n. 145); praise for, 82, 234 (n. 65); and Arthur de Gobineau, 237 (n. 131), 238 (n. 134); and Louis Agassiz, 238 (n. 133)

Pemon, 240 (n. 161)

Peri (from *Il guarany/O guarany*), 63, 90, 94, 95, 97, 99, 150, 220 (n. 28), 251 (n. 34)

Pernambuco (state), 81

Peru, 19, 35, 57, 118, 119, 122, 177, 215 (n. 69), 216 (n. 70), 224 (n. 60), 228 (nn. 122, 125), 232 (n. 38), 241 (n. 186), 243 (n. 13), 246 (n. 61), 248 (n. 86), 255 (n. 29), 256 (n. 29)

Peruvian Amazon Company, 241 (n. 186), 246 (n. 61)

Pio Lorenço, 96

Plurinationalism, 160. *See also* Transnationalism

Pocahontas, 230 (n. 4)

Political, the, 161, 168, 170, 173, 191, 192, 202, 226 (n. 91). *See also* Politics

Politics: indigenist, 4, 128, 152, 159, 162, 167, 182; indigenous uses of and engagements with, 5, 22, 24–30, 40–41, 55, 110, 156, 163, 166, 168, 175, 176, 178, 180, 182, 183, 191, 196, 202–5, 215 (n. 65), 226 (n. 91); of "epistemic murk," 8; dominant renderings of indigeneity in, 13, 90, 161, 175, 196, 202–5; national, 18, 36, 40–41, 106, 162, 167, 202–5; of identity, 19, 36, 50, 149, 152, 156, 157, 170; and sovereignty, 36, 174, 175, 191, 202, 258 (n. 64); and changing meanings of language over time, 73; Antônio

Carlos Gomes's view of, 67, 82, 93, 231 (n. 19), 233 (n. 52); of "race," 135, 148, 152, 237 (n. 132); and Indianism, 139. *See also* Biopolitics; Geopolitics; "Indian policy"; Indigenist policy; Political, the

Polygenism, 238 (nn. 133, 135). *See also* Agassiz, Louis; Darwin, Charles

Ponchielli, Almicare, 93

Ponchos Rojos, 229 (n. 125)

Pontos de Cultura, 255 (n. 27)

Poole, Deborah, 119

Popular culture, 1–30 passim, 38, 39, 40, 68, 70, 74, 76, 82, 88, 93, 94, 96, 107, 131, 136, 139, 147, 149, 152, 153, 154, 156, 160, 164, 181, 195, 197, 198, 221 (nn. 30, 35), 240 (n. 165), 262 (n. 21). See also *O Globo*; Globo TV; Journalism; Media; Xuxa; *and under specific media outlets*

Populism, 49, 66, 132, 136, 147, 165

Porto Seguro (Bahia), 153, 209

Positivism, 10, 37, 114, 116, 119

Postindigenism, 30, 162, 166, 195–205 passim

Postmodernity: conditions of, 19, 25, 26, 152, 161, 190

Postos indígenas. See Indigenous posts

"Posttraditional Indians," 42, 46, 48, 177, 193, 222 (n. 36). See also *Povos ressurgidos*

Potiguara, 181, 247 (n. 68)

Potiguara, Eliane (Eliane Lima dos Santos), 27, 181, 191–92, 193, 199. *See also* Grupo de Mulheres Indígenas; Indigenous writers; Jurupiranga; *Metade cara, metade máscara*

Potosí, 182

Poverty, 48, 65, 75, 98, 99, 113, 122, 126, 225 (n. 78)

Povos ressurgidos, 193, 209. *See also* "Posttraditional Indians"

Power: and representation, 4, 22, 23, 25, 38, 48, 49, 72, 89, 119, 132, 133, 134,

142, 153, 195, 199, 221 (n. 35), 257 (n. 47); distribution of, 5; of anthropology, 7; of Catholic Church, 10; of "Indianness," 11, 33, 38, 47, 49, 68, 90, 107, 149; of indigenous and subaltern peoples, 13, 25, 52, 56, 58, 110, 154, 156, 164, 170, 182, 183, 184, 199, 200, 201, 226 (n. 91), 257 (n. 62); of racism, 14, 37, 41, 66, 132, 136, 147; cultural, sociopolitical, and economic, 15, 28, 36, 38, 43, 51, 55, 56, 59, 78, 101, 115, 117, 126, 127, 128, 130, 161, 165, 169, 170, 172, 199, 200, 203, 207, 245; of state, 17, 119, 142, 223 (n. 48); struggles for, 18, 19; of dominant sovereignty, 51; and interculturality, 56, 57, 132; and education, 60, 61, 128; and land, 81; and nationalism, 77, 89, 90; military, 84, 123, 126, 127; tutelary, 107; biopower, 119, 168. *See also* Anthropology; Assimilation; Catholic Church; Colonialism; Coloniality; "De-Indianization"; Education; Ethnography; Governance; Interculturality; Land; Nationalism; Politics; Racism; Representation; Rights; Self-identification; Slavery; Sovereignty; Subalternity; Tutelage; Violence; War

Prado, Francisco Rodrigues do, 85
Prestes, Júlio, 245 (n. 39)
Preto (racial category), 214 (n. 49), 222 (n. 38), 225 (n. 89)
Price, David, 247–48 (n. 83)
"Primitiveness," 41, 42, 72, 105, 108, 109, 114, 124, 130, 137, 143, 171, 172, 216
Programa pela Aceleração do Crescimento (PAC), 6, 166, 185, 187, 190, 248 (n. 90)
Purutuyé, 83
Putumayo, 101, 122, 123, 241 (n. 186)

Quadros, Jânio, 109, 129
Quechua, 170, 256 (n. 46), 260 (n. 97)

Quilombolas, 193
Quincentenary celebration of Brazil's "discovery," 153–56, 178, 195, 207–9, 253 (n. 80)
Quiniquináo (*sic*), 67, 84, 85, 87
Quispe, Felipe, 217 (n. 87), 229 (n. 125), 260 (nn. 96, 103)

Raça brasileira. See "Race": "Brazilian"
"Race": "mixed," 11, 24, 28, 49, 50, 65, 67, 91, 152, 160, 232 (n. 39); "Brazilian," 11, 24, 28, 49, 50, 65, 147, 152, 160, 232 (n. 39); and law, 16, 41, 214 (n. 49); and Antônio Carlos Gomes, 67; debates over, 90, 93, 99, 135, 150; "Indian" as, 89, 101, 122, 150, 232 (n. 39); colonial notions of, 132; and self-identification, 133; categories of, 156, 221 (n. 35), 226 (n. 90); historically formed notions of, 202; and Paulo Freire, 229 (n. 127); and science, 237 (n. 132); and UNESCO study, 247 (n. 72). *See also* Affirmative action; Agassiz, Louis; Anthropology; *Caboclo*; Darwin, Charles; Ethnicity; Ethnography; "Indianness"; Indigeneity; *Mestiçagem*; *Mestiço*; Monogenism; *Mulato*/Mulatto; *Negro*; *Pardo*; Polygenism; *Preto*; Racial quotas; Racism
"Racial democracy," 24, 41, 49, 132, 139, 199, 225 (n. 86)
"Racial improvement," 66, 72, 159, 232 (n. 39)
Racial quotas, 214 (n. 49), 222 (nn. 40, 42), 225 (n. 89). *See also* Affirmative action
Racism: scientific, 11, 132, 248 (n. 2); and colonialist thought, 18, 21; North American "style," 41; and differentiated rights, 50; bases of, 54; recognition of, 54; during Paraguayan War, 74; in Italy, 93; and "progress," 119; and Eurocentrism, 135, 147; accusations against SPI of, 143, 146, 148,

Schwarcz, Lilia Moritz, 12

Schwarz, Roberto, 97

Secrets, 23, 160, 161, 240 (n. 161), 254 (n. 7)

Seismarias, 81, 235 (n. 81). *See also* Land; Land Law

Self-identification: and FUNAI, 4, 42; and terminology, 8, 14, 20, 23, 36, 41; and dominant society, 11, 13; politics of, 19, 23, 24–25, 28, 29, 36, 40, 52–53, 168–69, 178, 193, 202, 205; in activism and cultural production, 19, 182, 193, 197, 256 (n. 46); and national belonging, 28, 162, 258 (n. 70); and naming, 33; and power, 33; and legal status, 36; and census categories, 38, 133, 214 (n. 49), 220 (nn. 21, 24), 221 (n. 35), 222 (n. 38); and land, 44, 194; paradoxes of, 46; and ways of being and thinking, 47, 161, 193, 197, 205; and *mestiçagem*, 50, 152; and traditional indigenous knowledge and practices, 54; versus "Indianness," 54, 73, 149, 152, 153; and Lyrio Arlindo de Valle, 122; and hyperreality, 156, 194; and differentiated citizenship, 168; and Marcos Terena, 168; and Olívio Jekupé, 193–94; and affirmative action, 222 (nn. 88, 89)

Semana de Arte Moderna, 94

Sepúlveda, Ginés de, 39, 221 (n. 31)

Seringueiros, 123–24, 125

Serpa, Herbert, 32, 117, 219 (n. 11)

Serra, José, 187

Sertanejo, 241 (n. 176)

Sertanista: meaning of, 134, 212 (n. 8), 249 (n. 8); and Fundação Brasil Central, 134, 252 (n. 48); as profession of Ayres Câmara Cunha, 134–46 passim, 252 (n. 48); role in Brazil's modernity, 136; Villas-Bôas brothers, 243 (n. 10)

Sertão, 107, 112, 116, 122, 123, 128, 212 (n. 8), 249 (n. 8)

Serviço de Proteção aos Índios (SPI): Rondon and founding of, 12, 51, 101, 214 (n. 41), 218 (n. 7), 254 (n. 11); and "de-Indianization," 29, 32, 34, 37, 49, 101, 114, 249 (n. 8); and neo-Brazilianness and nationalization, 29, 33, 34, 115, 117, 118, 137, 144; and schooling, 31–32, 33, 35, 117, 118, 119, 124, 126, 137, 218 (nn. 6, 7), 247 (n. 82); and meanings of "Indianness," 34, 121, 138, 149, 150; tutelage and "protection" of, 43–44, 107–8, 114, 117, 129, 130, 138–57 passim, 162–84; and land use, 44, 83, 101, 223 (n. 53); critiques of, 53, 22–24, 125, 126, 130, 142, 144, 145, 232 (n. 34); and language of conquest, 72–73; and finances and capital, 101, 116, 121, 190; and propaganda, 115, 116, 119, 143; and Getúlio Vargas, 115, 121, 124, 136, 144, 245 (n. 39); and Ministry of Labor, Industry, and Commerce, 115, 134; and War Ministry, 115, 134, 249 (n. 12); and national security, 117, 118; and *caso* Diacuí, 133–53, 156–57; and "Indian improvement," 136, 148, 185, 186, 187, 188, 189; disbanding of, 212 (n. 12), 247 (n. 82)

Shaw, Karena, 173, 226 (n. 91), 257 (nn. 47, 62), 258 (nn. 62, 64)

Silva, Hédio, 219 (n. 16)

Simões Lopes, Luiz, 189

Simulacrum, 4, 253 (n. 76); "Indian," 153, 154, 156

SIPAM (Sistema de Proteção da Amazônia), 243 (n. 17)

SIVAM (Sistema de Vigilância da Amazônia), 110–14, 127, 128, 195, 243 (nn. 17, 19), 244 (n. 29), 261 (n. 2)

Sivamzinho, 112, 113 (ill.), 118, 121, 123

Slater, Candace, 107

Slavery: postabolition, 11, 41, 103; abolition movement, 78, 91; laws regarding, 78, 91, 103; conditions of, 83; of indigenous peoples, 83, 100, 230

Xavante, Hiparendo, 155

Xingu, xi, xxii, 16, 21, 149, 165, 204, 213 (n. 20), 243 (n. 10), 252 (nn. 46, 48), 255 (n. 25), 258 (n. 67), 262 (n. 21); Parque Indígena do Xingu, 109, 128, 129, 249 (n. 8); Parque Nacional do Xingu, 109, 249 (n. 8); Reserva Indígena do Xingu, 128–30; and *caso* Diacuí, 133–53 passim; people of, 137; Terra Indígena do Xingu, 243 (n. 10)

Xuxa (Maria da Graça Meneghel), 2, 3, 4, 5 (ill.), 6, 11, 13, 14, 16, 18, 19, 20, 195, 197, 214 (nn. 47, 48)

Yanomami, 47, 51, 112

Zapatistas, 175